THE *Coke* MACHINE

The Dirty Truth Behind the World's Favorite Soft Drink

MICHAEL BLANDING

AVERY
a member of Penguin Group (USA) Inc.
New York

Published by the Penguin Group
Penguin Group (USA) Inc., 375 Hudson Street, New York, New York 10014, USA • Penguin Group (Canada), 90 Eglinton Avenue East, Suite 700, Toronto, Ontario M4P 2Y3, Canada (a division of Pearson Penguin Canada Inc.) • Penguin Books Ltd, 80 Strand, London WC2R 0RL, England • Penguin Ireland, 25 St Stephen's Green, Dublin 2, Ireland (a division of Penguin Books Ltd) • Penguin Group (Australia), 250 Camberwell Road, Camberwell, Victoria 3124, Australia (a division of Pearson Australia Group Pty Ltd) • Penguin Books India Pvt Ltd, 11 Community Centre, Panchsheel Park, New Delhi–110 017, India • Penguin Group (NZ), 67 Apollo Drive, Rosedale, North Shore 0632, New Zealand (a division of Pearson New Zealand Ltd) • Penguin Books (South Africa) (Pty) Ltd, 24 Sturdee Avenue, Rosebank, Johannesburg 2196, South Africa

Penguin Books Ltd, Registered Offices: 80 Strand, London WC2R 0RL, England

First trade paperback edition 2011

The Library of Congress catalogued the hardcover edition as follows:

Blanding, Michael.
The Coke machine : the dirty truth behind the world's favorite soft drink / Michael Blanding.
p. cm.
Includes bibliographical references and index.
ISBN 978-1-58333-406-5
1. Coca-Cola Company—History. 2. Soft drink industry.
3. Bottled water industry. 4. International business enterprises. I. Title.
HD9349.S634C5333 2010 2010017095
338.7'66362—dc22

ISBN 978-1-58333-435-5 (paperback edition)

Printed in the United States of America
3 5 7 9 10 8 6 4 2

BOOK DESIGN BY MEIGHAN CAVANAUGH

For Alex—for everything

Contents

Part Two

TEACHING THE WORLD TO SING

Introduction

The Coca-Cola bottling plant in Carepa, Colombia, is an unlovely pile of brick on the outskirts of a sweltering Caribbean backwater. It sits past sad dogs blinking away flies on dirty streets, men loading yuccas and plantains into peddle carts, and gaudy open-roof *chivas* spewing diesel fumes as they idle by the roadside. Surrounding it, fields stretch to the horizon, studded with lonely palm and banana trees. The only consolation is a roadside Madonna on the edge of the gravel parking lot, a solitary benediction to bless the way of those leaving town.

On the morning of December 5, 1996, two men pulled a motorbike into the gravel driveway. They circled the parking lot a few times before coming to a stop in front of the gate. Inside the battered chain-link fence was a courtyard piled with soda crates waiting to be loaded onto delivery trucks. On either side was a wall of heavy pink brick, painted with the Coke logo. And to the right, a small gatehouse set into the wall looked through metal slats at the parking lot.

The motorcycle's passenger dismounted, while the driver sat with the engine idling. Walking up to the fence, he addressed the gatekeeper, a thin man with light brown skin, coffee-colored eyes, a mustache, and heavy eyebrows. That matched the description the visitor had been given, but he had to be sure.

"Are you Isidro Gil?" he asked.

Inside, the man hesitated slightly before replying. "Yeah. But why do you want to know?"

"We need to go inside and see a client."

"Wait a minute," replied Gil, who just then saw a delivery truck rumbling up from the yard. "Let me deal with this truck first, and then I'll help you out."

With nothing to do but his job, Gil unlocked the gate and pulled the chain-link fence toward either side to allow the truck to pass. Perhaps he suspected the danger he was in and simply resigned himself to his fate. More likely he somehow thought he would be spared from any potential violence by his position in the hierarchy of the bottlers' union, by promises the plant management had given ensuring his safety, by the fact that it was nine in the morning in a public location with plenty of people milling around the plant.

In fact, this was not the first strange motorcycle that he had seen this morning. A half-hour earlier, another had pulled up to the small kiosk by the side of the road that served Coke to workers before and after their shifts. Gil had watched one of his coworkers point him out, and the cyclist nod before driving off. Gil was still worrying about the incident when the second motorcycle appeared.

In Colombia, a motorcycle isn't just a motorcycle. It's also the transport of choice for the paramilitary death squads that target guerrillas and anyone remotely associated with them on the other side of the country's smoldering thirty-five-year-old civil war. In Medellín at the time, men were forbidden from carrying another man as a passenger, since it was so common for one to drive while the other pulled a trigger.

But Gil wasn't the kind of person to back down from confrontation. Among his coworkers, the twenty-eight-year-old was a natural leader. Gregarious and charismatic, he'd organize fishing trips to the river and soccer and baseball tournaments on the weekends. He started out on the production line, but was reassigned to his current job at the front gate in 1994, just around the same time the paramilitaries started ominously appearing in the region.

Ostensibly, the death squads targeted the guerrillas who exploited the coastal location as a launching pad for its drug and weapon trade. But the guerrillas were difficult targets, hiding in camps buried deep in the jungles. So soon the death squads turned their attentions to the civilians whom they suspected of supporting the guerrillas—a long list, including left-wing politicians, academics, health and human rights workers, teachers, and trade unionists.

The union at the Coke plant, SINALTRAINAL, was a natural target. Two of its leaders had already been killed by the time Isidro Gil was named secretary-general and put in charge of renegotiating the workers' contract with the bottling company. On November 18, 1996, the union submitted its final proposal for a new contract, demanding increased pay and benefits, along with protection from firing and new security measures to keep union leadership safe from violence.

The Coke plant's local managers and its Florida-based owners had until December 5 to respond to the collective bargaining proposal. As he stood at the gate that morning, Gil was mentally preparing for the meeting that day, not knowing it would never take place. As he opened the gate to let out the delivery truck, he stepped back behind the gatehouse. The truck rumbled past, its bright red Coke logo shining in the morning light. Before Gil could push the metal frame closed, the visitor walked right through the gate behind it. Pulling out a .38 Special, he raised it to Gil's face and shot him between the eyes.

On the face of it, this was just one more casualty in a Third World country's long and bloody civil war, a war that has claimed tens of thousands of lives—including more than 2,500 union members in the last twenty years. For the national leaders of SINALTRAINAL, however, this was something more: part of a coordinated campaign to stamp out union activism at the bottling plant, orchestrated by the bottler and the Coca-

Cola Company itself. Before it was over, eight union leaders would be killed in Carepa and the union driven to extinction. At best, they charged, Coke stood by and let it happen. At worst, they said, company managers directed the violence through regular coordinated meetings with paramilitaries inside the plant.

It's a shocking allegation to level at the company that has presented through its advertising one of the most compelling visions of international peace and harmony the world has ever seen. And yet it's not the only charge that has been leveled in recent years against the Coca-Cola Company, which stands accused of decimating water supplies of villagers in India and Mexico, busting up unions in Turkey and Guatemala, making kids fat throughout the United States and Europe, and hoodwinking consumers into swallowing glorified tap water marketed under its bottled water brand Dasani.

Perhaps it's not too much of a surprise to find the Coca-Cola Company on the stand for these injustices. In this era of cynicism, it's standard practice to believe corporations from Halliburton to ExxonMobil capable of every form of evil, trained by the profit drive of capitalism to turn a blind eye to the worst consequences of their actions. The Coca-Cola Company, however, represents a special case—at once the quintessential example of a giant American multinational corporation and a beloved pop culture symbol that has spent billions of dollars to present an image of wholesomeness and harmony that has made it cherished by millions of people around the world. Finding the Coca-Cola Company accused of murder is like finding out Santa Claus is accused of being a pedophile.

So how is it that a company that, in its own words, "exists to refresh and benefit everyone it touches" now stands accused of drought, disease, exploitation, and murder? To truly understand that contradiction, it's necessary to go back to Coca-Cola's origins as a cocaine-laced "nerve tonic" in the turn-of-the-century American South. It's there that the seeds of its inexorable drive to growth were planted, along with the decisions that have allowed it to disavow responsibility for its bottlers around the globe. That's the essence of Coca-Cola—what one of its legendary executives once called "the essence of capitalism."

Step, now, inside the Coke Machine.

Part One

"ALL THAT AMERICA STANDS FOR"

Coca-Cola represents the sublimated essence of all that America stands for, a decent thing, honestly made.

—NEWSPAPER EDITOR WILLIAM ALLEN WHITE, 1938

ONE

A Brief History of Coke

In Atlanta, Coke gets in your face. The drink is everywhere, from the Coca-Cola memorabilia store in the airport entry hall to the announcements on the subway train for Coca-Cola headquarters. All around the city, Coke's leading executives have lent their names to the city's major landmarks: Pemberton Park, the Candler Building, the Woodruff Arts Center, and the Goizueta Business School at Emory University to name just a few. But few authentic landmarks remain from the drink's history. The home of its inventor and the pharmacy where it was first served have both disappeared.

Those faithful seeking out the origins of Coca-Cola are directed instead to the World of Coca-Cola, a massive homage to the beverage in the center of the city that remains virtually the only place in the world where the public can come face-to-face with the history of its favorite soft drink. And come they do. One million visitors crossed under the thirty-foot Coke bottle hanging over its entrance in the year after it relocated here from a smaller space across town in 2007. Visitors still must call ahead to reserve a time for a tour, paying $15 for the privilege.

What they get when they do, of course, is an image of Coke completely mediated by Coke. Even before they enter, ambient advertising ditties—"Always Coca-Cola," "I'd Like to Teach the World to Sing"—float down from speakers above. Inside, the company early on establishes a spirit of benign internationalism, with a lobby full of giant "folk art" bottles decorated by artists from around the globe, set against a conspicuously multicultural portrait wall of world citizens—Japanese teenagers, a white-bread couple on the beach, three tropical dark kids, a pierced chick in a bar—all enjoying their Cokes.

The theme continues as the doors open into a blinding atrium whose walls churn with words like "refresh," "heritage," and "optimism" printed in every language. There are more multicultural portraits here, too. A phone receiver hanging next to each one, playing a recorded loop that describes Coke-funded work to tackle HIV/AIDS in Africa, water depletion in Pakistan, and child malnutrition in Argentina. There's even an American doctor from the Beverage Institute for Health and Wellness, which is pioneering research to counter the national childhood obesity epidemic.

If you knew nothing else about it, you'd think the Coca-Cola Company was incorporated for the sole purpose of spreading peace and social equality around the world. The real work of the museum, however, happens when visitors step out of the lobby and into the first exhibit—called "Milestones of Refreshment"—telling the story of how it all began.

"When John Pemberton invented Coca-Cola in 1886, he had no way of knowing what a phenomenon his creation would become," narrates a soothing baritone emanating from a video screen. Upon entering, visitors meet a bronze statue of the man himself, stirring a kettle with a wooden spoon. Broad-shouldered, bearded, and wearing overalls, the man in the statue looks more like a Soviet-era paean to the proletariat than one of the great progenitors of capitalism. "His idea," the video continues, "was to create a beverage specifically formulated to be served ice-cold." In doing so, he "invented a completely new category for refreshment, and his formula for Coca-Cola became one of the world's most closely guarded secrets.

Still, people began to discover the most exciting thing about Coca-Cola: that it's delicious and refreshing. And that's no secret at all."

The short video is impressive for hitting all of Coke's marketing leitmotifs—Delicious. Refreshing. Ice-Cold. Secret Formula. In reality, however, it was not so poetic. Pemberton's goal was hardly to create a new category of cold drink; like many people, he wanted to make himself rich. And in 1880, the quickest way to do that was found inside a bottle, through the creation of medicinal cure-alls called "patent medicines." The Coca-Cola Company doesn't like to talk about its early medicinal past; the sordid protohistory doesn't fit in well with the clean-scrubbed mythology it promotes in the World of Coca-Cola (and more broadly in the world of Coca-Cola). Even today, however, traces of the company's patent-medicine past are present in how it promotes and markets the drink.

The term "patent medicines" has nothing to do with the United States Patent Office, originating instead in the practice of British kings' granting "patents of royal favor" to favorite medicine makers. A few decades after bumping up against Plymouth Rock, colonists began importing medicines like Hooper's Pills and Daffy's Elixir to treat rheumatism, gout, tuberculosis—even cancer. Their inventors took great pains to guard the secret formulas of their proprietary combination of ingredients. As late Atlanta historian James Harvey Young writes in the definitive *Toadstool Millionaires*, "Rivals might detect the major active constituents, but the original proprietor could claim that only he knew all the elements in their proper proportions."

If Britons invented patent medicines, Americans became obsessed with them. After the Revolutionary War, vast swathes of the newly independent United States were a mucky, roadless wilderness. Doctors were scarce, and even when available, they were as apt to kill their patients as to heal them. The cutting edge of medical practice, after all, included bleeding with a sharp lancet and "purging" the bowels with mercury, thereby weakening and poisoning already sick patients. By the early 1800s, a backlash against doctors was in full swing, with many people avoiding them altogether in favor of whatever home remedies they could find. The practice grew into a fad with the publication of *New Guide to Health* by Samuel Thomson, a self-taught herbalist from New Hampshire who claimed any man could be his own doctor using plants readily available in the fields and woods of the young country.

Less scrupulous entrepreneurs and con men exploited the trend with their own American patent medicine blends that went far beyond the British concoctions in both claims and popularity. At the turn of the nineteenth century, Connecticut physician Samuel Lee, Jr., mixed up a batch of soap, aloe, and potassium nitrate and pressed them into "Bilious Pills," which he touted as a cure against indigestion and flatulence. Within a decade, they were sold as far away as the Mississippi River. Soon after, Thomas W. Dyott amassed a fortune of a quarter of a million dollars with concoctions such as the hot-selling Robertson's Infallible Worm Destroying Lozenges. These tycoons found a ready clientele with the rapid industrialization of the early 1800s, when laborers crowded into disease-ridden tenements. The Civil War brought new patients in the form of soldiers suffering from wounds and disease, many of whom received tonics along with their rations.

In truth, most patent medicines were little more than laxatives or emetics (to induce vomiting), often containing up to 50 percent alcohol. Consumers didn't seem to care. By the turn of the twentieth century, they were big business, with anywhere between 20,000 and 50,000 different concoctions on offer and total sales of $80 million. For every fortune, however, a dozen vendors went bankrupt. The winners were those who created the best story, the coolest shaped container, or the catchiest advertisements to cement their names in consumers' minds. Some relied on tales of exotic ingredients from Africa or the Far East. Others drew upon American Indian lore, pegging their origins, for example, to a secret formula given by an Indian chief to a trapper in exchange for rescuing his son from a bear.

No one exploited these gimmicks more relentlessly than a new breed of traveling salesmen who staged elaborate presentations known as "medicine shows." A fixture of American life for nearly a century, these roving productions traveled the country in the hundreds during their height, from 1880 to 1900. After a "ballyhoo" of musical bandwagons, magicians, and comedians to warm up the crowd, salesmen reeled in buyers with their pitches, often whipping up fears of disease before magically "healing" a planted crowd member. One of the most notorious showmen, Clark Stanley, publicly killed hundreds of rattlesnakes to advertise his Snake Oil Liniment, which was eventually discovered to be little more than camphor and turpentine—forever making the term "snake-oil salesman" synonymous with fraud.

But most customers convinced themselves that the elixirs they bought from these traveling road shows actually worked. As one 1930s-era pitch doctor explained, the key was to hypnotize the buyer into thinking he'd come up with the idea to buy the product himself: "First, attention; second, interest; third, suggestion; fourth, imagination; fifth, desire; sixth, decision," he explained. After years of shows, medicines such as Kickapoo Indian Sagwa and Hamlin's Wizard Oil sold themselves, bringing crowds flocking whenever their wagons rolled into town. It was this kind of success that Civil War colonel and pharmacist John Pemberton was seeking when he moved to Atlanta from nearby Columbus, Georgia, in 1870. Pemberton was an early devotee of Samuel Thomson's "every man his own doctor" philosophy, stirring local herbs and flowers into his own concoctions in a lab behind his pharmacy shop. He sold some, including Globe Flower Cough Syrup, marketed for consumption and bronchitis, and a "blood medicine" called Extract of Stillingia.

Yet Pemberton was no sleazy snake oil salesman. Wounded in one of the Civil War's last battles, he was constantly plagued with pain himself, and took to self-dosing in an effort to find relief for the rest of his life. In fact, one tidbit that doesn't make it into the official Coca-Cola myth is that he probably regularly dipped into his pharmacy cabinet for hits of morphine. Three of Pemberton's colleagues in the drug trade later named him an addict. If that was true, the addiction likely led him to the substance that would seal his legacy: cocaine.

"I am convinced from actual experiments that [coca] is the very best substitute for opium, for a person addicted in the opium habit, that has ever been discovered," he told *The Atlanta Journal* in 1885, adding that "the patient who will use it as a means of cure may deliver himself from the pernicious habit without inconvenience or pain." He wasn't alone in thinking so. Years before cocaine was found to be addictive, the little leaf from Peru was celebrated as a miracle drug. One Albany, New York, manufacturer marketed Cocaine Toothache Drops, picturing two contented children on a package trumpeting an "Instantaneous Cure!" (Indeed.)

But the most popular coca-laced "medicine" was a concoction called Vin Mariani, created by Parisian chemist Angelo Mariani by mixing red Bordeaux with a half a grain of cocaine. He cheerfully recommended three glasses a day for whatever ailed you—approximately one line of powder daily. A born promoter, Mariani landed endorsements for his product from celebrities on both sides of the Atlantic—including Thomas Edison, Queen Victoria, and three popes.

If imitation is the sincerest form of flattery, then Pemberton was obsequious in his 1884 invention French Wine Coca—a thinly veiled knockoff of Mariani. Pemberton's formula differed by only a few extra ingredients, the most significant being kola nut, a stimulant chewed by manual laborers in West Africa containing caffeine in higher concentrations than tea or coffee. After scraping along for fifteen years in Atlanta's patent medicine industry, Pemberton finally hit pay dirt with this new beverage, selling French Wine Coca by the case.

His timing, however, was impeccably bad. In November 1885, Atlanta declared it would be joining many states and counties in banning alcohol, taking effect the following July. That gave Pemberton only a few months to retool his formula to appeal to an America newly obsessed with sobriety. That obsession, which had been slowly gaining steam for almost a hundred years, led to the creation of the soft drink industry that would assure Pemberton's success.

In early years, in fact, most beverages in America had been alcoholic. Despite the dour image of Puritans and Pilgrims, beer was one of the first luxuries imported to New England, not to mention the cheapest form of water purification in a world of haphazard hygiene. Soon enterprising drunkards were fermenting anything they could get their hands on—Indian corn, birch bark, even twigs boiled in maple sap. Children drank hard cider at breakfast, and college students passed two-quart tankards down their cafeteria tables.

Not everyone was such a lush, however. Some abstemious colonists served nonalcoholic drinks flavored with sugar cane or juniper berries under the name "beverige," the direct ancestors of soft drinks. Meanwhile, the well-to-do made pilgrimages to effervescent mineral springs such as those at Saratoga Springs, New York, which were thought to have healing properties. In 1767, Englishman Joseph Priestley discovered how to produce the same carbonation artificially by mixing crushed chalk with sulfuric acid to create "fixed air" (carbon dioxide), and then pumping it into water or other beverages to make them fizzy.

The discovery coincided with a growing movement against alcohol led by Benjamin Rush, a signer of the Declaration of Independence who first identified alcoholism as an addictive disease in the 1780s and spoke out for the first time against drinking by children. Over the next few decades, the growing temperance movement founded the forerunner of Alcoholics Anonymous and passed statewide prohibition laws in some thirteen states. (Difficult to enforce, many were repealed by the end of the Civil War.)

Soon, teetotalers had a new venue for socializing as well. Just after the Civil War, a Philadelphia pharmacist improved Priestley's carbonation methods and added fruit and sugar, creating the world's first "soda fountain." Drugstores began sprouting elaborate marble beverage dispensers as a place for men, women, and children to all hang out together. As the patent medicine craze grew, they expanded their offerings with branded formulas, including the first trademarked soft drink, Lemon's Superior

Sparkling Ginger Ale, which appeared in 1871. Then came Hires Root Beer, a combination of pipsissewa, spikenard, dog grass, and other botanical goodies marketed as a blood purifier; followed by Dr Pepper, a Texas cherry drink touted as a digestion aid; and Moxie, a "nerve food" from Boston marketed—despite its high caffeine content—as a cure for insomnia and nervousness.

Nerves were something the newly prostrate South had in abundance. Broken by the Civil War as completely as Pickett's Charge was broken by the Union Army at Gettysburg, the South suffered a complete disruption in its social fabric, with newly liberated black slaves, deposed plantation owners, wounded veterans, and Northern carpetbaggers all anxious to find their place in the new order. Atlanta was better off than many locales—known as the "Phoenix City" for the speed with which it rebuilt itself after the war, the city's location at the terminus of major railway lines positioned it well for trade and manufacturing. All of the striving and ambition, however, only compounded the anxieties of urban life, providing the perfect market for a soothing nerve tonic. That's exactly what Pemberton set out to make.

Driven by the impending prohibition, Pemberton raced to remove the wine from his drink and tinkered with dozens of reformulations in the lead-up to the spring of 1886, when the annual soft drink season began. Frustrated by the bitter taste of the kola nut, he removed it entirely and replaced it with synthetic caffeine. Then, to further improve the taste of his new drink, he added sugar, citric and phosphoric acids, vanilla, lemon oil, and extracts of orange, nutmeg, and coriander. Just to make it a bit more exotic, he sprinkled in a few drops of oil derived from two trees found in China, bitter orange and cassia. To this day, no one knows the exact proportions that Pemberton used for the first batch of what would become Coca-Cola. But the vaunted secret formula is only the beginning of the lore built around Coke over the decades, which makes the drink's origins seem more like a religious creation myth than a product formulation.

Nearly every version of the drink's origins starts with a virgin birth in a kettle in Pemberton's backyard. In his 1950 book *The Big Drink, New Yorker* writer E. J. Kahn refers to a "three-legged iron pot" stirred with a boat oar. In his 1978 Coke biography, southern historian Pat Watters makes it a "brass kettle heated over an open fire" on the authority of long-time Coke archivist Wilbur Kurtz, Jr. (For good measure, he says the formula was perfected on the same day the Statue of Liberty was unveiled in New York Harbor, which didn't actually happen until October, some six months later.)

Reversing the spiritual order, next comes the immaculate conception, when Coke's trademark fizziness is added accidentally at Jacob's Pharmacy, the soda fountain around the corner from Pemberton's factory. In some accounts, it's a random soda jerk too lazy to walk to the fresh water tap who adds the soda water instead. In others, it's pharmacy owner Willis Venable himself. An heir to the Coca-Cola fortune, Elizabeth Candler Graham, even gives the name of a man, John G. Wilkes, who came in asking for a hangover remedy and accidentally got one with a fizz.

However romantic these accounts may be, all of them are fanciful revisions, if not outright fabrications. Firsthand accounts dug up by more recent Coke biographers such as Mark Pendergrast and Frederick Allen describe Pemberton's pharmacy laboratory as state-of-the-art for the time, with a forty-gallon copper kettle beneath an enormous sand filter built into the ceiling above. A contemporary account by Pemberton's nephew confirms that the idea from the beginning was to sell the drink carbonated; all spring, in fact, runners were sent back and forth from the headquarters of Pemberton Chemical Company to Jacob's Pharmacy for soda water to use in testing the drink. Even the claim made at the World of Coca-Cola that Pemberton created an entirely new category of beverage—cola—is a stretch, since fountain drinks containing kola nut, such as Kola Phosphate and Imperial Inca Cola, had been served for several years before 1885.

The truth puts the company into a bind, however, since dispelling the myth would force the company to explain the drink's origins in the shady patent medicine industry. Over the years, Coca-Cola has worked to construct its image as zealously as any medicine show barker hoping to win over a new potential client. Like them, the company has learned that it's not what the product actually contains, but what a customer thinks it represents that is important (even if that means distancing themselves from the showmen who first taught that lesson).

Maybe that's why the company's more recent official histories gloss over the truth, stating that Pemberton created the drink, "according to legend, in a three-legged brass pot in his backyard," and that "whether by design or by accident, carbonated water was teamed with the new syrup." In that way, the company is able to preserve its mythology while still technically being truthful. Whatever the facts, promotion of the drink was conceived right along with the drink. Everyone agrees the name Coca-Cola was coined by one of Pemberton's partners, Frank Robinson, who riffed off the alliteration popular in the names of Atlanta patent medicine at the time. A Yankee from Maine by way of Ohio, Robinson had shown up at Pemberton's door a year earlier with a special printer that could produce two colors at one time, quickly taking over advertising and marketing for Pemberton Chemical Company. One of his first acts was to write out Coca-Cola's distinctive cursive trademark, done with a flourish in Spencerian script, a flowing font then taught in grammar schools.

Hedging its bets between the twin crazes of patent medicines and prohibition, the label for the syrup advertised it as both an invigorating "brain tonic" and a refreshing "temperance drink." Company lore has it that initial sales were weak, at just twenty-five gallons the first year. Pemberton didn't live to see the drink's eventual success. Soon after inventing Coca-Cola, he took to his bed with illness. Within two years, he died of stomach cancer. Even from his deathbed, however, he set in motion a number of backroom maneuverings that took the drink away from his partners and eventually put it into the hands of an ambitious Atlanta pharmacist, Asa Candler.

Candler is Captain Coke, the hero of Coke's early history and the first man to espy the drink's potential to become the great American beverage.

His purchase of Coca-Cola for the paltry sum of $2,300 was hardly simple, however, taking years of legal maneuverings and possibly outright theft.

Napoleonic in stature and ambition, Candler was by all accounts a humorless workaholic who lived for his business. He neither drank nor smoked, he saved envelopes on his desk for scrap paper, and he was not above coming into the office on a Saturday to mix up a single gallon of Coca-Cola in order to make a sale. Initially, he aspired to be a doctor but changed course after realizing there was "more money to be made as a druggist." In later years, he loved to stress the Horatio Alger roots of his story, telling people he had arrived in Atlanta in 1873 with only $1.75 in his pocket. Within a decade, he owned a chain of drugstores.

Like Pemberton, Candler knew the real money was to be found in selling patent medicines. Rather than tinker with his own formulas, however, he bought those made by others, including Botanic Blood Balm and the unfortunately named Everlasting Cologne. It was Frank Robinson who convinced Candler to buy Coke just a few years after Pemberton invented it. Ill and in need of cash, Pemberton had sold two-thirds of the company out from under his partners in 1887, leaving Robinson—the adman who named Coke—with nothing. Livid at seeing his hard work taken away from him, Robinson cajoled Candler with visions of Coke's national potential—and with its efficacy at treating headaches, which Candler had suffered from all of his life. Swayed by the hard sell, Candler quietly began buying up outstanding shares by any means possible. On two occasions, according to Coke historian Mark Pendergrast, documents seem to include forged signatures, including Pemberton's own signature on a bill of sale signed with his son (who died soon after, under mysterious circumstances). Perhaps to cover his tracks from those early misdeeds, Candler later had all of the earliest records of the company burned.

At any rate, once he had the company under his control, Candler wasted no time spreading the drink around the country. His business model was simplicity itself—the company mixed sugar and water to create the syrup, added the flavoring, and sold jugs of the stuff to drugstores to peddle in their soda fountains for a nickel a drink. At those prices, however, the company wasn't going to make money unless it sold a lot of drinks. That is where Frank Robinson comes in, since it was Candler's quiet sidekick who directed the early strategy for selling the product.

Put in charge of sales and marketing, Robinson in large part literally gave the drink away, handing out tickets for free Cokes all over Atlanta and mailing them to Atlanta's most prominent citizens. Later he expanded the practice into a Victorian precursor to the now ubiquitous "reward cards" at stores promising discounts in exchange for customers' personal information. Each soda fountain operator got free syrup for 256 glasses of Coca-Cola, provided it gave the company names and addresses for 128 of its best customers, who then received free drink tickets. Soon the company was sending out coupons for more than 100,000 drinks a year. The buzz was well worth the cost. Sales took off as soon as Candler took over, multiplying nearly ten times between 1889 and 1891, from around 2,000 to nearly 20,000 gallons a year. Within another two years, sales had more than doubled again to nearly 50,000 gallons.

No doubt, those sales had something to do with the kick early imbibers got from the drink, from its namesake ingredient—cocaine. The World of Coca-Cola never mentions the word, of course, and the company goes out of its way to deny it whenever the issue crops up. Present Coke archivist Phil Mooney states flatly in a posting on Coke's corporate website: "Coca-Cola has never used cocaine as an ingredient."

At best, that claim is a technicality, since early formulas for Coke called for coca leaf, not cocaine, though it amounts to the same thing. Apparently no records survive showing how much Pemberton put in the drink, though one early copy of the formula held by a descendant of Frank Robinson calls for a relatively small one-twentieth of a grain per dose. When Candler took over the company, he reduced the amount of cocaine and caffeine over the span of several years in response to growing public controversy. Even so, an analysis by the president of the Georgia Pharmaceutical Association in 1891 found what amounted to one-thirtieth of a dose per glass, shrugging that off as "so small that it would be simply impossible for anyone to form the cocaine habit from drinking Coca-Cola."

Candler picked up on that diagnosis, including it in a 1901 pamphlet. That didn't stop him, however, from simultaneously touting the narcotic kick on his letterhead, identifying Coke as "containing the tonic properties of the wonderful COCA PLANT and the famous COLA NUT." Pamphlets he handed out to retailers claimed the syrup "contains, in a remarkable degree, the tonic properties of the wonderful Erythroxylon Coca Plant of South America." Candler even admitted on the stand in trial in 1901 that the drink contained "a very small proportion" of cocaine, which wasn't entirely removed until around 1906.

In the face of so much evidence that the drink contained cocaine, albeit a very small amount, it's a wonder the company continues to insist otherwise.

Of course, it took more than chemical appeal for the drink to expand as rapidly as it did. It also took money. With little cash on hand in 1891, Candler decided he needed to raise at least $50,000 to build a bigger factory and pay for salesmen and advertising. He found it in a relatively new form of business: the corporation.

Despite the ubiquity of corporations in our modern era, the arrangement is really only as old as America. One of the very first corporations chartered by the British Crown raised capital for the costly undertaking of exploring the New World. The Virginia Company wasn't particularly successful as a company—losing £100,000 before it was disbanded—but it did succeed in transplanting the survival of the corporation itself. After dozens of British families lost their fortunes from the collapse of the notorious South Seas Company in 1720, Parliament banned the risky propositions. When the father of capitalism himself, Adam Smith, wrote *The Wealth of Nations* in 1776, he spoke out against corporations, arguing that the "directors of such companies . . . being the managers rather of other people's money than of their own, it cannot well be expected that they should watch over it with the same anxious vigilance with which the partners in a private copartnery."

That was all very well in Europe, however, where a landed aristocracy could form partnerships to fund costly projects. In the United States, businessmen had comparatively fewer wealthy investors to fund their projects, requiring them to sell greater amounts of lower-priced shares to create the same investment. The corporation took off as the most popular form of business, with more than three hundred of them taking root in the United States in the two decades after the Revolution. And unlike their British counterparts, some American corporations such as the great maritime trading companies of New England were incredibly profitable. Their owners, in turn, created the textile mills that rapidly industrialized the United States beginning in the 1830s. No corporations were as successful, however, as the railroads, which raised huge reserves of capital—more than $1 billion by 1860—to build their networks, along with sophisticated management structures to operate them.

The increasing wealth of corporations led to an increase in their power. In their early days, corporations were chartered by states for specific purposes, with strict time limits, to prevent them from being "detrimental to, or not promotive of, the public good," according to a ruling by Virginia's top court in 1809. Some states even passed laws allowing them to revoke corporate charters whenever they deemed fit. That changed, however, in the mid–nineteenth century, when after increased lobbying at state capitals, some states began loosening their rules in an effort to attract more corporate dollars. Delaware and New Jersey led the pack, allowing corporations to exist in perpetuity for any purpose they desired, and codifying the concept of "limited liability," which shielded share owners from responsibility for the actions a corporation performed in their name. Then the courts, most notably in a California case won by Southern Pacific Railroad in 1886, declared corporations to be virtual "persons" who could sue or own property in their own rights. And in 1880, the federal government struck down state laws requiring companies to abide by local health and labor laws in order to trade in other states, allowing companies to sell their products nationally for the first time. "Had Coca-Cola appeared twenty years sooner, it might have withered inside Georgia, forbidden to trade outside its state of manufacture," writes social historian Humphrey McQueen. "Candler took over Coca-Cola just as the law assured capitalists of their right to spread geographically as well as financially."

Before the Civil War, in fact, there were few "national" products. Groceries were mostly made locally and sold generically out of the proverbial cracker barrel. The need to keep 4 million soldiers fed and clean while they shot at each other up and down the East Coast changed that, leading to innovations in shipping and packaging that allowed products to travel great distances. At the same time, the Industrial Revolution lowered the cost of manufacturing goods, and urbanization led to new markets in city department stores. Finally, the power of corporations was made complete when states starting with Delaware and New Jersey enabled them for the first time to merge, acquire, and buy stock in other corporations. In the four years between 1898 and 1902, there was a massive bloodletting, with the number of American companies falling from 2,653 to 269.

The companies that succeeded in the great winnowing, says Harvard business historian Richard Tedlow, were those that shifted from producing a small amount of high-quality goods to producing a large amount of goods at a low profit margin. With its nickel-a-glass price tag, Coke was the quintessential example. Candler incorporated the Coca-Cola Company in Georgia in 1892, creating one thousand shares of stock (five hundred of which he kept for himself) in order to raise the necessary funds for expansion. In first promoting the drink, he shrewdly limited the company's take of the profits, selling syrup wholesale at $1.50 a gallon, which retailers could then sell by the glass for $6.40 a gallon—ensuring them more than 400 percent profit.

Setting his margin low, however, meant that Candler had to rely on growth as a source of increasing profits. Coke employed legions of salesmen, usually off-season cotton farmers hired on a contract basis for the summer, who literally rode the rails to drum up business for Coke around the country. Known as "Coca-Cola Men," they epitomized the cult of the traveling salesmen in the era before Willy Loman died. Despite the fact they made only $12.50 a week—a low wage even at the time—they relished their freedom and expense accounts, proudly proselytizing for the beverage with a near-religious devotion. By 1895—less than ten years after it was created—Coca-Cola was sold in all forty-four states in the Union, with Hawaii, Canada, Mexico, and Cuba soon to follow.

After Candler, no "Coca-Cola Man" was as passionate as his nephew Sam Dobbs. Starting out sleeping on a cot in the back of the factory, he went on to drum up clients all over Georgia and the Carolinas in the first two years of the Candler era. Called back to headquarters, he was put in charge of all salesmen in 1900, freeing Robinson to concentrate solely on advertising. Strict where Robinson was lenient, he exhorted his troops like a one-man pep squad as they expanded the drink around the country. By the turn of the century, Coke was growing by leaps and bounds. In 1899, the company sold more than 250,000 gallons of syrup annually; by 1902, it surpassed 500,000 gallons; and by 1904, it was selling over a million, earning $1.5 million in sales. By this time, those sales were helped by one more factor that more than any other would lead to the dominance of Coca-Cola in the beverage industry: bottling.

Coke's relationship with its bottlers has been fraught with mutual conflict and benefit from the moment it began. In 1899, a Chattanooga lawyer named Benjamin Thomas saw a bottled pineapple drink in Cuba during the Spanish-American War; when he got home, he thought he'd try the same with Coke, which until then had been sold exclusively at fountains. He headed to Atlanta with some home-sealed bottles and a friend, Joseph Whitehead, in search of a contract. Candler, as the story goes, was unimpressed, but figured he had little to lose in giving the Chattanoogans a chance. With little thought, he granted them the rights for free, setting a fixed price of 92 cents per gallon for syrup for as long as they worked their territory.

The six-hundred-word contract would eventually revolutionize Coke's distribution, establishing the franchise system of bottling that remains to this day around the globe. In theory, the bottlers take on all of the risk and responsibility, while the parent company provides the product and the two split the profit. In practice, however, the company and its franchisees have tussled constantly over the years, in both the United States and around the world, each one fighting to minimize its risk and maximize its control—to say nothing of the lion's share of profit.

In the early days, at least, Coke and its bottlers existed harmoniously, in part because they had a common enemy against which to join forces. Hard-driving Sam Dobbs had been urging his uncle Asa to begin bottling for years—only to see a host of imitators crop up as soon as Coca-Cola bottling plants started roaring into operation. Some, like Chero-Cola, had been around as long as Coke. Others were fly-by-nighters capitalizing off king Coke's success, sporting copycat names like Coke-Ola, Ko-Cola, and even Coca & Cola. "Unscrupulous pirates," Candler fumed, "find it more profitable to imitate and substitute on the public than to honestly avail themselves of the profit and pleasure which is ever the reward of fair dealing and competition."

Asa Candler was a firm adherent to the principles of the free market; nothing infuriated him so much as government regulation or taxation, at least whenever it infringed on the company's right to make money. Taxes, he criticized in biblical terms, calling them "gourd vines in wheat fields" that strangled the ability for a business owner to make profit. Child labor he called "the most beautiful sight we see." And as for unions, he did everything he could to discourage their formation, calling them "a political parasite sprung from the feculent accumulations of popular ignorance and fattened upon the purulent secretions of popular prejudice."

When it came to imitators, however, he gave Dobbs free rein to bring the full force of government down on them to protect the business. Coke had the perfect cudgel in the recently passed 1905 Trademark Law, part of the nascent Progressive movement that had emerged in a backlash against the unbridled capitalism of the previous decade. By the turn of the twentieth century, the power of corporate interests had reached its peak, as muckraking journalists writing in the nation's first magazines such as *Collier's* and *McClure's* increasingly exposed the political corruption and excesses of the robber barons in the railroad, coal, and meatpacking industries. The diatribes led to a political backlash resulting in increased regulation, breaking up monopolies and ensuring quality standards.

The new trademark law was originally passed as a way to protect consumers against deceptive marketing. Coke, however, was one of the first and most aggressive entities to use the law to defend its own rights to profit. Dobbs enlisted the company's head lawyer, Harold Hirsch, to lead the charge against the "loathsome following," his name for the bottlers who tried to steal Coke's business. "I have spent my nights and my days thinking about Coca-Cola," Hirsch once said, and he wasn't kidding—eventually, he would amass a seven-hundred-page volume of case law that virtually created trademark law in the United States. Starting in 1909, he brought a case a week against other soft drink companies, arguing they had deliberately created their names to ape Coca-Cola.

It was a suit against one of Pemberton's old partners that finally put the imitators to rest. Years earlier, Pemberton had sold some of the rights of Coca-Cola to his partner J. C. Mayfield, who had begun selling the formula around Atlanta under the name Koke. When he revived the drink two decades later, however, Hirsch brought suit, arguing in 1914 that "Coke" was in such common use as a stand-in for Coca-Cola, Mayfield could only be trying to piggyback on its success. Despite a promising beginning, Coke lost the case in District Court. The Court of Appeals was even harsher, accusing Coke, not Koke, of engaging in deceptive practices by saying it hadn't contained cocaine when it once had, and did contain kola nut when it didn't.

At the darkest hour, however, the United States Supreme Court came to Coke's rescue. In a December 1920 ruling that Coke executives love to quote to this day, judicial lion Oliver Wendell Holmes, Jr., essentially declared that whatever its past practices, Coca-Cola had transcended its own name to become "a single thing coming from a single source, and well known to the community. It hardly would be too much to say that the drink characterizes the name as much the name the drink." In other words, Coke was so popular that no one in his right mind would consider its name as merely describing its two main ingredients. Therefore, any beverage with a similar name was merely riding Coke's coattails. In one fell swoop, the U.S. government had ensured Coke's right to exist, clearing the field of virtually anyone who would oppose it.

Dobbs's aggressive strategy of taking on all comers had paid off, setting the stage for the continued rapid growth of the company. Sales of the drink by 1920 were now in the tens of millions of gallons, leading to more than $4 million in annual net profit. As the money poured in, Candler bought up skyscrapers in Kansas City, Baltimore, and New York, each of which he inevitably named the Candler Building. Meanwhile, as Dobbs amassed power, Robinson's star waned. In a tiff over advertising, Candler sided with his nephew, making him head of advertising and sales, as well as his de facto successor. As the company grew bigger and more successful, however, there was one person who remained unsatisfied, even appalled, by the growth—Asa G. Candler.

The strict Methodist upbringing that made Candler frugal and austere also made him feel guilty about the obscene profits he made from such an ephemeral product, and envy his brothers Warren, a Methodist bishop, and John, a state judge. Finally as the decade turned, depression got the best of him. He fretted about his legacy and his four sons, who were almost universally disappointing to him. (The most entertaining of the lot, Asa Jr., eventually became an eccentric drunk, who kept a menagerie of zoo animals in his mansion and created a minor scandal when his baboon scaled a fence and ate $60 out of a woman's purse.) The only one of his sons who showed any promise was Howard, who followed him into the company. But while Howard showed aptitude in the technical side of the soda business, he lacked his father's vision and management skill.

Candler's disappointments came to a head in 1913, when he suffered a nervous breakdown and took a prolonged tour of Europe to "steady his nerves." As much as anything, the cause of his breakdown was financial. Over the years, Candler had treated Coca-Cola as his personal piggybank, intertwining his finances with the company's. Progressive changes in tax laws in 1913, however, prevented businesses from holding on to large cash reserves, requiring that they distribute dividends to shareholders instead. Candler bitterly resented parting with any of it. Fine with allowing the government to protect his profits against would-be competitors, he wasn't about to let Uncle Sam tell him how he had to distribute those same profits to investors.

After this "forced liquidation," wrote his son Howard, "he was ready to quit trying to make money and entirely willing to relinquish to others the task of conducting the affairs of the corporation." At the same time, he tossed out vast sums to philanthropic causes, assuaging his conscience, increasing his stature in Atlanta, and earning a healthy tax write-off in the bargain. In 1914, he made a contribution of $1 million to Emory University, where his brother Warren Candler was president, the first of an eventual $8 million in largesse. The same year, he earned the undying affection of Georgians when he mortgaged his own fortune to shore up the price of cotton in the wake of a market crash during World War I.

By 1916, he was ready to give up his company, but not his legacy, shocking his board by slighting his natural successor, Dobbs, and making Howard president instead. A year later, he gave away nearly all his stock to his wife and children as a Christmas present. As Asa Candler left Coke, he turned wholeheartedly to public service, running for mayor of Atlanta and winning a two-year term from 1917 to 1919. If voters hoped he would use his personal fortune to relieve the city's debts, though, they were disappointed. Instead, his administration proposed raising water rates, which would fall disproportionately on the poor, and urged rich citizens to voluntarily overvalue their property to pay more taxes (few did).

In fact, Candler was deeply ambivalent about the power of altruism—happy to give his money away for the greater good when he was in control of who received it, but resentful of sharing the spoils of capitalism with those he felt hadn't built the system. Meanwhile, the company foundered in his absence. Howard was a lackluster president, struggling to keep Coca-Cola afloat during the sugar rationing of World War I. Meanwhile, in 1919, in the wake of Candler's slight, Dobbs became head of the Atlanta

Chamber of Commerce, where he got to meet many members of the city's business elite. Just as Robinson had persuaded Candler to buy up the company decades earlier, Dobbs would persuade one of them, Trust Company president Ernest Woodruff, to take over the company now.

As a business tycoon, Ernest Woodruff was almost a caricature—a cross between Gordon Gekko and the Monopoly Man. His occupation was to make money, mostly through the takeover, restructuring, and sale of real estate and transportation companies. He had a reputation for playing dirty, not above breaking into a rival's office late at night to steal files. And he was even more of a skinflint than Candler, once supposedly strapping $2 million in bonds to himself and his secretary on a train from Cleveland in order to save $200 in shipping costs. This was the man to whom Dobbs turned to buy the Coca-Cola Company, enlisting the company's lawyer Harold Hirsch as go-between. By the summer of 1919, he had secured signatures from all five of Candler's children to sell the company for $15 million in cash and $10 million in stock, the largest financial transaction ever conducted in the South at that time. Not one of the children said a word of the sale to their father.

The buyer was a syndicate of three banks—Woodruff's Trust Company of Georgia, and two New York Banks, Chase National and Guaranty Trust. Woodruff engineered a deal that, while technically legal, relied on insider information to offer a killing to the businessman and his colleagues. Settling on 500,000 shares, they sold the first 417,000 to brokers at $35 a share—anticipating they'd turn them around to the public at $40 or more. Secretly, however, they kept back 83,000 shares for insiders to buy at the bargain price of $5 each, assuring control of the company and millions of dollars in profit for pennies on the dollar. The gambit worked, and the new Coca-Cola Company was incorporated in Delaware, a state known for its low business taxes and leniency on corporate bylaws.

One of Woodruff's first actions was to reward Dobbs with the presidency of the new company, even while he maintained control with a three-man Voting Trust. Surveying his new domain, Ernest Woodruff liked what he saw—one of the fastest growing companies in the world, with seemingly unlimited territory to expand.

Quickly, however, he identified an enemy within the ranks: the bottlers to whom Candler had given away franchise rights for a song. The bottling system had grown from nearly 250 bottling plants nationwide in 1905, to almost 500 in 1910, to more than 1,000 by 1917. War changed many things in the world, however, not the least of which was the price of sugar, which skyrocketed from 5 cents to almost 30 cents after war's outbreak, costing the company $20,000 a day. Meanwhile, the bottlers' contract stipulated a set price for syrup at 92 cents per gallon, no matter how much sugar fluctuated, leaving the parent company to eat the cost. Hirsch, who had been the bottlers' best advocate when he was going after the trademark imitators, was now made the go-to guy to lead the attack against them.

Company executives directed their particular animosity against the "parent bottlers," umbrella companies set up by Whitehead and Thomas, who had subcontracted out territories to smaller bottlers. They were now little more than paper entities, buying syrup at 92 cents a gallon and selling it to bottlers at up to $1.20 a gallon. Thus, they pocketed a quarter a gallon without even handling the syrup, which was shipped directly from the Coca-Cola Company. Hirsch called the current presidents of the parent bottlers, Veazey Rainwater and George Hunter, into his office, and informed them their contracts were now "contracts at will." The bottlers protested that the contracts had been signed by Asa Candler in perpetuity. Even so, not wanting to appear unreasonable, the bottlers countered with a sliding scale for syrup with a more modest profit of a dime per gallon. Woodruff saw no need to strike a deal; he simply fired the bastards—declaring that from now on, Coke would be sold directly to individual bottlers.

The bottlers sued, hauling Coke into court in April 1920 for a two-year trial that quickly became a bloodbath. Hirsch essentially called the bottlers leeches who had built a profit of $2.5 million but "who served no useful purpose." That's a funny thing to say, shot back Veazey Rainwater, by a syndicate that pocketed $5 million in profit in just one day during the sale of the company. Even while the bottler case hung in the balance, the company's—and Sam Dobbs's—fortune took a turn for the worse. In the summer of 1920, Coke chairman Howard Candler committed to buying two tons of sugar from Indonesia at 20 cents a pound, just before the worldwide price of sugar broke back to 10 cents. Despite Howard's catastrophic error, Woodruff blamed Dobbs, with whom he'd clashed egos from the beginning. He forced Dobbs to resign, a bitter payback for the deal he had engineered to put Woodruff in charge. In his place, Woodruff reinstalled Howard Candler as president—at least for the time being.

Finally, the verdict in the bottler case came down in June 1921 in favor of Hunter and Rainwater, declaring the bottling contracts permanent. Now with the upper hand, the bottlers again offered a compromise allowing them to make a profit of 15 cents a gallon, a nickel more than they'd originally offered. Even as the rift was repaired, it was never healed. From then on, the bottlers were always suspicious of the intentions of the parent company, and the Coca-Cola Company was always looking for schemes to take back what Candler gave away. It would take another sixty-five years to again consolidate the bottlers under its influence.

With the lawsuit over, however, Coke had successfully weathered several crises to come out on top. The stock price rebounded from a low of $25 a share to back above $40, and sales, too, soon rose again, to $24 million by 1923. Everybody was happy, except Candler. When he heard of the deal brokered by his children to sell the company under his nose, he was publicly enthusiastic but privately devastated. "They sold out a big share for a fancy price," he sniffed. "I wouldn't have done that, but they did." More and more, the man responsible for creating the world's most successful brand sank into self-pity. Writing to Howard, he said, "I sometimes think that once I lived in Heaven and, wandering, lost my way. . . . I was once counted with Atlanta's builders . . . now I am companionless, not needed nor called for any service."

As sympathetic Coke historian Pat Watters puts it, "The syrup of life by now had, for him, entirely soured." After the death of his wife, Lucy, he scandalized Atlanta society with his intention to marry, of all things, a Catholic suffragette from New Orleans. Under pressure from his brother the bishop, he called off the marriage and instead married a stenographer in his office building who was soon caught in a police raid drinking bootleg liquor with two strange men. "Everybody is dead but me, and I ought to be dead but I just won't die," he sputtered during a trademark infringement case in 1924. "There are too many days between my cradle and my grave now." It would be another five years before he was finally relieved of suffering, dying alone in a New York City hotel room in 1929.

The company he helped create, however, was prospering beyond the wildest dreams of Asa Candler or John Pemberton. After a sometimes rocky start, it hit its stride during the Jazz Age of the 1920s, with profits increasing by millions of dollars a year over the decade. More important, the product itself had begun to worm its way into the American consciousness. As the company steadily built its brand, what started out as a fizzy drink and a headache cure was taking on new life as a symbol of everything desirable about American life—even as a symbol of America itself.

TWO

Building the Brand

The Gaylord Texan Hotel and Convention Center, twenty miles north of Dallas, is a triumph of illusion. Inside its eighteen-story glassed-in atrium is a full-size Spanish hacienda, an Alamo-like fort, a box canyon, and a covered wagon, all kept a comfortable seventy-two degrees in defiance of the Texan sun. It might seem a strange place to hold the thirty-fifth annual convention for the Coca-Cola Collectors Club, dedicated to the devotion of a product known as "The Real Thing." And yet, here Coke is, the ultimate symbol in a sea of surfaces. Vintage Coke signs hang year-round at the resort's pool area, and rusting Coke coolers decorate the café, fixtures in the resort's vast evocation of Texan nostalgia.

That's nothing, of course, compared with the amount of memorabilia laid out this Fourth of July weekend in the guest rooms on four floors of an entire wing of the hotel, amassed over decades from some of Coke's biggest fans.

For Bob Bessenden, it started with commemorative Coca-Cola bottles—6½-ouncers emblazoned with insignias of different college and professional sports teams he picked up for his kids on business trips. From there, he attended a Coke memorabilia swap-meet in Minneapolis after seeing an ad in the paper, and found table after table of collectors' items, along with a whole subculture of acolytes. "There were people from as far away as Australia," says Bessenden, who is sixtyish with a trim white beard and glasses. "It was more like a fellowship."

It didn't take him long to join that society, hunting down souvenirs at flea markets and thrift stores; in one of his biggest scores, he acquired an entire room full of vintage Coke signs set to be thrown out by a distributor in Alaska. Now his hotel room at the Gaylord Texan is a veritable shrine to the drink, with signs, posters, and menu boards spread across both beds. Most sport the "fishtail" logo of the 1950s, a cherry-red oval with triangles cut out of both sides. "For a couple of years, we collected only fishtails," says Bessenden. "Some people only collect signs that say 'Things Go Better with Coke.' Some people collect Santas. Some collect only Olympic items."

For those who collect it, this accumulated flotsam comes with many more associations than just the sugary drink it advertises. "It represents an era, a much simpler time," says Bessenden's wife, Ann, who's got a down-home vibe that goes with her unfussy bob. "You know, when everything was more laid-back, soda fountains and ice cream and people socializing." Countless collectors with their own hotel rooms chock-full of Coke offer variations on the theme. "The nostalgia, the good times, when things were so much easier," explains Pat Vaughn, the club's western coordinator, when asked what Coke means to her. Her basement in Denver is set up as an imitation 1950s diner, complete with Coke ads on the walls, and among her prized possessions is a sandwich iron from the 1930s that could emboss the Coca-Cola logo into a grilled cheese.

Despite their earnest appeals, it's hard to imagine collectors holding a similar convention for any of dozens of brands surviving from the same era—Campbell's Soup, Morton's Salt, Kleenex Tissue. Coke, however, is something more, having long ago transcended its corporeal reality to become a stand-in for baseball games and soda fountains, national pride and international harmony—symbols worthy of devotion, even obsession. In another room down the hall, two brothers from Oklahoma have stacked crate upon crate of commemorative Coke bottles; they have some 40,000 in all. On the last day, participants sit through a live auction of Coke coolers, vending machines, billboards, a bicycle. As the rapid-fire patter echoes off the ceiling of the cavernous convention hall, cardboard signs fetch $1,000 and an 1899 calendar garners a high bid of $6,500.

Despite the free-flowing Coke in the back of the convention hall, the participants invariably get shy when asked about their love of the drink itself. “I drink way too much,” says Bessenden bashfully, patting his not-particularly-large stomach. “I limit myself to one can a day at work. Then I have one when I get home—a couple of cans.” He hesitates. “Sometimes breakfast . . .” Vaughn drinks a six-pack of Diet Coke daily. “I start with decaf coffee in the morning and then switch—too much caffeine is not good for your bones,” she says.

But of course, the appeal of Coke to the collectors has little to do with the drink itself. “In its simplest form, Coca-Cola is sugar water,” says Keith Duggan, perhaps the most fanatical Coke collector of them all, having attended every one of the club’s thirty-four past annual conventions. “But they don’t sell sugar water. They sell refreshment. They sell love. They sell good times.” As he says this, he is rummaging through crates of old ads in another hotel room, looking for one he might not already have.

Sitting in a rocking chair nearby, the club’s past president Dick McChesney concurs. More than any company of its time, he says, Coke invested in new techniques of graphic design and color. “Their philosophy was that you had to create an idea in their heads to get them to drink your soft drink,” he says, leaning back in a rocking chair. “As a collector, what could be better than a whole bunch of signs that create ideas of what those products stood for?” He motions to a poster-sized reproduction of a 1942 ad with two girls in a convertible, one tipping a bottle to her lips. “How could you not look at that and say, ‘That makes me feel good to see those two gals enjoying a Coke’?”

He’s right, of course. The Coca-Cola Company would never have succeeded without its advertising. And in the bargain, it helped change advertising itself, into something that sold customers less on products than on the ideas.

Advertising was literally created by America. Lurid English handbills in the 1600s urged country folks to witness oddities such as "a woman with three breasts," but the first serious ads touted something only slightly less obscene: free land and limitless opportunity in the New World, compliments of the Virginia Company. After their birth, ads followed the colonists across the ocean, posting real estate for sale and rewards for the capture of runaway slaves, and, as prosperity trickled down, wine, wigs, and perfumes, all described in increasingly over-the-top, flowery language.

A man named Volney Palmer opened the first advertising agency in Philadelphia in 1843, serving as little more than a middleman buying up space in newspapers and selling it to manufacturers at a markup. At the time, most companies dismissed advertising as "puffing," an ungentlemanly pursuit designed to unfairly trick the consumer—if not an admission that your product couldn't succeed on its own merit.

The first industry to throw good taste aside was the same one that gave rise to the creation of Coca-Cola: patent medicines. With few intrinsic qualities to sell their products, patent medicines had long employed an extra sleight of hand to lodge their names in the minds of consumers. The theatrical "medicine shows," however, reached audiences of only a few dozen people at a time. To maximize exposure, medicine makers blanketed streets with handbills and employed teams of young boys to hand out collectible trade cards.

In the countryside, they really went wild, painting every rock, fencepost, and barn with names of salves, elixirs, and potions. An English visitor in the 1870s lamented that travelers to the United States couldn't "step a mile into the open country, whether into the fields or along the high roads, without meeting the disfigurement." Niagara Falls, Yosemite, and Yellowstone Park were all covered in painted ads. One enterprising laxative maker even offered $25,000 to help build the Statue of Liberty's pedestal in exchange for posting "Fletcher's Castoria" in giant letters on it for a year (fortunately, the U.S. government turned him down). When, just before the Civil War, the number of newspapers exploded, patent medicine makers discovered a new way to reach the masses. It was a perfect match: Newspapers needed money, and patent medicine makers needed something on which to spend their obscene profits. By 1847, there were 11 million medicine ads in some two thousand papers nationwide. In some, they took up half the ad space. Oftentimes they consisted simply of the name of a tablet or salve repeated over pages and pages of dense text. But with increasing competition, the ones that succeeded were those that used the most creative or memorable slogans or artwork to sell their products.

As one medicine proprietor said, "I can advertise dish water, and sell it, just as well as an article of merit. . . . It's all in the advertising." Some early ads appealed to patriotism: "The Army protects our country against internal Dissension, Pe-Ru-Na protects our country against Catarrhal Diseases." Others, like Hembold's Extract of Buchu, peddled exotic ingredients, with pictures showing "Hottentots" gathering buchu leaves off the Cape of Good Hope. Then, of course, there was that old standby, T&A—with ads featuring a flash of cleavage or a half-robed girl entering or exiting a bath.

It was only a matter of time before other industries began to take a page from patent medicine makers to advertise their own products. "The greatest advertising men of my day were schooled in the medicine field," said advertising pioneer Claude C. Hopkins in *My Life in Advertising.* "It weeded out the incompetents and gave scope and prestige to those who survived." In many ways, advertising became a necessity for products sold nationally for the first time after the Civil War. In order to recoup packaging and shipping costs, companies such as Uneeda Biscuit, Quaker Oats, and Campbell's Soup needed something to persuade customers to pay a premium over the generics in the cracker barrel or sugar loaf.

In part, the new packages themselves served as ads. Tobacco companies literally branded their icons into the leaves with a hot iron—creating the concept of a "brand" as something that didn't involve cattle. But to keep up with the new demand for newspaper advertising, ad agencies transformed from mere middlemen to one-stop shops employing copywriters and artists to design ads for clients. Royal Baking Powder was the first company to picture its product in a newspaper advertisement in the 1870s. Quaker Oats did one better with the creation of its smiling behatted symbol, personally reassuring customers of the superior quality of its most pedestrian product. Manufacturers borrowed a toned-down version of the patent medicine maker's repetitive sales pitch, developing cloying catchphrases to figuratively brand their names into the mind of the consumer—"Do Uneeda Biscuit?" or "Good morning! Have you used Pears' Soap?"

The Coca-Cola Company used a bit of all of these tactics—and perfected them. As Coke spread rapidly across the country, it was advertising, not the secret formula, that kept it on top. After all, as business historian Richard Tedlow comments, "How really different was this product from other colas in taste?" In the early days, he continues, it probably varied as much "from soda fountain to soda fountain as it differed from similar soft drink products."

But the name remained the same, and from the beginning, Pemberton and his partners outdid other soft drink companies in getting it before the public. Their first year, they spent more than $70 on oilcloth banners and streetcar signs around Atlanta—despite reportedly earning less than $50 in sales. As profits increased, so did the advertising. Over the next few years, Coke's Spencerian script graced the sides of buildings and barns, along with soda fountain trays, fans, bookmarks, and paperweights—the Victorian antecedents of the advertising accrual that would one day fill the Gaylord Texan Hotel. By 1890, the advertising budget had swollen to more than $11,000, nearly a quarter of total sales.

Coke's slogans in those days hedged their bets, selling Coke as both a medicine to soothe jangled nerves and a cooling refreshment—a dichotomy encapsulated in Coke's very first ad in *The Atlanta Journal.* "Coca-

Cola. Delicious! Refreshing! Exhilarating! Invigorating! The New and Popular Soda Fountain Drink," the ad crowed, before stressing the healthful qualities of coca leaves and kola nuts. As Candler took over, he kept up the split personality, touting the drink as refreshment and "nerve tonic" that both "satisfies the thirsty and helps the weary."

Increasingly, those claims were made in a new genre—magazines. The first magazines, which helped to usher in the Progressive Movement with their muckraking investigations of big business, were paradoxically supported in large part by the advertising revenue of a raft of new products. And unlike newspapers, they embraced the use of artwork to fill their pages. Ad agencies produced more and more elaborate illustrations, at the same time streamlining flowery language or simple phrases into more sophisticated copy.

Ad titan Alfred Lasker, one of many early admen to earn the moniker "father of advertising," argued at the turn of the twentieth century that each ad should include a precise reason why customers should buy a product. Companies worked to create the next memorable catchphrase, from Procter & Gamble's new soap—"It Floats"—to Kodak's new instant camera—"You Press the Button—We Do the Rest."

With the pressure to pick one characteristic, and one only, the Coca-Cola Company made a strategic shift away from its medicinal use to emphasize the appeal as a soft drink. As Frank Robinson later explained, "Instead of advertising to one man in a hundred [who was sick] . . . we advertised to the thousands, by advertising it as a refreshing beverage." In truth, the switch had as much to do with the stubborn capitalist tendencies of Asa Candler. Looking for a source of income during war over Cuba in 1898, the U.S. government levied a tax on the fat patent medicine industry, including a total of $29,500 over three years on Coca-Cola. The amount was insufferable to Candler, who took the case to court in 1901—but not before almost totally dispensing with medicinal claims. (Coke eventually won the case when the government couldn't substantiate the drink's amount of cocaine, which by then had been almost entirely removed.)

The change in advertising was fortuitous for Coke, coinciding with the dawn of the Progressive Era, when journalists such as E. W. Kemble and especially Samuel Hopkins Adams began to increasingly attack patent medicines, blowing the cover off many of their fraudulent claims. Coke had already moved on, crafting an image based on relaxation and enjoyment. Working with Atlanta's Massengale Advertising Agency, the company turned out a procession of smiling, fancily dressed Victorian women raising flared glasses of Coke to their lips. Coke certainly wasn't the only company advertising with idealized upper-class images, but the sheer ubiquity of its ads set the tone for advertising nationally. Looking at them, you'd never know that the United States was going through convulsive demographic changes, with immigrants flooding the country, fueling a new manufacturing boom with long hours in the factory.

If those rigid images of upper-class refinement seemed an odd choice for a mass-market product such as Coke, contemporary economist Thorstein Veblen offers a reason for their success in his 1899 book *The Theory of the Leisure Class*, in which he invented the term "conspicuous consumption" to describe the consumer pretenses of the upper classes. The high-Victorian style of top hats and walking sticks had nothing to do with functionality, but were rather "evidence of leisure," he wrote, a message sent to onlookers that a person wasn't involved in "any employment that is directly and immediately of any human use." By associating Coca-Cola with such refinement, Coke in effect created the first "aspirational" advertising campaign, sending the uniquely American message that success could be achieved simply by buying the right brand.

And in Coke's case, the cost of admission to that "brand community" was remarkably low—a nickel, or a price that even the lowliest worker could afford. As Andy Warhol would later say: "The President drinks Coke, Liz Taylor drinks Coke, and just think, you can drink Coke, too. A Coke is a Coke and no amount of money can get you a better Coke than the one the bum on the corner is drinking."

Whether Coke realized it or not, it was on the vanguard of a new form of advertising. Just as Coke was establishing its new identity, Northwestern University psychologist Walter Dill Scott revolutionized the advertising field by applying the newly in-vogue principles of psychology. In his 1903 book *The Psychology of Advertising*, he argued that "the effect of modern advertising is not so much to convince as to suggest." So-called reason-why advertising was a blunt instrument compared with "atmosphere advertising," which would associate a product with the viewer's subconscious desires: to be well liked, to be healthy, to possess, to succeed.

In fact, the history of advertising might be seen as a pendulum swinging constantly back and forth between the "hard sell" advertising that spelled out specific reasons why a consumer should use a particular product and "atmosphere" advertising that emphasized the *idea* behind a product. Dill's principles were especially adopted by makers of luxury items such as cars and pianos, who increasingly crafted ads displaying how products would fit into their customers' desired lifestyles. Despite being one of the cheapest products on the market, however, Coke branded itself as the ultimate lifestyle symbol.

Looking for a way to distinguish himself when he took over advertising from the older Frank Robinson, Sam Dobbs dumped Massengale in 1906 in favor of up-and-coming St. Louis adman William D'Arcy. In D'Arcy's ads, the men and women shook off their top hats and petticoats to engage in golf, tennis, swimming—sports that were still out of reach of the vast majority of people in an industrializing society. The Coke bottles in the scenes, meanwhile, became a subtle part of the leisurely lifestyle, and sometimes weren't even pictured at all. Instead a simple tagline promised that "Coca-Cola provides a refreshing relish to any form of exercise." D'Arcy further created an aspirational lifestyle for Coke with celebrity endorsements—before Bill Cosby, Christina Aguilera, and "Mean Joe" Greene, there were actor Eddie Foy, opera star Lillian Nordica, and baseball legend Ty Cobb.

More than anything, however, D'Arcy pioneered Coke's main selling point for the next hundred years—pretty girls. "Sex sells" may be the oldest cliché in advertising, but until the turn of the century, sex was used only in sleazy products—circuses, cigarettes, and, of course, patent medicines. With the improvement of photography and color printing in the

1890s, companies began using pictures of women to sell everything from bicycles to cameras. But no one picked up the trend like soft drink companies did.

Before Coke, Moxie and Excelsior Ginger Ale both began revealing thighs and cleavage in their ads, and White Rock introduced its half-naked nymph in 1893. Sex was a natural match for beverages promising mental and physical stimulation from sugar and caffeine. "Interestingly enough," writes Tom Reichert in *The Erotic History of Advertising*, "reactions to sexual imagery provide a similar physiological response: dilated pupils, slight perspiration, and heartbeats that are ratcheted up a notch. Pairing the two, sex and beverages, served to provide a subtle link between the reactions to the image and the drinks' effect on us."

Let loose from their bodices, Coca-Cola girls became noticeably sexier. One 1910 ad flat-out said, "Nothing is so suggestive of Coca-Cola's own pure deliciousness as the picture of a beautiful, sweet, wholesome, womanly woman." Most ads, however, just implied as much, with foxy maidens offering a coquettish smile and a come-hither glint in the eye. Candler was adamant that there be no "hint of impurity" in his ad subjects—Coca-Cola girls would flirt but not put out. And yet they were arguably more effective for being ultimately unattainable.

Despite that bait-and-switch from a beautiful girl's smile to a mouthful of sugary refreshment, Dobbs was hailed as head of a movement for "Truth in Advertising," a crusade for "clean, truthful, honest publicity." As president of the Associated Advertising Clubs of America, he distanced the drink from the frauds of patent-medicine makers, saying the company was "claiming nothing for Coca-Cola that it did not do, no virtue that it did not have." And yet the company was pouring out astronomical sums to "truthfully" and "honestly" shape Coke's image.

By 1908, the company's ad budget topped half a million dollars a year. That number grew to more than $750,000 in 1909, the same year the Associated Advertising Clubs of America lauded Coca-Cola as the "best advertised article in America." Four years later, in 1913, the company spent

$1.4 million to churn out a mind-numbing take of logo-stamped junk, including 5 million lithographed metal signs, 2 million soda fountain trays, 1 million Japanese fans, 1 million calendars, 10 million matchbooks, 50 million paper "doilies," 20 million blotters, and 25 million baseball scorecards—all in just one year.

Given these efforts, it was a surprise in 1918 when Coke's sales declined for the first time in the company's history, dropping from 12 million to 10 million. The problem wasn't in demand, but supply. As the United States prepared to enter World War I in 1917, when access to international supplies of sugar would again be cut off, Dobbs and Harold Hirsch made frequent trips to Washington to argue against a quota. Their pleas fell on deaf ears, however, when the country's Food Administrator, Herbert Hoover, limited syrup producers to half their former amounts. Publicly, Coke took the defeat in stride, describing in an advertisement called "Making a Soldier of Sugar" how it selflessly cut production rather than water down the beverage. As Coke historian Frederick Allen writes in his book *Secret Formula*, the episode would establish Coke's way of handing setbacks: "Lobby furiously behind the scenes, give in gracefully when the cause is lost, and be sure to associate the product with the highest national interest."

At the same time, the company must have taken note of the success of other companies, such as Procter & Gamble, whose Ivory soap appeared in every soldier's mess kit, boasting in its own ads how it offered "the very joy of living to Our Boys when they are relieved from the front lines for rest, recreation, clean clothes, and a bath." What if, in addition to those other fine things, the Boys could be relieved with a Coke? The man who answered that question would transform Coke from a national beverage into an international phenomenon.

After the lawsuits and sugar rationing, the post–World War I Coke finally got on a roll, much of that because of the leadership of a new boss: Robert Woodruff—known as "The Boss" for the fifty-some years he effectively ran the company. The son of that cranky banker Ernest Woodruff, Robert Woodruff stands like a giant over the twentieth-century history of Coke, leading the company on an epic quest for expansion.

A lackluster student who was forever failing the test for his father's affections, he dropped out of Emory after just two years to work as a manual laborer, and then salesman at a truck company, White Motor Works. As bad as he was as a student, Woodruff proved to be a born salesman, encouraging an easy liking from clients and a reflexive loyalty from subordinates. By 1922, he was first vice president of the White Motor Works and a member of the board. Watching from afar, Ernest Woodruff both resented and admired his son's success. After canning Sam Dobbs, and knowing Howard Candler was not suited to be president forever, Ernest decided he'd rather see his son succeed him than succeed without him, and tapped him to be president of the Coca-Cola Company that year.

Whatever the elder Woodruff's motives, he made the right choice, at least as far as the company was concerned. By the 1920s, Coke had established itself as *the* national brand of soft drink, with a monopoly that few companies could ever hope for. As it became more and more a part of the landscape, lifestyle started imitating advertising: Films began incorporating the drink into scenes, music started spontaneously referring to it in lyrics.

The 1920s was also the decade advertising came into its own. As Europe cleaned up the wreckage from World War I, a newly confident American marketing machine churned countless new products off the assembly lines. "The chief economic problem today," wrote ad executive Stanley Resor at the time, "is no longer the production of goods but their distribution. The shadow of overproduction . . . is the chief menace of the present industrial system." To sell all of the new radios, telephones, and refrigerators, advertising increasingly seemed a necessary part of the industrial process. A new generation of ads took the psychological techniques of "atmosphere advertising" and ran with them to exploit the unconscious needs of consumers, probing for consumers' soft spots to promise the health, happiness, comfort, or love that a product would bring—or conjuring the anxieties of *not* owning a product, creating new afflictions such as "halitosis" and body odor, and then providing their solutions in Listerine and Lifebuoy soap.

Coke retained its positive outlook—and why shouldn't it? Coke was tailor-made for the Jazz Age, the first American generation of young people to rebel against their parents in a fast-moving culture of jitterbug and gin. As the Roaring Twenties roared in, D'Arcy's Coca-Cola girls strutted their stuff in flapper dresses and bathing suits, always with a beading bottle or glass at the ready. A brief attempt to increase rural sales with homey images of farms and storefronts was a flop—sales pointed upward only when the ads featured the young and rich.

Even so, Coke hadn't even begun to saturate its potential market. Robert Woodruff immediately set out to increase the company's profits and its share price with one word in mind—growth. If consumption of Coke increased just a few drinks per person per month, the company calculated, it would translate into millions in profits. The key to that, he reasoned, was making sure that people had access to a bottle of Coke whenever the urge to drink one struck them. It was Robert Woodruff's sales chief Harrison Jones, a six-foot-two gregarious redhead, who first coined the phrase of putting Coke everywhere "within an arm's reach of desire." Woodruff liked the phrase and repeated it so much that he adopted it as his own.

In order to further make that vision a reality, he enlisted a new ally with a gift for stoking that desire. Archie Lee started out as a newspaper reporter in North Carolina—but his ambition led him to advertising. "A man who can see life in its true colors and describe it in words can gain fortune and fame," he wrote his parents in 1917. Joining the D'Arcy Agency, Lee worked hard to distinguish himself. Soon he was virtually writing the entire Coca-Cola campaign by himself.

By the time Lee took over in the 1920s, Coke was taking advantage of new four-color printing techniques to run increasingly lavish advertisements painted by some of the best artists of the day—Hayden Hayden,

Haddon Sundblom, N. C. Wyeth, and Norman Rockwell. Before Lee, the company had never been big on slogans. He not only started to introduce them, but also came up with some of the most memorable slogans of the twentieth century. Unlike the increasingly hard-sell and negative advertising of the day, Coke stood apart as a small pleasure as simple as it was inevitable. Beginning in 1923, Lee started rolling out a new slogan every few months, all of them intentionally restrained—"Enjoy Thirst," "Always Delightful," and "It Had to Be Good to Get Where It Is."

The biggest breakthrough, however, came on July 27, 1929, when Lee coined the simple slogan "The Pause That Refreshes." The idea that Coke could be a momentary time-out captured the public imagination in the frenetic 1920s, when a booming economy and the new environment of fast-paced city life, motion pictures, and jazz were overwhelming the senses. Unlike Coke's initial pitch to soothe jangled nerves a generation before, the slogan promised that relief could come not through a secret formula of medicinal herbs but just through the simple momentary pleasure of drinking a cold beverage in the midst of a busy day.

Coke's ad slogans might have used the soft sell, but behind the scenes, its selling tactics were anything but subtle. In his quest to put Coke "within an arm's reach of desire," Woodruff created a Statistical Department to analyze highway car traffic and supermarket foot traffic to determine the most effective placement for ads. The department's research also identified a new market, home consumption, and created new cardboard "six-boxes" for housewives to take bottles home.

Meanwhile, the legions of Coke Men unleashed upon retailers around the country were told not to accept no for an answer. "Salesmen should keep calling unremittingly on their prospects," wrote sales chief Harrison Jones. "Continual chewing will enable you to digest your food." Ad exec William D'Arcy repeated the mantra: "No matter how many times you have talked to a dealer about Coca-Cola, there is always something new to say. Repetition convinces a man." By 1928, Woodruff could boast, "We can count on our fingers the soda fountains that do not serve Coca-Cola." Stock price increased along with sales, quadrupling from $40 to $160 in the decade since Ernest Woodruff's syndicate first took over the company. As the bull market roared, the elder Woodruff made a fortune—$4 million—in Coke stock, while Robert stashed a cool million.

But even when the market crashed, Coke continued to grow. In many ways, the Great Depression was Coke's finest hour yet, Archie Lee's "pause that refreshes" offering a temporary respite from the grinding headlines of job losses and bread lines. Buddy might not have been able to spare a dime, but he could always spend a nickel on a Coke. Coke pushed the point with new ads exhorting "Don't Wear a Tired Thirsty Face" and "Bounce Back to Normal."

The Depression was a hard time for advertising, with a backlash against the lifestyle ads of the 1920s and a return to hard-sell ad copy. Coke barely blinked, churning out an even more scantily clad parade of bathing-suited Coca-Cola girls, and adding celebrity endorsements from Joan Crawford, Clark Gable, Jean Harlow, and other Hollywood stars. As far as Coke's ads were concerned, there was no Depression; a better life was only the pop of a bottle cap away. In 1933, Woodruff blithely announced the company was putting an extra $1 million into its ad budget; during the period, it was one of the top twenty-five advertisers in the country.

Of all Coke's ads, however, some of its most successful featured the opposite of Coke's usual thin and beautiful people, showing instead a portly older gentleman with a white beard and furry red suit. Despite some claims, Coke didn't create the image of Santa Claus we recognize today. Throughout the nineteenth century, writers and artists were gradually following the lead of Clement Clarke Moore's 1822 poem "A Visit from St. Nicholas" in creating their picture of the gift-bestowing elf with "red garments . . . ruddy cheeks and nose, bushy eyebrows, and a jolly, paunchy effect," as *The New York Times* wrote in 1927. But even though the Coca-Cola Company didn't create the image, it did solidify St. Nick for generations of children when its ads of jolly Santa created by artist Haddon Sundblom became ubiquitous starting in the 1930s. More often than not, they featured a story line of children leaving a Coke in lieu of milk and cookies for Santa to pause and refresh himself on Christmas Eve, inspiring many children to adopt the practice as their own.

With its conquest even of Christmas, Coke became the darling of Wall Street. Profits of $14 million during the height of the Great Depression in 1934 more than doubled to $29 million by decade's end. Woodruff took to calling the beverage "the essence of capitalism"; he fetishized Coca-Cola, insisting that the company sell one product and one product only. In order to keep alive its mystique, he dragged the secret formula out of a company vault in New York and personally transferred it by train to a safe-deposit box in the Trust Company bank in Atlanta—where it supposedly remains to this day. In his mind he'd hit upon the perfect product, one that could sell in any economic time, and—with the success of its "Thirst Knows No Season" ad campaign—any climate. "Robert Woodruff could still look out on an America that justified his bedrock faith in laissez-faire capitalism," write J. C. Louis and Harvey Yazijian. "This faith informed his fundamental opposition to socialism, and later, to Franklin Delano Roosevelt."

Roosevelt's New Deal was, like the Progressive movement half a century earlier, a backlash against the greed of corporations, who were blamed by many for the crash. The government moved in to regulate the stock market and the banking industry, along with other businesses. Woodruff was, if anything, even more adamant than Asa Candler that he owed the government nothing. When Georgia began to tax stock held by residents in out-of-state corporations, he up and moved to Wilmington, Delaware, where Coke was incorporated, spending just over six months out of the year there to make it official.

And he had bigger plans as well. As Coke emerged unscathed from the Depression, its advertising constantly repeated two essential points: that it was available everywhere, and it was available for a nickel. But until now, Coke's claims of ubiquity included only the United States. "The opening of foreign markets is a costly undertaking," Woodruff wrote in the introductory letter to the 1928 Annual Report, laying out difficulties in distribution, trademark protection, and acceptance by foreign consumers. "Successful prosecution of this undertaking will require time, courage, and patience, as well as large expenditures." Though Coke had made tentative inroads into countries including Mexico, Canada, England, and Germany, it wasn't until the United States entered World War II in 1941 that it was able to expand its reach into more and more foreign markets. And as luck would have it, the American taxpayer footed the bill.

In the "Milestones of Refreshment" exhibit at the World of Coca-Cola, there is a whole room devoted to World War II, full of wartime advertisements and newspaper clippings. Among them, one black-and-white photo stands out: "Charles B. Hall was the first African-American fighter pilot to down an enemy aircraft in World War II," reads the caption. "His reward was a bottle of Coca-Cola."

When war struck America, it struck Coca-Cola, too, with the inevitable return to sugar rationing. Determined not to be left behind again, the company lobbied furiously for an exception, collecting a slew of testimonials from military bases about Coke's power to keep up morale. The crowning move was a twenty-four-page pamphlet titled "Importance of the Rest-Pause in Maximum War Effort," featuring pages of scientific "authorities" attesting to the increased productivity of well-rested soldiers and factory workers. Archie Lee's fanciful "pause that refreshes" was now opportunistically being applied to the real fight against the Nazis. "A nation at war strains forward in productive effort in a new tempo," it urged. "In times like these Coca-Cola is doing a necessary job for workers . . . bringing welcome refreshments to the doers of things."

Incredibly, the American government bought the line. One of Coke's own execs was appointed to the rationing board, and Coke was offered an exemption to quotas even as all other sugar users were limited to 80 percent production. Coke's next move was even more masterful. In an act of genuine patriotism, calculated scheming, or both, Robert Woodruff publicly promised that every soldier could buy a Coke for a nickel anywhere in the world—expenses be damned! In fact, Woodruff may very well have known that the company would never have to pay a dime, since Coke reportedly had been in talks with the government well before Pearl Harbor about aid in establishing Coca-Cola bottling plants overseas in order to spread American influence.

Sure enough, an order signed by General George C. Marshall himself informed commanders they could order bottling equipment to the front lines as an essential military priority—all paid for by Uncle Sam. The biggest taker was General Dwight D. Eisenhower, who requested 6 million Cokes a month during the North Africa campaign of 1943. (So much for the "military-industrial complex.") A war correspondent nearly met his end on a plane so overloaded with Coke bottles it could barely clear the sand dunes. "You don't fuck with Coca-Cola!" the pilot told him when he complained.

But the soda did seem to genuinely perk up morale. Thousands of letters poured in from dirty foxholes and heat-baked islands from soldiers grateful for the familiar taste of home. "If anyone were to ask us what we are fighting for . . . half of us would answer, the right to buy Coca-Cola again," wrote one. "To my mind, I am in this damn mess as much to help keep the custom of drinking Cokes as I am to help preserve the million other benefits our country blesses its citizens with," wrote another.

Never particularly patriotic before, Coke seized upon the sentiments for a new wartime ad campaign. Dozens of full-color ads depicted soldiers and airmen around the world, bottles in hands, greeting the natives with the words "Have a Coke!" In one, a soldier spots a sign for Coke; the caption reads: "Howdy, Friend . . . When you drink ice-cold Coca-Cola, you know it's *the real thing*"—the first appearance of Coke's most famous slogan. Almost overnight, Coca-Cola suddenly seemed worth fighting tyranny for, a stunning transformation from refreshing pause to all-American symbol in less than a decade.

And Coke's new association with its home country would stick well beyond the war. One ad in 1946 read, "As American as Independence."

A sign at Coke's own 1948 bottlers' convention crowed: "When we think of Nazis, we think of the swastika, when we think of the Japs, we think of the Rising Sun, and when we think of Communists we think of the Iron Curtain, BUT when THEY think of democracy they think of Coca-Cola."

One little fact, however, marred Coke's newfound support for its country: During World War II, it continued to do business with the Nazis. Germany had long been one of Coke's best markets under the leadership of American expat and Coke franchise owner Ray Powers, a fan of the rising Nationalist Socialist party who sent telegrams to Woodruff ending "Heil Hitler." But the real power was German businessman Max Keith, a six-foot-six giant with a Hitler-inspired mustache who distributed Coke at Nazi Youth rallies, advertised on Nazi educational pamphlets, and draped the stage in swastikas at bottler conventions.

That support of the regime may have been simple self-preservation, but Keith took it further. When Powers was killed in a bicycle accident, Keith wangled an appointment as overseer of all soft drink bottlers in the Third Reich, taking over bottlers as the blitzkrieg roared through Holland, Belgium, and France. At the same time Woodruff was securing special treatment for Coke as an essential item to keep up American troop morale, Keith was reserving the last bottles of Coke to succor wounded Nazi soldiers and using Coke trucks to deliver relief supplies to bombed-out enemy cities. When supplies of concentrate ran out, he created a new grapefruit-flavored beverage, naming his new concoction "Fanta," and using forced labor from concentration camps to produce it. He stopped short only of changing the name of the company, risking death at the hands of a Nazi general when he refused.

After the war, Coca-Cola investigators from the United States concluded that Keith himself had not been a Nazi. Nevertheless, during each of the years he had sold Fanta in Nazi Germany, he had made a modest amount of profit. The Coca-Cola Company was now only too happy to cash the checks, despite the advertising blitz assuring consumers it was leading America to victory against a ruthless enemy. The discrepancy, virtually unnoticed at the time, only shows how malleable Coke's allegiances were—and how, whatever genuine patriotism the company's executives might have felt in support of the American war effort, it paled before the *image* of that patriotism. In fairness, it might be said that Coke had no choice to but to play both sides of the war effort. Legally, its true allegiance was to its shareholders, who required only one thing: that the company continue to churn out a profit. If the company had an enemy, it wasn't a foreign country or tyrannical government, but the competition of a home-grown adversary that had been slowly growing to challenge Coke for years. Now that World War II was over, Coke went to war against its real opponent: Pepsi.

By the end of the war, Coca-Cola's supremacy seemed unassailable. Where decades of marketing had failed, American military might had succeeded overnight in cracking open the foreign market. By war's end, the company had sixty-three overseas bottling plants, financed for $5.5 million—just 20 percent of one year's net profits. And everywhere the GIs went, the natives seemed to develop a taste for the sugary beverage. In 1950, *Time* magazine published a cover image of a smiling planet Earth being suckled with a Coca-Cola bottle, praising without irony Coke's "peaceful near-conquest of the world."

In this new era, the company increasingly thought internationally in its advertising, shifting from D'Arcy to a new agency, global giant McCann-Erickson, to handle its accounts. Not that the ads themselves changed much; Coke did little more than translate the copy, producing a remarkably homogenized image as the quintessential American product. The ads worked for the same reason Coke's images of "conspicuous consumption" had worked half a century earlier—creating an idealized vision of luxury at a time when the war-torn world hungered for U.S. prosperity. Just at its moment of global triumph, however, Coke lost its way back at home. When Archie Lee died suddenly of a heart attack, the company was unexpectedly rudderless, floating a string of clunkers such as "Have a Coke and Be Happy." Halfhearted attempts at patriotic slogans were abandoned—the jingoism that worked in the epic battle against the Nazis falling flat in the messier conflict with Korea.

Fact is, advertising itself was changing after World War II. Faced with another postwar boom, Madison Avenue again turned to the hard sell, emphasizing the bells and whistles that made new cars, stoves, TV sets, and other durable goods indispensable. "Do you want fine writing? Do you want masterpiece? Or do you want to see the goddamned sales curve start moving up?" said ad guru Rosser Reeves of Ted Bates & Co., who encouraged companies to think of their "unique selling proposition," or USP—the one, and only one, attribute that sets a product apart. Suddenly there were as many products as there were unique reasons to buy one, and market segmentation was born. In this new selling environment, Coke might still be the leader in the soft drink category. But upstart company Pepsi-Cola could seek dominance in a new demographic: youth.

Like Coke, Pepsi had its origins in the patent medicine era, the creation of a North Carolina pharmacist named Caleb D. Bradham, who sold a brew of kola nut and the stomach enzyme pepsin as a cure for stomachache. It nipped successfully at Coke's heels for a while, with some three hundred bottlers in twenty-four states by 1910, but foundered during World War I, when the spike in sugar prices all but put it out of business. The company probably would have died if not for the intervention of a temperamental New York City department store owner, Charles Guth, who bought it out of bankruptcy in 1931 after Coke refused to cut him a discount for his soda fountains. Despite sweetening Pepsi's formula and reviving bottling, Guth failed spectacularly at first—even offering to sell the company to Coke for $50,000 in 1933.

When Coke refused, the company went for broke with a new strategy: bottling the drink in 12-ounce beer bottles and selling "Twice as Much for a Nickel." The tactic worked; Pepsi sales rocketed back during the value-conscious Depression, with profits topping $2 million in 1936, $3 million in 1937, and $4 million in 1938. The new medium of radio drilled the drink more firmly into the public's mind with an infectious jingle first introduced in 1940 that became the most successful radio spot in history: "Twice as Much for a Nickel, Too . . . Pepsi-Cola Is the Drink for You."

Coke wasn't about to take such vibrant free-market competition lying down. It went straight to the government to quash the young upstart, arguing in a series of court cases in the United States, Canada, and the United Kingdom that Coke had exclusive rights to the word "cola." Pepsi countersued, charging Coke with illegally trying to constitute a monopoly. In the end, Pepsi's arguments carried the day, with a British court finally ruling in 1942 that "cola" was a generic term any company could use. Coke sued for peace, with Woodruff personally agreeing with Pepsi's new president, Walter Mack, that the two companies would no longer compete in the court of law.

Instead, they competed in the arena of image—and here, for the first time, Coke was losing. In 1950, Pepsi hired as its president Al Steele, a former D'Arcy executive and Coke VP of marketing, who out-coked Coke with a new lifestyle-oriented campaign. While Coke still marketed itself as the product for everyone—workmen and businessmen, soldiers and socialites—Pepsi focused solely on young middle-class families moving into suburban tract houses in droves.

"Stay young and fair, be debonair, be sociable, have a Pepsi!" the new radio jingles urged. Pepsi's USP had nothing to do with its product, but in the idea that it represented: youth, energy, upward mobility. And the campaign was wildly successful. After dipping as low as $1.25 million in 1950, Pepsi's net profit shot up to $14 million by 1955. For the first time, Coke's market share began slipping, and sales slumped. "Coke can hardly be said to be foundering," wrote *The Wall Street Journal*. "But it is faltering." Pepsi, meanwhile, distilled its message to take advantage of the burgeoning "generation gap" with a new slogan: "For those who think young." Eventually, the campaign would become a direct appeal to the new generation of "baby boomers"—the Pepsi Generation—and establish the most important battleground for the Cola Wars: young people.

Despite Pepsi's upper hand in advertising, however, Coke had something the upstart could never match: money. In 1956, Coke poured $11 million into its advertising, one of the top ten ad budgets in the country. By 1963, it was number one, spending $53 million a year. Much of it was spent on increasingly targeted research, surveying customers in all of 1.6 million retail outlets. McCann-Erickson led the way in the newfangled approach of "motivational research," a doubling-down on the psychological advertising techniques of the 1930s that used "depth interviews" to plumb what consumers really wanted in their products. Maidenform, for example, exploited what it said was women's subconscious exhibitionist tendencies. GM put a convertible in the window to entice men with a "possible symbolic mistress," then once in the showroom pushed the security of the sedan.

Eventually, the practice paved the way for a new "creative revolution" in the 1960s, a backlash against the overly utilitarian USP that would forever put the *idea* of the product above the product itself. "The greater the similarity between products, the less part reason really plays in brand selection," noted the revolution's chief architect, David Ogilvy. "There really isn't any significant difference between the various brands of whiskey or the various cigarettes or the various brands of beer." (He might have included soft drinks.) As a result, argued Ogilvy, it was the advertiser's job to create an emotional response that consumers would unconsciously associate with a brand—the kind of advertising at which Coke had excelled for nearly a century.

In 1957, journalist Vance Packard exposed the "depth boys" in his bestselling book *The Hidden Persuaders.* The public outcry that followed, however, focused on a short section of the book about subliminal advertising—a part that directly implicated Coke. At the time, a researcher named James Vicary flashed the words "Hungry? Eat Popcorn" and "Drink Coca-Cola" for up to a three-hundredth of a second every five seconds during a showing of the movie *Picnic* in a New Jersey movie theater. According to Vicary, popcorn sales increased 57 percent and Coke sales 18 percent. Vicary later backtracked, all but admitting he made the whole thing up. Advertisers further denounced the practice, and the furor subsided. (Modern research has since debunked the technique.)

But the public missed the larger point of Packard's book: All advertising is on some level subliminal—utilizing only dimly conscious parts of our brains to get us to irrationally open up our wallets. As *New York Times* columnist Rob Walker points out, "You'd have to be an idiot not to recognize that you're being pitched to when watching a thirty-second commercial. But recognition is not the same as immunity." In fact, "it's precisely because we don't tend to think of regular advertising as something we have to be on guard against, or even take seriously, that it works on us in much the way we imagine subliminal advertising might."

After the challenge from Pepsi, Coke redoubled its efforts to associate Coke subliminally with almost *everything*. Of all of the agencies on Madison Avenue, none embraced the new "depth" techniques more than Coke's ad house McCann. According to the firm's research, when people thought of Coke, they thought not so much of the beverage itself as of the social interactions it helped facilitate—from the hostess serving Coke at dinner to the dads popping caps at Little League games. McCann copywriter Bill Backer used the insight to create the first successful Coke slogan in years: "Things Go Better with Coke." *What* went better didn't matter so much—Coke could just as well spark romance as childhood friendship. It was left to the consumer to fill in the blank.

That same year, Pepsi unveiled its "Pepsi Generation" ad campaign that challenged baby boomers to rebel against the conformity of their parents. Finally, both companies had an advertising style—and neither said a word about what the soda actually tasted like or contained. Despite the competition, the real winner was the soft drink market. Between 1954 and 1964, per capita consumption rose nearly 25 percent, from 174 servings per capita in 1954 to 227 in 1964. Along with the advertising face-lift, Coke also had a new face of the company. As the 1960s dawned, new president J. Paul Austin was the first in decades to emerge from the shadow of chairman

Robert Woodruff to drag the company into a new corporate era. Even as Pepsi merged with Frito-Lay snack company to become PepsiCo, Coke finally got over its single-product fetish to branch out with Minute Maid juices, diet soda Tab, lemon-lime Sprite, and fruit-flavored Fanta (a name it kept despite its Nazi origins).

Austin also confronted the changing reality of America, as blacks, women, and other groups were finally demanding their civil rights. The civil rights debate began, in fact, when four students at a Woolworth's counter in Greensboro, North Carolina, demanded their right to a *Coke*, by now the symbol of American prosperity. Caught between rumors it financed White Citizens' Councils on one side, and the National Association for the Advancement of Colored People on the other, the company stayed on the sidelines. "I've heard the phrase 'Stand up and be counted' for so long from both sides that I'm sick of it," groused one vice president. "Sure, we want to stand up and be counted, but on both sides of the fence." Taking a moral stand, after all, could only lose the company customers. Even as Woodruff personally risked his reputation in Atlanta to support a Nobel Prize dinner for Martin Luther King, Jr., the company dragged its feet on producing racially integrated advertising.

Similarly, when the war in Vietnam broke out, the company virtually ignored the controversial conflict; there would be no soldier made of sugar in Danang, no "Have a Coke" in Saigon. With nothing much to lose, Pepsi filled the gap, courting hippies and love children with the countercultural slogan "You've Got a Lot to Live, Pepsi's Got a Lot to Give." Not that Coke slipped behind the times. When the "depth boys" at McCann told Coke that youth of today didn't like phoniness in their leaders, lyricist Bill Backer reached into the World War II archive to pull out "The Real Thing," a slogan that could brilliantly appeal to disenfranchised youth searching for a more authentic world, as well as disaffected adults longing for a simpler time before all of the national discord.

The times were catching up with Coke, however. As the socially conscious 1970s hit, farm labor organizer César Chávez followed up his successful grape boycott with a campaign protesting the deplorable conditions in Florida orange groves—focusing particularly on Coke's Minute Maid subsidiary. An NBC documentary revealed substandard housing and inadequate toilet facilities for workers making less than minimum wage. Coke was livid at being singled out by the program but appeared publicly contrite. Testifying before the U.S. Senate, Austin sympathized with the "profound sense of futility" suffered by the workers, and promised to change. Eventually, Coke signed a union contract with the United Farm Workers in 1972, leading to higher wages and benefits for Minute Maid workers compared with other fruit pickers. (The contract lasted only until 1994, however, when Coke sold its Florida orange groves, which effectively ended union representation in the state.)

On some level, Austin's rhetoric about changing the world was genuine. Under a principle he dubbed the "halo effect," the company launched new initiatives on recycling and acquired a company called Aqua-Chem to produce desalinization plants to provide clean water in the Middle East—even though the subsidiary never turned a profit. The company's new social thrust, however, wasn't completely uncalculated. Now that love beads and folk music were safe cultural touchstones, Coke glommed on to the hippie movement for its biggest transformation in decades. The company had already gone from a medicinal cure-all to sign of good breeding, from refreshing pause to all-American icon. Now it would tackle world peace.

Bill Backer supposedly came up with the idea when his plane was fogged in in Ireland, and he saw his fellow passengers sharing Cokes to pass the time. At that moment, he realized Coke was "a tiny bit of commonality between all peoples." He set out to re-create the vision with a new commercial assembling two hundred international teenagers with stereotypical national clothing, to sing the earnest lyrics: "I'd like to teach the world to sing, in perfect harmony, / I'd like to buy the world a Coke, and keep it company. . . ." In reality, the shoot was a nightmare, with the unruly kids constantly breaking formation to run down the hill to get more Coke. But the ad worked, turning the act of buying a Coke into a nod to international harmony, and spawning a radio hit that *Newsweek* noted was a "sure-fire form of subliminal advertising."

As hope of the 1970s settled into economic malaise, however, Coke showed how easy it was to appeal to the other side of the political spectrum. A new series of ads featured lighthouses, redwoods, and corn silos, set to a song called "Look Up, America!"—a nod to the new "moral majority" backing conservative president Ronald Reagan. Through it all, sales of soft drinks continued to soar, from 242 cans per person in 1970 to 363 cans per person in 1980. As Pepsi's new CEO Roger Enrico once said, "At Pepsi, we *like* the Cola Wars. . . . The more fun we provide, the more people buy our products—*all* our products." It was Pepsi, however, that changed the rules of engagement, leading to the Coca-Cola Company's biggest blunder, and the Coca-Cola brand's greatest triumph.

What's amazing, in retrospect, about the Pepsi Challenge isn't that Pepsi had the audacity to compete with Coke on the basis of taste. It's that it hadn't done so before. Here, the two soda giants had been fighting it out for decades on which soda refreshed or relaxed you better, on which one made you feel younger or more nostalgic—as if to distract consumers from the simple idea that they could just drink the one they thought tasted better.

It took a state of near desperation to try it. Coke had trounced Pepsi on market share for years in Texas before a new regional manager decided on a fresh approach. He found it in television commercials inviting shoppers to try two sodas head-to-head, filming their surprised expressions when it turned out they liked Pepsi better. The campaign doubled market share in just a few months, and Pepsi eventually rolled it out nationally, reaching 90 percent of the market by 1983.

The campaign rocked Coke to the core, leading to its own tests revealing that Pepsi did actually outperform Coke on taste by a small margin. Nonetheless, both companies fired off competing ads, each claiming they actually tasted better, at the same time slashing prices and offering discounts at supermarkets to win back customers. After a year or two, however, they realized the scorched-earth tactics only hurt both of them.

"The Pepsi Challenge, if managed differently, might have resulted in a real Cola War, one that was price-based," says historian Richard Tedlow. "This, however, is precisely the kind of competition both companies want to avoid." Pepsi's incoming president, Roger Enrico, called off the campaign almost as soon as it began, and both companies soon returned to more traditional forms of advertising—with Coca-Cola releasing the new slogan, "Coke Is It!" which, like "Things Go Better," was ambiguous enough to open itself to any interpretation.

Inside Coke, however, executives continued to fret. Every year, Pepsi chipped away at the company's market share a little bit more. From a high of 60 percent after World War II, Coke's share had fallen to just 22 percent by 1984—compared with Pepsi's 18. What was worse, when Coke applied a pseudo-scientific measure called the Advertising Pressure Index (API), it found "advertising alone couldn't account for Pepsi's aggressive advance, or Coke's devastating decline"—as if the thought that a company could grow or falter due to something other than its advertising image had never occurred to them. That realization set them up for a drastic mistake under the leadership of Coke's new president, a Cuban chemist named Roberto Goizueta.

A member of Cuba's financial elite who fled the island before Castro's takeover in 1960, Goizueta got a job with Coke first in Miami, then Atlanta, where he gained the trust of the senior executives and even learned the secret formula. His eventual rise to the top came the old-fashioned way: sucking up to the boss. Robert Woodruff was now in his eighties, but he was still chairman, and when Paul Austin flared out in a very public bout with early-onset Alzheimer's, Woodruff was back in charge. As the aging Boss suffered illness and depression, Goizueta visited him every day, and in one of the old man's last acts, he tapped Goizueta for the hotly contested top slot in 1981.

Perhaps because of his unusual ascent, Goizueta immediately declared the company would no longer be afraid to take risks. "There are no sacred cows," he announced, up to and including Coke's secret formula. "Reformulation of any or all of our products will not stand in the way of giving any of our competitors a real or perceived product advantage." Case in point, he oversaw the introduction in 1982 of Diet Coke, violating the sacred dictum that Coke was a "single thing coming from a single source"; within two years, it had become not only the best-selling diet drink, but also the number three soft drink overall. That success led to the act of ultimate hubris: changing the sacred formula of Coke.

The company should have known better. While developing Diet Coke, marketers discovered that the word "Coke" alone was enough to drive sales: When they tested Tab against Pepsi, it lost by a 4 percent margin; when they poured the same drink into a Diet Coke can, however, it caused customer preference to jump 12 points. Despite these findings, marketing chief Sergio Zyman led a two-year search for a new sugar-sweetened formula that would beat Pepsi in *blind* taste tests, finally hitting upon a sweeter version that consistently outranked Pepsi by 6 to 8 points. The project was so secret the company didn't even tell its advertising agency McCann until January 1985, just three months before its introduction.

Company executives stood up before a packed press conference on April 23, 1985, forever after known as "Black Tuesday" among the Coke faithful. Unfortunately for Coke, word of the change had already leaked. The day before, Pepsi had taken out a full-page ad in *The New York Times* declaring victory in the Cola Wars with the statement "The Other Guy Just Blinked."

As Goizueta followed a montage of cowboys, the Grand Canyon, and the Statue of Liberty onto the stage, the press corps leaped: "To what extent are you introducing this product to meet the Pepsi Challenge?" "Have you simply added more sweetness to make it more competitive with Pepsi?" In the face of such direct questions, Goizueta temporized. New Coke wasn't any sweeter than old Coke, he said, rather it had a "rounder . . . bolder . . . more harmonious flavor." Pepsi had nothing to do with it.

The press didn't buy it, and neither did the public. Anguished calls and letters came pouring into Coke headquarters—more than 400,000 by the end of the ordeal. "You've taken away my childhood," read one. "Changing Coke is like God making the grass purple," sputtered another. Finally, Coke capitulated. "We have heard you," Goizueta assured consumers at a press conference in July announcing old Coke would return. Pepsi continued to bask, with CEO Roger Enrico rushing out a book, *The Other Guy Blinked*, in which he sneered: "I think, by the end of their nightmare, they figured out who they really were . . . caretakers. . . . All they can do is defend the heritage they nearly abandoned."

History, however, hasn't exactly seen it that way. Within a year after its release, New Coke faded into oblivion, while "Coke Classic" again topped Pepsi in market share. It was the ultimate triumph of image over reality. Consumers rejected the two sodas they actually liked better in blind taste tests, in exchange for the one whose brand image made them *feel* better.

Marketing exec Zyman, who was responsible for the debacle more than anyone, later claimed the disaster was all but intentional. "A lot of people said it was a big fat mistake. It wasn't," he wrote. "New Coke was incredibly successful in reattaching consumers to Coke." Zyman left the company in 1987, the apparent fall guy for the disastrous reformulation, but was hired back as chief marketing officer in 1993. Neither he nor the rest of the executive suite at the Coca-Cola Company ever forgot the lesson: Taste aside, image was the most valuable asset the company had. If the company was to succeed, it must be protected at all costs.

THREE

Biggering and Biggering

By the end of the 1980s, it seemed like the Coca-Cola Company could do no wrong. For nearly a hundred years, it had been growing larger and larger, selling more and more of its sugary sweet pleasure. Now, after the New Coke experience, it had survived its biggest stumble ever, and somehow come out stronger for it. After decades of advertising, Coca-Cola's brand had been cemented into the American consciousness as something good and patriotic that brought people together not only in the United States but around the world as well. And now, it represented something more: a part of every American they suddenly realized they'd be heartbroken to lose. For its hundredth-anniversary celebration in 1986, Coke pulled out all of the stops, turning Atlanta's convention center into a huge indoor party for 14,000 people, complete with floats, marching bands, and food including 66,000 pieces of shrimp, 9,000 barbecue ribs, and a fourteen-foot-high Coke bottle popping out of a 7.5-ton cake.

When the hubbub died down, the company's executives turned to the future—where they saw nothing but blue skies on the horizon. Growth had always been a priority at the Coca-Cola Company. Asa Candler had made expansion part of Coca-Cola's very business model; Robert Woodruff had pushed Coke's expansion "within an arm's reach of desire" around the world. But growth would become an obsession for the next generation of Coke executives, spurred by an unprecedented level of wealth in the stock market.

For the first time, average Americans began putting their money into the market in significant numbers—either on their own or through the vehicles of mutual funds or pension funds. These institutional investors began to push for higher and higher returns, and companies obliged them, focusing everything on their quarterly earnings statements in a new emphasis that became known as the "shareholder value movement." The ideas that sparked the movement date back to an obscure 1975 book by economist Alfred Rappaport. But the philosophy was articulated most famously by Jack Welch, the CEO of General Electric, who declared in 1981 that plodding growth of "blue chip" companies was no longer good enough for him. Instead, he pushed GE's earnings into high gear by cutting waste and inefficiency wherever he found it—including downsizing through massive layoffs. He set the tone for other companies, who rushed to please Wall Street by any means necessary—including accounting tricks, stock buybacks, and rampant acquisitions of other companies. Flush with stock options, CEOs profited handsomely, even as they sometimes hurt the long-term success of their companies through an emphasis on short-term growth.

Outside of Jack Welch, no CEO was associated with the "shareholder value movement" more than Roberto Goizueta, who became a darling of Wall Street in the 1980s. "I wrestle over how to build shareholder value from the time I get up in the morning to the time I go to bed," he once said. "I even think about it when I am shaving." In the days before the Internet, he had a computer screen installed in a conference room on the twenty-fifth floor of Coca-Cola headquarters with a live feed from the New York Stock Exchange that continually monitored Coca-Cola's stock price; he put another screen at the main entrance to Coke headquarters, so it would be the first thing employees would see as they walked in the door and the last thing they'd see as they left. The company sloughed off divisions acquired by Austin to create his "halo effect" that never turned a profit—such as his desalinization plants in the Middle East—and acquired lucrative new companies with nothing to do with soft drinks, such as Columbia Pictures, fresh off the success of *Ghostbusters* and *The Karate Kid.*

But more than anything, growth meant returning to the core business of the company: selling more soft drinks. After the New Coke fiasco, Goizueta changed his tune about "sacred cows," realizing he had acquired "a most unique company with a most unique product." He abandoned any attempt to change the formula, concentrating instead on increasing per capita consumption, or "per-caps," around the world. "If we take full advantage of our opportunities . . . eventually, the number one beverage on Earth will be soft drinks—our soft drinks," he crowed in 1986. Ultimately, he told *Fortune* magazine, he envisioned a world where the C on the kitchen faucet stood not for "cold," but for "Coke." So comical do those comments sound today that they call to mind the Once-ler, from *The Lorax*, Dr. Seuss's cautionary children's book about corporate excess, who crowed about "biggering and biggering and biggering and biggering," at least until the last Truffala tree was chopped down.

In Coke's case, growth was never an end in itself—it was always a means to constantly raise the share price. The more bottles or fountain drinks, the more earnings from syrup sales. The more earnings, the more investors would put into the company. As the 1990s dawned, Goizueta was promising annual volume growth of 7 to 8 percent a year—translating into some 20 billion additional drinks sold around the world. That, in turn, meant 15 to 20 percent annual growth in earnings. Goizueta personally called the Wall Street analysts who covered Coke to discuss the company's earnings, detailing the new markets where the company was constantly treading.

Not surprisingly, analysts rushed to jump on board the Coke gravy train, followed by institutional investors. "If you weren't owning Coke, you were losing," said one about the time. Another called Coke "the closest thing we know of to a perpetual motion machine." Upon learning that Goizueta had been declared CEO of the year in a trade magazine, he said, "Hell, considering all he's done for shareholders, you should make him CEO of the century." Stock prices rose with each of their predictions; if an analyst predicted lower earnings, they were frozen out. Goizueta profited handsomely—eventually earning more than $1 billion in stock, his reward for raising the value of the company by more than $100 billion throughout the late 1980s and early 1990s. In 1991 alone, he received a bonus of $80 million when he exercised his stock options—at the time, the largest single payout ever given to an American CEO.

Much of Coke's growth in those years came in the form of new markets overseas, as the company gradually expanded into countries it hadn't already colonized. At the same time, executives knew that to raise share value they would have to keep selling more soda in the country where it was created—and that increasingly meant selling not only in more places, but also in larger sizes. In all of the rush to expand volume, however, it never occurred to company executives to ask: Does the world really *need* that much Coke?

In the age of Big Gulps and supersizing, it's almost inconceivable that until the 1950s Coke was sold only in 6½-ounce bottles. Even as the company was selling in more and more venues around the country, it was still seen as an occasional treat for after meals or on Sunday afternoons. The arms race with Pepsi changed that. After the upstart company's "twice as much for a nickel" campaign, Coke was under constant pressure to offer bigger sizes, too. Finally, in 1955, it relented, rolling out 12-ounce "King Size" bottles. Almost at the same time, it released 26-ounce "Family Size" bottles, intended for home consumption with meals.

For decades, the price of sugar still kept a lid on how big Coke was able to go. That changed in the 1980s when Japanese scientists invented high-fructose corn syrup. Unlike sucrose—subject to the whims of international sugar markets—the new sweetener could be made here at home, where corn subsidies keep the prices at rock-bottom levels. "Cheap corn, transformed into high-fructose corn syrup," wrote Michael Pollan in 2003, "is what allowed Coca-Cola to move from the svelte 8-ounce bottle of soda ubiquitous in the '70s to the chubby 20-ounce bottle of today." Coke rolled out a 50 percent high-fructose corn syrup (HFCS) version of its trademark beverage in 1980, delighted to discover that consumers couldn't tell the difference. In 1985, it switched to a 100 percent HFCS version.

The rock-bottom price of syrup now allowed Coke to grow exponentially—especially in fountain sales. Fast-food execs had long known that the way to drive profits was not to offer bigger hamburgers but to offer bigger sizes of the high-margin items such as french fries and soft drinks that went with them. It wasn't until the late 1980s, however, that the concept of "supersizing" really caught on. By then, fast-food companies realized that they could make more money by bundling a burger, fries, and a Coke into a "value meal" and selling it at a discount. They offered further discounts on larger and larger sizes of fries and sodas—both of which could be more easily increased in size, and with a greater profit margin, than could a hamburger or fish sandwich.

As Eric Schlosser describes in *Fast Food Nation*, in the 1990s a 21-ounce medium soda at McDonald's sold for $1.29, while a 32-ounce large soda sold for only 20 cents more. But the cost for ingredients was only 3 cents more—for 17 cents of pure profit. Everyone won—the customer got exponentially more soda, the restaurant got more profit, and the company sold more syrup. And if that wasn't enough, customers could request to "supersize" their drinks—a stomach-busting 64 ounces and 610 calories a pop. By 1996, supersizing accounted for a quarter of soft drink sales. (It was the same story at the 7-Eleven chain of convenience stores, which introduced the 32-ounce Big Gulp, the 44-ounce Super Gulp, the 52-ounce X-Treme Gulp, and finally the 64-ounce Double Gulp. The true champion, however, was "The Beast," an 85-ounce refillable cup released by Arco service stations in 1998.)

With two-thirds of the fountain sales market, Coca-Cola was the clear beneficiary of the new drive to push volume. And as consumers became more and more accustomed to larger sizes of soft drinks at fast-food restaurants and convenience stores, the company quietly retooled vending machines and supermarket displays to increase package sizes as well. At the time, the company insisted, it was just following consumer demand. In the skittish days after New Coke, the company engaged in more and more consumer testing, all of which pointed in one direction: "Bigger is better," according to Hank Cardello, Coke's director of marketing in the early 1980s, who has since broken with his industry roots to become a health advocate. "The mantra was bigger packages, bigger servings, and more of everything per container," he writes in his 2009 book *Stuffed.*

In 1994, Coke began introducing a new 20-ounce bottle, fashioned from polyethylene terephthalate (PET) plastic in Coke's trademark "contour" shape—a variation on the old green-glass hobbleskirt bottle. It quickly replaced the 12-ounce can to become the standard serving size for Coke. The new container was a boon to the company—reversing years of discounts on multipack boxes of cans and allowing it to charge a premium price on the new, larger bottle. Along with the bigger sizes, Coke doubled down on Woodruff's "arm's reach of desire" strategy to put Coke anywhere and everywhere it could. "Our goal was to make Coca-Cola ubiquitous. At all times, at all places. . . . Coke Was It," writes former brand manager Cardello. "My job was to keep the logo in your face, and present it in the most positive light. And I had access to a huge war chest with which to accomplish this."

In 1997, Coke's annual report laid bare its strategy with striking candor, stating, "We're putting ice-cold Coca-Cola Classic and our other brands within reach, wherever you look: at the supermarket, the video store, the soccer field, the gas station—everywhere." A Coke marketing newsletter later distributed to fast-food restaurants encouraged them to push soft drinks for breakfast, recommending they put Coke on the breakfast board and introduce special Coca-Cola cups for "the most important meal of the day."

The big push to sell more volume worked. Annual soda consumption soared to 56.1 gallons—more than 600 cans—per person in 1998, up 30 percent from 1985, and two and a half times what it had been in 1970. And more and more soda drinkers were drinking Coke, which had reclaimed 45 percent of the market in the United States compared with Pepsi's 30 percent. Naturally all of those soda sales sweetened Coke's bottom line, leading to more than $4 billion in net income, and a whopping 3,500 percent increase in Coke's stock price over Goizueta's tenure—to a high point of $88 a share (after splitting several times) by 1998.

Even as consumption grew, Coke knew that it couldn't count on customers to drink that much Coke without a little nudge. Goizueta, more than anyone, realized how important advertising was to selling product. "We don't know how to sell products based on performance," he once said, shrugging. "Everything we sell, we sell on image." When Goizueta took over in 1981, Coke's annual spending on advertising in the United States was up to $200 million. Goizueta doubled it, to $400 million, by 1984. There it hovered throughout the next decade, until Sergio Zyman came back on board in 1993.

After the debacle with New Coke, everyone had assumed Zyman would be the fall guy. Coke's marketing chief not only was one of the prime movers behind the fateful change to Coke's formula, but he could also be abrasive and authoritarian, alienating many in Coke headquarters. His insistence on numbers with no excuses had earned him the title of "Aya-Cola" back in the 1980s, when he had famously killed the "Mean" Joe Greene ad, one of the most endearing and popular ads in Coke's history. His reason: it didn't "move the needle" to sell more product. "The sole purpose of marketing is to get more people to buy more of your product, more often, for more money," he would write later, in his 1999 book *The End of Marketing As We Know It.*

Whatever Zyman's past mistakes, that philosophy made perfect sense to Goizueta, who hired Zyman back as chief marketing officer in 1993. Once back, Zyman pushed the concept of "spending to sell"; every marketing campaign, he announced, would be weighed against how much it increased sales of soft drinks—if it didn't, then it would be cut. If it did, "we poured on more." The domestic ad budget rose to $500 million in 1994, $600 million in 1996, and $700 million in 1997 (with $1.6 billion spent on advertising worldwide).

And it wasn't enough to get more people to drink Coke products—it was also important for those already drinking Coke to drink more of them. Company statistics showed that of the 64 ounces the average person drank in a day, Coke products accounted for just a miserable two of them. It was Zyman's job to think of ways to get people to increase that number; after all, in his native Mexico, it was common for people to drink three or four cans a day. "These are the consumers you want," he said. "And you want to make sure that you capture all of them."

Zyman came up with a new concept he called "dimensionalizing," which he defined as giving people more reasons to drink beyond Coke's "original selling proposition." If a person had eight drinks a week because he was thirsty, then telling him to be sociable might drive that up to ten. "Then you have to create a new reason after 10," said Zyman. In order to get a better handle on the various reasons to drink Coke, the company had 3,600 super-consumers—whom they called, without irony, "heavy users"—to keep diaries of all of the occasions when they drank, which the marketers called "need states."

The research was enormously successful, revealing 40,000 separate occasions when the test subjects might pop open a can. Zyman distilled them down to thirty-five different reasons to drink Coke, or "dimensions," including: "Coke is part of my life. It understands me. Cool people drink it. People of all ages drink it. It has a bite and a distinctive taste. It comes in a contour bottle. It is modern, funny, emotional, simple, large, friendly, consistent, and everywhere." Of course, such an approach to advertising raises the question: At what point are you anticipating customers' needs and at what point are you creating them? Coke didn't dwell on the question long. For each attribute, the marketers designed a different ad, rolling them all together in a new campaign under the slogan "Always Coca-Cola" (which had the delicious double entendre of harkening back to Coke's heritage while encouraging consumers to drink it at every occasion).

At the same time, Zyman shook up Madison Avenue by spreading work among different agencies, having them compete for Coke's vast advertising war chest. Along with Apple and Nike, Coke even began to contract out to Hollywood powerhouse Creative Artists Agency, which created one of Coke's most compelling symbols. During the 1993 Academy Awards presentation, TV viewers were introduced to a computer-generated family of polar bears watching the northern lights in a vast expanse of ice with nothing to break up the monotony but the familiar logo of Coca-Cola. The bear clan returned for the following holiday season, Coke's most successful branding of Christmas since it introduced its Santa Claus ads in the 1930s.

The polar bears were the perfect new branding agent in an era when branding was king. A few years after New Coke taught the Coca-Cola Company the value of its brand name, the rest of Wall Street learned the same lesson when Philip Morris cut the price of its Marlboro cigarettes by 20 percent to compete with generics flooding the market. Immediately Philip Morris's stock dropped, along with Coca-Cola and many other brands, as the financial press rang a death knell for the brand.

A few weeks after the incident, Goizueta called Wall Street analysts down to an emergency meeting in Atlanta. "We are getting a bum rap," he whined. "It's one thing when your stock drops 10 percent because of a mistake your company has made . . . but it's something else . . . when it drops because of a business with totally different financial and social dynamics." For the next four hours, he patiently explained why people might not pay for a Marlboro but they would pay for a Coke. And he was right. Coke's stock righted itself in a few weeks.

As Naomi Klein recounts in her book *No Logo*, the real lesson of "Marlboro Friday" was that companies needed to invest more money in branding, not less. The companies that succeeded after the recession of the early 1990s were those that wrapped consumers in their products, creating not just an association with their product but a complete lifestyle—think Starbucks, Disney, Apple, Calvin Klein, and Nike. "And then there were companies that had always understood that they were selling brands before product," writes Klein, citing Coke at the top of her list. As Disney opened Disney Stores in malls across America, Coke followed suit on a smaller scale with Coca-Cola stores in New York and Las Vegas and the original World of Coca-Cola in Atlanta.

The man responsible for of Coke's new success, however, didn't live to see it for very long. In 1997, Goizueta was one of the wealthiest people in America—personally worth more than a billion dollars—and because most of his wealth was tied up in stock, he was able to avoid paying virtually any personal income tax. But just at his moment of greatest triumph, he discovered he had lung cancer. Within a year, he was dead.

Goizueta's sudden departure was a blow to the company's image on Wall Street, as well as a threat to its ties to the all-important beverage analysts that could keep pushing Coke's stock price into the stratosphere. Though no one knew it, Goizueta's death would coincide with a dramatic turnaround in the fortunes of the company. At the time, however, it seemed like the executive he left in charge would pick up his mantle without missing a beat.

Douglas Ivester was, if anything, more relentless about Coke's need to grow. Joining Coke as an accountant in 1979, he constantly had an eye on the bottom line. "From his earliest moments at the company, he saw Coke's business as a numbers game—one he could win," writes *New York Times* business reporter Constance Hays in her book *The Real Thing: Truth and Power at the Coca-Cola Company.* As Hays describes, it was Ivester who pushed through the greatest revolution in Coke's structure, ensuring unlimited growth in its stock, at the same time finally getting the bottlers under control.

Starting in the early 1980s, the company began buying up any bottlers that were for sale, spinning them off into a new company called Coca-Cola Enterprises. The Coca-Cola Company made sure to own 49 percent of outstanding shares of the new company, giving it control without any of the risk or liability. No longer bound by Thomas and Whitehead's original contract, Ivester and company forced the new bottling company to accept a new contract that allowed the price of syrup to fluctuate at whim.

Over the next decade, the Coca-Cola Company replicated the Coca-Cola Enterprises model with bottlers in other countries as well—creating less than a dozen "anchor bottlers" all over the world, including the San Miguel Group in the Philippines, T.C.C. Beverages Ltd. in Canada, Panamerican Beverages (later Coca-Cola FEMSA) in Latin America, and Coca-Cola Amatil in Australia. Meanwhile, the tremendous debt accumulated from buying these bottlers was rolled right off Coke's books, onto the balance sheets of the bottlers.

The new arrangement, called by Ivester "the 49 percent solution," was enthusiastically embraced by Goizueta, who called it "a new era in American capitalism." When the dust had cleared, however, it looked more like a scheme from the parent company to cook its books. By owning a controlling interest in its bottlers, Coke could ensure that it hit its earning targets throughout the '80s and early '90s. Whenever the company didn't grow in sales, it could still force bottlers to buy syrup, ensuring profits for the parent company; how they sold that syrup was the bottlers' problem.

Not that parent Coke was about to let its bottlers go under, of course. If it appeared that a bottler wasn't going to make ends meet, the company would give rebates at the end of the year in the form of "marketing support" so they made just enough profit. Even as the anchor bottlers were under constant pressure to sell as many soft drinks as they could to eke out a minimum profit, they were also free to take on enormous amounts of debt—at one point, Coca-Cola Enterprises' debt was half its annual revenues—since lenders rightly assumed that the parent company would never let its franchises fail.

The system worked beautifully through the late '80s and early '90s to drive stock price and soft drinks sales. When Goizueta suddenly died, it was only natural that Ivester should take control. Where Goizueta was charming inside and outside the company, however, Ivester had a reputation for being a cold numbers-cruncher—an "iceman" in the eyes of fellow employees. Employees were all but forbidden to talk about their work outside of Coke headquarters, and some even suspected their phones were tapped.

But Ivester was ambitious. Where Woodruff saw putting Coke "within an arm's reach of desire," Ivester waxed on about a "360-degree landscape of Coke," the red-and-white swoosh in every direction a customer looked. "What I always wonder is, Why not?" he said in a speech to the National Soft Drink Association. "Why can't we keep this up? Just look around! The world has more people, in more countries, with more access to communication and more desire for a higher standard of living and quality products than ever before." In his mind, Ivester lumped a higher "standard of living" with consuming more sweet sugary Coke, the ultimate international status symbol—shades of Candler putting Coke bottles into the hands of the fashionable set in turn-of-the-century ads.

In one notorious speech to employees, Ivester cued the background noise of howling wolves, comparing the Coke company to a wolf among sheep and all but howling along. In truth, though, Pepsi was on the ropes by the mid-1990s, its market share stagnating. Coke showed no quarter, forcing food distributors to refuse to carry Pepsi if they wanted to keep their accounts for Coke. Convenience stores, meanwhile, had to agree to increasingly restrictive advertising agreements if they wanted to stock Coke in their store—agreeing not to hang signs for other products, or committing 70, 80, or even 100 percent of the available shelf space for soft drinks to Coke. (Eventually, Royal Crown Cola sued in Texas for violations of antitrust laws, earning a $15.6 million verdict.)

Even as it was dominating the field, however, Coke was having difficulty meeting its high earnings expectations year after year, especially as the market for soft drinks became increasingly saturated. Pepsi solved its problem, in part, by diversifying, buying up first Frito-Lay and then Gatorade and becoming as much a snack food vendor as a soda company. (Soft drink sales now account for less than 20 percent of Pepsi's business.) But Coke saw its future in liquid, specifically in carbonated soft drinks, which still make up more than 80 percent of its sales. It would need new markets to swim in, and so it redoubled its efforts to put its red-and-white dynamic ribbon within all 360 degrees of customers' sight lines.

In all of the pressure to continue expanding, Ivester and company never asked: Did the world really *need* all of that Coke? The answer to that question took them completely by surprise. After years of drinking more and more gallons of sugar-laced beverages, people finally couldn't ignore the consequences of all of that consumption in one area: their health. As it turned out, increasing evidence showed that Coke was not only "biggering" its own beverage sizes, sales, and profits—but also "biggering" American waistlines. The ensuing controversy over soda's role in a burgeoning crisis of obesity and diabetes presented the company's biggest challenge in more than a century, finally putting the brakes on its engine for growth.

In actuality Coke had been here before. When Coca-Cola first gushed from Gilded Age soda fountains, it was touted as a panacea for anything that ailed you. Within just a few decades, however, the tide turned on Coke, with the public increasingly questioning whether that bottle full of fizz could really be all that good. The drink hadn't quite lived down its associations with cocaine, for starters. In the early years of Coke, the press stirred up sensational visions of "Coke fiends," hopped up on Coca-Cola terrorizing good southern women. (The overtly racist coverage said more about the anxieties of the South after slavery, since the fiends were invariably black and the women invariably white.)

By the turn of the century, however, there was a wide backlash against patent medicines in general, as muckraking newspaper and magazine stories, starting with a series by Samuel Hopkins Adams in *Collier's* in 1905, exposed what was really in those elixirs—including chloroform, turpentine, and an awful lot of alcohol. At the same time, the publication of Upton Sinclair's *The Jungle*, which blew the lid off the dangers and lack of sanitation in the meatpacking business, led to increasing strictures on what food manufacturers could put in the products that Americans ate. It was the dawn of the Progressive Era, a reaction to the excesses of Gilded Age capitalism, in which government increasingly clamped down with increased regulations.

In this general climate, one man emerged as the flawed hero of the consumer movement—Dr. Harvey Washington Wiley, the head of the government's Bureau of Chemistry. Wiley nearly single-handedly railroaded a new law, the Pure Food and Drug Act (commonly called the Pure Food Law), through Congress in 1906. It proceeded on a simple if suspect proposition—that adding artificial preservatives and colorings to food or patent medicines made them less wholesome. Due to the "increased amounts of poisonous and toxic matters in the system," Wiley testified before Congress, "the general vitality of the body is gradually reduced. . . . Even old age, which is regarded as a natural death, is a result of these toxic activities." Wiley proved his theories with his celebrated "poison squad," a group of young men to whom he and his colleagues fed all manner of suspect food additives, including large quantities of boric, sulfuric, and benzoic acid to see if it made them sick. The experiments weren't exactly scientifically rigorous—lacking, for example, a control group or measures to account for preexisting medical conditions of the unfortunate crew, but the publicity they engendered gave public support to the idea of a new law. Congress passed it on June 30, 1906.

Over the next few years, Wiley went on the attack against blended-whiskey producers and catsup makers (for adding benzoate of soda as a preservative), earning a reputation as a crusading health advocate, if a bit of an arrogant self-promoter. His nemesis, however, would be Coca-Cola. From reports early on that Coke contained cocaine and alcohol, he demanded that a sample be tested. When it came back negative, it hardly dampened his ardor against bringing Coke down. At the same, the Woman's Christian Temperance Union, hot against the scourges of alcohol, published pamphlets that—despite Wiley's tests—railed against Coke as hazardous to children because of its content of cocaine, alcohol, and caffeine.

It was this last ingredient that Wiley would eventually make into the crook that dragged Coke into court. In keeping with his theories of adulterated foods, Wiley argued that "free caffeine" added to products such as Coke was much more harmful and addictive than the caffeine that occurred naturally in coffee and tea, comparing the added substance to opium and cannabis. On this basis, he tried several times to seize Coke shipments to put the company on trial but was constantly overruled by the secretary of agriculture, James Wilson, whom he later blamed for protecting Coke. Finally, when an Atlanta newspaper editor caught wind of the interference, Wilson relented, if only Wiley would try the company in Chattanooga, headquarters of Coke's largest bottler and, after Atlanta, the territory friendliest to the beverage company. (Other accounts have it that it was Wiley who chose the venue for the trial, in an effort to get it in front of an Eastern Tennessee judge who was known to look kindly on progressive regulation.)

The case went to trial in Chattanooga in March 1911, coinciding with Wiley's honeymoon with his new bride, feminist Anna Kelton. Officially called *The United States v. Forty Barrels and Twenty Kegs of Coca-Cola*, the trial turned on two counts—the unhealthy addition of "free caffeine," as well as the fact that it was "misbranded" as Coca-Cola, since it contained neither coca leaves nor kola nut. In fact, however, the trial brought out all Coke's dirty laundry—from government inspectors who testified about the unsanitary conditions of Coke's factory and the discovery of bug parts in the drink, to medical experts testifying that Coke drove people insane. The evidence presented by the government about the harmful effect of caffeine on humans was equally dubious, relying on flawed experiments of frogs and rabbits; no one from the poison squad made an appearance. In the end, none of it mattered. The entire case hinged upon a technicality when the judge ordered a directed verdict, at Coke's urging, that Coca-Cola's formula had always had caffeine, so it couldn't be considered an additive.

Wiley wasn't there to see it, having left town a week earlier, perhaps seeing the way the wind was blowing. A year after the trial, he resigned rather than risk having Secretary Wilson force him out. The case wasn't done, however. Years later, the government appealed it all the way up to the Supreme Court, which ruled it had been wrongly decided and sent it back to the district level. Coke maneuvered to spare itself the indignity of appearing again in court, striking a deal with the government whereby it reduced the level of caffeine in the drink by half and adding more coca leaf (from which the cocaine had been removed) and kola nut to address the issue of misbranding. The government would keep the forty barrels and twenty kegs it had initially seized but refrained from bringing the case anew against Coke's new formula.

Coca-Cola had emerged victorious, and essentially intact, from the attack. Eventually the Pure Food Law itself was repealed, as prevailing scientific opinion decided there was nothing wrong with food additives, which became rampant throughout the twentieth century. Ironically, it's only now that the purity of foods has become an issue in health—fueled by the writings of Michael Pollan and the "slow food" movement, which has railed against the "nutritionism" that has dominated the last few decades of food science, and urged a return to unadulterated foods.

For Coke, it would take another ninety years for the next major attack on the grounds of health, and when it came, it focused not on any detrimental additives but on the core ingredient that made up most of the drink's contents—sugar. And unlike the prior skirmish, this fight wouldn't occur in a court of law—but in the court of public opinion.

Every day, it seems, there's new evidence of America's expanding waistline—from a policy on Southwest Airlines requiring customers to buy two seats if they are going to spill over from the eighteen inches allotted in one, to the motorized carts Wal-Mart now offers for people too large to amble around the store by themselves. In medical terms, a person is obese when his or her body mass index (BMI) tops 30.* And after holding steady for much of the last century, the percentage of American adults checking that box has more than doubled, from 14 percent in the 1970s to 34 percent today, translating into some 75 million people.

Another 34 percent of adults with a BMI over 25 are classified as "overweight," placing more than two-thirds of the adult U.S. population into one of those two categories. And along with those statistics come increased

*BMI, a measure used to estimate a healthy body weight according to height, is calculated by dividing one's weight by the square of one's height.

risks for diseases such as high blood pressure and heart disease. The prognosis for the next generation is just as bad, with the percentage of obese teenagers more than tripling, from 5 percent to 18 percent over the past thirty years, and the number of obese children climbing to 20 percent.

On the face of it, the reason people get fat is simple: They eat more than they burn off in exercise. Beyond that, however, it's enormously difficult to pinpoint exactly what has led to the explosion in America's waistline. "Obesity is not rocket science, it's more complicated," warned Frank Hu, a researcher at Harvard Medical School, at a 2006 conference in Boston looking at responses to childhood obesity. Nearly all scientists now agree that at least part of the equation is genetic; some people are just programmed with so-called thrifty genes that cause the body to retain fat more than others.

For the rest, recent papers have blamed the obesity epidemic on everything from an increased prevalence of air-conditioning to decreased rates of smoking. But by far the most likely culprit is diet—and on that score, an increasingly convincing stack of evidence lays at least part of the blame at the syrupy feet of the soda companies. The math is simple: At the same time that America's obesity rates doubled, so has Americans' soda consumption; between 1970 and 1998, it accounted for nearly half the increase in calories in the average diet. It now represents the largest *single* source of calories for the average person, at 7 percent for adults and up to 10 percent for children.

Several years ago, Hu led a team analyzing some thirty studies linking soda consumption to weight gain, concluding that they "show a positive association between greater intake of sugar-sweetened beverages and weight gain and obesity in both children and adults." The report recommended that "sufficient evidence exists for public health strategies to discourage consumption of sugary drinks." In scientific language that's not quite "Drop the soda can, fatty!" but it is enough to point the finger for obesity squarely Cokeward.

One of the most compelling studies Hu looked at was done by nutritionist David Ludwig and published in the British journal *The Lancet* in 2001. Ludwig followed five hundred eleven-year-olds for more than two years, and concluded that each soda added daily to their diets increased their chances for becoming obese by 60 percent. (A later study by Ludwig showed that removing a daily can of soda led to a weight loss of about a pound a month for already overweight teens.) The implications of that were literally enormous. "It's not the exceptional child who drinks a liter, two liters, or even three liters a day," says Ludwig, who runs an obesity clinic for kids at Boston's Children's Hospital. "It's actually remarkably common among my patients." Another analysis, of thousands of nurses, by Harvard University nutritionist Matthias Schulze found that women who increased soda consumption to at least one a day gained an extra pound a year, and were twice as likely to contract diabetes. That study was all but a "smoking gun" that soda was linked to weight gain, wrote Boston nutritionist Caroline Apovian in *The New England Journal of Medicine*, concluding that reducing soda consumption "might be the best single opportunity to curb the obesity epidemic."

Of course, linking soda consumption to obesity doesn't necessarily prove it is soda making people fat—soda drinkers could also be couch potatoes, or eat more french fries. A surprising study by Purdue University nutritionist Richard Mattes has shown, however, that soda is unique in its contribution to weight gain. Mattes gave patients an extra 450 calories a day of jelly beans, telling them they could eat whatever else they wanted. When participants returned a month later, however, they hadn't gained weight, since they'd compensated by eating less other food. But when Mattes repeated the study with an extra 450 calories of Coke, he found they didn't compensate, and their weight and BMI increased. He hypothesized that "when drinking fluid calories," people simply didn't register the extra energy, and continued to eat more calories to keep their bellies full.

Some researchers such as Harvard's George Bray have even hypothesized that soda's main ingredient—high-fructose corn syrup—also leads to increased weight gain, since fructose isn't broken down in the bloodstream in the normal way, instead building up in the liver and turning directly into fat. Other obesity researchers disregard the theory—arguing that sugar is sugar. They virtually all agree, however, that any sugar in large quantities disrupts with the body's natural mechanisms, causing cells to become more resistant to the enzyme insulin, and, over time, leading to diabetes.* Before the 1990s, this kind of diabetes was known as "adult-onset diabetes," since it typically occurred later in life. By 1996, however, so many children had developed the disease that the name was changed to simply "type-2 diabetes." Recently the Centers for Disease Control and Prevention issued the shocking pronouncement that of all children born in the year 2000, *one in three* will become diabetic in their lifetimes.

Despite the preponderance of evidence linking soda to obesity—to say nothing of the commonsense proposition that drinking gallons of sugar might not be super-great for one's diet—the awareness of soda's harmfulness was slow to hit. Back in the 1980s, the government was continually warning Americans about too much fat—not sugar—in their diets. As Michael Pollan explains, "The whole of the industrial food supply was reformulated to reflect the new nutritional wisdom, giving us low-fat pork, low-fat Snackwells, and all the low-fat pasta and high-fructose (yet low-fat!) corn syrup we could consume." Meanwhile, as the shareholder value movement gained momentum, Coke wasn't the only company pushing larger and larger portion sizes to satisfy shareholders' desires for growth, according to New York University nutritionist and *Food Politics* author Marion Nestle. After staying stable throughout the 1970s, the number of calories present in the food supply has risen steadily since 1980, up more than 20 percent from 3,200 to 3,900 per capita, mostly from carbohydrates and added fats and sugars.

Not that the food company execs at Coke or any other brand were evilly plotting to make America fat—they were thinking about their own survival. "When you come in in the morning, there is no sheet that says

*Even those disputing the existence of the obesity epidemic, such as Paul Campos and Eric Oliver (authors of *The Obesity Myth* and *Fat Politics,* respectively), single out soda as harmful for "wreak[ing] havoc on our bloodstream," as Oliver writes, "affect[ing] cholesterol, blood pressure, and metabolism."

you get 50 altruism points if you do something charitable," says Coke's former marketing director Hank Cardello, now an anti-obesity advocate at the University of North Carolina. "The sheet says here's how many cases I sold and is it above or below the target." Besides, he says, no one was thinking about soft drinks in terms of obesity or diabetes. "At the time, the product was perceived so positively, it was feel-good stuff. I talk to executives now and they feel like they woke up one day with a target on their back. It's like you wake up one day and all of a sudden someone is saying your kid is ugly."

If Cardello and his fellow executives thought about health at all, it was during periodic flare-ups such as the program CBS did about health concerns over aspartame—the sweetener better known as NutraSweet—which both Coke and Pepsi had started using to sweeten their diet beverages starting in 1983 (moving to a 100 percent aspartame formula by the end of 1984). Complaints about the chemical more than doubled in the latter half of that year, from 108 to 248, with regular diet soda drinkers complaining about headaches, dizziness, fatigue, depression, and insomnia within a few days of starting to drink the beverages. It's telling that the company treated the issue as one of brand image—not health. Cardello nervously wrote a memo to his superiors telling them it wasn't a big deal "unless the CBS story snowballed," which it never did. Eventually the Centers for Disease Control declared concerns about aspartame of minor importance, even as more than seven thousand complaints—three thousand concerning soft drinks—were received by the FDA in the first fifteen years. Concerns over the chemical continue to persist, with a comprehensive, if controversial, study conducted in Italy and published in 2006 over seven years that found aspartame statistically linked to an increase in cancer in rats. (The FDA dismissed the study as flawed by preexisting disease in the rat population.) Faced with the catastrophic upheaval that would come with a reformulation of Diet Coke, the Coca-Cola Company has reflexively held the line on aspartame, sending representatives to lobby against a bill to ban the substance introduced in New Mexico in 2006.

Coke intervened even more directly when another potentially dangerous chemical was discovered in diet sodas in 1990s. During product tests, chemists at rival company Cadbury-Schweppes discovered excessive levels of benzene—a chemical linked to leukemia and other forms of cancer—in some of its sodas, particularly diet orange sodas. The chemical, which apparently was formed from a reaction of the preservative sodium benzoate with ascorbic acid (vitamin C), was found in levels of more than 25 parts per billion (ppb), well above the legal limit of 5 ppb.

Representatives of the National Soft Drink Association—of which Coke was a member—met promptly with the FDA and expressed concern over the "potential for adverse publicity associated with this problem," according to a memo from the meeting. The government agency agreed to let the companies quietly reformulate their drinks to prevent a scare. (Earlier that year, Perrier water was found contaminated with benzene at levels up to 22 ppb, and the company forced to recall more than 160 million bottles worldwide at a cost of $263 million.) It hardly policed their efforts, however; the FDA's own tests from 1995 to 2001 show that 79 percent of diet soda samples tested were contaminated with benzene at an average of 19 ppb.

The public wasn't alerted until 2005, when one of the original chemists who discovered the benzene fifteen years earlier found it still present in some drinks. Under pressure, the FDA released its own tests, finding among other beverages that Coke's Fanta Orange Pineapple soda contained benzene at nearly 24 ppb. Coke's public relations team flew into action, stating "unequivocally that our products are safe," even while not denying the presence of benzene. Not trusting the companies this time, some consumers brought a class-action lawsuit against Coke, Pepsi, Cadbury, and other companies. Coke settled in May 2007, agreeing to reformulate the drinks and pay $500 each to four plaintiffs.

These kinds of strategies set the tone for the Coca-Cola Company's early responses to the obesity epidemic, in which it made common cause with its competitors to try to fly under the radar—worried above all about the possible damage done to the Coca-Cola brand. Almost from the beginning, however, the obesity fight would be different—dragging Coke kicking and screaming into the public arena to defend itself against attack.

The opening salvo was fired by a nonprofit group called the Center for Science in the Public Interest (CSPI), which released a report about soda in 1998 called *Liquid Candy* that teased out the connections between soda and health issues. "I had been watching soda sales rise for decades, ever since World War II," says CSPI president Michael Jacobson. "We always knew that soda was the quintessential junk food, but the concern was tooth decay. No one talked about obesity." The report would change that—drawing the connection for the first time between the corresponding rise in soda sales and obesity rates over the previous twenty years, and sparking a debate that eventually spilled out into a national backlash against sugary soda.

CSPI was founded in 1971, one of the first of the many "public interest" groups that proliferated in a period that business historian David Vogel calls the last of the "three major political waves of challenge to business that has taken place in the United States in [the twentieth] century" (the first two being the Progressive Era and the strong push by organized labor in the post-Depression 1930s). Groups such as the Sierra Club, Common Cause, and Ralph Nader's Public Citizen used any means possible to curb the power of big business at a time when public support for corporations was at a low ebb.

In CSPI's case, the group has held vocal press conferences, slapped complaints against companies with government agencies, and even threatened lawsuits in its usually successful attempts to remove what it sees as deceptive advertising and nutrition labeling for food. For its actions, CSPI has been labeled the "food police" and derided as a reactionary group for taking on everything from cheese to hamburgers. (Most recently, it has gained notoriety for its push to ban trans fats in New York City restaurants and its fight for calorie counts in chain restaurants.)

But Jacobson makes no apologies for sounding the alarm over soda. As he watched the parallel rise of obesity statistics and soda consumption, he says, he couldn't help putting the two together. All of that emphasis on growth pushed by Goizueta and Ivester, he argued in *Liquid Candy*, had created collateral damage—especially with some of the most vulnerable of the nation's citizens—children. According to the report, even young children drank more than a can of sugary soda a day. A typical teenage boy who drank soda consumed nearly two and a half cans—with some drinking up to five. Not that girls fared much better, averaging nearly two cans a day. To put that into perspective: One 12-ounce can of soda contains about 10 teaspoons of sugar; a Double Gulp has more than 50—just over one cup. Other statistics in the report spelled out the aggressive marketing tactics that the company was using to push even greater sales of soft drinks. (Indeed, when CSPI did an update of *Liquid Candy* in 2005, the percentage of calories from soft drinks in the average person's diet had gone up 25 percent.)

The report was catnip to the media, which ran story after story about the findings—singling out Coke more often than Pepsi as a harmful substance fed to youth. The Coca-Cola Company sat back silently, even as its surrogate, the National Soft Drink Association, aggressively contradicted CSPI's claims. "Soft drinks make no nutritious [*sic*] claims," said a spokesperson for the trade group. "We are simply one of the nice little refreshments people can enjoy as part of a balanced diet." Furthermore, the group said, there was no conclusive evidence that soda caused obesity any more than any other added calories to the diet. The NSDA went on to dismiss CSPI's attack as a histrionic overreaction to a food that the vast number of people enjoy—akin to its previous attacks against theater popcorn and fast-food hamburgers.

If there was a corporate playbook to respond to public-interest group attacks, the soda companies had taken a page directly from it. The classic response had been established several decades before by the makers of an even more obviously harmful product—cigarettes. When studies first started casting aspersions on smoking in the 1950s, the tobacco companies hired the industry consulting group Hill & Knowlton, which in turn established the Tobacco Industry Research Committee (later the Center for Tobacco Research) in order to respond to the claims.

Rather than face them head-on, however, the group pulled a rope-a-dope, calling scientific studies into question all the while it stalled by holding out for more evidence, which eventually took decades to emerge. "Industry has learned that debating the science is much easier and more effective than debating the policy," writes David Michaels in his recent book *Doubt Is Their Product*, a title taken directly from a statement in an actual memo from a tobacco company exec. Knowing that it is nearly impossible to establish proof beyond a reasonable doubt in science, industry execs—whether from tobacco companies speaking on secondhand smoke or from oil companies addressing global warming—have very effectively changed the terms of the debate by encouraging further research as a way of holding off any government action—or as another tobacco executive wrote in a memo, "creating doubt about the health charge without actually denying it . . . encouraging objective scientific research as the only way to resolve the question of health hazard."

Cardello admits that Coke and its competitors followed a similar tactic of stalling on scientific evidence in dealing with early health concerns. "Clearly that is the playbook, and I think most companies whether it's sugar or salt or whatever the demon du jour is, follow that playbook," he says. "I'm not even making a moral judgment on it." But he also insists there are limits to the kind of stall tactics that a company will employ. "If someone finds salmonella in a product, I get that off in five seconds," he says. But Coke and other soft drink companies were taken aback by the way they were singled out for obesity—after all, many marketing executives in the industry had made a conscious decision not to apply for positions in liquor or tobacco companies because they didn't want to push harmful products on the populace. Now suddenly, they were the problem. "Without a crisis you don't change your core business model," says Cardello. "It took the crisis of obesity to make a change."

That assessment gives Coke too much credit, perhaps, ignoring the fact that even as it was adjusting its business model in the face of the obesity epidemic, it was continuing to use advertising and public relations efforts to deflect attention from its role in that crisis. When that didn't work, it followed a dual strategy of simultaneously denying its role and positioning itself as a partner in developing solutions to the problem. At no point did Coke seriously disavow its strategy of pushing more and bigger sizes of sugary soft drinks—in fact, after drawing back temporarily in the face of public opposition, it has redoubled its efforts in that core market.

One thing, however, is for sure—for Coke, the obesity crisis could not have come at a worse time. Faced with an increasingly saturated market, the company failed for the first time in years to meet earnings expectations in 1998. Ivester, meanwhile, went through a series of missteps—first a contamination scare in Belgium, in which the company seemed to drag its feet and not respond fast enough when some two hundred people, many of them children, got sick. Then came news that Ivester was considering a new type of vending machine overseas that would change its prices depending on the temperature outside—a cynical form of price-gouging even for Coke.

The coup de grâce, however, came when a certified public accountant in Indiana named Albert Meyer took a closer look at Coke's books, setting in motion a chain of events that would bring down all of Goizueta and Ivester's financial machinations. Meyer determined that through Coke's majority ownership in its bottlers it was able to exercise near complete control over their financials, ensuring the parent company would always make a profit. If Coke reported its bottlers' profit alongside its own, Meyer concluded, it would show nearly none at all. "One cannot transact with oneself," he told the *Philadelphia Daily News.* "If you are labeled America's most admired company, you should have accounting policies that live up to the name." Another analyst later called Coke's shenanigans simply "smoke and mirrors."

As Coke's sales stagnated, the bottlers began to balk. Ivester raised syrup prices, and they further dug in their heels, enlisting two of Coke's largest shareholders in their cause. In a private meeting in December 1999, they told Ivester he was through. If they hoped to rescue the stock price with the ouster, however, they failed. Coke's share price continued to fall, leading the company to lay off a third of its ten thousand U.S. workers, along with a similar amount overseas. Most of the lost jobs were outsourced to contract workers or private companies, even as longtime workers lamented the end of Coke's image as a benevolent employer. Meanwhile, new CEO Douglas Daft, who replaced Ivester, downgraded volume targets to 5 to 6 percent for the year 2000—and still missed them. When Daft tried to orchestrate a purchase of Quaker, maker of Gatorade, he was voted down by the board.

All of this bad news, however, was just a prelude to Coke's biggest crisis, when the anti-obesity activists opened up a new front in the fight against soda—one that took aim directly at the core of Coke's strategy to increase sales among its most valuable set of consumers—schoolchildren.

FOUR

The Battle for Schools

The first time Jackie Domac heard of her school's soda contract, it was an early fall day at the beginning of the school year in 1999. The high school health teacher was having lunch with students in her classroom in Venice, California, when one of them pulled out a can of 100 percent juice she'd brought from home. "Do you think we could have this in the vending machines?" she asked. Domac hadn't been aware that the school didn't have juice for sale, but she figured it would be an easy fix. After lunch, she dropped a quick note in the financial manager's mailbox. The reply she received in her own box was short: "No. Selling juice would conflict with our exclusive soda contract." Domac was taken aback. "I said soda contract, what's a soda contract?" she recalls now from her home in Southern California, where she has been studying to be a lawyer.

She asked the school office for a copy of the contract, and after some initial denials was given one. Sure enough, the deal the school had signed with the Coca-Cola Company prohibited it from selling juice. In fact, the school wasn't allowed to sell anything that hadn't been approved by Coke, which had inked a deal to sell its drinks, and only its drinks, in the vending machines. For the privilege, Coke gave the school $3,000 a year—about $1 per student.

"I was pretty much horrified," says Domac. "As a health teacher, it was pretty disturbing to discover that a private industry had more influence over students' health than their own teachers did. Even if a student wanted to drink something else, it didn't matter because we had sold all of our rights to this one company." She promptly sent the contract to the *Los Angeles Times*, and was rewarded with a sharp rebuke by the school, which censured her for violating the contract's confidentiality agreement.

But Domac wasn't just the school's health teacher. She was also the leader for a school "peace and justice" club. After she told the students what she had learned, some formed a new group, called the Public Health Advocacy Club, to investigate. What they found went far beyond their high school. As they picked apart the contract, they found that high schools across the country had adopted similar contracts with similarly restrictive beverage choices. Eventually that simple question asked by that one high school student would grow into a national movement combating soda for its role in the epidemic of childhood obesity. After all, the increase in consumption of sugar-filled soft drinks over the last three decades of the twentieth century wasn't a happy accident for Coke; it was a deliberate strategy. And schools were right at the center of it.

By the late 1990s, Coke had hit a wall. Despite executives' push for ubiquity, the company was running into the inevitable fact that the market for soft drinks in America was beginning to be saturated. Beverage analysts began to wonder aloud whether Coca-Cola would be able to continue to expand in its home country. Now with the unraveling of the bottling scheme and sales starting to lag, the company redoubled its efforts to find whatever new markets it could—and found a captive one in schools that could not only ensure a steady source of new sales but also inspire the early brand loyalty that was so important.

In fact, the soda companies, led by Coke, had been slowly pushing open the door to school contracts for decades. In the 1960s and 1970s, sales of soda and other food of "minimal nutritional value" were strictly regulated during school hours. In the 1980s, the National Soft Drink Association fought back, suing the federal government on the grounds that the regulations were "arbitrary, capricious, and an abuse of discretion." Though they lost in district court, the soda companies won on appeal when the court ruled the United States Department of Agriculture could restrict vending machine sales only during lunch hour. The USDA reluctantly revised its rulings, which went without challenge for more than a decade. When Vermont senator Patrick Leahy tried to bar soda machines again in 1994, Coke leaped to action with a letter-writing campaign that enlisted school principals, teachers, and coaches to complain about lost revenue. Unsuccessful in his efforts, a frustrated Senator Leahy complained that "the company puts profit ahead of children's health. . . . If Coke wins, children lose."

With the door now ajar to selling soda in schools, however, Coke pushed it open even further with a new strategy to win big in the hallways. So-called pouring-rights contracts began as agreements by soda companies to sell their products in fast-food restaurants, such as Coke in McDonald's and Pepsi in Burger King. Sometime in the early 1990s, they began to expand into sports stadiums and state fairgrounds, gaining exclusive access to sell only their own brand's products in exchange for a premium paid to the facility.

Based on this model, the first school contracts followed with little fanfare: Woodland Hills, Pennsylvania, for example, signed a ten-year contract with Coke in 1994 for twenty-five Coke machines in exchange for $30,000 up front and commissions on further sales. Sam Barlow High School in Gresham, Oregon, signed a contract with Coke in 1995 and received four scoreboards valued at $27,000.

For schools hamstrung by budget cuts, the contracts were a godsend, promising easy money for big purchases they couldn't squeeze into their yearly numbers. Schools had recently been hit hard by the double whammy of the "tax revolt" in the 1980s that lowered property tax revenues and decreased federal funding in the 1990s. The soda money offered discretionary income administrators could use as they saw fit; some put the cash toward awards for gifted students; others funded field trips or parties. (A $2 million district-wide contract in DeKalb County, Georgia, even included $41,000 set aside for all fifth-graders to visit the World of Coca-Cola.)

In some of the contracts, schools could even earn additional money by selling more Coke. An early report to hit the media was the strange affair of the "Coke Dude"—the self-chosen moniker of John Bushey, a superintendent in Colorado Springs. Bushey wrote his principals explaining the district had to top 70,000 cases annually or risk reductions in the payments from Coke, which ranged from $3,000 to $25,000 per school. He suggested they place machines in classroom corridors and allow kids to buy drinks throughout the day. Even if soda wasn't allowed in class, he urged teachers to consider allowing juices, teas, and waters. Sadly, the district fell short, in part because of loopholes that counted only direct sales from vending machines, and not Coke sales at sporting events. "Quite honestly, they were smarter than us," Bushey later told *The New York Times.*

Coke sweetened the pot for some educational honchos, paying the heads of the National Parent Teacher Association and the National School Boards Association $6,000 each in "consulting fees" to fly to Washington and Atlanta as part of a group called the Council for Corporate and School Partnerships. In a testimonial on the group's website that was later removed, a Coca-Cola official raved about the quality of consulting the educators provided, claiming, "They have become our friends!"

Perhaps the person most responsible for the growth in pouring-rights contracts nationwide, however, was a former college athletic director from Colorado named Dan DeRose, who reinvented himself as DD Marketing, a consulting company to guide schools on striking the hardest bargain with soda companies. Between 1995 and 1999, DeRose inked $300 million in contracts (the consultant pocketing a healthy 25 to 35 percent of the total).* "My basic philosophy," he told *The Denver Post* in 1999: "Schools have it; they're offering it. If we can assist them in maximizing their revenue then I think we're doing a great, great service." He even used his own daughter Anna to underscore the value of soda contracts, boasting to school administrators when his daughter was in first grade: "From now until she's graduated, all she'll drink is Coke. . . . She doesn't even know how to spell Pepsi."

As the contracts got more and more lucrative, however, some parents and activists began expressing misgivings about the amount of advertising by soda companies in schools. "There should never be a situation on public property where commercial advertising is permitted," says Ross Getman, a lawyer from Syracuse, New York, who launched a website to track the contracts nationwide, starting with the one signed by Cicero–North Syracuse High School in 1998. That one included up-front payments from Coke of $900,000 to construct a new football stadium—in which the Coke logo would be prominently displayed on a six-foot-high scoreboard provided by the company, with athletes on the field required to drink out of red Coke cups.

The deal was inked with the help of the president of the state assembly, Michael Bragman, who had a home filled with antique Coca-Cola memorabilia that would set the collectors at the Gaylord Texan to drooling, including two fully stocked Coke machines in the basement. Over the years, Bragman had been a good friend to Coke, helping to repeal a 2-cent-per-container soda tax imposed back in the 1990s. In exchange, Coca-Cola had consistently been one of the biggest contributors to Bragman's reelection campaigns.

Now, standing next to Bragman at the announcement, Coca-Cola Enterprises CEO Bob Lanz gave a heartfelt speech, saying that Coke "wanted to give something back to the community." Neither of them

*Still hustling, DeRose would agree to speak for this book only in exchange for $20,000 and 5 percent of the profits. This offer, it should go without saying, was declined.

mentioned that the majority of the money for the stadium—some $4.6 million—would come from state funds.

The floodgates had now been opened—the school stadium success was written up in Coke's hometown newspaper *The Atlanta Journal-Constitution*, and once administrators began hearing about the cash payments, school districts from Portland, Oregon, to Edison, New Jersey, got religion in a big way. By 2000, according to the Centers for Disease Control and Prevention, 92 percent of high schools had long-term soda contracts, along with 74 percent of middle schools and 43 percent of elementary schools. And at almost all of them, the number of vending machines increased, jumping from a lonely Coke machine by the locker room to dozens of machines scattered around the cafeteria, the auditorium, or even in the halls outside classrooms.

While the additional revenue for the company added only slightly to its massive balance sheet, the schools gave Coke access to customers at an early—and vulnerable—age. "If a high school student drinks a Coke while he's at school, the likelihood that he'll turn to Coke again when he's outside school and actually has a choice becomes much greater," says former brand manager Cardello. "Thus in the end, the goal is not just about getting kids to spend money, it's about getting kids to choose the right brand."

Getting inside the school building with the active support of administrators also gave Coke a back door around its long-standing strictures against advertising to children. For years, after all, Coke had directly targeted kids with special come-ons, from nature cards with the Coke logo in the 1920s to "Know Your Airplanes" decks of cards during World War II. Even back then, however, the company fretted about appearing to advertise a sugary drink to young children. The D'Arcy Agency's ad rules included a proscription against showing "children under 6 or 7 years old," which by the 1950s, McCann extended to children under twelve—a policy Coke supposedly continues to the present day.

Despite its restraint, however, Coke has been remarkably successful in penetrating even the youngest minds. Research has shown that babies recognize brands at anywhere from six to eighteen months, specifically requesting them by age three. Of those brands they know best, Coke is in the top five, along with Cheerios, Disney, McDonald's, and Barbie. In a society where Coke is within an arm's reach of desire—or part of a 360-degree landscape—even children can't escape the ubiquitous Coke logo. But familiarity and brand loyalty, of course, are very different things. As another former Coke marketing chief once said, "With soft drink consumption, early preferences translate into later life preferences. It's a lot easier than getting consumers to switch their brand preferences later on."

And so, Coke has constantly found ways to do that. For decades, for instance, it has blithely produced "collectors' items," including Barbie dolls, playing cars, board games, delivery trucks, and other toys supposedly targeted to adults. Then there are all of those Santa ads, which subtly package the meaning of Christmas in the delivery of a bottle of Coke, imprinting the two concepts together in minds that aren't cognitively well developed enough to distinguish the difference. Those cute polar bears serve a similar purpose. "You take any character that is cute and cuddly and fun and have them drinking down a Coca-Cola and smiling," says Daniel Acuff, an industry ad consultant for years who created the M&M's characters and worked on campaigns for Cap'n Crunch cereal. "That is very clearly playing on the soft spot in people in general and the cognitive unawareness of children under twelve in particular."

Coke has found other ways to get around its policies as well, especially on television, where it defines kids' shows as those in which 50 percent of the audience is under twelve. At least since the last decade, however, the programs children watch most are those originally intended for teens or adults. In 2000, Coke helped foment the concept of "product placement" with a $6 million deal for primary sponsorship of the WB show *Young Americans,* in which characters were seen drinking Coca-Cola in ways one television critic called "ludicrously conspicuous." But Coke found absolute product placement gold with its sponsorship of the runaway television hit

American Idol, which happens to be the second most popular show among children under twelve (second only to *SpongeBob SquarePants*).

In addition to commercials during the program, Coke puts Coke cups into the hands of judges and brands a backstage "red room" with Coke pictures on the walls, Coke coolers, and a "red couch," where performers are interviewed among Coke logos. "You couldn't ask for better TV," enthused one Coke VP in *USA Today*. "If you look at ratings, it's got universal appeal—everything from kids to 35- to 64-[year-olds]."

Television shows aren't the only realm where Coke has used product placement to appeal to kids. In 2001, Creative Artists Agency brokered a $150 million deal for Coke to be the exclusive sponsor for the Harry Potter movies—based on the wildly popular book about a child wizard that spurred a generation of tweens to start reading. In the deal worked out with Warner Bros., Coke wouldn't appear in the movie, nor would any of the characters be seen drinking it (after all, the film's young star, Daniel Radcliffe, was only eleven years old at the time). However, characters and symbols from the film were plastered on packages for Coke, Minute Maid juices, and Hi-C, leaving no doubt who the company was pitching to. "Kids love Harry Potter, and we are confident the affiliation will be very good for us," said a spokesman for Minute Maid, even as a Coke spokeswoman insisted, "The target is really families and not *just* kids."

The movie earned nearly $1 billion worldwide—the second-highest-grossing film at the time behind *Titanic*—and Coca-Cola Enterprises spokesperson John Downs called Potter the most successful campaign of the year. It was enough to spur a push to product placement in movies. Coke appeared in eighty-five of them between 2001 and 2009, third behind Apple and Ford in frequency. While many were marketed to adults, several were even more conspicuously aimed at kids, including the 2005 DreamWorks film *Madagascar*, featuring animated zoo animals escaping from New York, as well as such preteen fare as *Elf*, *Are We There Yet?*, *Scooby-Doo*, and the Disney live-action princess fantasy *Enchanted*.

Finally, in 2002, Coke made the leap to online advertising with Coke

Studios, an online world where users could create avatars called "V-Egos" and put together their own music mixes with different virtual instruments. In 2007, the company followed it up with an entire branded world, CC Metro—which must look much like what Doug Ivester imagined when he envisioned the concept of a "360-degree landscape" of Coke. In this world, avatars move around an entire three-dimensional city, buying cool clothes, riding on hovercraft and skateboards, and talking with fellow fans of Coke. And while they are doing all these cool things, they are surrounded by Coke's advertising images—with logos on billboards, blimps, and park benches, fountains and statues in the shape of Coke's hobbleskirt bottle, and various stores and restaurants where you can spend real money to buy virtual glasses and bottles of Coke products. (Strangely, there are very few ads for anything but Coke Classic.) Soon after it opened, it was getting more than 100,000 visitors a month—no doubt many of them children, given the video game interface and the range of activities available.

With that kind of success reaching young audiences, schools must have seemed to Coke just another avenue to "getting them young." But in doing so, it failed to see how cynical it seemed to sell to children who had no other choice but to spend eight hours a day in the glow of the Coke machine.

Almost immediately after forming the new Public Health Advocacy Club, Jackie Domac and her students took action, attempting to persuade the school to cancel its contract with Coke and implement healthier choices in the vending machines. They knew it would be difficult to convince their fellow students that the soft drinks they enjoyed were actually bad for them. *Liquid Candy* had only just been published, and studies were only beginning to link soda to obesity and other health problems. Even so, the students worked to raise awareness, creating whimsical T-shirts and holding taste tests for organic soy milk in the cafeteria.

Momentum grew after Domac and her students met directly with a representative from Coke's bottler, who reluctantly agreed to stock half of the slots with juice and other more healthful beverages (but only if the school accepted a 15 percent commission on those items, compared to 36 percent on soft drinks). When Domac triumphantly took a French film crew to show them the vending machines a few weeks later, she found the company had changed virtually nothing. "I had asked them to meet us halfway, and now I just embarrassed myself," she remembers. "That was it, they were out." She adopted more confrontational tactics, running for and winning a spot on the parents' advisory council and bringing students in to raise the issue during meetings.

It was money, however, that eventually did the talking. Domac and her students applied for a state health grant in 2002 to serve as a model school for nutrition. When they received a windfall of $250,000, the administration agreed to cancel the deal with Coke on a trial basis to see if the new strategy could work. "You can scream all you want about how healthy beverages prevent obesity and diabetes, but unless you can show a school that it has enough money to run its programs, that's going to fall on deaf ears," Domac says. With the new money, the students worked to get an array of juices and soy beverages into the vending machines at last, along with baked chips and trail mixes. While vending machine sales initially dipped, they eventually rose higher than before—$6,163 in 2002 versus $7,358 in 2003, according to Domac, who still keeps the figures.

Flush with their sense of victory, the student health club took the issue to a higher authority even before those numbers came in—arguing for a ban on soda in the entire Los Angeles Unified School District, the second largest school district in the country, with more than 700,000 students. Again, they used creativity to make their point, storming meetings dressed in necklaces of plastic fruits while performing a foot-stomping chant, "Take Back the Snack." "Facts are great, but they are also quite boring," says Domac. "Having kids being vivacious and happy with a positive message went a long way." The students made impassioned speeches about the new health craze at their school, at the same time marshaling data from a new

UCLA study showing that 40 percent of students in the Los Angeles district were already obese.

Coke waged a creative campaign of its own, threatening to pull its sponsorship of the district's Academic Decathlon events at the school in a blunt attempt to silence opposition. But in the end, the grassroots strategy worked: In August 2002, the Los Angeles Unified school board unanimously voted to cut their contract with Coke. Starting with the 2004 school year, the district would sell no soda at all, stocking its vending machines with only milk, water, and drinks with at least 50 percent juice and no added sweeteners.

After three years of struggle, the students had won—an empowering and humbling experience. "I've never been part of anything like that where people so young can have so much sway," says Faisal Saleh, one of the student leaders, who is now majoring in theater arts at Santa Monica State College. "That's something I take pride in." The success in Los Angeles, however, was hardly the end of the battle against Coke in schools—in fact, it was only the beginning. Even while Coke was losing ground in California, the company soon roared back, determined not to lose out on a hard-won new market for its products at a critical time.

By the time L.A. passed its resolution, word had already spread to other school districts, spawning similar resolutions in San Francisco, Sacramento, Madison, and Oakland. It wasn't just Coke that stood to lose from the backlash—but Pepsi as well. The two companies, bitter rivals in the press, closed ranks to defend themselves through their trade organization, the National Soft Drink Association. As with the initial criticism of CSPI's report, the group painted Domac and her students as misguided. "This is like using a squirt gun to put out a forest fire," said NSDA spokesman Sean McBride. "The LAUSD missed an important opportunity to stem rising obesity rates by having more physical education in their schools and better nutrition education."

That notion that "it's the couch, not the can," became a rallying cry for Big Soda. Coke quickly launched a pilot program in Houston, Philadelphia, and Atlanta called "Step with It!"—distributing Coke-red pedometers to kids to encourage them to exercise more by taking 10,000 steps a day. The program won praise from Health and Human Services secretary Tommy Thompson, and expanded to 250 schools around the country by 2003. Even as Coke was playing nice in the media, however, it was funding studies to cast doubt on the connection between soft drinks and obesity.

Along with Tyson Chicken and Wendy's, Coke reportedly "donated" $200,000 to a new group called the Center for Consumer Freedom (CCF), which took the lead in ridiculing the fight against soda and other unhealthy food, all without revealing its funding. (Pepsi publicly disavowed the group.) "There is a rush to blame soda companies that far outstrips any scientific evidence," said CCF senior analyst Dan Mindus. He pointed to competing studies, one showing that soda had no effect on weight gain, another contending that it was lack of exercise that caused weight increases. What CCF doesn't advertise, of course, is who is paying for those studies. A recent review by David Ludwig—the author of the previously mentioned study on kids and soft drinks—found that beverage studies paid for by industry sources were four to eight times more likely to deny the connection between soda and weight gain than those funded by government or private sources. He makes the connection between soda and the tobacco industry, which funded studies attacking the connection between smoking and lung cancer for forty years. "Is that happening today with the soft drink industry?" Ludwig asks. "Only time will tell, but there certainly is a precedent." As its name implies, CCF argues that consumers should be free to eat what they want—without the "food police" looking over their shoulder at the dinner table. "Their ultimate goal is to restrict our access to certain food," says Mindus. "If they don't believe that we are to be trusted with the decision of choosing the food we eat, how can Americans be trusted with anything?" The argument has resonance. Shouldn't Americans be free to choose what they eat and drink? And if it makes them fat, isn't that their own fault? The argument hits deep in the American psyche, evoking images of founding fathers dumping tea and the Marlboro Man bestriding the Western plains. It also evokes the spirit of free-market capitalism, which enshrines free choice as its highest value.

Ultimately, however, the argument is a cynical one—since the very success of Coke and its fellow companies has given the company the ability to narrow kids' choices. In 2009 alone, Coke spent $2.8 billion in advertising to push its products to the general public. And in schools, the deck is even more stacked against students, since they can choose only from a preselected array of beverages, all the while subjected to the advertisements of the exclusive brand. "Certainly students should be taught to make healthful choices and take individual responsibility," says Lori Dorfman, of the Berkeley Media Studies Group, who has analyzed the way that the soda/obesity issue has played out in the media. "But students do not determine what is made available to them in the vending machines. It's the adults who are responsible for ensuring that schools are doing right by children in their care."

Even so, the Coca-Cola Company appealed to "choice" in 2001 when it staged a strategic retreat with a new school beverage policy. Coke would continue to allow its products in schools but prohibit exclusive school contracts or up-front payments to school districts. "We just don't think that schools are an appropriate venue for marketing," said Coca-Cola America president Jeffrey Dunn during a luncheon announcement in Washington. Coke received a rush of positive publicity, but there was only one problem—nobody bothered to tell the bottlers. Whether by design or benevolent neglect, Coca-Cola Enterprises was caught flat-footed by the announcement. A spokesperson for CCE promised that the bottlers would comply if schools stopped putting out requests for proposals. That promise lasted for all of a week—until Portland, Oregon, put out a request and Coca-Cola Enterprises ponied up a bid.

When the Los Angeles plan passed in August 2002, CCE president John Alm appealed to his chief lobbyist and public relations head John Downs, asking, "What is the plan?" Truth is, the bottler didn't have one. It would take ten months to declare that it was keeping exclusive contracts, even as the bottler encouraged salespeople to offer schools more choices and eliminated big up-front payments. While Alm was announcing the policy, he also produced a private video for friendly politicians calling obesity "a war that's been declared on our company." At the same time, CCE proactively became a chief sponsor of the National Parent Teacher Association in June 2003 with an undisclosed contribution; Downs was placed on its board.

In partnering with teachers and parents, Big Soda emphasized the importance of the money they provided to schools. "They are a win for the students and the schools and the taxpayer," said the NSDA's McBride. "I think everybody benefits as a result of these business partnerships." It was a meme that was picked up by the media. A review by the Berkley Media Studies Group of news articles in 2001 and 2002 found 103 references to obesity threatening children's health but 115 references to soda sales providing money for schools.

Later analyses, however, showed they weren't quite the panacea they seemed. A review by Oregon nonprofit Community Health Partnership found contracts yielded on average only $12 to $24 per student annually—and most of that money came from commissions on purchases themselves. Another analysis by CSPI found that soda commissions averaged only 33 percent—meaning that schools made back only a third of each dollar students spent. The most detailed sections of the contracts, CSPI found, were those delineating just where and how the Coke logo was to be displayed—with stiff penalties to schools for noncompliance.

When Coca-Cola Enterprises finally announced its own new policy at the end of 2003, it did little to change any of the existing pouring-rights contracts. According to Downs, the company would prohibit sales of soda to elementary school kids during school hours—an empty gesture, as most elementary schools didn't sell soft drinks anyway. In addition, it would encourage bottlers to voluntarily control vending machine operating hours in middle schools and high schools. As a response to the criticism against advertising to kids, it announced, it would also end the practice of distributing book covers with the Coke logo (even while the vending machine signs and scoreboards stayed).

As soft drink executives hunkered down at an industry conference in

New York City at the end of 2003, the mood was grim. Coke's sales growth for the year was a disappointing 2 percent overall, and sales volume of Coca-Cola Classic actually *declined* 3 percent. Then there were other problems: A young accountant recently laid off by Coke, Matthew Whitley, had lashed out with allegations that Coke had committed fraud in consumer tests for a new frozen Coke drink at Burger King. According to Whitley, the company had hired thousands of young people to buy the drink, skewing results. Eventually Coke admitted the scheme, settling for $21 million. In separate proceedings, Coke's practice of "channel stuffing"—selling more syrup to bottlers than they could sell in order to pump up Coke's growth targets—finally caught up with it when the Securities and Exchange Commission opened a case against the company, eventually finding that the company had made "false and misleading statements," though Coke paid no fine.

Far from Coke's glory days in the 1990s, the picture was one of a company willing to do anything, legal or illegal, to sell more soft drinks. Nothing made the company look so bad, however, as its insensitivity on childhood obesity. In one 2003 poll in California, 92 percent of respondents declared obesity a serious problem; 65 percent blamed food and beverage company advertising as an important contributor; and 66 percent felt the best solution was tougher regulation in schools. At the soft drink industry's year-end meeting, CEO Douglas Daft directly acknowledged the issue, calling obesity the biggest challenge the industry had faced in fifty years. Giving cheer to his fellow executives, however, he assured them "a simplistic piece of government regulation will not solve the problem," an idea he brushed off as "absurd and outrageous." But that was exactly what activists were now gearing up to do.

The first anti-soda bill was submitted by longtime health advocate and state senator Deborah Ortiz in California in 2002, shortly after Jackie Domac's health class booted Coke out of Venice schools. If passed, it would categorically ban all soda in schools K–12. Immediately, Coke's lobby machine descended upon Sacramento. According to Domac, legislators would slip out the back door while she and her colleagues were waiting to meet them, later emerging in the hall talking with a Coke lobbyist. At the same time, a host of industry-paid experts testified against the bill on nutritional grounds (including one nutritionist representing CCF who did not disclose his affiliation). In the end, the bill passed, but only after being watered down to apply solely to elementary and middle schools, exempting high schools. That effectively gutted the bill, since most soda in California was sold just in high schools anyway.

Over the next few years, the California experience would be repeated over and over in other states, with Coke leading the way to kill anti-soda bills. "When it came to the two major companies, Coca-Cola stood out as the particularly bad actor," says Michele Simon, head of the Center for Informed Food Choices and author of *Appetite for Profit.* "They were just nefarious and nasty in their tactics, sending teams of lobbyists to state capitals to lobby hard against the bills."

The most notorious example of Coke's lobbying was in Connecticut, where legislators introduced the most sweeping anti–junk food bill to date in 2005, proposing a complete ban on selling anything but water, milk, and juice during school hours. For this battle, Coke and Pepsi spent a combined $250,000 on lobbying, Coke paying $80,000 up front and an additional $8,000 a month to hire Sullivan and LeShane, the most influential lobbyist in the state. Patricia LeShane, in fact, was a large contributor and campaign advisor to Connecticut governor Jodi Rell.

"It's not a level playing field," says Simon. "Here we are doing cute things like putting sugar in a bag to show how much is in a can of Coke, and meanwhile, Coke is having these closed-door meetings making deals over campaign contributions. These multinational companies have many times more over the resources than the average mother or teacher or nutrition advocate." In the debate over the bill, lawyers for Coke, which had the majority of pouring-rights contracts in the state, selectively shared revenue data with legislators in opposition. The debate in the House was the longest in the Connecticut legislature in 2005, stretching for eight hours, during which time opponents, according to *The New York Times*, "derided their colleagues for second-guessing local superintendents and school boards"; some even reminisced about painful times when their parents had denied them candy as children. Pushing the situation to the point of absurdity, a "well-stocked" cooler of Coke mysteriously appeared in the Democratic caucus room on the night of the vote.

Lost in the debate was the support of 70 percent of the public, according to one poll, along with the American Academy of Pediatrics, the state PTA, and other public-interest groups. Once again, the bill passed, but not without a provision allowing sales in high schools. The biggest shock, however, came when Connecticut governor Jodi Rell vetoed the bill, accusing it of "undermin[ing] the control and responsibility of parents with school-aged children." The justification was ironic, to say the least, given the lack of control parents and teachers had over the exclusive beverage contracts.

Even while, for the time being, it held the line against the onslaught of anti-soda legislation, Coke was reeling from the suddenness of the backlash against soft drinks—not only in the United States but in Europe as well. The United Kingdom's Food Standards Agency was already making noises about binding regulations against soft drinks; and in France, lawmakers voted to ban all vending machines from elementary and middle schools in the summer of 2004, forcing companies to remove them entirely by the end of the school year. Back in the United States, CCE's John Downs admitted to *The Atlanta Journal-Constitution* that the company was blindsided by the attack. "Clearly we are playing catch up," he said.

By late 2004, however, industry began to formulate a line of defense, not just in the back rooms of state legislatures, but in its public image as well. For starters, the National Soft Drink Association changed its name to the American Beverage Association "to better reflect the expanded range of nonalcoholic beverages the industry produces." Shortly afterward, the group's president of fifteen years resigned, putting in charge a new director, Susan Neely.

Most recently a PR exec in the Department of Homeland Security, Neely had previously created the "Harry and Louise" ads that torpedoed the proposed health-care legislation during the early years of the Clinton administration. Now she took the helm specifically to deal with the obesity crisis. She laid out an immediate new strategy: simultaneously denying soda's role in causing obesity and presenting industry as part of the solution. "The industry thinks [obesity] is a real concern and something we as a country need to address," she said. "What we are concerned about is when state legislators or anyone else tries to leap to quick solutions to a complex problem."

At the same time, a new white knight rode in to rescue Coke itself. Since Goizueta died and Ivester was pushed out, the company had drifted aimlessly under the leadership of CEO Douglas Daft. Buffeted by the obesity crisis, he turned the company away from sugary soft drinks, emphasizing other brands such as Powerade and the new diet drink Coke Zero. In March 2004, Coke created the Beverage Institute for Health and Wellness, a new organization, whose mission was to promote "global health and nutrition." The new institute sponsored a conference in Mexico City that fall to explore the ways in which sugar might be nutritionally beneficial. But that did little to restore investor confidence. While PepsiCo's stock rose 74 percent, Coke's fell 28 percent during Daft's stewardship. Morgan Stanley's Bill Pecoriello, the dean of beverage analysts, predicted stagnation in the U.S. soft drink market for the next five years, writing that "the glory days of the big mass-marketed soft drink brands are probably over."

Coke's board had had enough. By the middle of 2004, it had quietly pushed Daft out. Amid intense speculation, the man who emerged to take his place was Neville Isdell, a thirty-five-year veteran of the company who had retired after being twice passed over for the top job. A patrician-looking man of Irish descent, Isdell had grown up in Zambia and studied social work before deciding—as he put it—that he could "help more people by working for Coca-Cola than I would be able to individually as a social worker." From the moment he arrived, he made his message clear: The future of Coke lay not overseas or in health beverages, but in the core of the brand—carbonated soft drinks, and in its core markets—the United States and Europe.

Isdell predicted it would take eighteen to twenty-four months to turn around the company's fortunes—a remarkably accurate prediction in retrospect. "I came back to the Coca-Cola Company to make sure that we are the leading growth company in our industry," he said, reiterating on another occasion: "Regardless of what the skeptics may think, I know that carbonated soft drinks can grow." Almost immediately, he committed an extra $400 million to marketing and innovation, mostly for cola drinks. In public appearances, he adopted an almost identical tack to the ABA's Neely—denying soft drinks' role in the obesity epidemic, while at the same time offering up the industry as part of the solution to the problem. "Carbonated soft drinks are going to be carriers of health and wellness benefits," he assured analysts in a November 2004 conference call. At a food industry conference, he added without irony: "Healthier consumers are going to be good for us. . . . They will grow older, healthier, wealthier, and hopefully therefore able to buy more from us. Which at the end of the day, let's face it, is our goal."

In the meantime, the juggernaut of anti-soda legislation continued to roll over statehouses. By this time, Chicago and New York had joined Los Angeles and Philadelphia in banning soda on the city level. The first hole in the dike keeping sugar-sweetened soda in high schools, however, started at a small middle school in New Jersey. In April 2005, students at the East Hampton Middle School boycotted food from their cafeteria, demanding they receive healthier options. A few months later, New Jersey passed the first state junk food ban with a ban of soft drinks in high schools. The soft drink companies got together to debate new guidelines, emerging in August with rules nearly identical to those Coke had pushed all along—no sugar soda in elementary schools; no soda in middle schools during the day; and half non-soda choices in vending machines in high schools.

But that wasn't enough to stave off soda's biggest defeat yet. Three years after California's anti-soda bill went down in defeat, new governor and former bodybuilder Arnold Schwarzenegger championed a new bill to victory that included a blanket ban on all soda in schools—including even diet drinks. When Jackie Domac heard the news, she was ecstatic. "I was very, very happy because I felt like my students' efforts had really come to fruition," she says. Her only disappointment was that the law included a long phase-in period; schools wouldn't be required to comply until July 2009.

No Sundblom Santa Claus could cheer the Coke faithful when it got the news just before Christmas 2005 that PepsiCo had for the first time ever passed Coke in total market capitalization—$98.4 billion to $97.7 billion. Much of that rise was based on Pepsi's food divisions; Coke was still the undisputed leader in selling soda. At least there was a bright spot with the first inkling that Isdell's strategy paid off. The company saw a 4 percent increase in all products, including a 2 percent rise in carbonated drinks in the last quarter. "There is growth still in carbonated soft drinks and we have demonstrated that," crowed Isdell.

Emboldened by the rising tide against soft drinks, however, activists were preparing for their endgame. Finally, they had a plan to make Big Soda into the next Big Tobacco and turn the Coke polar bears into Joe Camel. They were going to sue.

The window outside Dick Daynard's office at Boston's Northeastern University still says "Tobacco Control Research Project." Inside, the decor includes several antique tin cigarette advertisements ("Chesterfield—They *Satisfy*!") and a stuffed Joe Camel atop a bookcase stuffed with binders labeled "Philip Morris," "Brown & Williamson," and "R. J. Reynolds," along with bound back issues of the *Tobacco Industry Litigation Reporter*. Daynard has been called the "intellectual godfather of tobacco litigation," and that's by his detractors. He was one of the original lawyers behind the lawsuits against the tobacco industry for fraudulent practices in the 1990s. That campaign succeeded in 1998 with a $250 billion settlement by the tobacco companies, who admitted they'd lied about the addictiveness of their products, followed five years later by a global tobacco treaty to limit cigarette sales overseas.

In the summer of 2005, however, he was pursuing a new quarry—soda. "The number of analogies [is] very surprising," says Daynard, now director of something called the Public Health Advocacy Institute (PHAI). "You are dealing with an addictive product sold to kids, where, if not the addiction, at least the taste is acquired at a young age. You are dealing with a product that, at least when initially produced, was not understood to be deleterious, yet as the evidence kept coming in, companies kept marketing it and stonewalling."

The idea of suing the soda companies over the issue of childhood obesity had been percolating since a conference organized by PHAI in 2003. As long as the anti-obesity advocates were forced to go after soda one school or one state at a time, they reasoned, Coke and Pepsi could stonewall indefinitely. If they were going to succeed, they'd have to speak the language companies understood—hitting their bottom lines with legal damages, or besmirching their brands so badly they'd be forced to settle.

Shortly after the confab, one of the lawyers, John Banzhaf, threatened to sue the Seattle School Board if it renewed its contract with Coke, but eventually backed down. It was one thing to brand multinational corporations as greedy, but it was simply too risky to go after a school that was already hurting for cash. It took another two years for lawyers to get up the courage to go after those they argued were really calling the shots: the companies themselves. "I look at Coke and Pepsi as the Colombian cartel, the bottlers are the middlemen, the school is the one who is actually selling the drugs," reasons Stephen Gardner, litigation director for the Center for Science in the Public Interest, which joined with PHAI in seeking a lawsuit. "The best way to stop it is to go after the cartel, the ones who are actually selling the product." (The imagery is ironic given Coke's origins as a cocaine-laced nerve tonic, to say nothing of its later problems in Colombia.) As the lawyers prepared a class-action lawsuit in the fall of 2005, they modeled their strategy after the tobacco case, arguing that the companies knew the damage their products could do, yet pushed them anyway. The situation was made even worse by the presence of caffeine in the drink, which rankled the lawyers as much as it did Harvey Washington Wiley a century earlier. According to one study at Johns Hopkins University, consumers couldn't tell the difference in taste between caffeinated and noncaffeinated sodas, contradicting soft drink makers' claims that the substance was added for taste, and implying that it was there to addict consumers.

No matter how they spun it, however, soda wasn't cigarettes, and caffeine and sugar weren't nicotine and cocaine. In painting them that way, they risked a backlash of their own, similar to a case a few years earlier when Banzhaf had sued McDonald's on behalf of a man who accused the company of making him fat. Coca-Cola's surrogates sought to paint this lawsuit in the same light. "There are trial lawyers who see dollar signs where the rest of us see dinner," said the Center for Consumer Freedom's Mindus. "It's the height of silliness."

Despite their ridicule, behind the scenes the soda companies weren't finding the threat silly at all. The public anger over soda—especially sold to the captive audience of kids in schools—was too palpable to risk in a jury trial. Sometime in the fall of 2005, Pepsi general counsel Robert Biggart quietly approached Gardner about putting this mess behind them. The first face-to-face came in December 2005 in Washington, including Jane Thorpe, a lawyer with Alston & Bird who represented Coke, as well as Patricia Vaughan, general counsel for the American Beverage Association, on one side, and lawyers from CSPI and PHAI on the other.

From the beginning, the soda reps made it clear they were willing to agree to some kind of settlement to get soda out of schools—but only if the lawyers held off in bringing a lawsuit. The other side reluctantly agreed—since, unbeknownst to the soda companies, they were having trouble finding plaintiffs anyway. They'd made their decision to file in Massachusetts, a state with strong consumer protection laws, but where most schools had already canceled soda contracts. The lack of a stick to hold over Coke's head, however, put the anti-obesity lawyers at a disadvantage.

In meetings throughout the winter, the two sides hashed out an agreement, with sugary soda being the first to go, followed by sports drinks—noncarbonated beverages like Coke's Powerade that have almost as much sugar as an equivalent amount of soda. Diet soda, after some debate, stayed. But the real sticking point was advertising—with the companies balking at removing all of those brightly lit logos on the sides of their vending machines that preserved that all-important early brand recognition, and arguing for half-measures like stickers with nutritional information placed on the machines. Finally, the anti-soda advocates thought they were able to prevail on the issue. On March 30, 2006, their lawyers drew up a confidential document summarizing their understanding of the proposed settlement. It included a promise from Coke to "refrain from all product marketing and advertising in school buildings, or on the school campus," as well as an outline to get rid of all beverages with more than 10 calories per bottle (with the exception of milk and fruit juices) by the beginning of the 2009–2010 school year.

"Somewhere in there, the stalling began in earnest," says soda activist Simon, who watched negotiations unfold. "We didn't hear from them to schedule a meeting, and I got nervous and said something was going on." As it turned out, she was right. Coke was barraged by negative publicity that spring, and even Governor Rell bowed to public opinion, supporting a new bill in Connecticut to ban sugary soft drinks, and diet drinks and Powerade. Coke threatened to pull school scholarships if the ban passed, prompting state attorney general Richard Blumenthal to decry Coke's "unconscionable practices" and announce an investigation of the Coca-Cola Foundation for violation of its nonprofit status. Despite Coke's threats, the state legislature passed the bill in April 2006.

Coke had had enough, calling a press conference a week later along with other soft drink companies to announce its surrender. Reporters from *The New York Times*, *The Washington Post*, and other newspapers assembled to hear the details, when Bill Clinton, former president of the United States, strode to the podium. By his side was Arkansas governor Mike Huckabee, the American Beverage Association's Neely, and Coca-Cola North America president Don Knauss. "I don't think there are any villains here," said Clinton with his patented earnest delivery, going on to call the soda companies "courageous" for dealing with the obesity issue head-on. Then with great fanfare, he announced new guidelines that the industry had agreed to limiting soda in schools, which had been negotiated by the Alliance for a Healthier Generation, a partnership between the Clinton Foundation and the American Heart Association.

The agreement—which had been in the works since fall 2005—was significantly weaker than what the companies had already agreed to with Daynard, Gardner, and the other anti-obesity activists over the same period, allowing diet drinks, sports drinks, and juice drinks of up to 12 ounces to be sold in high schools. Moreover, unlike the enforceable guidelines under discussion with the lawyers, the deal would be completely voluntary and implemented over the course of three years. Advertising wasn't even addressed.

Daynard found out about the agreement the way most people did—reading the newspaper. "I think there was considerable bad faith on their part," he says. "They did not tell us they were simultaneously negotiating with another group." Daynard now thinks their talks were nothing but a sham to stall litigation. Even so, he puts the best face on the agreement—arguing that if not for the threat of a lawsuit, the companies would never have taken even the more modest measure of getting rid of sugary soda within three years. "When we began, we thought that was impossible," he says.

Even as they were staging a tactical retreat, Coke and Pepsi were able to save face, stressing at the news conference that soda could be part of a well-rounded diet. In the fall, the ABA rolled out a $10 million ad campaign to "educate" parents about the new policy. They failed to mention that some schools with long-term contracts would not be able to participate, at least not without buying out the companies to amend the contracts. One school in Wisconsin learned it would have to pay $200,000 to remove high-calorie beverages from vending machines. The Portland, Oregon, school district was told it would have to pay back $600,000 to remove diet soda after the district's wellness policy banned them. Local activists with Oregon's Community Health Partnership cried foul—pointing out that a contract is something that can be renegotiated at any time if both sides are willing. It took six months, however, for Coke to agree to new terms, under which the school forfeited all commissions from drink sales, though it was allowed to keep the up-front fee for signing the contract.

The very public deal has led to perceptions that the school issue had been dealt with, saving Coke's image and taking the wind out of a push for stronger legislation. Oregon is one of the few states to move ahead with a binding state law against soda in schools after the Clinton soda agreement—pushing through a law similar to California's tough standards in 2007. Even so, says the health partnership's Mary Lou Hennrich, an initial proposal to ban sports drinks and marketing fizzled when legislators, supported by the school administrators, pointed to the Clinton guidelines as the new standard. "Their attitude was that now you've crammed this down our throats and we can't have sugar-sweetened beverages for sale, haven't you done enough?" A similar phenomenon happened in Utah, when the new state law to ban soda was specifically written with the Clinton guidelines in mind. In Oregon, Massachusetts, and Rhode Island, the local affiliates of the American Heart Association told Simon that their national headquarters had requested they stand down in supporting tougher laws. (A past president of the AHA denies this, saying that affiliates weren't counseled either way.)

By 2008, thirty-four states had some combination of regulation or legislation curtailing soda in schools. Just eleven banned all sugar-sweetened soda; the rest allowed some portion of soda sales for some portion of the day. Only a few go beyond the voluntary guidelines adopted by the Clinton agreement: six ban sports drinks, five set calorie limits, and only one provides any kind of penalties for noncompliance. On a federal level, an effort led by Senator Tom Harkin and Representative Lynn Woolsey to pass a bill to ban soda and sports drinks as foods of "minimal nutritional value" failed in 2007.

In the three years since the first announcement by the Alliance for a Healthier Generation, there's mixed evidence that the voluntary guidelines pushed by industry have been successful. According to a study by a consultant funded by the American Beverage Association, 98.8 percent of schools under contract with soda companies were in compliance with the guidelines by the 2009–2010 school year. Even more important, shipments of carbonated soft drinks to schools dropped by 95 percent compared to another ABA-funded survey in 2004. In high schools, sugar soft drinks fell from 47 to 7 percent of offerings, and water grew from 12 to 39 percent. While sports drinks did increase, from 13 to 18 percent of the total, total calories for all beverages were still down 88 percent. "It's a brand new day in America's schools when it comes to beverages," said the ABA's Neely in 2008. "Our beverage companies have slashed calories."

Some anti-soda activists, such as CSPI's Margo Wootan, have grudgingly accepted the ABA report, though they point out that much of that decrease in soda in schools has been due to binding state legislation. Others, however, look at the industry-funded study with a jaundiced eye, knowing how favorable those studies have been to the soda company biases in the past. At least one independent study leaves serious reason to doubt the trade association's figures. An annual survey by the University of Illinois at Chicago and the University of Michigan found that in the 2008–2009 school year, only 30 percent of school administrators said they were implementing the guidelines, up from 25 percent the previous year. By contrast, 14 percent said they were not implementing them, and 55 percent—more than half—said they had never even heard of them.

Generally, the fight over schools has been a qualified victory for the anti-soda activists; if nothing else, it was a win in the area of perception; no longer would it be possible for people to drink soda without thinking about the potentially negative health consequences waiting for them inside the can. The fight affected Coke's bottom line as well—stopping the runaway increases in soda sales for most of the previous century. In early 2006, soda sales fell in the United States for the first time in twenty years, by nearly 1 percent over the previous year. That was followed by several more consecutive years of sales drops—by 2.3 percent in 2007, 3 percent in 2008, and 2.1 percent in 2009.

Where the campaign was successful in changing the public's consumption of soda, it succeeded through a combination of public support and the vigorous support of the media, which thrives on stories of conflicts with clear battle lines and combatants on both sides—company executives, school administrators, dogged activists, and parents. However unfair it may have seemed to the soda companies to single out soft drinks as the primary cause of obesity and diabetes, the issue resonated with the public, who after all must have secretly suspected that pouring all of that sugar down their throats just couldn't be good for them in the long term.

The tactical decision to focus the fight on schools also helped to frame the issue in a way that was impossible for the public not to understand. As the campaign against tobacco did with Joe Camel and other instances of child marketing, it garnered the sympathy of the populace, which instinctively understands that even if adults are free to choose what they put inside their bodies, children need protection. Finally, the campaign made effective use of the power of the purse, speaking the language that school administrators and soda companies understood, whether it was Jackie Domac's grant to implement healthy food choices or Dick Daynard's threat to sue Coke for damages.

Where the anti-soda forces failed, it was in removing the pressure it had so expertly marshaled just as it was beginning to bear fruit. They took away the cudgel of the lawsuit, their biggest weapon, as they began negotiating with Coke and the other companies, who then had every incentive to stall until they could find a more favorable deal elsewhere. And by focusing so completely on the school issue, the campaign against soda lost a chance to talk about the messier but arguably more significant influence that runaway soft drink consumption has had on both adults and children outside the school walls.

In the end, it's debatable exactly how effective the fight against soda in schools has actually been in schools themselves. A 2008 study in Maine published by the Society for Nutrition Education compared intake of soda by kids at high schools where soda was banned with intake in schools where it wasn't, finding no difference in overall consumption. Another study, of 11,000 fifth-graders in forty states, found soft drink consumption by kids decreased just 4 percent after soda was banned at their elementary schools. After expending all of their political capital on the fight to get soda out of schools, however, activist groups have found it hard to make headway outside that realm. Putting warning labels on bottles or restricting serving sizes are almost a nonstarter, while recent attempts to push a state or national "soda tax"—Asa Candler's old nemesis—have failed to catch on. Modest soda taxes were passed in Washington, Colorado, and Maine in recent years, only to be undone after heavy lobbying by the American Beverage Association. The group spent $4 million to sponsor a ballot initiative that tapped into anti-tax sentiment to successfully repeal Maine's 42 cent per gallon soda tax in early 2010, and $17 million for a similar initiative to repeal Washington's 2 cent per can tax in November (compared to $500,000 spent by the other side). The biggest fight occurred in New York, where Governor David Patterson proposed a 1 cent per ounce tax widely supported by health advocates. After a $9 million advertising campaign by the ABA painting the proposal as a regressive "sin tax," however, the state dropped the effort.

Whether or not the Clinton deal was a victory for activists, it certainly was one for Coke, which was spared a public thrashing in the courts while tying their ship to one of the country's more popular public figures. Most important, the brand was kept intact, with Diet Coke and Coke Zero in the vending machines, and the Spencerian-script logo flashing brightly in the hallways. And there was evidence Isdell's pledge to turn around the company was being kept. Throughout his tenure, overall company growth continued to surpass analysts' expectations—with increases of 6 percent in 2007 and 5 percent in 2008. Much of that growth was thanks to the overseas market, which represents 80 percent of Coke's total sales. But the Clinton deal staved off the worst of the slide in the United States. While sugar soft drinks continued to decline by a percentage point or two a year in the past few years, today's youth has hardly been the "lost generation" for soda, as one analyst had predicted in 2006.

And to make up the difference domestically, Isdell started a new round of product launches and acquisitions that took the battle to Pepsi on several new fronts, including a big new push on bottled water. Coke might never achieve its once-upon-a-time dream of seeing the C on the tap stand for "Coke." But if it couldn't beat water, it could do the next best thing: brand it.

FIVE

The Bottled Water Lie

The noise is deafening on the bottling floor of the Needham Heights Sales Facility, the largest Coca-Cola bottling plant in Massachusetts and the sixteenth largest in the country. Cans of Diet Coke swirl around in a giant silver whirligig, blinking lights indicating each is being filled with the proper amount of carbonated water and syrup. The din dies in the warehouse next door, where hundreds of thousands of cans and bottles of Coke, Sprite, Nestlé iced tea, Minute Maid juice, and other products under the Coca-Cola umbrella are stacked in rows as far as the eye can see, calling to mind the last scene of *Raiders of the Lost Ark*.

But tucked amid these boxes is another whirring collection of machinery. Test tube–sized nipples of polyethylene terephthalate (PET) plastic are dumped into a giant centrifuge, where they are blown by compressed air into 20-ounce bottles. On an adjoining piece of equipment, the full bottles reappear, filled to the brim with water. They trundle naked down the assembly line to get sealed and slapped with their label: Dasani.

It's here that Coke's vaunted brand of bottled water is made, and where, by extension, the fortunes of the Coca-Cola Company were rescued. The actual process by which ordinary water is turned into Dasani is hidden inside a separate "water room," which the plant manager describes as a bunch of twenty-foot stainless-steel tubes through which the water is shot at high pressure to be filtered. No amount of pleading will persuade the Coca-Cola Enterprises press agent giving the tour today to allow a peek inside. Like the secret formula for Coca-Cola hidden deep inside an Atlanta safe-deposit box, the process behind creating Dasani is equally shrouded in mystique. And no wonder, since Dasani's brand image is even more important than Coca-Cola's to sell the product.

In coming to dominate the bottled water market, Coke has had to pull a feat of behind-the-curtain wizardry every bit as impressive as turning Coca-Cola into a symbol of American pride and international goodwill a century earlier. Despite promising beginnings, however, Dasani has faced an even more damaging backlash, based not on individual health but on the health of the environment itself.

Even as awareness of the obesity crisis was beginning to hit, threatening sales of Coke's trademark carbonated sodas, the company was readying its Plan B. In the summer of 1998, CEO Doug Ivester began toying with selling the most basic of beverages—water. The company had watched from the wings as other companies had made a fortune on the beverage, which the French company Perrier had introduced in the United States in the late 1970s. The fad had taken off quickly, after Perrier's marketers appealed to a new demographic of yuppies as conscious about their health as they were about the conspicuous consumption of paying top dollar for something others were getting for free. Perrier's profits from water rose from $20 million in its first year to $60 million by its second.

Starting in 1984, another French company, Evian, pioneered the use of lightweight bottles made of a clear plastic called polyethylene terephthalate (PET) just as the fitness craze was taking off, making the pink-and-red logo ubiquitous at the gym. Perrier stumbled briefly in 1990 when the supposedly pristine water was found contaminated with trace amounts of benzene, leading to a $160 million recall and cutting sales in half overnight. But the industry quickly recovered, led by the Swiss company Nestlé, which swooped in to acquire Perrier, as well as dozens of other brands—Deer Park, Arrowhead, Calistoga, Poland Spring—that were left from America's first flirtation with bottled water at the turn of the last century. Between 1990 and 1999, bottled water sales shot up from $115 million a year to more than $5 billion.

With profit margins on water as high as 50 cents on a $1.50 bottle, Coke and Pepsi couldn't resist entering a market that had been dominated by foreign companies. Instead of selling natural spring water, however, the cola giants didn't see why they couldn't just take the same water flowing through their bottling plants and package *that.* Pepsi was first, shooting its purified water into a blue bottle with a squiggle evocative of snow-covered mountains. *Voilà*, Aquafina.

Coke could have gone the same route, licensing a new brand to its bottlers. But the Coca-Cola Company had always sold syrup, and there was no syrup that you could use to create water. Ivester stewed for the better part of 1998 before he hit upon the solution. Coke scientists would formulate a proprietary mix of minerals that it would ship to bottlers to put in their purified tap water. This was its *new* secret formula, which it could market as every bit as unique as Coke's own. After much focus-grouping, Coke created the perfect pan-national combination of syllables for its new beverage. Intended to signal relaxation and refreshment, the name Dasani could just as well be that of an Italian winemaker or an African tribe.

Dasani actually wasn't Coke's first entry into bottled water; it had bought Belmont Springs in the 1980s and Mendota Springs in the 1990s, both times suffering lackluster sales. But that was when water was a mere side venture to the runaway growth in sugary soda. Now water itself was the growth market. Coke put the full weight of its advertising power behind a new $20 million campaign intended to both sell the product and grow the market itself.

Coke targeted women, who consumer surveys showed were more focused on healthy living (and not coincidentally, more concerned with their kids' drinking so much soda). In the same way that "The Pause That Refreshes" had addressed the anxieties of workers suffering from grueling production schedules, Coke played on the stresses of women struggling to balance the demands of the workplace and their responsibilities to home and family with new slogans such as "Life Simplified" and "Replenish the Source Within." In 2002, Coke teamed up with *Glamour* magazine to give away an all-expenses-paid weekend in New York to the woman who wrote the best one hundred words about "Women at Their Best." Applicants were "encouraged to list the ways in which they pamper themselves, thereby replenishing their own spirit everyday" (no doubt scoring extra points if they replenished themselves with Dasani).

The marketing worked—by 2003, bottled water was the one bright spot in a disastrous year for Coke. Bottled water sales were up to $8.5 billion overall—and Dasani had passed Perrier, Evian, and San Pellegrino to become the second-best-selling brand behind Pepsi's Aquafina. And Coke had yet to go international with Dasani—the arena where it always outfought Pepsi. As the company planned to launch Dasani across the Atlantic, it seemed there might actually be life after soda pop after all.

For its big overseas splash, Coke followed the same playbook it had for its soft drinks a century earlier, tackling the English-speaking world first. The launch for the United Kingdom was planned for March 2004, with drives the following month into Belgium and then France, the ultimate prize. The average French person drank more than twice what an American drank in bottled water, some 145 liters a year. Cracking *that* market would be a sweet victory for the company. Just a couple of decades after France had introduced bottled water to the United States, America would be returning the favor under the banner of the quintessential American brand. For the UK, Coke spared no expense, pouring £7 million ($13 million) into advertising, trumpeting the slogan "The more you live, the more you need Dasani." For weeks, billboards around London declared,

"Prepare to get wet," and just before the launch, high-divers plummeted ninety feet with flaming capes into tanks of water to draw attention to the brand.

No amount of theatrics, however, could prepare Coke for what happened next. Just weeks after the launch, a British newspaper broke the story that Coke's "pure" water was actually bottled in the southeast London suburb of Sidcup, which got its water from the River Thames. It was the equivalent of discovering that bottled water served in New York came from the Hudson. Immediately, Coke came under fire from the Food Standards Agency (FSA), the British version of the FDA, for the improper use of the word "pure."

Of course, Dasani wasn't exactly tap water. While Coke might not let prying eyes into one of its water rooms, it touts a multistep scouring to turn pedestrian water into the final product. First, there is "ultrafiltration" to remove particles, followed by a carbon filter to remove odors, and a zap of ultraviolent light to kill bacteria. Most important, it passes through a reverse-osmosis filter—a technique, Coke told the skeptical British public, "perfected by NASA to purify fluids on spacecraft" to remove 90 percent of anything still remaining. Only then does Coke add back in its mineral mix, as the company has oxymoronically explained, to "enhance the pure taste." Finally, the water is given a dose of ozone to get rid of hard-to-kill parasites such as giardia and cryptosporidium. The result, Coke claimed, was "as pure as water gets."

Despite such assurances, the launch was a disaster. Soon, Dasani was being handed out for free in train stations and supermarkets in a desperate attempt to win customers. But the death blow was what happened next: Two weeks after the Sidcup jokes started, consumers stopped laughing when Coke tersely announced it was voluntarily recalling half a million bottles of Dasani. The water, it explained, had been contaminated with levels of the carcinogen bromate at 22 parts per billion, twice the amount allowed by the FSA (or FDA).

In the ultimate irony, then, Coke's water was not only no more pure than London tap, but also more dangerous to drink. Quickly, Thames

Water declared *its* water safe. Soon it became apparent the contamination hadn't come from the pipes, but rather from a by-product of ozonation, one of the very methods Coke boasted of to "purify" its water. In a statement, Coke all but blamed the British government, saying that it was legally required to add calcium chloride into the water in the UK. The high level of bromide in calcium chloride, it continued, led to the formation of bromate when exposed to ozone.

That explanation might have held more water if the tendency to create bromate through ozonation wasn't already well known in the industry. Just two years before, the FDA had warned manufacturers to use care in ozonation and test finished products for the presence of the chemical. An industry trade publication at the time went so far as to provide a formula for how much bromate can be formed given the amount of bromide in the source water. As a result of the warnings, Nestlé stopped using ozonation for Perrier in June 2001, even as Coke and Pepsi continued the process.

Whether through carelessness or arrogance, Coke had turned a public relations hiccup into a disaster, as Britons now vocalized their anger at the American company. "Should I Really Despise Coca-Cola?" read a typical headline, and there were plays on Coke's own branding, such as "Things Get Worse with Coke" and "Dasani: It's a Real Disaster." In the face of such criticism, Coke declared an end to its European conquest, swallowing a cost of more than $45 million and giving up dreams of converting the French.

For the Europeans, it was the perfect opportunity to stick it in America's eye during a time when the continent was chafing under George W. Bush's invasion of Iraq and anti-American sentiment was at an all-time high. Any Coke exec tempted to write off the fiasco as the cranky proclivities of another continent, however, was due for a rude awakening back on American shores.

It's a blustery spring day in Cambridge, Massachusetts, where sets of four blue Dixie cups are arranged on a folding table in the middle of a city square. Three of the cups contain bottled water from the country's most popular brands—Dasani, Aquafina, and Nestlé's Poland Spring. The fourth cup is full of tap water from a café up the street. One by one, passersby stop by to sample them and guess which is which. If you think it'd be easy to tell the difference between the bottled water and the tap, you'd be wrong. The success rate of folks is only slightly better than random. Typical is Joe Marsden, a Cambridge resident, who stares in sullen disbelief at the table after identifying tap water as Dasani. "I thought I would have at least gotten Dasani or Aquafina right because I drink them the most," he says. "I couldn't tell the difference at all."

Dubbed the "Tap Water Challenge," the update of the Pepsi Challenge is run nationally by young activists belonging to the group Corporate Accountability International (CAI), which has made bottled water the latest front in what it sees as the excesses of corporate power. Like anti-soda lawyer Dick Daynard, CAI cut its teeth in the fight against Big Tobacco in the 1990s, when it waged a boycott against Kraft, parent company of Philip Morris. However, the group dates back to two decades before, when it was originally founded as the Infant Formula Action Coalition (INFACT) to attack Nestlé for its promotion of baby formula over breast milk overseas. After a bitterly fought campaign, Nestlé eventually agreed to stop pushing its formula in 1984. Now, twenty years later, Nestlé was profiting off another product that the activists thought should be distributed for free, as one of the four largest bottled water producers along with European giant Danone (parent company of Evian), PepsiCo, and Coca-Cola.

If it seems a stretch to brand soft drinks as the next tobacco, then bottled water seems an even more unlikely villain. Here's a product with no harmful tar or sugar, no addictive nicotine or caffeine. Yet CAI was affronted by the way in which the bottled water corporations were taking over local water supplies, often paying next to nothing for the privilege. In Nestlé's case, the company was tapping underground aquifers around the United States, as citizens from Maine to California and Michigan to Texas complained about dried-up streams and dropping water levels around their plants. But at least Nestlé could legitimately call its "spring water" a unique beverage. Coke and Pepsi were bottling municipal tap water, passing ostensibly clean water through additional purification processes, and then selling it for a huge markup. Meanwhile, Coke's huge advertising campaign touting Dasani's "purity" further undermined public confidence in tap water, they argued, leading to more bottled water sales and less investment in public infrastructure.

By the time CAI began sounding the alarm in 2004, consumers were spending some $9 billion annually on bottled water in the United States, consuming an average of twenty-three gallons of the stuff per person (those numbers have since risen to $11 billion and twenty-nine gallons). Each year, sales increased by almost 10 percent—reminiscent of Goizueta-era Coke before the backlash over obesity began. In fact, as soft drinks started to decline in sales for the first time, Coke increasingly promoted water as a healthy alternative, spending tens of millions of dollars to rebrand itself as a "hydration" company, and replacing Coke signs with Dasani signs on the sides of vending machines. All of those marketing messages sunk in; a Gallup poll at the time found three in four Americans drank bottled water, and one in five drank *only* bottled water.

Despite its popularity, however, a growing body of evidence has shown bottled water to be no purer or safer than tap—and in some ways, potentially *less* safe. That's because tap water is regulated by the Environmental Protection Agency (EPA), which imposes strict limits on contaminants and mandates daily testing and mandatory notification of problems. Bottled water, on the other hand, is regulated by the Food and Drug Administration (FDA), which by its own admission has set a "low priority" for regulating bottled water plants. Its standards are slightly lower on some contaminants, and it requires only weekly testing and voluntary recalls in the case of problems.

And sure enough, the benzene scare over Perrier and the bromate controversy in Britain are just the beginning of the problems with bottled water quality over the years. A classic study by the Natural Resources Defense Council of more than one thousand bottles of water in 1999 found that while most samples were safe, nearly a quarter tested above state standards for bacterial or chemical contamination (only 4 percent violated weaker federal standards). More recent studies have continued to find problems: In 2000, the American Medical Association found some bottled water had bacterial counts twice the level of tap. A 2002 study by the University of Tuskegee of brands including Dasani, Aquafina, and Poland Spring found mercury, arsenic, and other chemicals above the EPA limits. A 2004 study by the FDA found low levels of perchlorate, a derivative of rocket fuel, in samples of spring water. As recently as 2008, the nonprofit Environmental Working Group (EWG) found thirty-eight different pollutants in bottled water, ranging from bacteria to fertilizer and Tylenol, and concluded that consumers "can't trust that bottled water is pure or cleaner than tap water." (The study did not reveal the types of water it tested, saying only that they were "popular" brands.)

That spotty safety record of bottled water doesn't let tap off the hook. The same analysts at EWG found that tap water from forty-two states met federal standards for contaminants but still included a range of toxic goodies, including gasoline additives and endocrine disruptors, for which the government had not set limits. In early 2008, the Associated Press reported traces of pharmaceutical drugs and hormones in the water in twenty-four American cities, affecting 41 million people. True, the amounts were virtually microscopic—present in parts per billion or parts per trillion—but doctors cautioned even those small amounts can have effects with repeated exposure. "After learning about all the things that can go wrong with tap water, I don't know what to think, or drink," sighs Elizabeth Royte, author of *Bottlemania*, a 2008 exposé of the bottled water industry.

Despite all of the conflicting studies and alarms, the truth is that in the United States, both tap water and bottled water are generally safe to drink. And that might be the most damning charge of all against bottled water, given the price difference between the two. On average, convenience-sized bottled water costs just over $2 per gallon, while tap water costs just one- or two-tenths of a cent per gallon—a difference of one thousand times. With statistics like these, it was only a matter of time, perhaps, before people began thinking what comedians from Dennis Miller to Janeane

Garofalo have been telling us for years—that "Evian is just 'naive' spelled backward."

Even as some newspaper stories questioning bottled water began to appear, however, the activists from CAI realized that none of the charges against bottled water would mean anything if they couldn't address the issue of taste. The idea of the Tap Water Challenge grew out of a late-night brainstorming session in CAI's Boston office in 2005, as the activists groped for a way to take the issue head-on. Not knowing what they'd find, they pitted the tap water in their office against bottles of Dasani and other brands; they were genuinely surprised to find that they couldn't tell the difference.

In the early spring of 2006, CAI rolled out Tap Water Challenges in seven cities—including Boston, Austin, Minneapolis, and San Francisco—adding others every few weeks over the next six months. Everywhere they went, people were amazed to find they couldn't distinguish between bottled and tap. Just as decades of advertising had convinced people they liked Coke Classic more than Pepsi or New Coke, it seemed the millions spent on branding bottled water had made people think it tasted fresher and purer than tap. And just like the Pepsi Challenge a generation earlier, the ready-made conflict of pitting two beverages against each other was irresistible to the media. Newspapers began running on-the-scene reports of die-hard Dasani or Aquafina drinkers chagrined to find they'd mistaken their favorites for Newark or Philadelphia tap water.

CAI's Gigi Kellett, the national director of the Think Outside the Bottle campaign, admits the group first chose cities they already knew had good water—including Boston and San Francisco, which pipe in water from reservoirs so pristine they don't have to filter it. Soon, however, they realized they could hold them almost anywhere—even places such as South Florida that had a reputation for poor-tasting tap water. Oftentimes, the most skeptical taste-testers hadn't tasted the water in years. When they held challenges in Miami—which sources its water from an underground aquifer before submitting it to a high-quality filtration and treatment system—they got the same results as anywhere else.

As awareness of the Tap Water Challenges spread, however, the activists found the issue that resonated most with consumers had less to do with the quality of the water, much less privatization and control of water resources. Instead, they were most concerned with the bottles themselves. In 2006, former Vice President Al Gore had just released the documentary *An Inconvenient Truth*, warning of the apocalyptic consequences of climate change and spurring consumers to measure their personal carbon footprints and carry canvas bags to the grocery store instead of wasting excess plastic. Likewise, there seemed something especially galling about wasting all of that plastic for a product that could just as easily be had from the tap. According to a 2009 report by the nonprofit Pacific Institute, it takes the equivalent of 17 million barrels of oil to produce the plastic for all bottled water consumed in the United States in a year—enough to power 1 million cars. Add in the cost of production and transport, and that number increases to between 34 and 58 million barrels. (And worldwide production takes three times that.)

Then there is disposal. Nationwide, the average container recycling rate was 33 percent in 2009, down from a high of more than 50 percent in 1992. Much of that decrease was due to the introduction of bottled water, which has doubled over the past decade to nearly 33 billion liters sold by 2008—nearly all of it in single-serving PET containers. Since bottled water containers have been recycled at notoriously low rates of less than 20 percent, the Washington, D.C.–based Container Recycling Institute concludes that these containers have brought the overall recycling rate down. Add it all up, CRI says, and that translates to some 3 billion pounds of plastic bottles in the waste stream each year. Bottled water companies, of course, dispute the notion that bottled water containers are more to blame than other products for plastic waste. According to Joe Doss, president of the International Bottled Water Association (IBWA), PET bottles represent only a third of 1 percent (.0033) of all trash. "If you can get your head around that, it's very clear that these efforts to target bottled water are misguided at best and totally ineffective in dealing with the problem at worst," he says. In some ways, he has a point—what makes bottled water any worse than soda, juice, or beer, which also use plenty of water in their production and are nearly as likely to end up in the trash? And in an increasingly on-the-go society, isn't it better for people to grab a bottle of water at the convenience store rather than a sugary soda?

That's long been the line of the bottled water folks, who argue that bottled water isn't competing against tap water so much as against other beverage choices, like soda. "Every day in newspapers and on TV you see stories about increasing obesity and diabetes," says Doss. "These actions against bottled water will have no good consequences if they discourage people from drinking a healthy beverage."

Without trashing soda, Coke makes virtually the same argument. "Consumers are making a choice of bottled water versus another beverage," said Coke's director of water stewardship, Greg Koch, in 2007. "Do I want a Coca-Cola? Do I want a coffee? Or is it happy hour? There's a time and a place for bottled water, as there is for milk and juice and beer." In a sense, it's the same argument that the company used for years to support drinking soda—consumer choice—updated for a new beverage.

As for recycling, Doss says the IBWA has lent support to curbside recycling initiatives—adding that two-thirds of bottled water is consumed at home, at work, or in offices, places where curbside recycling is readily available. Those also happen to be places where tap water is readily available, however, contradicting the argument that bottled water is necessary as an alternative beverage "on the go." When that discrepancy is pointed out, Doss, too, falls back on the mantra of "choice": "It is a choice, it's always a choice, they should have that choice, bottled water consumers are choosing to drink both and there is nothing wrong with that."

While that argument might float to some degree, it's hard to say Coke and its fellow companies aren't competing against tap water when they are churning out advertisements full of mountain streams and rivers emphasizing how pure and tasty their water is—not how easy it is to grab at the 7-Eleven on the way to the gym. As bottled water has caught on, it has taken over in more and more places that tap water used to be available—and even replaced tap water entirely in many homes and offices. Just as pouring-rights contracts led to a proliferation of soft drinks in the 1990s, now water fountains have disappeared at schools, airports, and municipal buildings, which all have contracts with bottled water producers instead.

The most dramatic consequence of that shift occurred at the inauguration of the University of Central Florida's new stadium on a sweltering day in 2007. The stadium had been built without any water fountains, a fact discovered by fans when concession stands ran out of the Dasani they'd been selling at $3 a bottle. Some sixty people ended up suffering from heat exhaustion as a result of dehydration; eighteen were sent to the hospital. Initially, school officials apologized by handing out a free bottle of Dasani to each ticket holder at the next game; after widespread fan outrage, however, they eventually agreed to install fifty water fountains, an amenity that had somehow previously escaped their minds.

Incidents such as these, coupled with the Tap Water Challenges, turned awareness of bottled water's environmental consequences into a full-fledged backlash—driven by the unlikely champions of those most responsible for tap water's production: U.S. mayors. Sick of being criticized about the water quality of their cities, mayors began canceling city contracts with bottled water companies and even began reinstalling water fountains in their city halls. Taking the issue further, San Francisco mayor Gavin Newsom took a resolution to the meeting of the U.S. Conference of Mayors in June 2007 that would commit all member cities to phase out bottled water at municipal buildings and events. Joining him to cosponsor the resolution were two mayors from more conservative political territory: Salt Lake City's Rocky Anderson and Minneapolis's R.T. Rybak. When the American Beverage Association, led by Coke, showed up to lobby aggressively against its adoption, arguing that it was only the first step in banning bottled water citywide—a direct affront to capitalism—their efforts backfired. While the mayors stopped short of passing a resolution encouraging members to ban bottled water, they did approve a resolution to study the issue and its effects on municipal trash systems. More surprisingly, the study actually occurred, and a year later, resulted in passage of the earlier, tougher call for a ban.

By then, more than sixty cities has already joined the backlash, with Los Angeles, Seattle, Boston, Austin, and Providence all either canceling bottled water contracts or instructing city departments not to buy bottled water. At the same time, restaurants moved to take bottled water off their menus, starting with chef Alice Waters, the godmother of "California cuisine," who nixed bottled water from her Berkeley restaurant Chez Panisse in March 2007. Soon after, Food Network favorite Mario Batali followed suit at his empire of restaurants, including Manhattan's swish Del Posto.

If the summer of 2003 was the season that childhood obesity exploded into public view, the summer of 2007 was the season the United States woke up to bottled water. Even *The Economist* has called the success of bottled water "one of capitalism's greatest mysteries" in an online editorial in July 2007, conjuring the patent medicine era by calling it the new "snake oil." Kellett remembers the exact day when she realized CAI had won—July 15, 2007. While organizing a day to call in to Pepsi's corporate headquarters, she was taken aback by a strange playback message saying executives were meeting to determine how to respond to activist concerns—a response CAI hadn't heard in decades of organizing.

Finally at the end of the day, Pepsi declared that, from then on, it would label Aquafina with the words "public water source," identifying its origins from municipal sources. If it had hoped through the action to stave off further criticism, it failed. Within two days, the activists were doing round-the-clock interviews with every major television and news organization to talk about how not only Pepsi, but also Coke, sourced its water from the tap.

Within just a few years, bottled water had gone from trendy to gauche. In the fall of 2007, CAI began circulating a "Think Outside the Bottle" pledge, asking people to drink public water over bottled water whenever possible. Within just a few weeks, it signed on several thousand people, celebrities among them, including actor Martin Sheen. In late 2007, actors Sarah Jessica Parker and Lucy Liu supported a project to charge $1 for tap water in New York City restaurants to raise money for UNICEF's clean water efforts abroad. They raised $100,000. By that fall, Nestlé had joined Pepsi in revealing the source of its water on its labels—and went even further by including detailed water quality information on its website for all brands by 2009.

Alone among the Big Three bottled water producers, Coke held out. "The FDA's definition of purified water does not require [revealing] the source," argued Coke spokesman Ray Crockett. "We believe consumers know what they're buying." Unfortunately, his words turned out to be too true. After a decade of near double digit growth, bottled water suddenly plummeted in 2008—with sales volume dropping 2 percent over the previous year. Dasani fared even worse, with sales dropping 4 percent, despite slashing its prices by 40 percent in the previous three years.

Part of that was due to the major recession that hit that fall; as consumers tightened their belts, they cut down on luxuries such as a $1.50 bottle of water at the convenience store to fill their own bottles at the tap. But they might never have made the choice to do that had they not already been assured they'd be safe doing so. As the recession hit, CAI moved from city hall to the state house, encouraging governors to cut state bottled water contracts to save scarce state resources. By then, Coca-Cola had already planned its response, and true to form, it was more in the vein of changing its image than changing its reality. Over the last hundred-some years, Coke had gone from a health tonic to an all-American drink to a symbol of worldwide harmony. Now it would work to undergo its biggest branding change in decades to become an environmental steward.

Lined up outside the bottling plant in Needham are eight tractor trailers, their polished sides gleaming red in the sun. Another, pulled around in front of several rows of foldable chairs, is hung with a big sign on the side: "Do You Know This Hybrid Electric Truck Helps Reduce Emissions in Our City?" The press conference today has been called to announce the addition of fifteen of these new hybrid trucks to the Massachusetts fleet, part of Coca-Cola Enterprises' "Commitment 2020," a new initiative to become an environmentally sustainable company within the next decade.

"We've set pretty aggressive goals," says Fred Roselli, CCE's press officer, standing in the parking lot before the press conference. Wearing big black sunglasses and a black suit despite the eighty-degree heat, he looks like a Mormon door-to-door missionary, and has the enthusiasm to match. "We're reducing absolute numbers of carbon 15 percent from our 2007 levels," he patters. "We've installed energy efficient lighting, we're putting in water-saving technology, we've started a whole new company to do recycling." The tractor trailers, he says, are part of the largest fleet of hybrid trucks in North America—some 237 by the end of 2009, each one spewing 30 percent fewer emissions into the air.

All of these environmental initiatives are "part of CRS," says North American president for Coca-Cola Enterprises Steve Cahillane, as he takes the podium. On cue, employees circulate through the crowd, handing out pins in the shape of a green Coke bottle reading "Corporate Responsibility & Sustainability." "CRS is all about making a difference wherever our business touches the world," Cahillane continues. "We not only work here, we also live here, so we are doing everything we can to create sustainable communities."

The concept of socially responsible business practices isn't new—though usually it's called CSR, for "corporate social responsibility" (perhaps inverting the letters is a way for Coke to claim ownership of the concept). In fact, Coke's environmental initiatives follow a script that dates back to the 1950s. It's then that corporations, having survived the Progressive Era and FDR's New Deal, began to proactively affirm the power of businesses to benefit society. "Business managers can more effectively contribute to the solution of many of the complex social problems of our time," wrote Frank Abrams, chairman of Standard Oil of New Jersey—which would become Exxon—in 1951. "There is no higher duty of professional management." The concept emerged as a sort of noblesse oblige of corporations, who responded by spreading a set amount of their profits to social causes in their communities.

Of course, there were limits to what a corporation could do—since legally its obligations were to increase profit for its shareholders, not spread its wealth to solve the world's problems. Henry Ford had found that out in 1916, when his Ford Motor Company was sued for using profits to give discounts to customers instead of dividends to shareholders. The judge in the case sided against him, ruling that "a business corporation is organized and carried on primarily for the profit of its stockholders." It's that principle that has caused Joel Bakan to argue that corporations are essentially "pathological" entities—maximizing profit at the expense of any other good—whether workers' rights, environmental improvements, or even its own customers' pocketbooks. "The corporation's legally defined mandate is to pursue, relentlessly and without exception, its own self-interest regardless of the often harmful consequences it might cause to others," he writes.

That's not to say that corporations can't do good, however, so long as their efforts align with their profit motive. The second wave of corporate social responsibility began in the 1970s, when, faced with challenges from consumer advocates like Ralph Nader (and CSPI's Michael Jacobson), corporations realized that investing in social causes could serve as a kind of insurance against criticism. It was in this era that Coke's Paul Austin pursued his "halo effect" with hydroponic shrimp farms, desalinization plants, and soybean beverages that he argued could help earn goodwill in the developing world at the same time they helped make Coke's vision of global harmony a reality.

Surprisingly, the practice of CSR was further entrenched by the Reagan administration, which encouraged voluntary corporate giving as a way to fill the void left from cutbacks in social programs. Even while Goizueta sloughed off the do-gooding subsidiaries acquired by his predecessor Austin, Coke established the Coca-Cola Foundation in 1984 in an effort to "enhance our ability to meet the growing needs of the communities we serve, and to provide the company with an established, forward-looking program of charitable giving." Historically, of course, Coke had long given to charity, dating back to Asa Candler's first gifts to Emory University. But while Candler resented the obligation to give, and Robert Woodruff earned the nickname "Mr. Anonymous" for the lengths he went to avoid credit for his charitable giving in Atlanta, Goizueta ensured that the new Coca-Cola Foundation would go out of its way to gain publicity for its actions. "It's not that we plan to be boastful now, but we plan to step out in our name and give at a level that we can be proud of," said its first president at the time.

While the Coca-Cola Foundation was ostensibly independent from the corporation itself, it focused its efforts in areas closely aligned with the goals of the company, concentrating particularly in the area of Coke's most important market—children. Neatly getting around Coke's policies about advertising to children, Coke instituted a $50 million giving program to elementary and middle schools throughout the 1990s, and followed it up with a $60 million gift to Boys & Girls Clubs that came with an exclusive beverage agreement with the organization in 1997.

In fact, Goizueta was one of the pioneers of "strategic philanthropy," the newest trend in CSR that emerged in the 1990s. Instead of spreading money around broadly to a number of causes in an effort to be seen as a good corporate citizen, corporations increasingly began tying their non-profit foundations to the image they were trying to achieve for their brand—from Exxon investing heavily in conservation issues after the Valdez oil spill in 1994, to AT&T pouring money into kids' art and education programs as it expanded into cable and the Internet. Some companies even competed to sign exclusive contracts for particular causes, as yogurt maker Dreyer's discovered when it asked to support the largest breast cancer foundation, only to discover that Yoplait had already signed on.

The "social branding" was working. One survey found that, all things being equal, 84 percent of people would switch brands to a company that supported a good cause. While some financial purists such as Milton Friedman declared CSR "evil" for perverting the free market, most financial analysts saw it for what it was: "a cool appraisal of various costs," in the words of one *Financial Times* columnist, since "companies less exposed to social, environmental, and ethical risks are more highly valued by the market."

No one could argue, after all, that CSR was fundamentally changing the character of business—in an era when the United States saw some of the worst examples of corporate wrongdoing in history in WorldCom, Enron, Tyco, and other companies that cooked their books to shovel record profits into the pockets of executives and investors at the expense of their own customers and employees. As the real threat of global warming emerged at the turn of the twenty-first century, companies rushed to tout their environmental consciousness. The most notorious example is British Petroleum, which rebranded itself BP and vowed to move "Beyond Petroleum" to alternative energy. After years of positive publicity, however, alternative fuels have never amounted to more than 5 percent of company spending; in 2009, a new CEO announced he'd be scaling back on even that commitment in an effort to improve profitability. The following year, of course, BP was responsible for one of the worst environmental disasters in U.S. history when one of its deep-sea oil rigs exploded in the Gulf of Mexico, discharging more than 4 million barrels of oil over the course of a five-month spill. After the incident, it was revealed, BP had lobbied against a simple safety measure that could have prevented the accident.

Even when the environmental branding isn't such obvious "greenwashing," it obscures one simple fact: Most of the initiatives companies have taken to increase efficiency and drive down their carbon footprints are also just good business. That's certainly the case with Coke, whose efforts to reduce emissions, water use, and electricity, after all, also mean reducing costs. Asked to name anything the company is doing that is actually costing it money, Roselli hesitates. "Well, the hybrid trucks cost more," he says. "It will take three years to recoup the money we spend on those." Asked if any of the projects will cost the company money *in the long run*, he responds, "Well, the bottom line is the bottom line," he says. "I think big corporations want to be able to do that, but we're trying to figure out which projects to prioritize."

There is nothing wrong with companies profiting from doing good—a win-win for business, consumers, and causes. The danger of CSR initiatives is that they have become such a branding tool that they make it seem like companies are somehow investing in causes out of a motive of self-sacrifice, rather than *partnering* with causes for mutual benefit. And as branding has become the primary reason for CSR, the appearance of doing something can become more important than actually doing it. That's certainly the case with Coke's biggest environmental advertising initiative, touting its recycling efforts at the same time that the bottled water backlash has been drawing attention to all of that wasted plastic in Dasani bottles.

Just as the criticism against bottled water was going mainstream, in late 2007, Coke announced a new partnership between the Coca-Cola Company and Coca-Cola Enterprises to create Coca-Cola Recycling, with the stated goal of eventually recycling 100 percent of its PET plastic bottles. The cornerstone of the effort was a new $50 million facility in Spartanburg, South Carolina, that it announced would be the world's largest "bottle-to-bottle" recycling plant. By 2010, the company boasted, the plant would have a capacity of 100 million pounds per year, making it the most ambitious effort ever by a company to recover and recycle all of its own packaging materials.

To celebrate its effort, the company created an "eco-fashion" line of clothing made from recycled plastic; and, of course, it launched a new ad campaign, premiering during *American Idol* in January 2009. Called "Give It Back," it featured people tossing Coke bottles into recycling bins, only to see them pop out anew from slots of Coke machines. To drive home the message, Coke began working with parks, zoos, and sports stadiums to prominently display red recycling bins in the shape of Coke's hourglass bottle.

Despite the happy imagery, the truth about Coke's recycling efforts was much less impressive. An initial pledge by Coca-Cola Enterprises to use 30 percent recycled PET (rPET) in its bottles in the United States by 2010 was quietly downgraded to a more modest 10 percent "where commercially viable," creating a loophole big enough to drive a hybrid trailer through. In fact, that goal was even less than what Coke had pledged back in the early 1990s, one in a long line of promises on recycling it had reneged on because of "sustainability issues." Recycled PET, the company claimed, was just too expensive in the United States to use on any wide scale. In other words, the environment was worth taking into account only when it didn't cost additional money.

Now with the creation of the Spartanburg plant, the company claimed to have solved the problem, assuring that "the demand for recovered bottles remains strong," according to Scott Vitters, Coke's director of sustainable packaging. The problem with PET, however, has never been one of demand, but of supply. Carpet and car part manufacturers have always competed to get their hands on PET for industrial uses. But to get the high-quality PET needed to make into bottles is much more difficult. Unlike other materials, which can be recycled many times without degrading, PET quickly degrades when melted down repeatedly, making clear, transparent PET hard to come by—to say nothing of the additional costs to clean the material to make it "food-grade."

The only thing that could drive down those costs, then, was a greater availability of PET—especially high-quality PET needed for beverage containers. Coke's new plant, however, does nothing to address this side of the equation, since it purchases 98 percent of its material from already existing curbside recycling programs (the other 2 percent will come from Coke's recycling bins at NASCAR races and other events). In fact, according to industry trade sources, Coke's plant will if anything make the situation worse by driving up the cost for recycled PET with a huge new demand for raw materials.

Meanwhile, Coke has done relatively little to help the supply side of the equation. In addition to its branded recycling bins, it has supported education programs such as Keep America Beautiful, which gives grants to local communities to support curbside programs, and a new program called RecycleBank, which gives consumers coupons for local businesses depending on how much they recycle. Such efforts have increased recycling rates in some municipalities with low rates to begin with, but so far hasn't succeeded in driving rates above the 30 percent national average—a far cry from Coke's 100 percent goal.

"It's a series of building blocks," says Lisa Manley, a spokeswoman for Coke on sustainability issues. "[We] start with recycled content in our packages, then continue to support community recycling efforts, and with that we'll be able to drive more material to Spartanburg. It's a longer journey, but they are the right steps." Even while Coke urges incrementalism, it has led the fight against the most proven means of increasing recycling rates—state bottle bills that charge a 5 or 10 cent deposit on containers that is redeemable when they are returned. In the eleven states with bottle bills, recycling rates average 70 percent for bottles. The higher the refund rate, the higher the percentage—up to the 10 cent return in Michigan, where the recycling rate is 95 percent.

Coca-Cola and its trade association, the American Beverage Association, have lobbied hard against such legislation, arguing that they unfairly single out bottles from all other packages and compete with curbside recycling efforts. "If you take away the incentive for curbside recycling, which oftentimes happens when you take away the materials with the highest value, oftentimes you see the system itself disappear," says Lisa Manley. Of course, nothing of the sort has happened in the states that do have bottle bills, where public support for them averages around 80 percent.

Sometimes, too, the largesse from the company comes with an implicit threat. Coke entered into a recycling partnership with the city of Miami to provide recycling bins in public places—until the mayor of Miami publicly supported the Council of Mayors resolution to ban bottled water from city functions. According to CAI's Gigi Kellett, Coke then pulled its part of the funding for the program, leaving the city to pay for its own recycling bins and providing another example, as if one was needed, of how CSR efforts provide cover for other company goals.

Despite its efforts to save the bottled water market by emphasizing environmental sustainability, Coke found itself back where it had been only a few years ago—with a consumer backlash driving down sales. And in a larger instance of "coming full circle," the one area where bottled water was still growing by 2009 was that in which Coke had originated more than one hundred years before: health beverages. Even while Neville Isdell was rallying for a return to soft drinks in 2005, he was making good on his promise that Coke would eventually carry health benefits.

Coke formed a partnership with Nestlé in 2006 to roll out a green-tea drink it called Enviga, which was "proven to burn calories." The claim hinged on the antioxidant EGCG, the active component of green tea, which had been found in some controlled tests to speed metabolism. A study by Coke and Nestlé claimed that when thirty-one already thin adults drank Enviga for three days, they burned an average of 100 extra calories on the third day. Even to burn that modest amount of calories, you'd have to drink three 12-ounce cans of Enviga, at between $1.29 and $1.49 each. But Coke was bold enough to say the drink had "negative calories."

That was too much for the "food police." Still smarting from being double-crossed on the school soda deal, Coke's old nemesis CSPI filed a class-action lawsuit against the companies. Coke hedged, claiming ridiculously that it had said only that Enviga burned calories, not that it led to weight loss. "You can stop that, it's about weight loss," said a judge, swatting down the distinction during a hearing. In the end, the company cut the calorie-burning claims, and eventually Coke and Nestlé pulled Enviga entirely in the face of poor sales.

The same could not be said of VitaminWater, the leader in a new trend of "enhanced beverages," which Coke had paid an eye-popping $4.1 billion to acquire through its parent company Glaceau in 2007. Vitamin-Water promised a cocktail of exotic ingredients—guarana, açai, and green tea—that in another era would seem straight out of the carpetbag of a snake oil salesman. But consumers have literally drunk it up, with sales in recent years growing by double digits, comparable to bottled water sales a few years before (or, for that matter, soft drinks two decades ago). It has even found its way quietly into schools, when the American Beverage Association and the Alliance for a Healthier Generation amended their agreement from allowing sports drinks and juices to allow any "other drinks" with fewer than 66 calories per 8-ounce serving into school vending machines. In all of its advertising of vitamins and health additives, however, Coke failed to advertise one ingredient in VitaminWater: a whole lot of sugar. In fact, a 20-ounce bottle of VitaminWater has 32.5 grams of sugar and 125 calories—nearly half of the calories in a comparable-size Coke.

"When I bought VitaminWater, frankly I thought I was doing myself a favor healthwise," says James Koh, a San Francisco gym rat who drank the stuff regularly. "I had no idea I was actually getting almost a Coke's worth of sugar and calories." Koh is now the lead plaintiff in yet another class-action lawsuit filed by CSPI, which may finally get its day in court. This time, CSPI didn't even bother calling Coke before filing the suit in January 2009. As a sign of the increasing acrimony between the company and its nemesis, Coke blasted the lawsuit as "ridiculous and ludicrous." Using language rare even for a company under attack, the company went on to call the suit an "opportunistic PR stunt" and "grandstanding at a time when CSPI is receiving very little attention."

At the same time, in response to press inquiries, Coke claimed it hadn't yet had the opportunity to read the complaint, so it couldn't respond to specific charges. Had the company read it, they would have found it alleged a grab bag of bogus health claims on behalf of Coke to hide the fact that the drink is essentially watered-down soda.

The FDA allows food companies a lot of leeway in making claims about the nutritional effects of supplements—for example, that calcium supports the formation of strong bones. It prohibits companies from marketing food items as drugs intended to treat or cure disease (though in practice enforcement of this has been lax). VitaminWater's claims have skirted and in some cases crossed the line with claims that antioxidants in one flavor "may reduce the risk of certain chronic diseases," and vitamin A in another "may reduce the risk of age-related eye disease."

Even more egregiously, says CSPI's Stephen Gardner, the brand has deliberately misled consumers through a practice of "double labeling"—listing the good stuff like vitamins and other nutrients by the bottle size, while listing the bad stuff like sugar and sodium by the serving size in order to minimize their appearance, since there are two and a half 8-ounce servings in a 20-ounce bottle. "They say there are only 50 calories, but in effect there are 125 calories," Gardner says, bristling. "Why should consumers assume they are being lied to in the front? Why should they have to study the very hard-to-read fine print to know the ingredients?"

Remaining a step ahead of the backlash, Coca-Cola recently released VitaminWater 10, with just 10 calories per serving (that is, 25 calories per bottle)—and finally VitaminWater Zero in the fall of 2010. Both products contain stevia, a plant-derived sweetener that has faced its own controversy over claims it contributes to infertility and cancer, even though it has just won approval as safe by the FDA.

If Coke doesn't succeed on VitaminWater, they may have few options left in the United States and European markets. While the key to capitalism is constant innovation, the company may have simply reached a plateau in developed countries. While Coke has survived the backlash against soda in schools, the sugar-sweetened carbonated beverage market has stopped growing. Bottled water, too, has stagnated, and if it doesn't revive, it will spell a big loss to Coke's profit center.

Fortunately for the company, it isn't dependent on the U.S. and European markets—and hasn't been for a long time. Like the tobacco companies, which looked overseas when they came under fire in the United States, Coke has increasingly looked to countries like Brazil, China, and Russia as its next big markets. In addition to the growing populations of countries in the developing world, the company has the added benefit of a more lax regulatory environment, allowing Coke to take advantage of lower costs. In doing so, however, it has created an even bigger conflict between the image of international harmony the brand projects and the reality of the company's operations on the ground.

The world of Coca-Cola isn't the World of Coca-Cola.

Part Two

TEACHING THE WORLD TO SING

I'd like to teach the world to sing, in perfect harmony,
I'd like to buy the world a Coke, and keep it company,
That's the Real Thing . . .

–Coke commercial, 1971

SIX

"¡Toma lo Bueno!"

Salamandering along the ridges of the Chiapas Highlands in southwestern Mexico, you might miss the small sign announcing the village of San Juan de Chamula. But you'd never miss the painted Coke advertisements that surround it on all sides. As visitors come down the hill into the town of 60,000, it takes on the appearance of an army camp, with bright red tents bearing the red Coke logo pitched all over town. Like most Mexican towns, Chamula centers around a huge central plaza where vendors sell bright Mayan textiles, piles of fruits and vegetables, knockoff clothes, and, of course, soft drinks. But the visibility of Coke only hints at the complete cultural integration the fizzy beverage has achieved in Chamula. Facing the plaza is the Church of St. John the Baptist, a white colonial-style cathedral built in 1522, where Coke has literally been turned into a means of religious veneration.

Nearly every day, gringo tourists line up outside the church, clutching tickets to observe the bizarre rituals within. Once through the entrance, they are enveloped in the warm, woodsy smell of pine incense, supplemented by fresh pine needles strewn on the floor. A soft light filters in from windows set below the ceiling some eighty feet above, while thousands of candles burn on tables before glass cases containing gaudily dressed statues of saints. As musicians near the altar play a repetitive dirge, small groups of women and children burn clumps of small, tapered candles stuck into the flagstones. Some are so close together, their combined flames look like a small campfire.

As bewildered tourists wander among them today, a young girl opens up a cardboard box to lift out a clucking brown chicken. Her mother takes it, holding it by its neck and feet, as she rubs it over each of her children. Then laying it on the ground in front of her, she talks to it and soothes it before calmly breaking its neck. The ceremony is a healing art; the chicken is intended to take away the problems of those upon whom it is rubbed. When it dies, the problems go away.

By far the most prominent rituals in the church, however, are those involving soft drinks—which are used by the indigenous people here as a means of directly communing with God. Half-empty bottles of Pepsi and local drinks Big Cola and Gugar are scattered all over the ground amid the pine needles. The most common drinks, though, are half-liter bottles of Coke. By the altar, one man opens up a canvas bag full of them, along with clear bottles of a homemade sugarcane rum called *pox* (pronounced "posh"). He passes two small glasses to each member of the group, one full of *pox*, the other of Coke. Then the eldest man, who stands in the middle dressed in a black sheepskin vest and is missing most of his teeth, chants for five minutes. When he's done, he takes a gingerly sip of the cane liquor—then tosses back the whole glass of Coke in one long guzzle, holding his hand out for a refill as the other members follow suit.

All around the church, in fact, the groups of people are performing the same ritual, explains Carlos Gallegos, an English-speaking tour guide leading a quiet group of Germans. "People drink the *pox* first, then they drink the Coca-Cola," he says. "Then they make a little burp, and that is your spirit floating up into the air. It makes a confession to God and it comes back to your body." The burps are virtually undetectable, done discreetly as a personal communication with God. The different colored candles, continues Gallegos, represent different supplications—yellow for health, green for the harvest, and so on, which are carried upward along with the little belches. "People drink different ones now, but Coca-Cola is still the official one, the best one," says Gallegos. So significant has Coke become to the ritual life of the village that neighbors give it to celebrate births, deaths, and marriages, and judges order it as a means of payment in small claims court. "Here," says Gallegos, "Coca-Cola is cash, poison, magic, passion, pleasure, torture, love, and medicine."

How a caramel-colored drink from Georgia came to be everything to a remote Mexican village is a long story, intertwined with Coke's international expansion after World War II. When Asa Candler forecast Coke's unstoppable growth, and Robert Woodruff imagined Coke "within arm's reach of desire," they might have been picturing modern-day Mexico. "*¡Toma lo bueno!*" read ads blanketing the country—"Drink the good stuff!"—and Mexicans do, 635 cups of Coke beverages annually per person, half again as much as the United States' 412. In part, it is Coke's role as a symbol of the American way of life that has made it so popular, and in part, it's the extremes the company has gone through to get its soda into every village shop and dispensary. It's nearly impossible to describe the ubiquity of soft drink ads in Mexico, with Coke's logo painted on houses and buildings along the roads at least every hundred feet.

Along with Canada and Hawaii, Mexico was one of the first foreign countries to sell Coke, dating back to 1897. For the next few decades, the company sold small amounts in Cuba, the Philippines, England, Germany, and other countries. Early sales abroad ranged from sporadic to anemic. In 1927, Woodruff focused on the market with a new Foreign Department, which contracted out with local companies and businessmen to operate plants overseas, eventually spinning off into a separate subsidiary called the Coca-Cola Export Corporation.

The franchise system put into place when Candler accidentally gave away the store proved useful in foreign markets, allowing the company to expand more rapidly and with less risk—not to mention decreasing the company's liability if anything should go wrong. The company took delight in calling itself a "local" company wherever it went, pointing out that only 1 percent of Coca-Cola Export's employees were American. Then again, the bulk of the profits—up to 80 percent in some cases—flowed back to Atlanta. And not all countries were created equal. In developing nations, bottling companies were often contracted out to American corporations, such as the powerful United Fruit Company in Guatemala and Nicaragua, or owned outright by Coke, as in India.

However much it championed local autonomy, the company was not above using its lobbying clout to force its way into countries that weren't so receptive. In Brazil, for example, a law prohibited drinks containing the preservative phosphoric acid, necessary to prevent degradation of caffeine. (Since Brazilian colas contained caffeine naturally derived from the guarana plant, the preservative was not needed locally.) As part of a bilateral trade agreement with the United States in 1939, the country was forced to repeal the law. The agreement also reduced taxes on soft drinks sold in 6½-ounce bottles, a transparent sop to Coke, since local sodas were sold in 12-ounce bottles.

Despite expansion into South America and Europe in the 1930s, Coke's sales overseas didn't really pick up until after World War II—thanks to Woodruff's promise to give soldiers Cokes for a nickel and the taxpayer-funded bottling plants it engendered. In many ways, the company's international success mirrored that of the country that created it. As Europe lay in ruins, the United States suddenly found itself, along with the Soviet Union, as one of the world's two superpowers. With the new economic and cultural hegemony came a new resentment from some foreigners, particularly in Europe, where the Marshall Plan facilitated the entry of American corporations, at the same time creating anxiety about the crass commercialism of American culture. In some cases, the opposition spilled out into open protest, often directed against the most obvious symbol of the United States: Coca-Cola.

Local communists, in particular, spread wild rumors about the American drink—warning that it turned children's hair white overnight, or that its bottling plants were cover for atomic bomb factories. Nowhere was opposition stronger than in France, where the French Communist Party lamented the growing "Coca-Colonization" of the continent, and the left-centrist newspaper *Le monde* warned that nothing less than "the moral landscape of France is at stake!" Joining the leftists in an unlikely alliance were conservative wine growers who feared Coke's effect on French viniculture—the liquid symbol of France's own way of life.

When the communists and their allies tried to pass a law in the French National Assembly to effectively ban Coke in France and its colonies, Coke reacted with immediate furor. "Coca-Cola was not injurious to the health of American soldiers who liberated France from the Nazis," fumed Coca-Cola Export head James Farley, a former political operative in the Roosevelt administration. "This is the decisive struggle for Europe," cried Coke's top lawyer, as if describing a military conquest. The company called in all of its troops. At its urging, the State Department warned France of "serious possible repercussions" if it pushed through a ban so "prejudicial to American interests." One Georgia congressman forswore French dressing (in an eerie precursor to the "Freedom Fries" protest by Republican congressmen preceding the invasion of Iraq); another more seriously threatened a trade war on French wine, cheese, and Champagne.

As the combined political pressure defeated the anti-Coke alliance in the National Assembly, the company was in fact living up to the fears of those opposing it—becoming a cultural bully that imposed its will, and its products, on a country whether it liked it or not. Despite its victory in France, a 1953 poll there found that only 17 percent of respondents liked Coke "well enough" or "a lot," while 61 percent liked it "not at all." Company officials justified their forceful entry into Europe in the name of the free market, in contrast to the totalitarian control by communists.

"My guess is that the commies don't dislike us so intensely just because we're American," mused one Coke executive. "It's because Coke is a champion of the profit motive. . . . Everyone who has anything to do with the drink makes money." Coke had good reason to resent communists, who had nationalized bottling plants in Cuba and China after World War II.

For years, Coke steered clear of the communist world, even as Pepsi broke into the Soviet Union with the help of former Pepsi counsel Richard Nixon in the 1960s.

With the exception of its stand against "the commies," however, the company was as flexible in its politics internationally as it had been at home. In the Middle East, it used every excuse not to open a franchise in Israel so it didn't upset the wealthy sheiks who owned bottling franchises in Saudi Arabia, Egypt, and other Arab countries. When American Jews protested in a boycott in 1966—Mount Sinai Hospital and Nathan's Famous Hot Dogs both suspended sales—Coke backtracked and granted a franchise in Tel Aviv within days. The Arab League predictably retaliated with its own boycott. Coke did the math, and stayed with the Jews, closing up shop in the rest of the Middle East for the next two decades. In an interview, company head Paul Austin said it would simply be against company policy to give in to a boycott, despite the fact that the company seems to have done exactly that.

As president of Coke in the 1960s and chairman in the 1970s, Austin spent more than half his time flying around the world to cultivate new countries for Coke. By 1976, the overseas market accounted for 40 percent of consumption and 55 percent of profits. By this time, the concept of the "multinational corporation" had become the established way of doing business around the world. All across the business world, companies spawned international subsidiaries to exploit local markets, while profits invariably flowed back to New York, London, Paris, or Stockholm. Coke was virtually unique, however, in spinning off not only control but also ownership to its franchises.

"We're not multinational, we're multilocal," said Austin, who after the Arab boycott began actively trying to walk the walk in living up to the image of international harmony espoused by Coke's "Teach the World to Sing" commercials. As the idea of corporate social responsibility (CSR) caught on, Austin set out to make Coke a leader. In addition to buying Aqua-Chem, the subsidiary that made desalinization plants to provide fresh water in the Middle East, he invested money in sports programs and nutritious milk-based drinks to sell in Latin America alongside sugary sodas. Austin's efforts to create his so-called halo effect seemed genuinely aimed at improving the lot of people in countries where Coke was sold. If it had a secondary effect of selling more Coke in markets where Coke struggled, that was just the "perfect harmony" of the company's business plan.

In the campaign for president in 1976, Austin cultivated corporate peanut farmer–turned–Georgia governor Jimmy Carter, throwing the candidate multiple fund-raisers and offering free use of Coke's corporate jet. "We have our own built-in State Department in the Coca-Cola Company," Carter said in one interview, claiming Coke execs gave him "penetrating analyses" of foreign countries, "what its problems are, who its leaders are, and when I arrive there, provide me with an introduction to the leaders of that country." The strategy paid off for Coke after Carter's election, when Portugal suddenly reversed its long-standing resistance to a Coke bottling plant (maintained out of deference to citrus growers). Shortly after Coke went on sale there, the State Department approved a $300 million loan to the country, a coincidence that did not go unnoticed by U.S. editorial writers.

The limits of Austin's "halo effect" were most evident—violently so—in Guatemala, a sliver of a country southeast of Chiapas that shares its indigenous Maya population. The Coke franchise in Guatemala City had passed from United Fruit in the 1950s, and was now run by Texas businessman John Trotter. A lawyer who loved polyester suits and hated communism, Trotter flew in on his Piper Club plane every few weeks to give pep talks to local managers. Mostly he harped on one theme—the evil of unions, which he ranked second only to communists in their desire to snatch away the god-given profits of the working businessman. Under no circumstances, he told them, should the cancer of unionism be allowed to affect the plant.

Workers at the Coke plant at the time suffered under inhuman working conditions, spending twelve-hour shifts loading crates at the minimum wage of $2 a day. By spring of 1976, more than 80 percent of the two hundred–some workers signed papers to unionize in an effort to improve their lot. When union leaders Israel Márquez and Pedro Quevedo presented the petition to Trotter, however, the Texan refused to recognize it, firing 154 workers. With the law on their side, the workers successfully sued for reinstatement—but Trotter and local executives continued to break up the union, subdividing the bottler into other companies to make it more difficult for workers to organize. The Coke workers reached out to the Catholic Church for help, and were answered by a Philadelphia-based order of nuns called the Sisters of Providence, who owned two hundred shares of Coca-Cola stock—as a way to generate wealth for their order and to influence policy abroad.

Horrified to hear of the situation, its leader, Sister Dorothy Garland, contacted the Coca-Cola Company to demand changes. Coke's president, Luke Smith, admitted tension, but said the franchise agreement tied the company's hands. "There is no provision in the bottlers' agreement . . . which give us any right to intervene on such a dispute," he explained. Undeterred, the nuns filed a shareholders' resolution at the company's annual meeting in 1977 to demand an independent investigation into the issue.

Before the vote, Coke announced its own investigation, which came back a few months later, exonerating Trotter. The nuns cried foul, even as a new president assumed power in Guatemala in 1978. General Romeo Lucas García was one in a long line of military leaders who had ruled the country since a CIA-sponsored coup in the 1950s. But the avowed anticommunist was particularly brutal in his crackdown on "subversive elements," directing his secret police to rout any leftist influences in government, academia, and industry—including unions.

Taking advantage of the situation, Trotter threatened the union organizers with violence if they didn't give up their efforts. Shortly thereafter, Israel Márquez was sprayed by machine-gun fire in his jeep, narrowly escaping with his life. Pedro Quevedo wasn't so lucky. Sitting in his truck during deliveries, he was ambushed by two men, who pumped four rounds into his face, then another eight into his throat before driving away on waiting motorcycles. Another union leader, Manuel López Balán, was also killed, his throat slit while making deliveries on his route.

Even as most of the workers resigned from the union, Márquez traveled to Wilmington to confront Coke chairman Paul Austin at the 1978 annual meeting. In a soft voice, he detailed the murders of his colleagues, before directly appealing to Austin's business sense. "Coca-Cola's image in Guatemala could not be worse," said the small Guatemalan man through a translator. "[In Guatemala,] murder is called 'Coca-Cola.' I have come here today to ask your immediate help so that blood no longer flows through the Coca-Cola plant." Unmoved, Austin tabled the resolution as out of order. Then amid cries from the audience, he gaveled the meeting to a close.

In truth, Austin's hands were tied—intervene in the dispute and he'd call the entire franchise system into question, potentially opening the Coca-Cola Company up to a flood of labor complaints from other countries. At the same time, if he didn't intervene, he'd abrogate all the goodwill he'd so eagerly sought through Coke's CSR efforts. Even as Coke execs privately decided not to renew Trotter's contract, they declined to break it, instead sending another company exec to investigate the situation. He, too, exonerated the franchisee—and no wonder, since he never even questioned Trotter or set foot inside the plant. Unconvinced, the Guatemalans appealed to the International Union of Food and Allied Workers (IUF), a Geneva-based super-union, which issued a call to boycott Coke in November 1979 and instigated work stoppages at Coke plants in Finland, Sweden, and New Zealand.

As the situation quickly grew out of hand, the company assured critics that it would not be renewing Trotter's contract when it expired in 1981. Meanwhile, the rampage continued, with four more union organizers killed. Street protests against Coke in Guatemala led to a dramatic fall in the company's market share. Finally, the pressure was too much for Coke to stall any longer. Even though it had repeatedly claimed it could do nothing until the contract expired, company execs flew to Houston in July 1980 to present Trotter with an offer he couldn't refuse—a generous buyout by two handpicked bottling executives, with most of the financing provided by Coke Atlanta, and no questions asked. The new owners approved a contract with the union after the sale.

But Coke's stalling had left eight workers dead—a legacy in Guatemala that would come to haunt the company again in more recent years.

For the time being, however, the company was able to breathe a sigh of relief when it put the Guatemala incident behind it, and could focus again on expanding the company. When Roberto Goizueta took over the Coca-Cola Company in August 1980, he targeted international growth as a critical part of his plan to increase shareholder value and make Coke, as he would later say, "the number one beverage on Earth." The yardstick he chose to measure that growth was "per-caps"—the number of drinks per capita claimed by Coca-Cola in a country in a given year. He salivated as he looked at the numbers. Per-caps in Latin America at the time were just a third of those in the United States; those in Europe, less than a quarter; and in Africa, only 4 percent.

Goizueta's mantra was "Think globally, act locally," a phrase first attributed to him and only later appropriated by social activists. Under his leadership, Coke concerned itself with the minutiae of foreign markets, installing automatic drink dispensers on street corners in Tokyo and slapping thousands of Coke stickers on every available surface in Bordeaux. "Our success," Goizueta wrote, "will largely depend on the degree to which we can make it impossible for the consumer around the globe to escape Coca-Cola."

Again, politics took a backseat. When activists threatened a boycott of Coke if it didn't divest from South Africa's repressive apartheid regime, Coke brushed them off. It could ill afford to lose the country, which accounted for 70 percent of sales on the continent. When the Atlanta-based Southern Christian Leadership Conference (SCLC)—the civil rights group established by Martin Luther King, Jr.—joined the call, however, Coke compromised by moving its concentrate plant supplying the bottlers to black-ruled Swaziland, and establishing a $10 million fund to support African-Americans administered by Nobel Prize winner Archbishop Desmond Tutu.

That mollified the SCLC, even as Coke—and the apartheid government—continued to profit from its South African bottling franchises. For years after his release from prison, Nelson Mandela denied Coke's offers of travel aid, and even required hotels to remove Coke products from his sight during his stay. The company assiduously courted the sainted leader, putting its highest-ranking African-American executive on the case. By 1993, Coke was contributing heavily to Mandela's campaign to be elected president of a new South Africa, and he was flying around on one of Coke's corporate jets. A year later, Coke returned to South Africa, picking up where it had left off by assuming ownership of the company it had contracted with after it departed.

By 1988, more than three-quarters of Coke's profits came from outside the United States. That year, it topped $1 billion in profits for the first time in history. While it had taken a hundred years for it to reach that mark, it doubled its profits to $2 billion just five years later, in 1993, when it became the sixth most valuable company in the United States. When new CEO Doug Ivester took over in 1997, he wasted no time exploring ways to scrape more profits from foreign countries—including an attempt to pilot a new vending machine in Brazil that would vary its price based on the temperature. "This is a classic situation of supply and demand," Ivester told a Brazilian newspaper reporter. In hot weather, "the utility of an ice-cold Coca-cola is very high. So it is fair that it should be more expensive." The comments resulted in an uproar, not only in Brazil but also in the United States, where they were reprinted and lambasted on late-night talk shows.

Lost in the same interview, however, was a statement at least as outrageous, and with much more lasting implications. Asked about health concerns regarding Coke, Ivester brushed them off. Sugar, he said, was "a good source of energy, of vitality. . . . We have a very healthy product." If Coke's contributions to obesity and disease were apparent in the United States, however, they'd become even more of an issue in the developing world, where a balanced diet is hard to come by even on a good day. Nowhere are those negative effects starker than in Mexico, and nowhere in Mexico is it starker than in Chiapas. It's here, just a few miles from Chamula, that the latest call for a boycott against the company has emerged.

Even though Mexico was one of the first countries to see Coke served outside its homeland, it wasn't regularly drunk here until the 1950s, when Coke began the ad blitz to wallpaper the country in red and white. Before then, even the poorest farmers ate a relatively healthy diet of corn and beans. A study two decades later found white bread and Coca-Cola were the two food items *campesinos* bought as soon as they could afford them—and sometimes even when they couldn't. "It is not uncommon, doctors who work in rural villages report, for a family to sell the few eggs and chickens it raises to buy Coke for the father while the children waste away for lack of protein," wrote Richard J. Barnet and Ronald E. Muller in 1974 in *Global Reach*, one of the first books to look critically at the growing power of multinational corporations.

Along with the proliferation of advertising, Coke followed the same early sales plan that it had in America, with enticements such as branded chairs, tables, and refrigerators for shopkeepers who sold above a certain quota. It also used more aggressive tactics, threatening shopkeepers if they sold any competing brands. In Mexico City in 2002, for example, Coke distributors told a forty-something shopkeeper named Raquel Chávez they'd stop delivering Coke to her store unless she got rid of a Peruvian import called Big Cola. Chávez reported them to the Federal Competition Commission, which fined the Coca-Cola Export Corporation $68 million for unfair competition. ("You may call the shots everywhere else, but I'm the boss in my store," she told the BBC.)

Coke's sales tactics have paid off in Mexico, however, raking in profits for its Mexican anchor bottler, Coca-Cola FEMSA, and its parent company, FEMSA. The latter company is a member of the Forbes International 500 list, with a value of nearly $6 billion. The company's profits tripled in the past decade following the acquisition of several smaller bottlers, including Venezuela-based Panamerican Beverages (Panamco). Between 2002 and 2007, FEMSA's stock price tripled, from $35 to more than $115 a share. Much of that wealth found its way to Atlanta—since in addition to making money on syrup sales, the Coca-Cola Company owns more than a 30 percent stake in Coca-Cola FEMSA.

The increase in Coke sales was felt directly in Chiapas, where the first crates of Coca-Cola were brought up to Chamula by horse in the early 1960s. At first, the growth of Coke in the region coincided with a welcome decrease in the consumption of homemade alcoholic beverages. Years ago, says City University of New York anthropologist June Nash, the men and boys of the highland villages drank copious amounts of *pox*—the homemade sugarcane rum seen in the Chamula church. In part, the drinking was pushed by the village elders, called *caciques*—local political bosses who tightly controlled *pox* production and profited from its sale.

When Nash lived in the nearby village of Amatenango in the 1960s, boys and men drank *pox* daily in both religious and civil ceremonies, holding competitions to see who could drink the most. Not surprisingly, the practice led to rampant alcoholism with serious health and social problems. "There are problems with Coca-Cola, but nothing compared with the alcoholism, which was debilitating in every way," says Nash. Some peasants even converted to Protestantism to exempt themselves from having to drink so much. Fearing they were losing control, the *caciques* turned to a new drink that was just then beginning to penetrate the market: Coca-Cola.

In many communities, the same *caciques* who monopolized production of *pox* retained the concessions to Coke and later Pepsi. In some, such as Amatenango, concessions were granted politically, with officials of the Institutional Revolutionary Party (PRI) controlling Coke and the Party of the Democratic Revolution (PRD) controlling Pepsi. It was easy enough to substitute the new drinks for many of the same rituals that previously used *pox* (though in some cases, such as the church in Chamula, *pox* is still maintained in limited quantities). Those owning the concessions of the soft drinks became rich, reaping huge profits in villages with little other commerce or industry, and passing the concessions along to family members to create dynasties. Before long, however, the increasing consumption of soft drinks brought its own problems—tooth decay, diabetes, and obesity. "Ugh, they drink a lot of soft drinks, they really push it," says Nash. "They never used to have decayed teeth before, and you can really see it now."

In an interview with American anthropologist Laura Jordan, the current owner of the concession to distribute Coca-Cola in Chamula and the surrounding area, Carlos López Gómez, enthused about the popularity of soft drinks for the local people. "[It is] part of daily life," he said. "Like drinking water—every day. Instead of water, they learn to want soda. They want Coca-Cola."* A Chamula city councillor for the minority party, the PRD, elaborates further. "Indigenous people, the number-one thing they consume is Coca-Cola, and the number two thing is Pepsi," says Cristóbal López Pérez. So nervous was he about speaking about the beverage, he insisted on arranging the interview in the back room of a local human rights organization. Sitting at a cramped table wearing a cowboy hat and zip-up cardigan over a collared shirt, he paints a picture of cradle-to-grave consumption of which U.S. marketers could only dream.

"When a child is born, they give soda. When a woman is married, they give soda. When someone dies, they give soda," he says. The amount is directly related to the wealth of the family, ranging from three or four boxes up to one hundred depending on the occasion. No event, however, matches election time, when all candidates buy astounding amounts of

*Despite several attempts, López Gómez was unavailable for an interview himself. When I arrived for an appointment at the distribution center, I was told he had just left. I traded several messages with him over the next three days, but he always seemed to be in Chamula when I wasn't.

Coke for their supporters. For López's council election, he bought five trailers, each with 180 boxes, totaling more than 20,000 bottles for just one candidate. On election day, he says, people bring straps to the polling booth to cart home the expected case of soda. "Whoever gives Coca-Cola has more of a possibility of winning," he says. "If you give another kind of soda, it's not as good."

No one is obligated to buy soda, says López, but *not* buying it is the easiest way to acquire social stigma in the village. Families who serve the locally made corn beverage *pozol* at parties are looked down upon. "People say, 'They shouldn't have invited me. I can make that at home.'" López is one of the few people in the village who is critical of all of the soda consumption, which he blames for the poor health of the community. "There are many headaches, people have gastritis, they have sugar in the blood [diabetes]," he says. "We are just beginning to realize that this is not nourishing for our bodies, that it is making us sick." Asked if he's tried to broach the subject with his neighbors, he sighs. "It is not possible to change people today or tomorrow. I don't know when this is going to end. To change the mentality of people is very difficult."

Health problems in the villages of Chiapas have been exacerbated by recent changes in patterns of physical activities by the peasant population. As mining and oil interests have taken up arable land, men from the villages have increasingly gone to the United States to find work, leaving behind women and children to live a more sedentary lifestyle—using their money transfers from America to buy more junk food. Local indigenous health coalition COMPITCH has done surveys of communities in the highlands and jungles of Chiapas, finding that problems with obesity and diabetes are greater in communities closer to the roadways plied by delivery trucks for Coca-Cola and other processed foods. "We can't blame Coca-Cola," says the group's Juan Ignacio Dominguez, "but we can situate Coca-Cola as a detonating component. When we put together all these social factors, Coca-Cola is the last drip that makes the cup overflow." He shakes his head. "There is something that makes Coca-Cola really formidable for us. Maybe it has to do with the sugar," he says, laughing. "We are a very sweet culture."

In fact, he may not be far off. Research by the Chiapas-based medical NGO Defensoría del Derecho a la Salud (Health Rights Defense) has found the taste for sugar is established at a very early age, with most women in indigenous villages serving their children soft drinks even below the age of three. "These three years in many ways define the future of the child, and it is when malnutrition and diabetes can be prevented," says the group's director, Dr. Marcos Arana. "If babies are exposed to a high intake of sugar, they will be conditioned to depend on sugar for the rest of their lives." While breast-feeding is still the norm for younger children, says Arana, there are still instances of mothers putting Coca-Cola into baby bottles.

Anecdotally, Arana says he has seen a steady increase in obesity and diabetes in the communities he serves. Official evidence, however, is hard to come by. While government statistics show Chiapas has the highest rates of obesity in the country, for example, it has one of the lowest rates of diabetes, which Arana says is due to an underdiagnosis of the disease. Compounding the problem is the lack of safe drinking water at homes and schools in highland communities. "The teachers know this and sometimes they are convinced by Coca-Cola to promote the consumption of soda in schools among the children," says Arana. As in the United States, many schools still have exclusivity contracts with Coke or Pepsi—and despite phasing out sugary beverages in schools in the United States, they are still frequently sold here. "They do in other countries what they would not do in the United States," sighs Arana, a statement that represents a lot about Coke's strategy around the world. Because the company's franchise bottlers aren't directly owned by the company, they don't have to live up to the same standards.

In addition to contracts in schools, Coke also drives up soda sales by selling beverages for a cheaper price in indigenous communities. In the city of San Cristóbal de Las Casas, for instance, a liter of Coke sells for 10 pesos (about 90 cents), while just up the mountain in Chamula it is sold for half that. In the same shops, a 1.5-liter bottle of Coke's water brand Ciel costs 10 pesos, making Coke actually cheaper than its main ingredient. The most logical explanation for the difference is that the company is hoping that the taste for sugar will result in more sales over time.

Arana is part of a group of doctors who pushed for a soda tax to curb consumption nationwide. In 2002, in fact, the country imposed a 20 cent tax on all soft drinks made with high-fructose corn syrup, affecting Coke and Pepsi but not local sodas made with sugar from sugarcane. (The rumor persists that Coke in Mexico is made completely with natural cane sugar, which the Coca-Cola Company does nothing to dispel. However, that hasn't been the case for a decade, since the North American Free Trade Agreement flooded the market with cheap corn, and Mexican bottlers began using cheaper HFCS. In past years, Coca-Cola FEMSA has used up to 60 percent HFCS in Mexican Coke. By 2009, that ratio was down to 30 percent, but with plans to raise it because of an increase in sugar prices.)

When the tax was passed, however, the United States promptly filed a dispute on Coke's behalf in the World Trade Organization (WTO), arguing it was discriminatory against American products. The WTO ruled in the favor of the United States in 2005 and again in 2007, after which Mexico repealed the tax. An effort by Mexican president Felipe Calderón to impose a 5 cent tax on all soft drinks failed in the legislature, amid heavy lobbying from soft drink companies. Arana is hopeful that in the future another tax might succeed—or if not, then at least the government might be able to pass a law outlawing the selling of soft drinks at different prices, or prohibiting exclusive school beverage contracts.

The health issues surrounding soft drinks, however, are not the only issues here that have led to a backlash against the company. Down the mountain from Chamula and the highland villages, residents of the city of San Cristóbal have raised questions about how the company produces the drinks themselves.

Geckos scamper underfoot during the steep climb up Huitepec, a dormant volcano on the outskirts of San Cristóbal de Las Casas. The path weaves its way through a forest of ancient-seeming oak trees, all twisted trunks and gnarly burrs with moss and vines clinging to their sides. It's easy to see why the mountain holds a special place in the folklore of the indigenous Maya, many of whom still believe the spirit of the place watches over them. Unlike the dry, piney hills around, Huitepec is lush and green, supporting not only white oaks but also a fragmentary cloud forest with an array of wildlife, including more than one hundred species of birds, squirrels, deer, and coyote.

The largest mountain in the hills encircling San Cris (as the municipality is known), Huitepec collects water from the rains that blow through the valley, then percolates the water through the volcanic soil and limestone into a huge underground aquifer that serves as the major municipal water source. The apparent abundance, however, is an illusion—hiding a chronic shortage of water that plagues the surrounding communities. "During the dry season there is huge water scarcity here," says Erin Araujo, an American graduate student who has studied the water table, pausing for breath in a clearing near the top of the mountain. "Most people get their water only from the municipal water supply, and during the dry season all of the rain that replenishes the aquifer has dried up." At those times, residents of San Cristóbal are rationed—some limited to only a few hours of water a day in outlying communities, even as residents in the city center are allowed twenty-four-hour, seven-day access.

Even more egregious to some residents is the presence of a Coca-Cola bottling plant on the other side of the mountain, which always seems to have enough water for its beverages. Coke's presence at the foot of Huitepec dates back to the late 1980s, when it first established a bodega here. Soon Coca-Cola FEMSA moved its bottling operations to San Cristóbal from the state capital, Tuxtla Gutiérrez, to take advantage of the more abundant water supply there. By 1994, the plant was churning out five thousand cases a day, ramping up production year after year. By 2004, it had doubled that to ten thousand cases a day, serving not only the entire state of Chiapas, but also part of the neighboring state of Tabasco. By 2008, it was serving part of Oaxaca as well.

According to government statistics, the company has the right to extract up to 500 million liters a year from the aquifer—an amount translating to 1.37 million liters a day. Coca-Cola FEMSA denied a request for an interview, asking that questions be transmitted through the Coca-Cola Company, which in turn directed them back to Coca-Cola FEMSA. A company spokesperson, however, defended the company's water usage to American anthropologist Laura Jordan, who wrote her thesis on Coke and corporate social responsibility in the Highlands in 2008. The plant's human resources director, Graciela Flores, told Jordan the company takes no more than 2 percent of the total water consumed by "all of San Cristóbal"—at the same time providing a number of well-paying jobs to the community.

Those who live in the vicinity of the plant, however, see things differently. On the other side of the mountain, the Coke plant squats in a massive gray installation beneath Huitepec's bulk. On the rutted dirt road behind it, an elderly woman named María de la Asunción Gómez Carpio sells fried snacks to school kids. "The water here used to be very abundant, but all of the springs here dried up since the plant came here twenty years ago," she says. Now she says residents in her neighborhood, which sits on one of the richest aquifers in Mexico, get water brought in by tanker trucks called *pipas*—pipes—at the cost of $240 pesos ($22) a month.

Asked about employment the company provides to locals, she laughs. "No, they don't give employment to people with low education; you have to be educated to work there." Meanwhile, she says, the company has refused requests for assistance in repairing the road behind the plant. "They provide no benefit. On the contrary, they take from us." The story is repeated by several other residents in the vicinity of the plant, including Rosa María Reazola Estevané, who lives in a nice house at the top of the hill. "There used to be a lot of water," she says. "Now there is a scarcity. They are not paying anything, and they are just taking our water away. I am really pissed off about it. I want them to leave."

From the looks of things, the company isn't just taking—it's also leaving a foul-smelling stream that flows from one side of the plant. In the central Mexican state of Tlaxcala, the outspoken mayor of the town of Apizaco, Reyes Rúiz, accused Coke of polluting the land with a milky effluent that killed trees in a river a short way from the plant. In addition, as in San Cristóbal, he has accused Coke of decreasing the local aquifer and drying up farmland. FEMSA has denied the charges, pointing out that it stays within the 450 million gallons allowed by the National Water Commission, and that the plant accounts for less than 1 percent of the total water usage in the region. "We comply with the law," Marco Antonio Dehesa, project engineer with Coca-Cola FEMSA, repeatedly told researchers with the American nonprofit Grassroots International.

For all of the water that it takes from communities such as Apizaco and San Cristóbal, however, Coca-Cola FEMSA pays them nothing for the privilege. That's because the company has negotiated contracts for the water extraction directly with the federal government in Mexico City, thanks to a law passed with the help of a former Coke executive who happened to be Mexico's president. Whatever influence Coke has had with U.S. presidents from Eisenhower to Carter, Coke FEMSA surpassed it in the unprecedented access to the halls of power it had through former Mexican president Vicente Fox. Back in the 1970s, Fox was director general of Coca-Cola Mexico, a division of the Coca-Cola Export Corporation that is fully owned by the Coca-Cola Company; during his tenure, he boosted Coke's sales to topple Pepsi as the nation's best-selling soft drink.

"Working at Coca-Cola was my second university education," Fox told *The New York Times* in 1999. "I learned strategy, marketing, financial management, optimization of resources. I learned not to accept anything but winning." Nicknamed "The Coca-Cola Kid" during his campaign, Fox used focus groups and heavy television advertising he learned from his Coke days to win. He also drew heavily upon his former Coke connections, including hiring as his finance director a former Coke executive, who raised millions from Coke bottlers and other businesses to put him on top. After he became president in 2000, Fox had no compunction about helping out his former employer. He appointed another former Coke director general, Cristóbal Jaime Jáquez, as national water commissioner; together, they pushed privatization of much of the country's water network and sold extraction rights directly to big agribusiness and other corporations.

Coca-Cola FEMSA, the anchor bottler in Mexico and the owner of the Chiapas plant, was one of the big winners of the new policy, according to an investigative news report in 2003. In all, FEMSA negotiated twenty-seven concessions to extract water from aquifers and rivers, along with another eight concessions to dump waste in public waters. For all of these, it paid a reported $29,000 in U.S. dollars—a pittance compared with its $650 million in annual profits. According to San Cristóbal's former right-wing mayor, Victoria Olvera, the company has continued to pay next to nothing for the community's water, with an outlay of only 1.75 million pesos ($150,000) annually—or as little as three-hundredths of a cent per liter—to the federal government. "Nothing for the municipality. Nothing," Olvera told anthropologist Jordan. "They say, 'We generate employment.' But there is not as much employment as the damage they cause us, and they could be doing us so much good if they *could* pay that tax."

Even more than its effect on health of the local community, resentment over water use has turned many in the environs of San Cristóbal against the company, making it a symbol of greed in an environment already hostile to American capitalism. Like France in the 1950s, Chiapas has become deeply distrustful of the motives of American corporations. After all, it's the home of the most famous revolution in the last twenty years.

They came out of the jungle on New Year's Day, 1994, wearing black ski masks and carrying assault rifles as they took control of the main square of San Cristóbal de Las Casas. For years, San Cris has been a laid-back tourist town, blending Maya and gringo culture in the cafés and street festivals. Now the tourists locked in their hotels had no idea what to make of the hooded revolutionaries in their midst. Finally, their leader identified himself as Subcomandante Marcos. His comrades, he said, were Zapatistas, after the revolutionary peasant leader Emiliano Zapata, and here to demand land and rights for the indigenous people. It was no accident that the revolutionaries appeared on the day the North American Free Trade Agreement was implemented in the United States and Mexico, since Zapatistas saw the free-trade deal as a continuation of the policies that had allowed privatization and sale of their land to ranching, mining, and natural gas interests.

While the Zapatistas stemmed from the Marxist revolutionaries once common in Latin America, they didn't espouse the traditional communist ideology with a top-down command structure. Instead, they supported autonomous village groups that could stand outside Mexico's notoriously corrupt political structure. After clashes with the army in which several hundred people—mostly Zapatistas—were killed, the group renounced violence. Soon the tourists came back, and in greater numbers, as the Zapatistas became a cause célèbre among lefty activists. Peace was short-lived, however, as the army raided several Zapatista bases, and paramilitary groups staged massacres in several villages known to sympathize with the rebels.

When Coca-Cola Kid Vicente Fox won the presidential election in 2000, he tried to negotiate with the Zapatistas, compromising on a new law to protect indigenous rights and demilitarize Chiapas. After the law had been weakened, however, Marcos rejected it as a joke and the Zapatistas went back to the jungles, where they've remained ever since. Strangely enough, while the Zapatistas have fought exploitation by other foreign multinationals—most recently drug companies they accuse of driving them off their land in search of new medicinal plants—they've had no problem with Coke. Even as Marcos has barred drugs and alcohol from rebel-controlled areas, he has encouraged consumption of Coca-Cola, whose trucks have reportedly been the only traffic allowed through the front lines during skirmishes with the army. "We have a way to get rid of Coke," he once joked. "We will drink every last bottle."

The revolutionary spirit the Zapatistas kicked off, however, has spurred others to take opposition against the Coca-Cola Company, especially in San Cristóbal, where Coke's presence on Huitepec, the sacred mountain of the Maya, is too egregious for some to ignore. Since 2006, Zapatista rebels have manned a "peace camp" on Huitepec to guard its forest against cutting by logging interests. The real opposition to Coke, however, has come in the city, where a coalition of neighborhood groups under the acronym COCIDEP (Comité Ciudadano para la Defensa Popular) has protested the water rationing faced by residents of outlying neighborhoods, refusing to pay for water and illegally turning their water back on when the water company shut it off. The group has also argued that Coke's consumption should be limited, especially during dry season when there is scarcity. "We know Coca-Cola is extracting massive amounts," says César Morales, one of the group's leaders, as he sits in the back room of a local café. "They don't ask for public consent. All of the water is from underground—it's the same—so when you open one well, it affects the whole community."

Since Coke FEMSA has negotiated a twenty-year contract directly with the federal government, however, COCIDEP has had no legal say-so to limit the company's extraction. Frustrated, the group has joined a local boycott of the company, urging its members to drink fruit juices and traditional indigenous beverages such as *pozol.* While boycotts of Coke may have worked for New York Jews in the 1960s or southern blacks in the 1980s, however, none of them had to contend with the cultural integration that Coke has achieved in Mexico. "We have Coca-Cola in our blood, and in our heart," sighs Gustavo Castro, a leftist intellectual with bushy hair and a beard who has helped lead the boycott through his group Otros Mundos (Other Worlds). "You can talk about politics, but you put the idea of Coca-Cola on the table and it creates huge controversy. It's so deeply a part of Mexican culture that we can't question it."

In Castro's brightly colored office hang posters for various campaigns around water usage and health, including a sign poking fun at Coke with the slogan "Always Gastritis!" In theory, says Castro, a boycott could do real damage to the company. Castro and his colleagues have calculated that the communities around San Cristóbal spend some $50 million annually on Coke products. Getting people to make the connection between Coke and the affect on health and the environment, however, has been difficult. The boycott has fallen far short of its relatively modest goal to register ten thousand people.

Part of the problem with boycotting Coke is the lack of alternatives to the drink, especially in an area where local water supplies are commonly contaminated. Castro's group tried to strike a deal with a Mexico City juice company whose beverage Boing! sells for 15 pesos for 1 liter (versus 10 or 11 pesos for a 2-liter Coke), but they were unable to come to an agreement that would bring prices down to a competitive level.

With the boycott in Chiapas failing to gather much steam, and the municipal government checkmated by federal law, at least one civil society organization is looking ahead to the future—the next generation. "The adults aren't salvageable," says Teresa Zepeda Torres, director of Alianza Cívica, which has campaigned to raise awareness of water issues. "The young people and adolescents are the ones who are going to have the problems, and they are the remedy for this, so it's more important to talk with them."

Zepeda's office in San Cris is covered with brightly colored posters made by young people as part of a contest to draw attention to environmental issues. Even as they embrace campaigns against pollution and water conservation, however, Zepeda says that Coke consumption is difficult to broach. "We are trying to teach children what it does to their health—that it's why they are so chubby," she says. "When I talk about natural resources and the water cycle, the children are very receptive. They propose things. When I talk about Coca-Cola, however, that complicates things."

Perhaps, in part, that's because of the pouring-rights contracts that expose them to Coke products in schools. In Mexico, Coke has gone far beyond the advertising and exercise programs, to concentrate its CSR efforts on building schools themselves. In 1999, the Coca-Cola Foundation put $10 million toward creating the Coca-Cola Foundation/Mexico, which has partnered with government to build, at last count, eight day schools and four boarding schools throughout Chiapas. Of course, the foundation isn't actually building the schools but rather putting up money toward their construction—generally 20 to 30 percent of their total cost. For a $180,000 boarding school, Coke donated $55,000; for a $680,000 secondary school, it put up $155,000.

As in the United States, that investment has often gone hand in hand with supporting the Coca-Cola Company's goal to sell more soft drinks to kids. For one school in Huixtán, a dozen miles east of San Cris, the bottler prevailed upon the community store next door to exclusively sell Coca-Cola drinks, with a bright sign painted right next to the school. In other cases, it has splashed Coke logos all over school basketball courts behind the schools. In one, the backboards and foul circles are covered in the Coke logo, while Coke signs hang in the stands and spectators swig Coke as they watch.

And some critics of the company see an even more sinister attempt at water privatization in Coke's school-building operations. COMPITCH's Juan Ignacio Domínguez alleges that Coca-Cola FEMSA has put its schools in communities with the richest water resources, even while it bypasses communities with greater needs that don't have access to aquifers. "There are two communities where Coke proposed to bring a high school, and communities nearby don't even have middle schools," he says.

In Huixtán, according to a former town councilor, the company came back just a few weeks after the inauguration of the school in 2002 to request authorization for a small bottling plant in the village. The offer sparked intense debate, with a majority of residents afraid the company would deplete its water. When put to a vote, some 80 percent voted against the authorization. According to Domínguez, however, Coke had already requested the rights from two private landowners. When the town council found out, it protested, forbidding the sale. "They said, The water is public," says Domínguez. "You have to ask everyone, and Coca-Cola didn't want to go through that process."

It's nearly impossible to verify the story, which might be just another version of the European communist rumors of children's hair turning white or the atomic bomb factory at the bottling plant. If nothing else, however, it shows the deep distrust some people in the area have of the multinational's motives, even while it is ostensibly doing something positive for the community. Rumors such as these, however, have failed to turn the majority of people in Chiapas—much less Mexico—against Coca-Cola, which continues to see record growth throughout the country.

Just a few hundred miles south, however, another boycott has taken root, based on a more serious set of disputed facts. Conjuring the deadly history of Coke's bottling plant workers in Guatemala, the campaign has rocked the company all the way to its headquarters in Atlanta.

SEVEN

"Syrup in the Veins"

Clouds shroud the windows of the fifty-seat turboprop flying to Apartadó, the capital of the Colombian region of Urabá on the Caribbean coast. As it rises to clear the crest of the mountains, suddenly sunshine breaks in through the clouds, revealing the dark green ridges of the surrounding Andes. It's easy to see how the guerrillas who first appeared here in the 1960s were able to avoid capture for so long in this forested fortress. As the plane finally begins to descend, the color changes from forest green to a tropical shade of lime and suddenly acre after acre of banana plantations stretch in all directions.

The airport itself is surrounded by towers and fences topped with barbed wire. Just past the open-air parking lot, a bright red billboard sports the familiar hourglass silhouette of a Coke bottle. Printed over it are the words *"El Lado Coca-Cola de Urabá"*—The Coca-Cola Side of Urabá—a riff off Coke's latest advertising slogan, "The Coca-Cola Side of Life." Spurting out of the mouth of the bottle is a riot of birds, butterflies, and flowers, surrounded by multicolored splatters of paint. It's an unfortunate irony that, in the present context, they look like nothing so much as splatters of blood.

On the road into Carepa, miles upon miles of banana trees speed past, their leaves splayed lazily in the sun. After twenty minutes, the town appears, choked with dust and clogged with a dozen cafés of concrete and corrugated steel, each advertising with a sign for Coca-Cola or its Colombian rival Postobón (distributed by PepsiCo). The Coca-Cola plant is a few hundred meters past the town center on a desolate stretch of highway.

Owned by a bottling company called Bebidas y Alimientos de Urabá, it was built relatively recently by Coke standards, beginning operations in 1979, around the same time that the banana processing plants run by United Fruit Company (which later became Chiquita) set up shop in the area. While the company initially did a good business, sales languished over the years, in part due to the violence gripping the region, which had become a stronghold of guerrillas during the country's increasingly violent civil war.

By all accounts, the conflict began sixty years ago in a period appropriately called La Violencia, a sectarian bloodletting pitting the two major parties, Liberal and Conservative, against each other following the killing of a popular liberal leader in 1948. Caught in between, communist rebels fled into the hills around Bogotá for protection, eventually consolidating themselves under the leadership of a guerrilla captain called Manuel Marulanda—better known by his nickname Sureshot for the quickness with which he dispatched any government forces encroaching on his territory.

When the two major parties reached a power-sharing accord in 1958, the communists were left out. The army attacked their bases, scattering them into the jungles, where they took on the new name of Fuerzas Armadas Revolucionarias de Colombia (Revolutionary Armed Forces of Colombia), or FARC, and adopted a Marxist philosophy and guerrilla tactics of ambushing government troops and bases operating in their territories. While most fled south, some spread northward into the relatively unpopulated area of Urabá, where they used their Caribbean location to import weapons from Panama and tax drug shipments bound farther north, kidnapping or killing anyone who opposed them. By some accounts, the FARC also infiltrated the unions in the banana-processing plants run by United Fruit Company.

At any rate, businessmen throughout Colombia had much to fear from the guerrillas, especially from a smaller guerrilla offshoot known as the ELN (National Liberation Army), which operated in the center of the country along Colombia's largest river, the Río Magdalena, and pioneered the guerrillas' most feared tactic—kidnapping and holding wealthy people for ransom. When it wasn't doing that, it was extorting money from the oil refineries and other businesses—including the ultimate symbol of capitalism, Coca-Cola. Starting in the 1990s, the ELN "taxed" bottling plants 20 cents for every crate of Coke sold. When the company didn't pay, it declared war, stealing and burning its delivery trucks and killing several distributors.

It was these kinds of tactics against businessmen that led to the formation of the first paramilitary groups to fight back. Civilian "self-defense" groups, or *autodefensas*, had existed in Colombia for decades, authorized by law in 1965. But the paramilitaries didn't come into their own until the mid-1980s, when some businessmen and ranchers banded together in Colombia's Middle Magdalena Valley under a grizzled rancher named Ramón Isaza.

Boosted by drug money from Pablo Escobar's Medellín cartel, they began killing FARC and ELN "tax collectors," cutting up their bodies and sinking them in the rivers. Soon they were conducting increasingly brutal massacres in villages and towns suspected of giving support to guerrillas and targeting policemen and liberal politicians to silence opposition. The paramilitaries went too far in 1989, when they killed a judge and a team of government prosecutors, and were declared illegal by the federal government.

But they didn't disappear; they merely went underground, reconstituting themselves under the leadership of a murderous band of brothers, Fidel, Carlos, and Vicente Castaño. The Castaños originally came from the coffee belt of Córdoba, just south of Urabá, but soon expanded their operations nationally to create the Autodefensas Unidas de Colombia, or AUC. Openly declaring itself in 1997, the new paramilitary coalition began a reign of terror against anyone it suspected of collaborating with guerrillas, including community leaders, human rights activists, and union workers.

Urabá was controlled by the brutal Freddy Rendón Herrera, also known as "El Alemán" (The German) because of his light hair and eyes, and whom human rights groups accuse of killing, disappearing, or forcibly displacing as many as two thousand people in six years; and José Ever Veloza, known as H.H., who by his own count confessed to ordering the deaths of three thousand. "More innocents than guilty died"—he shrugged—"but that's because the war is irregular." Their men were known for brutal massacres where civilians were gored with chain saws and hacked to death with machetes. In one, paramilitaries raided a school during a "peace education day" and decapitated a boy in front of the crowd; in another, they cut off the head of an elderly man and played a pickup game of soccer with it in the town square.

Even as the paramilitary violence was beginning in Urabá, the bottling plant in Carepa was struggling to survive, subsisting on personal loans from its majority shareholder, Richard Kirby, a businessman who split his time between Bogotá and Miami and owned significant interests in several other Coca-Cola bottling franchises in Colombia. Management responded by squeezing workers, forcing them to work sixteen-hour days and firing workers who had more seniority in order to save money on higher salaries and benefits, according to former workers at the plant.

The union at the time reluctantly went along with the changes, trying to eke out concessions where it could. In 1993, however, a new food and beverage union called SINALTRAINAL began to organize workers with a more militant strategy, taking a hard line in negotiations. Particularly vocal were two of the union's new leaders, José Eleazar Manco and Luis Enrique Giraldo, who pushed management for higher wages and increased job security. By Colombian law, workers can be fired at will—unless they are members of a union executive council, who are protected against dismissal.

At the same time that SINALTRAINAL began making noise at the plant, paramilitary graffiti began appearing around town, and rumors circulated about trade unionists coming under attack in neighboring towns. Then, on April 8, 1994, Manco simply disappeared. Two weeks later, it was Giraldo's turn. On April 20, 1994, his motorcycle was stopped on the way to work, and he was dragged into the woods and shot. "There was an investigation," says his brother, Oscar Giraldo, interviewed at SINALTRAINAL's headquarters in Bogotá, a nondescript building with a double-reinforced door in a residential neighborhood just outside the center of the city. "A couple of reports were written, but not much happened. My mother suffered a lot." Over the next year, he and other union members started receiving death threats, culminating in the killing of another union leader, Luis Enrique Gómez, who was shot while drinking on his front stoop.

The company was silent about the murders, even as the remaining members of the executive council fled the region. With opposition gone, Bebidas pushed for more concessions from workers. "The company was always sucking the blood of workers, just work, work, work," says Giraldo, who joined with some of his fellow employees to re-form the executive committee. The situation intensified with the arrival of a new manager at the plant, a man by the name of Ariosto Milan. In a small town where everyone knows everyone, workers say they began seeing Milan socializing with local paramilitaries, including the regional commander known as Cepillo (The Brush), a light-skinned man with jet-black hair and almond-shaped eyes, and his lieutenant Caliche (Saltpeter—the active component in gun powder), who was squat and harsh-faced with dark skin. On several occasions, workers say they saw Milan sharing Cokes with the paras at the kiosk outside the gates of the plant or drinking beers with them in bars around town.

Worse, they say, he began publicly boasting that he would "sweep away the union." To one worker, he said the only reason the union "hasn't been destroyed is [that] I haven't wanted to destroy it yet." Alarmed by the developments, SINALTRAINAL's national leadership sent a letter to Bebidas and to Coca-Cola Colombia—a fully owned subsidiary of the Coca-

Cola Company—in November 1995 protesting Milan's associations and urging the company to provide protection for workers. They received no response.

Tensions were running high when the union began negotiating a new labor contract in 1996, pushing for an ambitious pay raise of 35 percent within a year, along with increases in maternity leave, disability insurance, and life insurance, and a fund for sporting activities. Finally, there was a clause demanding increased security for workers and prohibitions on managers consorting with paramilitaries. As chief negotiator, the union tapped secretary-general Isidro Gil, the well-liked gatekeeper at the plant.

Born in a small town one hundred miles northeast of Carepa, Gil was the seventh of ten children. Even as a child, he'd been ambitious, always studying and selling the local newspaper on the side. Before he finished high school, he followed his older brother Martín to Urabá, marrying and raising two daughters. When Martín got a job in the administrative office of the Coca-Cola bottling plant, Isidro again followed him, finding work on the production line. After cutting his finger in a workplace accident, he moved to the front gate instead. Gil thrived at the plant, organizing weekend sports tournaments—soccer, volleyball, baseball—and inviting coworkers to fishing trips on the nearby river. Soon he was friends with everyone at the plant—or almost everyone. When he had a motorcycle accident on the way to work, he argued for a workers' compensation payment from Milan, who refused to grant it.

On the day the company's reply to the labor petition was due, December 5, Giraldo was talking with Gil at the front gate. The two of them watched nervously as a motorcycle pulled up in the driveway. "We'll talk in a bit," Giraldo said, quickly excusing himself and walking back toward the yard. He was only halfway there when the crack of a pistol rang out behind him. He turned just long enough to see Gil fall to the ground. Ice coursing through his veins, Giraldo broke into a run, even as he heard the shots continue to ring out behind him.

The union's president, Hernán Manco, was working the packaging machine in the courtyard. He watched Gil's head snap backward as he fell back toward the gatehouse. The killer's pistol followed him down, firing point-blank into his jerking body. In all, he emptied ten bullets into his body—four more into his face, four into his heart, and one into his groin—as he lay lifeless on his right side, his head inside and feet outside the gate.

After the assassin walked casually back to his motorcycle and rode away, another worker, Adolfo Cardona, ran to the body. Cradling Gil's head, he watched his friend's skull come apart in his hands. Back in Carepa, Gil's brother Martín received the news by phone. He immediately jumped on his own motorcycle and flew off to the plant, leaving so quickly he must have passed the assassins as they drove in the other direction. Arriving at the plant, he threw himself down on his brother's body, crying and embracing Isidro. He was still there when investigators with the Fiscalía, the Colombian attorney general's office, arrived to declare him dead.

As the machines stopped and the workers filed out into the yard, the workers stood paralyzed, not knowing if Gil's murder was a personal vendetta or the beginning of a rampage against the union as a whole. At last it was Gil's friend Cardona who volunteered to investigate. He was better known as "El Diablo" (The Devil), mostly as an honorary title after his father, who was "El Diablo," too. But it also suited his headstrong personality.

Pedaling onto the highway on his bicycle, he ran into the paramilitaries almost immediately. "Cepillo wants to see you," shouted a man pulling up alongside on a motorbike. Cardona started at the name of the known regional paramilitary commander. But he tried not to show fear. "Well, I need to speak to him, too," he shouted. "Meet him at La Ceiba," spat the paramilitary, naming a soda shop in the center of town.

Cardona followed the motorcycle into the crowded commercial district, past storefronts overflowing with cookware, CDs, knock-off T-shirts, and plastic kids' toys imported from Panama. Pedaling up to the shop, he saw seven or eight tough-looking men sitting at the outside tables. In a moment, the local paramilitary lieutenant, a squat, unattractive man named

Caliche, drove up. El Diablo went on the offensive. "I need to meet Cepillo," he said. Caliche shrugged, saying the commander was across town washing up, but would be there shortly.

As Cardona waited, he says, a white Toyota minibus pulled up. Seeing the face of the driver, Cardona went numb. Around Urabá, that car was known as the "Pathway to Heaven." People got in and never got out. *Oh my God, they are going to kill me,* he thought, eyes quickly darting from side to side in an attempt to find some line of escape. That was when he saw the two men who had shot Gil coming out of the shop. "Hey, man, you come with me," one of them said. Cardona began to move in the direction he indicated, looking to put a little distance between himself and the minibus.

When he had a little opening, he took it. "Catch me if you can!" he yelled, starting to sprint down the street in the direction of the police station two blocks away. Expecting bullets to hit him any moment, he saw a banana waste truck parked up on the sidewalk next to a billiards hall, and ducked behind it. He watched as Caliche parked his motorcycle on the opposite side of the truck —between him and the police station—sending another man around the back. At that moment, El Diablo ran again, narrowly skirting by Caliche as he tried to grab his shirt. "Son of a bitch!" Cardona screamed, running down the street in a zigzag pattern so he'd be more difficult to shoot. "Why are you running?" yelled a startled friend as he careened past. "Can't you see, these sons of bitches are going to kill me!" he screamed back as he ran for the safety of the police station.

Meanwhile at the plant, the union leaders waited in vain for their friend to return. Finally, word came that he had been seen at his house escorted by police, staying just long enough to get a suitcase. (He eventually fled to Bogotá, and later the United States, where he currently lives in asylum in Detroit.) As the unionists took in this information, a company representative emerged to say Bebidas would buy plane tickets for anyone who wanted to leave town tomorrow. As they dispersed to spend a sleepless night, the paramilitaries were busy breaking into the union hall in a cramped neighborhood across town. They grabbed the typewriter and petty cash before burning the hall to the ground.

The next day, a friend appeared at the hiding place of union president Hernán Manco, to summon him to La Ceiba before he could go to the airport. He went to the soda shop resigned to die. As he climbed the stairs, the gate rattled shut behind him. Sitting at a table in the dark bar was Cepillo. "That kid was murdered at the plant because of you," said Cepillo. "The burning of the union hall was because of you. Tomorrow we are going to have a meeting at the plant," he continued. "Anyone who doesn't want to resign, well, we're not responsible for what happens." Addressing Manco directly, he added, "Since you are the president of the union, I don't ever want to see you again."

Manco didn't need to hear more. He and Giraldo headed to the airport to fly to Bogotá along with several other executive committee members. The rest of the workers assembled at the plant the next day to find the yard full of paramilitaries, including Caliche. They passed out prepared resignation letters, and one by one the workers signed them. In all, forty-five members signed letters or fled town. The union was finished.

The destruction of the union in Carepa wasn't an isolated occurrence—at least not in the minds of the union leaders. "From the beginning Coca-Cola took a stand to not only eliminate the union but to destroy its workers," says Javier Correa, SINALTRAINAL's national president, speaking in the union's Bogotá headquarters. Short and serious with short-cropped dark hair, he talks in almost a monotone, a stoic expression on his pockmarked face. As unions go, SINALTRAINAL is unapologetically militant, pushing for wholesale changes in the state laws to protect people and the environment.

"Our country, our resources, have been plundered by multinationals for over forty years now," says Correa. And yet, far from reining in the power of big business in the country, he says, government has just facilitated the violence against people pressing for changes, branding them as guerrillas. "What the government has done is to say there are no social movements—only terrorists," says Correa. He himself has received multiple death threats from paramilitaries and has been imprisoned several times as an accused guerrilla, each time found innocent. "My kids say kiddingly that walking with dad is like walking with a time bomb—you never know when something is going to happen," he says. "But I can't leave this struggle. The reality of the situation is that it's better being in a union than being without one."

In addition to the letter Correa and his fellow union leaders sent to Coca-Cola Colombia in 1995, a year before Gil's murder, they followed up with requests to discuss the situation after the murder with Bebidas's lawyer and with its majority shareholder, Richard Kirby. Both told the union they had nothing to say about the situation. Nor did the Coca-Cola Company itself, which later said it learned about the murder days after it occurred, but never provided support for the displaced workers.

Bebidas gave them money only for a plane ticket out of town, telling the workers they couldn't provide them any pay since it was the fault of the paramilitaries, not of the company, that they had to flee. Soon thereafter, they were all terminated for "abandoning their place of work." Since the day they had to flee Carepa, Manco and Giraldo have known little peace. "You have to leave your work, your family, your wife, your kids, your mom," sighs Manco, who has the chiseled good looks of a movie star, now lined and weathered with age. "You are used to a tropical climate, and you come to a city where it's really cold. You get old, you get tired." Asked about his family, he rubs his face with the side of one of his big calloused hands. "I wasn't able to bring my family here," he says. "We're separated now. [My wife] went with her family."

Giraldo has fared little better, living now in a small town outside of Bogotá with his wife and four children and working occasional jobs as a doorman. "If I get enough money to buy some food, I don't have enough money to pay bus fare," he sighs. "If I get enough money to buy bus fare, I don't have enough money to buy food." Even so, violence has followed him. Five years after leaving Carepa, in 2001, Giraldo was grabbed by two men on a bus and forced to accompany them to a house where they threatened him at gunpoint. They finally let him go, but not before telling him, "The next time we find you, we'll kill you." Since then, both workers have lived in constant fear. "We don't come out of the woodwork much," says Giraldo. "You don't know who might be waiting for you."

Asked if either of them ever drink Coca-Cola, they both laugh, breaking the tension for a brief moment. Manco turns serious again. "No, we do not drink Coca-Cola. Cola-Cola is death," he says. In the early days of the Coca-Cola Company, when a worker was particularly enthusiastic and loyal to the company, it was said he had "syrup in the veins." Manco turns that exactly on its head: "Drinking Coca-Cola is like drinking the blood of the workers."

Even while it remained silent at the time, the Coca-Cola Company has since vehemently denied any involvement in the violence against its workers in Colombia. "Conducting business in the current environment in Colombia is complex," a company spokesman wrote several years later in a letter to the United Steelworkers Union in the United States. "The loss of life and human rights abuses we read, see, and hear about in some regions of the country are sadly all too frequent and very troubling." Even so, he continues, "the recent allegations contending that the Coca-Cola Company has resorted to illegal and reprehensible tactics in the conduct of its business in Colombia are untrue. Accordingly, the Coca-Cola Company adamantly denies these serious violations regarding human rights violations in Colombia, and does not condone such practices anywhere in the Coca-Cola system."

On at least one score, the company is right: The situation is complex. Because of the franchise system of bottling established by Asa Candler more than one hundred years before, Coke has devolved responsibility for its labor standards to its independent local bottlers. At the same time, in keeping with the vision of international harmony that is integral to its brand, the company has established a code of ethics for its bottlers, upholding freedom of association and freedom from violence. The question is not only how much Bebidas's local managers aided paramilitaries in committing the violence against the union but also how much Atlanta knew about it and whether it did anything to stop it.

In its defense, the company says Gil's murder was investigated by Colombian authorities, who ultimately dismissed charges against the bottler. On paper, at least, the investigation into Gil's murder is impressive. The Fiscalía's Human Rights Office opened an investigation just a week after the killing, and over the next few years conducted hundreds of man-hours of interviews with workers, officials, and witnesses in an attempt to bring the killers to justice and determine what role, if any, Coca-Cola's bottling franchise played in the crime. On the first score—finding the actual killers—it came up spectacularly short. By the time officials determined the identity of "Caliche" as Ariel Gómez, he'd already been killed himself, gunned down in the street a few months after Gil's murder. Cepillo, meanwhile, was identified as Enrique Vergara, a henchman of El Alemán, who had been involved in some of the country's most notorious massacres, before disappearing without a trace.

Multiple witnesses attested to the fact that Milan had socialized with known paramilitaries. In addition, witnesses including two security guards and the plant's head of human resources said that the plant's chief of production, Rigoberto Marín, was also friendly with paramilitaries and known to hang out with them. According to the security guards, Marín let the paramilitaries into the plant, ordering them not to record the names in the visitors' book kept at the gate.

By this time, both managers had fled the scene of the crime. Milan had resigned a week before Gil's murder, citing "the health of my dear mother." Marín left six months later, resigning for "personal reasons" in a tersely worded letter. Prosecutors with the Human Rights Office didn't buy it. In September 1999, they issued an arrest warrant not only for Cepillo, but for Marín and Milan as well, declaring them under investigation for murder, terrorism, and kidnapping. The evidence "leaves not the slightest doubt that [Milan] and [Marín] were behind inducing and encouraging the paramilitary group to finish off the union organization at the company," prosecutors wrote, saying their behaviors "demonstrate there was a preconceived plan . . . leading to the dissolution of the union."

Both Milan and Marín declared their innocence, claiming that they'd never met with paramilitaries or threatened the union—in fact, they said, they'd been threatened by paramilitaries themselves. Milan said he had even agreed to pay money to the army post up the road in Apartadó, led by General Alejo del Río, for protection. Marín admitted that paramilitaries had entered the plant, but only to buy drinks; if they weren't recorded in the logbook, it was simply because watchmen were afraid of them. Meanwhile, he claimed that he'd been called to a meeting with a regional paramilitary commander named "Pablo," and been accused of collaborating with guerrillas himself.

With this new information, the Fiscalía reversed itself, releasing Marín from prison on June 19, 2000, on the grounds that it didn't have sufficient evidence to prove he was behind the violence. Six months later, prosecutors closed the investigation into Gil's death. The outcome was deeply disturbing to Gil's surviving family and union colleagues. But it is typical of the Colombian justice system, says Dora Lucy, an attorney with the Bogotá-based José Alvear Restrepo Lawyers' Collective, which has worked to combat impunity for paramilitaries. "There are a great number of cases where there will be all this conclusive evidence, but then the Fiscalía will say there's not enough, so we are going to have to close the case."

Of the more than 2,600 reported murders of trade unionists in the past twenty years, there have been fewer than a hundred convictions—most of those in the past few years. Much of that impunity can be traced to the political pressure prosecutors face. Right around the time of the Gil verdict, the power of the guerrillas was at its height, spawning a public backlash against any measures that seemed soft on terrorism. At the time, the attorney general's office was increasingly exposing ties between the army and paramilitary forces. In July 2001, the Fiscalía even arrested General Alejo del Río—the man Milan says he turned to for help—and accused him of colluding with paramilitaries for years in joint military operations.

That same month, however, a new attorney general, Luis Camilo Osorio, sacked the head of the Human Rights Unit and purged prosecutors he said were overzealous in prosecuting paramilitaries. He overturned del Río's detention, freeing him a month later. "Osorio did severe damage to the Fiscalía, and they have never really recovered from that," says Adam Isacson, director of programs for the Center for International Policy, a Washington think tank focusing on Colombia among other countries.

In addition to the allegations of ties to paramilitaries by the managers at the Carepa plant, there is other troubling evidence that Coke had a more than cozy relationship with paramilitary groups. Longtime National Public Radio reporter Steven Dudley—author of the definitive study of Colombia's civil war, *Walking Ghosts*—has reported that paramilitaries have deliberately set up their bases near Coca-Cola bottling plants. And in 1999, Colombia's respected magazine *Cambio*—the Colombian equivalent of *Time*—reported that officials with Coke bottler Panamco actually met with AUC head Carlos Castaño in August 1998 to negotiate free passage for Coke products in the Magdalena Medio, Colombia's largest river.

At the time, paramilitaries under Ramón Isaza were demanding a tax for transporting Coke in the region; when Panamco refused to pay, they prohibited trucks from making deliveries for four months. In response, Panamco officials reached out to paramilitaries through a human rights group to arrange the secret meeting. Sitting down at an AUC camp outside the Colombian city of Montería, Castaño reportedly chastised Isaza for holding up the Coke trucks. "Ramón, we can't turn into mercenaries against the multinationals," he said. "Our objective is the guerrilla." Isaza nodded without saying anything, but acquiesced to lifting the ban, after which the executives and paramilitaries shared a meal of chicken, rice, and Cokes.

On the one hand, the incident speaks well of Coke's bottler that it held out against paying paramilitaries, who were then committing some of their most violent massacres under the orders of Castaño and Isaza. On the other, it's shocking that the executives were secretly negotiating with a group that the Colombian government had declared illegal and the United States has since declared a foreign terrorist organization. "You didn't hear about any other U.S. corporations meeting with Carlos Castaño," says Isacson. "The question is, What did Coke in Atlanta know? Your bottlers are meeting with narcotraffickers to move your product, did this bother you at all?"

True, the company was caught between two conflicting groups in a complicated civil war that it had no role in creating. It's possible that Coke's executives—whether in Colombia or in Atlanta—truly believed that they were improving the situation by being there. If the Colombian government couldn't protect them from the violence perpetrated by two warring factions, why shouldn't they sue for their own separate peace? In Colombia at the time, however, there was simply no sitting out the conflict as Coke had done in other political issues in its past, when it had been able to "stand up and be counted," as one executive famously said, "on both sides of the fence."

"I don't think it's valid to say the state couldn't protect us, so we had to seek our own protection," says Maria McFarland, who follows the country for Human Rights Watch. "If you can't do business in a region without supporting a group that is supporting atrocities, you don't do business in that region." That's exactly the conclusion that the U.S. Department of Justice came to years later under the Bush administration when another company—Chiquita Brands International—admitted in March 2007 to paying $1.7 million in protection money to the AUC in Colombia over the course of eight years, from 1997 to 2004 (along with previous payments to the FARC for the prior eight years).

In fact, the company kept paying even after its own internal counsel advised it to "leave Colombia," despite making profits of $10 million a year. While the company insisted it paid the money to protect its employees, lawyers with the U.S. Department of Justice concluded the cash also fueled the massacres of trade unionists and human rights workers in the banana plantations of Urabá during almost the same time when the union was stamped out of the Carepa plant. "Simply put," the U.S. Justice Department wrote, "defendant Chiquita funded terrorism." In a deal with the United States, Chiquita agreed to pay $25 million in damages, even as it has remained in Colombia.

Nor was Chiquita the only company to pay off armed groups, according to evidence that has come to light thanks to a recent "peace and justice" law that offered amnesty or reduced sentences to paramilitaries who agreed to disarm and admit their crimes. "The companies that benefited from this war . . . had to pay," said paramilitary commander Ever Veloza, aka H.H., in his testimony. "It wasn't funds to kill people specifically, but with these funds we did indeed kill many people." Another paramilitary from a neighboring province described an arrangement with Chiquita as well as Dole that went beyond providing protection. "The Chiquita and Dole plantations would also call us identifying specific people as . . . 'problems,'" said that province's commander Carlos Tijeras in testimony released in December 2009. "Everyone knew that this meant we had to execute the identified person. In the majority of cases those executed were members or leaders of the unions."

A local businessman in Urabá named Raúl Hasbún, who was himself a secret paramilitary commander, told *The Miami Herald* that Dole and Del Monte coughed up cash as well. In addition, he said, the Colombian soft drink company Postobón paid $5,000 a month in protection money after the AUC started kidnapping its truck drivers. In one of his testimonies, Hasbún said Coke paid money as well—but later recanted that fact, saying he was mistaken.

Without blinking, however, he did admit to ordering the deaths of several members at the Coca-Cola bottling plant, including Isidro Gil, who he said in March 2009 was "collecting money for the guerrillas." The testimony was in some ways damning to Coke—after all, here is a businessman who admitted to extorting money from international corporations to kill people also admitting to murdering Coke workers; on the other hand, his testimony could just as easily exonerate the company, since he said Coke didn't pay him any money directly to carry out the murders.

Whether or not Coke was paying money to the paramilitaries to wage their war of terror, the company has clearly benefited, not only in Urabá, but also in other parts of the country where there is more evidence of links between bottling plant managers and paramilitaries. In the Magdalena Medio, for example, the lazy current belies a dark past—hundreds of bodies have been cut up and thrown into it over the past three decades. As the paramilitaries under Ramón Isaza consolidated their power throughout the 1990s, only the working-class city of Barrancabermeja was outside their control, an island of left-wing sympathies in a reactionary region.

As in Urabá, however, that was about to change. "The threats started in 2001, when the graffiti started appearing inside the plant," says Juan Carlos Galvis, SINALTRAINAL's vice president, who works in the city. "Some mentioned me by name, saying Juan Carlos Galvis leave Coca-Cola, written right in the bathrooms." Short and gregarious, with a sharp nose and intense beady eyes, Galvis arrives at the airport in a gray SUV with dark tinted windows driven by two bodyguards who stay with him at all times as he drives around town. As in Bogotá, the local union hall in Barrancabermeja (locally known as Barranca) is unlabeled and well protected with bulletproof doors, but the atmosphere here is more laid-back, with workers filing in and out, constantly cracking jokes, usually at one another's expense.

Galvis's easygoing demeanor fades as he sits down at the head of a long conference table, twisting two rings on his fingers as he talks. After he ignored the threats, he says, he began receiving calls at home, with the voice on the other end calling him a "son of a bitch unionist" and threatening to kill him. The callers knew where his children went to school, they said, and could act at any moment. While they didn't realize it at first, the union workers were witnessing the beginning of a paramilitary takeover.

As Galvis talks, the metal door clangs open suddenly and the local president of the union, William Mendoza, enters, guffawing loudly at his version of a practical joke. He nonchalantly takes off his button-up shirt and removes a pistol from a shoulder holster, laying it on the table. Mendoza's nickname is Cabezón (Big Head), he says with a smile, a name needing no further explanation. He's been with the union eighteen years, working on the loading docks, and can remember back to a time when the plant was owned by a company called Indega, which enjoyed an uneasy truce with the union throughout the 1980s. At its high point in 1993, SINALTRAINAL had nearly two thousand members throughout the country.

That's when the plant in Barranca was bought by a new company called Panamco, which had been operating in Colombia since 1945, gradually buying up most of the country's bottling territory as well as expanding throughout other South American countries. Back in Atlanta, Coke CEO Doug Ivester was pursuing his "49 percent solution" to finally get the company's bottlers under control. Coke acquired a 10 percent share in Panamco in 1993 that it increased to 15 percent by 1995 at a time when it declared Panamco its "anchor bottler" in South America, and 25 percent by 1997.

Over the years, Panamco consolidated seventeen plants in Colombia (leaving out three small bottlers, including Bebidas y Alimientos in Carepa), going heavily into debt in the process. Antiquated machinery and distribution systems at the new plants further drove up costs—to say nothing of the wages and benefits negotiated by the unions. Because Coke set the price of both the syrup that bottlers bought and the prices at which finished beverages could be sold, the company had few options to increase revenue other than to cut labor costs. Some 6,700 Coke workers were laid off nationally from 1992 to 2002, the vast majority at Panamco plants. In 2003, Panamco simply shut eleven of its seventeen plants, cutting contracts with its workers. That same year, it was acquired by Mexico's Coca-Cola FEMSA to create a new Latin super-anchor bottler.

Even as SINALTRAINAL protested the job cuts, they were in little position to put up much of a fight, as they were increasingly targeted by the paramilitaries, who accused them of collaborating with guerrillas to burn and steal Coke trucks. Mendoza adamantly denies the union's involvement with any armed groups. "In this country, anyone who thinks differently is considered part of the guerrillas," he says. "That was just a way for the company to get us on a list of people who could be murdered." Even as he says this, it's hard not to notice a portrait of Che Guevara that looms above Mendoza's head. The union doesn't see any contradiction in venerating Latin America's most famous guerrilla, even as it disassociates itself from guerrillas itself. "We consider ourselves to be a left-wing union. We respect the armed struggle," says Mendoza. "Sometimes the people who choose to use weapons can bring about the change we need in the country, but that is not the option the union chooses."

Even as the graffiti attacking the company intensified around town, Panamco provided water and soft drinks to paramilitary protests against guerrillas in the area. According to Mendoza and Galvis, company officials met directly with a member of the AUC inside the plant. Shortly after the city was taken over by paramilitaries, a former union member named Saúl Rincón reached out to Mendoza, offering to set up a meeting with a paramilitary commander to strike a deal—be a quiet union and don't cause any trouble, they were told, and they'd be spared any violence. After they rejected the offer, sure enough, Galvis saw Rincón inside the company talking with the head of sales a few months later. Eventually, he was arrested and convicted for conspiracy in the murder of a leader of the oil workers' union in March 2002. As he was sent to prison, he was identified as a member of the Central Bolívar Bloc of the AUC.

Meanwhile, in 2002, the threats against Galvis and other members of the union began to intensify. Galvis contacted the secret police, known as the DAS, which provided him with a security detail—but applied only to him, not to members of his family. Men began harassing his wife on the street, blocking her way and telling her they'd kill her husband. In 2002, when she was pregnant with their second child, says Galvis, a motorcycle blocked her way, shining a light in her face. Riding the bike was the paramilitary commander in Barrancabermeja, who threatened to kill her—and then her husband.

Galvis looks down at his hands, spread out on the glass top of the table, and absently twists his rings. "I felt impotent, because you are totally in their hands," he says. The threats on his family were the worst, he says. His wife began demanding he leave the union, and when he refused, the stress on their marriage was too much, exacerbating existing problems and forcing the couple apart. "We never could reach an agreement on that. I always said no," he says.

Galvis isn't the only one whose family members have been threatened. In the summer of 2002, several men tried to pull Mendoza's four-year-old daughter, Karen, out of her mother's arms. The following day, claims Mendoza, he got a call on his cell phone. "You son-of-a-bitch guerrilla, you are really lucky," the caller menaced. "We were going to kill your girl and return her to you in a plastic bag." He continued, claims Mendoza, by directly linking his actions with the union. "You are speaking out against what we do in Barrancabermeja and the alliance we have with Coca-Cola. And if you continue to do that we are going to murder one of the members of your family." Mendoza reported the incident to the authorities, and a human rights organization came back with an offer of asylum in Switzerland, which Mendoza declined.

Nevertheless, he couldn't sleep for a month after the attempted abduction of his daughter. "This is an innocent life and she is already getting death threats," he says quietly. "My wife said she got attacked because of what I do. It destroyed our relationship." Mendoza's wife eventually left him, as Galvis's had left Galvis, but Mendoza retained custody of their daughter, who is now ten. He sends her to school with bodyguards and forbids her to go outside. "Sometimes she asks me why she can't go out and play like a normal girl," he says. "But it would destroy me as a person if anything happened to her."

After the initial spate of violence, the threats against the union subsided somewhat, but not before Galvis himself was subject to attack. He was driving home with his bodyguards in August 2003, when he turned the corner to find a man in the middle of the street pointing a pistol at the car. One of his bodyguards opened the door to shoot, and the man started firing. After a few exchanges of gunfire, the assailant drove off on his motorbike, and Galvis reported the incident to the police as an attempt on his life. He heard nothing until 2007 when the attorney general's office informed him there was an investigation against *him* for making a false claim. According to police, witnesses reported that an armed robbery was taking place at the time, and the gunman shot at Galvis's SUV only because his bodyguard pointed a gun at him. "I am being criminally investigated for being a victim," he says. "It's a great way for the government to demonstrate internationally that we make things up."

In Colombia, making false charges is so common there is a name for it, *montaje judicial*—judicial setup. In the 1990s, the setups against union members and social activists were increasingly elaborate in the means they took to implicate the innocent. The charges against Galvis in Barranca, in fact, were mild compared with those against three union members fifty miles east in the city of Bucaramanga, in which Panamco bottling plant managers were directly involved.

In contrast to the beaten feel of SINALTRAINAL's headquarters in Bogotá or the gallows humor of Barranca, the union hall in Bucaramanga recalls an armed bunker. The Colombian Central Labor Council—known by the Spanish acronym CUT—occupies the building with several affiliated unions, including two rooms for SINALTRAINAL. Going out for a breakfast of black coffee and *arepas* (corn meal pockets) with his colleagues, the local president, Nelson Pérez, casually sticks a pistol in the back of his pants. On the way, the union workers pass a non-union laborer in a red Coke shirt pushing a cart stacked with sixteen full crates of Coke bottles up a steep hill. Every muscle in his arms bulges as he strains to get the cart up the hill. "He'll work a year before his back goes out," says Álvaro González, a twenty-seven-year veteran of the company. "After that, he'll end up selling fruit on the street."

González should know, since, at forty-four, he spends most of his days at the Coke plant loading dock, lifting those fifty-pound crates onto and off of trucks. González's smooth skin and slightly slanted eyes have given him the nickname "Japonés" among his coworkers. Skinny and smartly dressed in a checkered Tommy Hilfiger shirt, khaki pants, and leather loafers, he hardly looks like a manual laborer. Yet he started at the company at age eighteen as a janitor cleaning toilets, gradually moving up the ranks to syrup maker, he says, sitting down in a virtually barren room at the union hall to tell his story.

In the beginning, González had "syrup in the veins." Excited to be working for the prestigious American company, he put even the most rabid collector of the Coca-Cola Collectors Club to shame. "I used to have Coca-Cola memorabilia all over my house, because I thought I worked at the best company in the world," he says. "I had Coca-Cola socks, I had Coca-Cola shirts, I even had underwear with Coca-Cola on it. I never thought that I would think of the company in the way I think about it today."

When he first started, he says, he was a "spoiled brat"—he came to work early and left late, drank on the job, and no one cared. But everything changed in 1990 when he first joined the union. "As soon as I joined the union and said 'I think differently,' my whole life changed." First, his supervisor tried to talk him out of it, he says, offering him a higher-paid warehouse job if he'd reconsider. After the ELN burned ten Coca-Cola trucks in 1992, González says, his supervisors began actively harassing him, threatening to write him up and punish him whenever they saw him away from his post.

Without warning, González breaks down and starts crying. He grabs for a roll of toilet paper on the table, dabbing at his eyes. "This is just so difficult to talk about," he says. "They made our life impossible. To talk about this I live it again." The *montaje judicial* that made González's life a living hell started in the spring of 1994, just a year after the Coca-Cola Company had acquired a minority ownership in the company.

That morning, he says, federal agents from DAS showed up at work and ordered González and two fellow members of the union executive council to strip naked in the locker room and lie on the floor. As the head of security Alejo Aponte looked on, they rummaged through their lockers, telling them there had been a reported bomb threat.

Over the next two years, according to González, the harassment increased. One day in May 1995, Aponte called a company-wide meeting to show workers a device he said was a bomb, which he said he found underneath the carbonation tank. He showed workers another spot where a bomb allegedly did detonate, even though González says there was no visible damage at the spot.

Finally, on March 6, 1996, seven months before Isidro Gil was to be killed in Carepa, the last part of the plan was sprung. González was having lunch at the company cafeteria at the end of his shift when his fellow worker and union leader Domingo Flores returned from his job as a delivery driver. Just as he came up to the gate and called to his friend, four men came up behind Flores and jumped on top of him, wrestling his arms behind him. González watched helplessly from the other side of the fence while Flores screamed—"They are going to disappear me, they are going to kill me!"

At the time, forced disappearances were also common in the Magdalena Medio, and the executive committee of the union had been holding trainings to prepare for them. That was fresh in Flores's mind when he was grabbed, he says when interviewed a few hours later in the same room. Arriving right from work, he is still wearing the dark green pants and red

Coke shirt that bunches over his belly, a feature that has given him the union nickname Gordito—that is, "Fatty" (which in Spanish is more of a term of endearment than in English). Square rimless glasses sit on his dark, round face. Almost immediately, tears well up behind them as he talks, trickling down rough cheeks after he refuses the roll of toilet paper.

"I told them they were going to have to kill me, that I wouldn't be taken alive," he says. "That's when they started beating me." The agents tried to handcuff him but could get a cuff around only one wrist; it bit into his skin as they dragged him along the parking lot, spilling blood. As Flores was being dragged toward a waiting pickup truck, González says he ran to the manager, who went out to talk to the uniformed agents, and motioned for González to join him. As soon as he left the plant, however, González, too, was jumped from behind by two men and pushed roughly against the fence. Standing there afraid, González felt a hot trickle of piss run down his leg and into his shoe. As the men dragged him across the parking lot to the truck, he stamped his damp sock in a futile attempt to get it out. Thrown into the pickup along with Flores, González shouted at the top of his lungs for anyone who could hear him to call a human rights group. "Shut up!" Flores yelled at him. "You are just making it harder on us." "Fuck that." González hissed. "We haven't done anything wrong. If they want to kill us, they can kill us right here."

As the two sat arguing, another delivery driver and fellow union leader, Luis Eduardo García, pulled into the parking lot. García has worked at the company for thirty years, starting as a driver in 1978. For the last twenty years, he and Flores have been best friends. Both fifty-three, they share the same delivery route and even share an e-mail address. The two are an odd couple, García skinny where Flores is chubby, and fiery where Flores is gentle. When he began working at the company, he earned the nickname "Chile" after he got into a heated argument with a manager, and a workmate exclaimed, "Wow, you are like a Mexican chile pepper!" Even in death threats he is referred to by that nickname. Chile comes to the interview with an entourage—his adult daughter and his seven-year-old granddaughter (the daughter of his other daughter), whom he promised he'd take shoe-shopping and who sits silently as her grandfather details the atrocities he faced.

When Chile first pulled into the parking lot on that spring day in 1996, he says, he saw González in the pickup motioning to him. "What is happening, Japonés?" he cried. Immediately, an agent walked up to him and grabbed him, slapping cuffs on him and throwing him into the truck. The three were driven to the local police station, where they were put in a jail cell and kept for three days before being arraigned before a judge. They listened in disbelief as the charges were read: terrorism and conspiracy to plant explosives. A witness wearing a mask—a practice at the time to protect identities—fingered them, saying he had seen them bringing bombs into the Coke plant by truck and planting them around the facility. As evidence, the prosecution showed pictures of the two supposed bombs found by the company the year before. Bail was denied, and they were taken to La Modelo, the medium-security federal prison in Bucaramanga.

That was the start of a six-month ordeal for the union leaders. In Colombia, the worst thing you can be is an accused terrorist. The three were mixed in with guerrillas, paramilitaries, and common criminals, all of whom thought they had masterminded a plot to blow up the factory. "We couldn't trust anyone," says González. "I would cry every day." The whole block had only four bathrooms, which the unionists avoided anyway since they were frequently the site of attacks. "If you wanted to use the bathroom, you had to bring a soda pop bottle and a bag into your cell," says Chile, who shared a four-by-six-foot cell with his best friend, Flores.

At the time, González's daughter was only four years old, just beginning preschool. He used to bribe guards for admittance to a third-floor courtyard, where she could see him in the afternoons when his wife drove her home. On weekends, the daughters of all three prisoners stood in the street as they threw down notes wrapped around pieces of candy.

Life became more difficult for their families, as the three workers were fired from their jobs and stopped receiving income. When word came out about the accusations, their children were taunted by other children as terrorists, murderers, and worse. Eventually, they had to leave school for the year and began collecting cans on the street or begging for money from other workers at the plant. "Our friends would reject us and we didn't have any food to eat," says Chile's daughter, twenty-year-old Laura Milena García, who has sat throughout the interview listening to her father and his friends talk about their suffering. She, too, breaks down crying, wiping her eyes as her voice falters.

Throughout the interview, Flores sits with his head in his hands for long stretches, periodically lifting up his glasses to wipe both eyes with one big hand as Chile talks for him. In all, the three spent 174 days in La Modelo before the case went to trial in August 1996, just a few months before Gil was shot dead in Carepa. When evidence was finally presented, however, the case started falling apart almost immediately. The only witness provided by the company was the masked one, whose statements about how and where the union members entered the plant were contradicted by dozens of workers and official company documents. Moreover, the masked witness constantly contradicted himself, leading a regional prosecutor to declare that he would need to have been in three different places at the same time to have seen everything he said he had. Prosecutors dismissed his testimony out of hand as completely false, ending the investigation and allowing the three unionists to go free.

Still, according to SINALTRAINAL, prosecutors declined to press charges against the company managers who had accused them of setting the bombs, or even reveal the identity of the masked witness. In a civil suit against Panamco, a judge found the evidence inconclusive to hold anyone at the company to blame. "There has been impunity," says González angrily. "Everyone remains unpunished. There was a pardon and forgetting." Even today, the attorney general's office refuses to reveal the identity of the masked witness.

For the workers, however, being released from prison was just the beginning of their personal ordeals, as they started regularly receiving death threats against them and their families. In 2002, González's daughter, then twelve, answered the phone to a voice telling her that her "son-of-a-bitch terrorist father" had to give them 20 million pesos ($10,000) or they would kill his daughter. His wife left soon afterward. "She would say, 'You ruined my life, my family, my daughters.'" González halts again, choking back tears. "Everyone starts to distrust you, even the neighbors." As the tears flow, so do the words. "They want to destroy the union and because of that the collective bargaining gets worse, and the conditions for the workers get worse. I'm not a guerrilla member, I'm not a paramilitary member. I just have convictions that the country needs to change."

He suddenly explodes in a sardonic laugh. "You get so fucking pissed off by your helplessness that you want to put a bomb in the place and blow it up. You get in such an extreme psychological state you want to be a suicide bomber and just finish it off."

Despite the deep ambivalence they now feel about the company that tried to have them imprisoned for life, all three of them still work at the plant, every day lifting and depositing crates with the bright red-and-white Coca-Cola logo. Since the day he walked through the gates of the prison, González hasn't drunk a single Coke. As soon as he goes through the gates of the company, "I become another Álvaro. I look at the bosses and I know they are my enemies. We left the jail in 1996 and today it's 2008 and we are in another prison."

Whether the company colluded with the violence against the union or just benefited from it, the union has been decimated by the constant threats and attacks. In 1993, when Panamco began buying up bottling plants, SINALTRAINAL had 1,880 workers at the company. By 2009, according to SINALTRAINAL researcher Carlos Olaya, that number was 350. Much of the decline has been due to outsourcing of the workforce to contract or temporary workers, he says; from 10,000 full-time workers in 1993, the company now employs only 2,000. Most of the other workers are so-called cooperative workers who are responsible for their own health insurance and other benefits, and of course excluded from collective bargaining.

Even the direct workers have seen wages decline from a high of $800 a month to near $500. For nonunionized workers, wages are even worse—only $150 a month. In addition, workers have lost overtime and holiday bonuses. All of the consolidation and downsizing, however, has been tremendously successful for the company; Coca-Cola now controls 60 percent of the nonalcoholic beverages market in the country; with the acquisition of Panamco by Coca-Cola FEMSA in 2003, the country has been one of the new anchor bottlers' primary growth markets.

Despite the supposed demobilization of the paramilitaries in Colombia, however, the threats against SINALTRAINAL continue, sent from a new generation of "successor groups" to the AUC, which have picked up where they left off. In Barranca, there is a new paramilitary boss who is rumored to be the brother of Urabá's El Alemán. Death threats appear regularly at the union hall, slipped under the door or even e-mailed. "DEATH TO ALL LEFTIST COMMUNISTS—TOTAL EXTERMINATION TO THESE DOGS!" read one e-mail received in November 2008. "WE GIVE A DECLARATION OF DEATH TO ALL . . . TRADE UNIONISTS OF OUR BELOVED BARRANCA."

In Bucaramanga, paramilitaries kidnapped Flores's son as he was leaving his high school in November 2007, throwing him in a black SUV and pistol-whipping him before dumping him on the side of the road. Chile's daughter Laura Milena García was targeted in the summer of 2008, she says, when she was walking home from her university and noticed two men following her. One caught up and hissed, "Don't scream," pressing a gun to her side. Luckily she was close enough to her home to recognize a groundskeeper and greeted him loudly, scaring her assailant away. It's suddenly clear why Chile has brought his daughter and granddaughter to hear him speak—they need to know what has happened to their father because they are targets themselves.

"Now I don't go alone to the university anymore," says García, who on the outside looks like your average MTV-watching twentysomething, with a sparkly, midriff-baring shirt and big hoop earrings. Inside, however, she is clearly a chile pepper like her father. "When I'm at the university and a professor starts talking bad about unions, it really makes me angry," she says, wiping away the tears. "I say, 'What are you talking about—they defend the rights of workers. How many workers' rights are violated at his university?'" If there is hope for the union, it clearly lies in the next generation. This one is just struggling to survive. "I started working at the company when I was eighteen—my whole life," says González. "I was more sane when I was eighteen than I am now. They say, 'You are just resentful.' I say, 'Of course, I am resentful. You threw me in jail.'"

Back in Barranca, Galvis goes out with other union members to a café across the street after being interviewed, downing beer after beer while a regional blend of folk music called *vallenato* blares on television. Afterward, he asks his bodyguards to take him to the town square. A balmy wind rustles through the trees, as couples and groups of friends lounge at outdoor tables over beers and Cokes. Even the bodyguards seem to relax, one of them talking on a cell phone on the corner while the other stands astride the front wheel of a scooter in the park, flirting with a woman on the seat. An old man with a hunchback stops by to show us little metal bicycles he has fashioned from beer cans. Galvis takes the time to talk with him for several minutes, asking whether he has a family and how he hurt his back. The man explains he injured it falling off a roof, and obligingly lifts up his shirt to show it. Galvis hands him some small change without taking a bicycle.

"We must enjoy our lives," he sighs. "We can't just work, work, work. That is what the capitalists do." The constant pressure of driving around with bodyguards waiting for the next death threat has clearly gotten to him. "We union leaders talk a lot of shit," he sighs. "It is good to be self-critical. But we must continue to struggle, because there are many who get off the bus." He leans across the table with a hazy stare. Behind him, a waiter is rolling out a stack of red plastic Coke crates full of empties. "It is tough," he says, "we are on the brink of death, but we keep surviving. We bring in new members to the union, but the company fires them. If it weren't for international solidarity, we would have been eliminated long ago. That is the truth."

As in Mexico, the Colombian activists have responded to their perceived injustices by declaring a boycott of Coke in the country. Unlike Mexico, however, they have also been successful in reaching outside of their country's border to spread their movement to the United States as well. Starting with a response from the United Steelworkers Union, the movement has snowballed to the point where the Coca-Cola Company could no longer stay silent about the charges.

EIGHT

The Full Force of the Law

It's not hard to find the United Steelworkers building in Pittsburgh, Pennsylvania. Just past the bridge over the Monongahela River, it's the one covered on the outside by an enormous diamond-hatched truss of steel. Dan Kovalik is sitting at his desk in front of the window, framed inside one of those diamonds like he's on some working-class version of *Hollywood Squares.* Boyish-looking despite his bushy black hair and beard, he is a senior associate general counsel for the union, dealing with all manner of cases involving unfair labor practices involving steelworkers.

But Kovalik's interests are not limited to the concerns of his own union. A black-and-white picture of Kovalik with Nicaraguan president Daniel Ortega sits on his desk, taken on the eve of Ortega's election in 1985, before the socialist president was subject to a U.S.-supported revolt by the right-wing contras. Above his desk is a giant black-and-white portrait of a figure familiar in the union offices in Colombia: guerrilla leader Che Guevara. Kovalik, who grew up in a conservative Catholic family in Ohio, became, in his words, a "Latin American–phile" at age twelve after seeing a documentary about the killing of Archbishop Oscar Romero by right-wing death squads in El Salvador. By nineteen, he was traveling to Nicaragua with the Nicaraguan Solidarity Network, a group of activists who supported the Sandinistas in their civil war against the contras.

"At a pretty young age, I decided the U.S. was on the wrong side of the war in Latin America," he says. Over the years he traveled to many Latin American countries to do what he could to counter that undue U.S. influence, with its support for military dictators and paramilitary groups. He took his first trip to Colombia in September 2000, two months after the approval of a new infusion of military aid from the United States to eradicate the guerrillas and end coca production, otherwise known as Plan Colombia. Since then, the $6 billion the United States has spent on the plan has succeeded in helping to defeat the FARC and other guerrilla groups, but has done nothing to stem cocaine production, which has actually increased under the plan. To Kovalik, the aid was never about eradicating drugs as much as it was protecting U.S. oil and mining interests.

With that view in mind, he traveled to Barrancabermeja that first trip to gather stories of union officials, including the local president of SINALTRAINAL, William Mendoza. On his second trip, in March 2001, he heard about the case of Isidro Gil, which immediately struck him as a flagrant use of paramilitaries to rub out union organizing. "Here you have a guy killed within the walls of the plant by paramilitaries," he says. "He was killed after the manager threatened to wipe out the union. The paramilitaries returned, gathered all the workers within the plant, told them to resign from the union or they would be killed." In his mind, the finger pointed all the way up to the top.

"I don't think necessarily someone from Atlanta said do this," he says, "but it seemed like a combination of complicity and turning the other way and allowing things to happen." Whether it was a sin of commission by giving tacit approval for violent tactics to its bottlers, or a sin of omission by not taking stronger action to condemn the violence with the full weight of Coke's corporate power, it amounted to the same thing in Kovalik's mind. What was less clear to him was how the Coca-Cola Company could be held accountable for actions that were at best taken by a foreign bottler, if not the managers of a foreign bottler, in a foreign country, with its own set of laws and system of justice. Only months before, the Fiscalía had officially ended its own investigation into Gil's murder without even staging a trial.

Talking it over with SINALTRAINAL leadership, Kovalik hatched a new idea. If the union couldn't get a fair trial in Colombia, he would try Coca-Cola in the United States. And Kovalik knew just the person to talk to—a Washington, D.C.–based lawyer named Terry Collingsworth, who had made a career out of holding corporations accountable for not just freedom of association, but also things like murder, slavery, torture, and imprisonment in far-flung places around the world—the exact kinds of crimes that Coke had been accused of by SINALTRAINAL.

Together Kovalik and Collingsworth crafted a case in order to determine exactly how much Coke knew about the violent activities at its bottling plants in Colombia—and hold it responsible for any actions it had played in profiting from that violence. Just a few months after Kovalik's first trip to Colombia, in July 2001, the lawyers filed suit in U.S. District Court in Miami on the basis of a little-used law dating from the eighteenth century called the Alien Tort Claims Act. That law, they contended, gave them the right to sue Coke for crimes committed in a completely different country.

The road that took Collingsworth to court that month began in Malaysia nearly two decades before. After graduating from Duke Law School in 1982 and paying off his law school debts, Collingsworth set off on a backpacking trip across Asia. Arriving in Kuala Lumpur, he ran upon a protest of workers fighting for their right to unionize at their company, U.S.-based Harris Semiconductor, which had been exempted from collective bargaining by the Malaysian government. Impulsively, he offered to help them when he returned to the United States, even though it had little to do with his own dreams of becoming a lawyer who, like Kovalik, would defend the rights of American workers to unionize.

Although he now looks like the very picture of a buttoned-up lawyer, Collingsworth grew up in unions himself, following his father and uncle into a copper plant near his hometown of Cleveland. His job was to operate a crane dumping copper ore into a molten furnace, and he admits the union made it a cushy one. "My total collective work time was probably like an hour and a half a night," he says. "Looking back it's almost outrageous." He used his free time to get a college degree, attending Cleveland State by day and studying books in the crane cab by night with the goal of helping people like his father and his uncle who were getting increasingly squeezed.

By the early 1980s, it was clear that manufacturing was in trouble. The same shareholder value movement pushed by Jack Welch and Robert Goizueta was leading to massive downsizing of employee rolls and reliance on temporary workers or relocation of plants overseas in search of cheap labor. (Collingsworth's own plant eventually was moved to South Korea.) The protest he saw in Malaysia was the flipside of the equation—whereby developing countries were easing up on human rights and environmental standards in order to attract companies from the United States and Europe.

The question Collingsworth faced then—and the one that he and Kovalik would face two decades later—was how to impose morality on multinational corporations driven by economic factors that were inherently amoral. As long as competitors were doing everything they could to increase their own profits, taking moral questions into account in their business plans was a sure way of going out of business. At the same time, developing countries were in effect competing against one another to attract foreign investment to lift themselves out of poverty, giving them even less incentive on their side to push for more stringent labor requirements.

As it happened, when Collingsworth returned from his Asia trip he found a representative from his home state of Ohio, Don Pease, who was working on legislation to deal with this very issue. Pease's idea was to give those incentives in the form of preferential trading status to countries "taking steps to afford internationally recognized workers' rights" such as collective bargaining and a minimum wage. After it was passed, Collingsworth partnered with one of Pease's staffers, William Gould, to form the International Labor Rights Fund (ILRF) in an attempt to enforce the new law by filing petitions on behalf of workers around the world. Their very first petition dealt with the computer workers in Malaysia. Unfortunately for them, however, the law's language that a country could retain benefits as long as it was "taking steps" to change provided enormous wiggle room to companies and to the panel appointed by the Reagan administration to interpret the new law.

After years of getting nowhere with the countries, Collingsworth and his colleagues eventually gave up, and began to work on companies instead. With the second wave of corporate social responsibility rolling over corporate America in the mid-1990s, companies were eager to present themselves as responsible to the needs of the less fortunate around the world—as long as it didn't cut into their profits by disadvantaging them against their competitors. Collingsworth and other labor and environmental activists reasoned that if everyone could agree to the same standards, then companies could "do the right thing" without worrying about losing ground to competitors. At the same time, they could earn that much-sought-after boost to their brands by showing sensitivity to the social concerns their consumers cared about.

The idea emerged as a voluntary "code of conduct" that companies would commit to following for their factories and suppliers overseas. The idea especially caught on after university students began criticizing apparel companies such as Nike for using sweatshop labor to create campus athletic gear. In a short time, the issue was national news, shaming everyone from Liz Claiborne to Kathy Lee Gifford. As he would several years later with the soda companies over obesity, Bill Clinton mediated a compromise in 1999. Then president, Clinton brought apparel companies and unions together to agree on a new voluntary set of standards similar to those of Pease's law a decade before, along with a new nonprofit organization called the Fair Labor Association, to monitor them.

While Coke was not a signer to that agreement, it did participate more broadly in the "code of conduct" movement of which it was a part through other means, including the Sullivan Principles, a set of standards first established by a Pennsylvania minister in the 1970s in an effort to commit companies to racial equality in their doing business with apartheid-era South Africa. After the principles were ineffective in dealing with the issue (and, according to some critics, even counterproductive since they stalled the more powerful divestment campaign), their creator abandoned the principles. But in the midst of the Nike debate, they were reconstituted in 1999 through the United Nations as the brand-new Global Sullivan Principles, which committed companies to respecting freedom of association, paying workers enough to at least make basic needs, and providing a "safe and healthy workplace."

Around the same time, Coke took the lead in working with the United Nation's International Labour Organization (ILO) to create a set of principles against the use of child labor overseas and established its own "code of conduct" for bottlers that went further than either of the United Nations codes that it had signed. But these codes had problems. In addition to the fact that they were completely voluntary, Coke also interpreted them to apply only to companies in which it held a majority ownership. And thanks to Ivester's "49 percent" solution, Coke intentionally held minority ownerships in nearly all of its "anchor bottlers," which made up most of the Coca-Cola system overseas, and certainly most of the employees in places like Colombia who might benefit from those worker protections. With the increasing use of contract workers, many of those employees weren't even employed by companies in which Coke had a *minority* share.

Similarly, Collingsworth found the Fair Labor Association to be a bust. Whatever good intentions those signing the agreement might have had, the mechanism to enforce it was underfunded and weak. Nike reaped gobs of positive publicity, yet a 2005 report by the company found that workers in up to half of its factories were still forced to work sixty-hour weeks, made less than minimum wage, or were denied use of bathrooms and drinking water. "At the end of the day, it turned out to be a real whitewash," sighs Collingsworth, who admits to being at a loose end in the late

1990s, no closer to holding corporations accountable for their sins overseas than he had been during that trip through Asia.

That's when a man with the felicitous name of U Maung Maung walked into his life. General secretary of trade unions in Burma—a country taken over by a military junta in 1962, and known also as Myanmar since 1989—he told Collingsworth about an alarming new trend. Refugees crossing over into Thailand told horrific stories about being forced by the army to clear the jungle with machetes or search for land mines; those who refused were tortured, raped, or murdered. More shockingly, the work was being done for the benefit of two foreign companies—French-based Total and California-based Unocal. Maung appealed for help. "You're a smart lawyer," he told Collingsworth. "Here's a case where you can show there's slave labor, there's brutality, and it's being done on behalf of a U.S. multinational company."

However much he wanted to help, Collingsworth was stymied. The favored-nation legislation created by Pease had failed to create any meaningful changes in company operations, and the code of conduct movement had turned out to be a weak Band-Aid on the problem. And here Maung wasn't talking just about poor working conditions or subsistence wages, but about rape, torture, and murder. Obviously, the ILRF couldn't file suit in Burma. And ironically, given that Unocal was just six miles away from his office at Loyola Law School in Los Angeles, he didn't see any way he could sue in the United States either.* The problem was discussed with other lawyers for months, and it was finally a summer associate named Doug Steele who came up with the solution: the Alien Tort Claims Act.

The law is ancient to say the least, going back to the 1789 Judiciary Act that set up the U.S. federal justice system. In its entirety, it reads: "The district courts shall have original jurisdiction of any civil action by an alien for a tort only, committed in violation of the law of nations or a treaty

---

*A New York judge hearing a case against Union Carbide for its gas explosion in Bhopal, India, that killed more than three thousand people dismissed it as "another example of imperialism . . . in which an established sovereign inflicted its rules, its standards and values on a developing nation."

of the United States." Translated into common speech, that essentially means a foreigner can sue in U.S. courts providing it is over a violation of international law. The law's history is murky; apparently passed to protect American diplomats or possibly American ships from piracy on the high seas, it had been used exactly twice before 1980.

That's when a Paraguayan by the name of Joel Filártiga used it to sue the policeman who had tortured and murdered his son after the policeman had moved to Brooklyn, eventually winning $10 million in a wrongful death suit. Filártiga was never able to collect, and the policeman was shortly deported back to Paraguay. But the floodgate had been opened. Soon Ethiopian prisoners were using it to sue their torturers, Guatemalan peasants to sue their foreign defense minister, and a group of Bosnian rape victims to sue Bosnian Serb leader Radovan Karadžić, in the last case leading to $4.5 billion in damages in 2000.

While no one had ever used the law against a corporation, there was nothing in theory stopping them. The same legal precedent that established a corporation as a "person" for the purposes of owning property more than a hundred years ago in the Southern Pacific Railroad case could also be used against them to drag them into court like any other person who committed human rights abuses.

Not that it wasn't a stretch. To sue Unocal under the ATCA statute, the lawyers with the ILRF had to prove that the actions rose to a violation of international law, and that the Burmese villagers couldn't get adequate relief in their own country. Furthermore, no one was saying that Unocal directly raped and tortured anyone—only that they willingly aided and abetted the military in performing those acts. First filed in 1996 in California, the case was thrown out of court by a judge who argued that the company had no control over the Burmese military. That decision was overturned in 2002 by an appeals court that ruled it could go forward. Rather than proceed with a trial, Unocal settled for an undisclosed amount, without admitting any wrongdoing.

Nevertheless, the case was a huge victory for the human rights lawyers, giving them a new tool in their arsenal to hold corporations accountable. Collingsworth was elated. "We had tried negotiating with companies, but now we finally had a real tool to get their attention," he says. "Believe me, this is what got them to care about this stuff." The group giddily went about bringing cases against corporations for a grab bag of injustices around the world—among other cases, suing ExxonMobil for funneling money to brutal Indonesian dictator Suharto to protect its oil pipeline and a Del Monte subsidiary in Guatemala for meeting with paramilitaries before beginning a campaign of torture and intimidation of union members.

Back in Pittsburgh, Dan Kovalik had closely followed the burgeoning use of ATCA, contacting Collingsworth in 2001 to ask for his help in bringing a case against Coke. Collingsworth was enthusiastic about the prospect, accompanying Kovalik to Colombia in May 2001 to gather testimony. The two filed suit almost immediately afterward, on July 20, 2001, against the two bottlers, Bebidas y Alimientos and Panamco, as well as Richard Kirby and his son Richard Kirby Kielland, Coca-Cola Colombia, and finally the Coca-Cola Company itself. All of them, it argued, had "hired, contracted with or otherwise directed paramilitary security forces that utilized extreme violence and murdered, tortured, unlawfully detained or otherwise silenced trade union leaders."

The case was similar to those involving Unocal and ExxonMobil, Collingsworth and Kovalik argued, in that a U.S. company had aided and abetted violence for its own monetary gain—with one important twist. According to the union lawyers, even though Coke didn't directly conspire with the paramilitary forces that perpetrated the violence, the company worked through its bottlers to do so, which—given the tight control Coke had over the bottlers in other areas—they argued amounted to the same thing.

"There is no way that Coke didn't know that paramilitaries were infesting their bottling plants down there and killing union leaders," says Collingsworth. "When the first guy is killed, you could say, 'Oh my, what a surprise.' When the second guy is killed, you say, 'Oh geez, I hope that doesn't happen again.' Number three, number four, number eight. At some point you've got to say they knew it and they were willing to accept it as the cost of doing business."

In addition to the bottlers' agreements that spelled out in detail how they should produce and sell Coke products, the lawyers argued that the Coca-Cola Company's quarter share in Panamco, and two seats on its board of directors, gave it direct control over the company. As for Bebidas, Coke had so much control it could block the Kirbys from selling it. A year after Gil's murder, Kirby and his son Kirby Kielland told Colombian investigators, they had tried to sell, even lining up a potential buyer. There was only one problem. "I sought the permission from the international Coca-Cola Company to sell that company," said Kirby Kielland, "a request that was denied. . . . We could sell the bottling plant, land, trucks, installation, etc., of the bottling plant in Urabá, but we could not guarantee that the franchise contract we have with Coca-Cola would be transferred."

With that level of control over its bottlers, Collingsworth and Kovalik argued that the situation in Colombia was essentially no different from the one in Guatemala in the 1980s, when Coke intervened directly in Trotter's franchise agreement after political pressure from the nuns when workers were murdered there. In this case, the lawyers argued that Coke could have curtailed the violence, or, in an extreme case, severed its bottling contract with any company in Colombia it felt was violating its international labor standards. If it didn't, it was for the same reason that Chiquita stayed in the country for years while paying off the murderous AUC—it was simply making too much profit.

The Coca-Cola Company, of course, vehemently disagreed with that logic. As soon as the suit was filed, a spokesperson in Atlanta dismissed it out of hand, saying that "wherever we operate, we adhere to the highest ethical standards" (a somewhat empty statement, since the same spokesperson then averred that "the Coca-Cola Company does not . . . operate any bottling plants in Colombia"). Panamco and the Kirbys, meanwhile, didn't deny that paramilitaries targeted workers but vehemently denied any association with them. "You don't use them, they use you," said Richard Kirby. "One day they showed up at the plant. They shut it down, put everybody up against the wall, and started shooting. Now it has been turned around so that it's our fault."

The two sides first appeared in Miami for a hearing on June 6, 2002. Coke's lawyer, Marco Jiménez, began by arguing that the acts of violence allegedly committed by the company were not war crimes, and therefore had no business being hauled into U.S. courts as violations of international law. "For all we know [the paramilitaries were] moonlighting to go and take violence or action against union members not for any purpose related to the war, but for a corporate campaign of terror in order to get rid of a union." It hardly made a difference, responded Collingsworth, whether the paramilitaries were furthering their war against guerrillas or whether the company was simply taking advantage of the war to get rid of the union. "The fact that this war is going on and that leftist trade union leaders can be killed with impunity allowed this to happen, and Coke and Panamco and the Kirby defendants stepped in to take advantage of that."

As for the Coca-Cola Company itself, Coke's lawyer argued that it shouldn't even be there—since its bottler agreement with the franchise didn't control labor relations anyway. Frustrated by a lack of specifics about the actual agreement, the judge cut to the chase: "Shouldn't I have a copy of that?"

"I would like to see one myself," interjected Collingsworth.

At the judge's request, Jiménez said that Coke could furnish the bottlers' agreements with Panamco and Bebidas within a few days.

"Try to get here before five o'clock tomorrow," concluded the judge, calling an end to the hearing. When Coke's lawyers came back to the court, however, they claimed they didn't have time to translate the exact agreements between the company and the bottlers in Colombia. In its place, they submitted a sample bottlers' agreement, a boilerplate document representing the kinds of agreements it had with its bottlers all over the world.

Even as the judge deliberated, SINALTRAINAL received news of another murder in Colombia, when Adolfo de Jesús Múnera was shot dead on the doorstep of his mother's house in the northern seaport city of Barranquilla. Branded as a guerrilla after organizing a successful strike against a Panamco plant, he had come out of hiding for only a brief time to see his family when the paramilitaries caught up with him. It was a brutal reminder, if one was needed, that the workers at the Coca-Cola plants in Colombia still faced daily threats of violence.

In Miami, meanwhile, a new judge had been put on the Coke case: José Martínez. Known for his conservative opinions and his off-the-cuff style, he pleased no one with his ruling in March 2003. Essentially, Judge Martínez found that Gil's murder wasn't a war crime, since it hadn't happened during an open battle—however, it was still a violation of international law given the Colombian government's close ties to paramilitary forces. Score one for the union.

At the same time, he ruled that the sample bottlers' agreement backed up Coke's claims that it had no control over the bottlers. "Nothing in the agreement gives Coke the right, the obligation, much less the duty . . . to control the labor practices or ensure employees' security at Bebidas," the judge wrote. Because of that, Martínez dismissed the Coca-Cola Company from the case, at the same time he kept in the local bottlers—Panamco, Bebidas, and the Kirbys.

As Collingsworth and Kovalik celebrated keeping the case alive, they privately fumed that the judge had prematurely dismissed Coke Atlanta without even looking at the actual bottling agreement—or at least giving them the ability to question the Colombian bottlers to see if there were any differences between their agreements and the sample agreement. Frustrated with the mixed ruling in the courts, Collingsworth and Kovalik immediately appealed the case against Coke Atlanta. Procedural rules, however, required them to wait until the case against the bottlers was finished before it could go forward—a process that could take any number of years, depending on how many motions the other side presented. "We needed to figure out a way that Coke sees delay as bad," says Collingsworth. They found it—and so much more—in an aging labor activist by the name of Ray Rogers.

The attempt to hold Coke accountable in the United States might have died a slow death in fruitless hearings and procedural motions had it not been for Rogers, whom Coke eventually considered the biggest threat to its brand in more than a hundred years—and in some ways more serious than the fight over childhood obesity it was engaged in at the same time. The lawsuit might have made Coke listen, but it was Rogers's tactics—brash and confrontational—that made Coke actively take steps to defend itself.

The contrast between Coke's gleaming headquarters towering over downtown Atlanta and the office from which Ray Rogers has launched his attack to bring down the giant could not be greater. The Manhattan Bridge runs directly outside the window of his ramshackle Brooklyn warehouse space, drowning out all conversation every few minutes as the subway rattles noisily overhead. The dimly lit space overflows with file cabinets piled high with flyers, books, and DVDs, and the air is musty with the smell of the office's full-time resident, a long-haired crossbreed cat named Melvin.

Sitting amid the confusion this Saturday morning, Rogers is wearing a navy blue sweatshirt and matching sweatpants, as if he's just returned from the gym. At age sixty-five, he has a shock of white hair and the physique of a longshoreman, a fact he attributes to his earliest education as an activist. "One of the best things to happen to me was when I was beat up in the third grade," he says. After the incident, he took up weightlifting and boxing, and the next time someone picked a fight with him, he gave as good as he got. "I never liked the bully syndrome," he says. Only these days, he's the one picking fights—as a self-described corporate-thug buster. "There is tremendous imbalance of power, with corporations having far too much of it," he says. "What we want to do is equalize that balance."

Rather than use legislation or the courts, however, Rogers's favored tactics have been loud and contentious activist campaigns that target companies' financial connections and corporate image. In 2003, he was gearing up for his most ambitious campaign yet—an attempt to take on ExxonMobil over its failure to pay for the *Exxon Valdez* oil spill. Knowing Collingsworth had himself sued ExxonMobil in the past, he sent him an e-mail asking for help. Instead, Collingsworth called him with a very different proposal: developing a campaign against Coke. "Look, we've got a very serious life-and-death situation," he said. "But we don't have any money." Rogers didn't hesitate. He knew that he couldn't build a campaign against ExxonMobil without a boatload of cash. But Coke was different. "I said, you know, we could really try to build from scratch. There are some good elements that make it vulnerable."

Rogers should know. He coined the term "corporate campaign," now in common usage among activists, back in the late 1970s. The son of two union factory workers, he began working as a union organizer after college, including a stint with César Chávez's Farm Workers Association, whose members popularized the idea of product boycotts to pressure agriculture companies. In 1976, Rogers was working with the Amalgamated Clothing and Textile Workers Union (ACTWU) in their fight to unionize at North Carolina textile giant J. P. Stevens. He quickly ruled out a boycott, since few of the company's products were sold retail. At a loss one day, he drew a big circle in the middle of a chart and said, "That's J. P. Stevens." Then, getting more and more excited, he began drawing arrows representing all of its business and financial interests. With some research, he developed a list of banking and insurance companies, each with interlocking members on their boards of directors, who could all be subject to personal pressure.

He launched his new "corporate campaign" with a big punch at the company's 1977 shareholder meeting, when six hundred textile workers attended, bringing the meeting to a standstill as one by one they stood up to denounce the company, threatening that anyone involved with them be held accountable. Thus putting them on notice, Rogers moved against one bank where two Stevens board members served as directors, threatening to pull out millions of dollars of union money if it didn't dump the two executives. The bank blinked, and the two directors stepped down. Only emboldened, Rogers moved against insurance giant MetLife, which did a huge business insuring union pension funds. In a panic over the prospect of negative publicity, MetLife's president cleared his schedule to meet with the union, and eventually pressured Stevens to come to the bargaining table. The contract eventually signed on October 1980 ensured the unions' rights to organize, but only if they agreed to never "engage in any 'corporate campaign' against the company." Stevens employees dubbed it the "Ray Rogers clause."

Business advocates spared no criticism for Rogers's tactics, which they saw as little more than extortion. "Because Stevens can't be beaten in a fair and square stand-up fight, Amalgamated has now resorted to terrorizing businessmen who do business with Stevens," wrote *The Wall Street Journal* in an editorial. And they weren't the only ones who took issue with Rogers. Some union leaders as well derided his scorched-earth tactics as overly confrontational, leaving little room to negotiate. Throughout the campaign, Rogers constantly ran afoul of the ACTWU's own lawyers, who feared a countersuit on defamation charges. Rogers pushed ahead regardless, leaking information to the media behind the lawyers' backs. "What the labor movement has done that I really criticize is they have turned more and more to lawyers to fight their battles," he said at the time. "You can't confront powerful institutions and expect to gain any meaningful concessions unless you're backed by significant force and power yourself."

Rogers's tactics bear an obvious debt to the controversial father of modern community organizing, Saul Alinsky, the Chicago radical who published the seminal *Rules for Radicals* in 1971. In detailing tactics for successful organizing, Alinsky turned common conceptions of power on their head, arguing that the goal of those wanting to change the world was not to *fight against* power, but to *gain* power themselves. With that view, the morality of what was fair was a luxury for those removed from any real stake in the situation—or as Alinsky put it, "rhetorical rationale for expedient action and self-interest." For those in the fight to win, the question isn't what was right, but what is effective. Situations were always complicated and murky—a fact that corporations and governments always use to their advantage in shifting responsibility for problems—the way that Coke can always say that obesity is a complicated problem with many factors beyond soft drink consumption; or that bottled water bottles account for only a small amount of the entire municipal waste stream; or that Colombia is a complicated country with a long history of violence by conflicting forces.

"In a complex, interrelated, urban society, it becomes increasingly difficult to single out who is to blame for any particular evil," says Alinsky. "There is a constant, and somewhat legitimate passing of the buck." If an activist wants to be effective, it is his job to stop that inevitable game of hot potato. "Pick the target, freeze it, personalize it, and polarize it," says Alinsky. "If an organization permits responsibility to be diffused and distributed in a number of areas, attack becomes impossible." It's for this reason that anticorporate activists have tended to pick one company—usually an industry leader—to focus their efforts on. When it came to the evils of tobacco companies, Corporate Accountability International and others focused their efforts on Philip Morris. When it came to sweatshops overseas, United Students Against Sweatshops publicly shamed Nike.

Not only does personalizing a corporate target help crystallize a complicated issue in the mind of the public, but it also quickly leaves them bereft of allies, as their competitors (say Brown & Williamson or Adidas) trip over themselves to avoid association with the now toxic target. That is the principle that Rogers's newly formed Corporate Campaign, Inc., used to great effect after the Stevens battle, picking off other companies involved in labor battles, and in successful campaigns against Campbell's Soup and American Airlines.

In the mid-1980s, however, Rogers met defeat in a disastrous strike against the meatpacking company Hormel when he became the polarizing figure. After Hormel made heavy cutbacks in the midst of a national recession, the local union called Rogers to put on the pressure. Rogers butted heads immediately with the international union, which advocated a more cautious approach. When a judge forbade pickets at the plant, Rogers and the local went ahead anyway. Police called in tear gas and dogs, carting off more than two dozen people, including Rogers, to jail. Eventually demoralized, the union gave up their fight, and 650 people lost their jobs. In an Oscar-nominated documentary about the struggle, *American Dream*, Rogers comes across as a caustic carpetbagger, seeking confrontation and publicity at the expense of a more reasoned settlement with the company.

By 1988, *Time* magazine was referring to Rogers as "one of the labor movement's most controversial and innovative figures," writing that "while supporters describe his approach as a welcome addition to strike tactics, critics attack him as a glory hound who seduces local unions into pursuing his interests—publicity and influence over the rank and file—rather than theirs." The head of the local union, Jim Guyette, however, continued to praise Rogers—at a recent sixtieth-birthday party for Rogers, he gave a heartfelt tribute to his courage and personal sacrifice in the fight. Rogers himself lost everything and was forced to relocate Corporate Campaign, Inc., from a spacious office in Manhattan to a dark warren in Brooklyn, the predecessor to his current ramshackle office.

It wasn't long before Rogers found his footing again with several more victories against companies. By the time he got the call from Collingsworth, his strategy of going after interlocking financial interests was well established. From the very beginning, however, he saw a new weakness he could exploit in the fight against Coke: its brand.

The Campaign to Stop Killer Coke began in April 2003 with a letter to Rogers's Rolodex of union contacts. "We need your help to stop a gruesome cycle of murders, kidnappings, and torture," the letter began, bearing an image of a Coke can with—in the same expressive Spencerian script

Frank Robinson had so indelibly created more than a hundred years before—the words "Killer Coke." From the beginning, Rogers did everything he could to tweak Coke's brand image to highlight its culpability in the Colombian murders, producing posters with the slogans "The Drink That Represses" and "Murder—It's the Real Thing." One particularly gory image titled "Colombian Coke Float" featured a flared soda tumbler with dead bodies floating on top and the caption: "Unthinkable! Undrinkable!" Another depicted two blue, wrinkled feet, tagged with the words "Colombian Union Worker" as if in a morgue, along with the caption, "Ice Cold."

A parade of union carpenters carried the posters in front of Coca-Cola's shareholder meeting in Houston on April 16, 2003. Inside, William Mendoza, up from Barrancabermeja, challenged Coke's general counsel, Deval Patrick, to intervene against the ongoing violence against Coke workers in Colombia. The action was hardly more than a jab, but it was enough to get Coke's attention. Immediately, the company released a statement emphasizing all that it was doing to protect its workers, providing transportation, housing loans, and bodyguards for threatened union leaders. SINALTRAINAL was quick to point out that the company had nothing to do with those protections, which were afforded by the Colombian government. And still the violence continued, with the alleged attempt on Juan Carlos Galvis's life in August 2003, and the kidnapping and beating of the son of Limberto Carranza, a union leader in Barranquilla, the day after the union rejected a company demand to change its retirement plan.

Besides the new Killer Coke campaign, SINALTRAINAL released a list of demands—including that the Coca-Cola Company establish a human rights policy that would apply to its bottlers and compensate the families of slain workers. Watching the early splash of the campaign, Collingsworth saw it as just the kind of pressure the lawyers needed to bring the company to the bargaining table. "The Nike campaign in particular always burned me, because it had no end point," he says. "There was nothing you could say to necessarily end that campaign. I like the fact of tying the campaign to a [court] case, because the end point would be to resolve these issues."

The campaign was almost derailed before it really began, when SINALTRAINAL called for a yearlong boycott of Coke products in July 2003. Immediately, the International Brotherhood of Teamsters, which transported Coke products and was having its own union difficulties with Coca-Cola Enterprises, balked, fearing it would cost them jobs. In conference calls with the lawyers and the union, Rogers hastily concocted a new strategy he called "cutting out markets." While the campaign wouldn't ask consumers to stop drinking Coke products, it prevailed upon unions and other allied organizations to ban Coke from their facilities. It was a boycott in everything but name, and the media reported it as such, but the Teamsters were mollified and continued their support.

In the meantime, Rogers explored how he could attack Coke's financial interests, including its interlocking board of directors with SunTrust Bank, the descendant of Ernest Woodruff's Trust Company of Georgia, which still owned some 50 million Coke shares. Without any money to create a sustained campaign against the bank, however, Rogers was unable to create much momentum. But as summer turned to fall, the Campaign to Stop Killer Coke hit upon a new target to put pressure on the company's image almost completely by accident. As luck would have it, it took virtually no resources at all: college campuses.

Colleges have been centers of activism at least since the Vietnam War; even as unions were fighting downsizing in the 1980s, however, labor issues were hardly on the radar of the privileged, middle-class, mostly white students who gravitated toward global issues such as the wars in Central America or the nuclear-freeze movement. As environmental issues took prominence in the 1990s, unions were frequently on the opposite side of battles pitching jobs against the environment.

Then came Nike. In the campaign against sweatshops, students led the boycott against apparel companies on behalf of workers overseas. By the late 1990s, activists were making connections between environmental, labor, and human rights issues, which they saw as casualties of a globalizing economy pushed through by international institutions such as the World Trade Organization (WTO) and the International Monetary Fund (IMF) for the benefit of multinational corporations and politically connected elites. The backlash burst into view in protests at the WTO meetings in Seattle in 1999, when thousands of activists locked themselves together on street corners and skirmished with riot police and tear-gas-wielding National Guardsmen to shut down the talks.

The inevitably dubbed "Battle in Seattle" inaugurated the modern antiglobalization movement (or as some within the movement insisted on calling it, the "anticorporate globalization" movement). This time, unions were allied with environmentalists, marching side by side in Seattle with activists dressed as sea turtles under the slogan "Teamsters and Turtles Together!" After Seattle, a patchouli-scented caravan of activists and black-masked anarchists followed the economic elite to meetings of the WTO, IMF, G8, and Free Trade Area of the Americas (FTAA) in cities across the world, stalling much of their agenda.

Even after energy was siphoned off from the movement in the wake of the September 11, 2001, terrorist attacks, the new alliance between environmental and labor activists against corporate globalization held strong. It's that attitude students brought with them when they returned to campus in the fall of 2003, at the same time the Campaign to Stop Killer Coke was finding its feet. Suddenly, here was a campaign against the very symbol of American capitalism, accused of horrific crimes of murder and intimidation in a far-off country. Rogers encouraged anyone who wanted to run with the campaign to download literature and campaign materials from the Campaign to Stop Killer Coke's website. But even he was surprised when word came that a 1,200-student college in Illinois had removed Coke from its campus in favor of Pepsi after a student petition. Soon after, 1,400-student Bard College in upstate New York followed suit, on the basis of violations to the code of conduct it implemented for vendors after the sweatshop campaign.

It was enough for the Coca-Cola Company to take notice. "Unfortunately, Bard College officials appear to be relying on discredited allegations that have been reviewed and repeatedly rejected by courts and independent investigations in the United States and Canada," Coke spokeswoman Lori Billingsley told the *Atlanta Business Chronicle* (without elaborating on which investigations she was referring to). "There is no factual or legal basis that our company and its bottling partners were responsible for wrongful conduct in Colombia."

Despite Coke's denials, the college campaign really took off across the Atlantic when the 20,000-student University College Dublin scheduled a referendum on dropping its contract with Coke. With three thousand votes cast, the measure passed by fewer than sixty votes. Coke flew into action, sending in a public relations representative from Latin America to give a presentation in support of the company; SINALTRAINAL countered by sending Luis "Chile" García to present its side. When a revote came down on November 19, 2003, the campaign won by an even higher margin than before—causing the first serious blow against the company, and putting the Campaign to Stop Killer Coke on the map.

In a sense, colleges seemed the perfect venue for the campaign—a way to "cut out markets" in the one place that Coke was most eager to keep them in order to develop that key early brand loyalty. Meanwhile, Corporate Campaign could rely on a virtually unlimited amount of foot soldiers that cost it virtually nothing—a not insignificant fact given that the campaign never had more than a $100,000-a-year budget, compared with Coke's $30 billion. The college battle also created waves far from campus, as the media piled on Coke's alleged misdeeds overseas. Coke's hometown *Atlanta Business Chronicle* wrote a long, unflattering article, and business magazine *Forbes* ran a cover story titled "Coke's Sinful World" that mentioned the situation in Colombia. Rogers's strategy of publicly embarrassing the company was working—and the company only dug itself into a deeper hole when it tried to fight back. When Carleton College invited Coke spokeswoman Lori Billingsley to speak in the spring of 2004, Rogers was in the audience. When she repeated her assertion that an independent investigation had cleared the company, he leaped up, yelling, "They're lying! They're lying!" The investigation, he told students, was done by the company's own law firm White & Case, the same firm representing them in the ATCA case in Miami. "There's a moment in history that's very rare where students have the power to change one of the largest corporations in the world," he continued, urging them to boot Coke from campus. Following the meeting, the student senate voted twelve to eight to remove Carleton's Coke machines.

Meanwhile, students started campaigns at more than a hundred other colleges, lured by the opportunity to do something concrete about the overwhelming issue of global injustice. "It's something that students feel personally connected to, because it's something they can hold in their hand," said Avi Chomsky, a professor of Latin American studies at Salem State College in Massachusetts, the next campus to sever its ties with Coke.

As the student campaigns started to gain momentum, they rallied around the idea of a truly independent investigation into the Colombia murders that would determine once and for all the truth of the situation: What hand did local bottling plant managers play in fomenting the violence against the union, and how much and when did bottling heads and the Coca-Cola Company itself know about that violence. The stakes for Coke were high in such a scenario—agree to an investigation and it would be able to put the case behind it once and for all; but if something turned up in the investigation that was unflattering to Coke's image, it would cause a backlash even greater than the one it was currently facing, not to mention potentially open it up to hundreds of millions of dollars in damages. And in 2003, Coke could ill afford any more controversy. It was already fighting for its life in the midst of the obesity crisis, not to mention dealing with the fallout from its catastrophic dip in earnings after the death of Goizueta and the rejection of Ivester.

Given that context, it's surprising that the company executives actually considered giving in to activist demands on this point—even in one case agreeing sincerely to carry one out. When Coke's general counsel Deval Patrick was being honored as a civil rights pioneer by the legal nonprofit Equal Justice Works, the campaign saw an opening. Patrick had formerly headed the civil rights division in the Clinton administration Justice Department, before becoming a corporate lawyer for the likes of Ameriquest, Texaco, and finally Coke, which he joined in 2000. He was hailed as a reformer, trying to extricate the company from its legal troubles in the nineties with the channel-stuffing allegations and the frozen Coke fraud revealed by whistle-blower Matthew Whitley. Collingsworth sent a letter to his colleagues at Equal Justice Works criticizing Coke, which he said profited "from human rights violations while limiting liability to a local entity that is a mere facilitator for the parent company's operations." When one of the nonprofit's members raised the issue publicly at the awards ceremony, Patrick impulsively pledged to create an independent delegation to Colombia "so we could see that those workers were in fact organized and were able to be organized."

When Patrick got back to headquarters, however, CEO Doug Daft nixed the idea, telling Patrick in March 2004 that it wouldn't happen. Patrick resigned a month later, with *The Washington Post* quoting "sources close to the situation" as saying "the frustration played a role in Patrick's decision." Coke denied it, saying Patrick's decision to resign was "predominantly personal." Running for governor of Massachusetts a year later, however, Patrick said that even though Coke's internal investigations hadn't turned up links between the Colombian bottlers and paramilitaries, he had pushed for an independent investigation to give consumers "confidence in the brand." In his mind, he said, "either of two things would happen. . . . Either that independent investigation would confirm what we had found with our internal investigation, or we would find something we didn't know, in which case we needed to know and the bottling company needed to know it and deal with it." The company refused, he said, and "that's why I resigned." His devotion to principle, however, hardly stopped him from accepting a $2.1 million consulting contract with the company on the eve of his successful gubernatorial campaign.

Rogers takes credit for forcing Patrick out of the company—the first casualty of Killer Coke's corporate campaign. He also suspects that the campaign played a role in Daft's own retirement from the company shortly thereafter. Whether or not that's true, Rogers did at least ensure he went out with a bang. Unlike the tepid protests at the previous year's shareholder meeting, Rogers intended the 2004 meeting to be an affair to remember.

Rogers had a love-hate relationship with shareholder meetings. It was his one opportunity all year to confront his enemies in the ring, *mano a mano.* But he also hated the pressure of direct confrontation. He couldn't sleep the night before Coke's annual meeting in April 2004, and he was still scribbling notes as he sat in the audience in the ballroom of the Hotel Dupont in Wilmington, Delaware, not exactly sure what he would say.

At least he had a new weapon in his arsenal. Just a month earlier, a New York City councillor, Hiram Monserrate, had released a report from a fact-finding mission to Coke plants in Colombia. In ten days, Monserrate and his team had met with dozens of Coke workers and Coke FEMSA managers who admitted that it was possible that bottling plant managers may have worked with paramilitaries without authorization. Shockingly, however, those officials said neither Coca-Cola nor any of its bottling companies had ever done any internal investigations into the violence. The report's conclusions were damning to the company. "Coke has shown—at best—disregard for the lives of its workers," it stated, adding that the company "has allowed if not itself orchestrated the human rights violations of its workers, and it has benefited economically from those violations, which have severely weakened the workers' union and their bargaining power."

Sitting in the audience, Rogers grew increasingly angry listening to Daft standing at the podium. After he declared record first-quarter profits of $1.13 billion—an increase of 35 percent over the previous year—

Daft addressed the Colombia situation, saying not only that Coca-Cola was innocent of any violence but that no union member had ever been harmed on the grounds of a Coca-Cola bottling plant in Colombia. That was too much, for Rogers, who leaped to the microphone as soon as Daft opened the floor to comments.

"After months of investigation into Coca-Cola," he began shouting, "all evidence shows that the Coca-Cola system is rife with immorality, corruption, and complicity in gross human rights violations including murder and torture. Mr. Daft, you lied earlier today about the situation in Colombia," he continued. "Isidro Gil was assassinated, murdered, in one of your bottling plants in Colombia." As Rogers's voice boomed off the ballroom's high ceiling, Daft impatiently tried to break into his speech, warning Rogers had exceeded his two-minute limit. "Please do not interrupt me, Mr. Daft!" Rogers yelled, as audience members started joining in the call for him to be quiet.

Rogers continued on about the Monserrate report and the ATCA lawsuit, as Daft ordered his microphone shut off. Security guards moved in, but the former boxer wouldn't be taken out of the ring without a fight. "You're getting out of here," said one guard, trying to put an arm around Rogers's neck in a chokehold. "Oh no, I'm not," said Rogers, struggling free. Three more guards came to help, knocking out Rogers's legs and tackling him to the floor, knocking off his glasses. "I'm not leaving," he continued to yell, even as Daft pleaded from the podium for the police to be gentle. Finally, Rogers relented and they carried him out of the room. "We shouldn't have done that," Daft said to a fellow executive on the podium, even as more members of the audience—a fired-up member of the Teamsters, several student activists—repeated the call for an independent investigation into the murders.

To this day, Rogers insists he hadn't intended the meeting to turn physical—but he doesn't regret what happened. "It certainly got more attention," he grins. One person who noticed was B. Wardlaw, a descendent of a member of the 1919 syndicate and the company's largest individual shareholder, with 77,000 shares of common stock worth more than

$4 million at the time. "The cops didn't have to choke you and drag you off to earn my respect," he wrote in a handwritten note to Rogers. "But, hey, Ray, I certainly admire the way you handle yourself!" Enclosed was a $5,000 check to Corporate Campaign, Inc.

Meanwhile, major stories on the incident appeared in *The Washington Post* and *The Atlanta Journal-Constitution*, casting an unflattering light on Daft. And a month later, a new *Fortune* cover story slamming Coke mentioned its refusal to investigate in Colombia a "public relations nightmare." Encouraged by so much success just a year into the campaign, Rogers redoubled efforts for the coming school year—looking for a big campus in the United States that could serve as a poster child for the campaign. By that time, however, Colombia wasn't the only issue being talked about on campus. Rogers's open invitation to take part in the Campaign to Stop Killer Coke was taken up by a campaign against Coke in another country. While less sensational than murder, the allegations were potentially damaging to Coke's core business in one of its key growth markets overseas—India.

NINE

All the Water in India

The sun has yet to come up over the horizon as a boy pushes his wooden skiff into the current of the holy river Ganges. Already the city is waking up. Yellow lights shine from the tiers of steps along the bank, and men stripped to the waist and women in colorful saris descend for ablutions to Ganga Ma in a ritual as ancient as anything on earth. Nowhere in the world is water as revered as in Varanasi, the holiest city of Hinduism, where every Hindu Indian is expected to bathe at least once in life, and where, Hindus believe, to be cremated is to skip to the head of the line of reincarnation straight through to liberation.

Temples built centuries ago by maharajas from desert lands line the steps along the river, or ghats, where the sacred and profane intermingle now with the dawn. Tourists with zoom lenses watch from rowboats as ascetics smeared with ash strike yoga poses on concrete walls and *dhobi-wallahs* soaked thigh-deep in the river beat the city's dirty laundry against stone blocks. Ads painted on the ghats boast of guesthouses and bookstores, silk emporiums and German bakeries. Amid piles of trash and scavenging children, someone has painted in English: "Fortunate are those who live along the banks of Ganga."

Among all of the ironies of the river, however, the deepest is how much the water of this holy river is rife with pollution. The upstream side of Varanasi has a fecal coliform bacteria count of 600,000 per liter—more than one hundred times what's considered safe for bathing. At the downstream end, levels approach 15 million. Meanwhile, a toxic soup of heavy metals—including cadmium, chromium, and lead—flows downstream from the electroplating factories, tanneries, and brick kilns. All of that makes the Ganges, as *The Economist* put it, "a cloudy brown soup of excrement and industrial effluent."

It's not a lack of environmental laws that makes it that way—regulations in India are as strict as those in the United States or Europe. Nor is it insufficient resources or political will. Since 1985, the government has spent some 14 billion rupees ($300 million) on an ambitious cleanup plan that includes sewage treatment and chromium recovery. Sadly, the plan has been a colossal disappointment, beset by power failures and local indifference, lack of enforcement, and outright corruption. Nearly half of those who bathe regularly in the river suffer from skin diseases and stomach ailments, according to local health officials. The World Health Organization estimates that Ganges river water accounts for the deaths of 1.5 million children each year. This is the environment the Coca-Cola Company reentered in 1991 after more than a decade away from the country. The question is whether the company would follow the prevailing laxity in environmental enforcement or set a higher standard in keeping with the image of international harmony it so assiduously projects. As with water issues in Mexico or labor protections in Colombia, however, it has been accused of falling far short of the mark.

On a drive through the outskirts of Varanasi, the smells of diesel, shit, and curry assault the nostrils, carried through the open window of the taxi with a blast of 110-degree heat. For those unused to it, the humidity makes even breathing a chore. The car narrowly avoids countless collisions as it merges onto the Grand Trunk Highway, a chaos of cars, motorcycles, bicycles, and honking cargo trucks running clear between New Delhi in the west and Kolkata (Calcutta) in the east. Just as suddenly as it entered the highway, however, the taxi veers through a claustrophobic alley to break suddenly into agricultural fields. Water buffalo and wooden carts amble slowly past orderly plots of green wheat and sugarcane, pixilated with the bright saris of women stopping to weed and till. The landscape looks almost biblical—or would if not for the Bollywood music screeching from the Lok Samiti school in the middle of the village of Mehdiganj.

Several hundred people, mostly women and children, sit on blankets spread on the grass between smudged yellow walls. Onstage, teenage girls in saris of crimson, saffron, and cobalt shake their hips and arms to the Bollywood numbers, seemingly impervious to the heat. In contrast to Chiapas, there is no obesity here. The peasants live lean and close to the bone, and children sport the sallow eyes and sharp angles of malnutrition. After the dancing, the head of the school, Nandlal Master, steps up to the podium to congratulate the girls on completing a summer certificate program, with courses including candlemaking, sewing, and computers. With speakers buzzing, he announces the name of each girl along with that of her father, as one by one they rise to accept their diplomas.

The school is only the most visible project of Lok Samiti, which translates to "people's committee" in Hindi. "Lok Samiti follows the Gandhian idea of village democracy," Nandlal says after the ceremony, once the girls have piled into a three-wheeled pickup to be taken home. The air fills with the woodsy smell of burning cow dung, as the men congregate around a buzzing electric light. "Our idea is that people in the villages should have jobs and stay rather than go to the city, and that production should be done by hand and not by machines."

The villages around Varanasi are prized for their silk saris, and Nandlal himself comes from a family of weavers. His father died when he was only five years old; perhaps because of that loss, he in turn has become a father figure to some of the village children, teaching weaving skills and eventually opening his own school. Over time, the group grew into a one-stop social services agency, called upon to settle land disputes and domestic squabbles, and performing a group marriage ceremony for couples each spring. So it was only natural that farmers would come to the committee when they began having problems with their neighbor, a Coca-Cola bottling plant.

The plant here dates back to 1995, built by Indian company Parle to produce local soft drinks Thums Up, Limca, and Gold Spot. In 1999, however, a division of Coca-Cola India purchased the plant and almost immediately workers began clashing with the company over working conditions. As in Colombia, only a fraction of the workers in the plant—some thirty-five or forty people—are permanent. The rest, up to two hundred workers, are employed only on short-term contracts, allowing the company to save on pay and benefits. Unhappy with the arrangement, workers appealed to company management for a more favorable deal—the company said no.

The real problems with the company, however, began when the farmers surrounding the plant began to experience problems with their crops and livestock they had never had before. The day after the graduation ceremony, Nandlal introduces a group of villagers who have gathered under a thatched awning to tell their tale. "The first major problem was that Coca-Cola used to discharge this wastewater. It was reaching the farmers' land and destroying the land, making the land barren," states Urmika Vishwakarma, a woman who has worked with Lok Samiti to administer microloans to women in the village. "All the animals who drank it died; anyone who touched it got blisters."

Originally, Coke channeled its wastewater through a culvert under the Grand Trunk Highway into a canal that eventually made its way into the Ganges. In December 2002, however, the government blocked the culvert during highway reconstruction, spilling effluent into the fields. For months, the water pooled by the side of the highway, turning the fields into a rank, fly-drawing soup.

At that time, several villagers came to Lok Samiti to help. As they began to investigate, the farmers told Nandlal about a more insidious practice by which the bottling plant had been distributing the sludge from the plant's wastewater treatment—a dry, white-colored ash—to farmers as fertilizer.

After they used this ash, says Vishwakarma, "nothing would grow." Then there was the drought. The entire state of Uttar Pradesh—of which Varanasi is a part—began experiencing water shortages in 2002, when the yearly monsoons began to fail. But the villagers around Mehdiganj say that their problems began several years earlier, when water levels began to drop precipitously around the Coca-Cola plant. The villagers now gather around an open well in the center of the village, sending a metal bucket down on a rope some sixty or seventy feet. Only in the last few inches does it hit water. Another well nearby is completely dry—one of ninety-seven wells that Lok Samiti says have dried out since the plant began operation in 2000, nearly half of the 223 wells they have surveyed in villages neighboring the plant.

The villagers name a number of factors in that decline—including lack of rainfall and drought. But as in Chiapas, they blame also Coke's deep bore wells for literally sucking their land dry—exacerbating an existing problem if not causing the problem itself. Under the leadership of Lok Samiti, the villagers staged their first rally in front of the plant in May 2003, drawing only a few dozen people to protest. At the same time, they appealed to the local district magistrate, who ordered Coke to clean up its spilled wastewater and install a pipe under the highway to divert wastewater into a canal flowing into the Ganges. Not that the new drain fixed the problem; it just moved it to a less visible location. Across the highway from the plant in Mehdiganj, Nandlal leads the way through fields to a spot in one canal where a pipe protrudes. "There, that's where the Coca-Cola plant discharges their water," he says, pointing to an area where the water is scummy and green, with dried patches of white powder on the rocks.

A local farmer who lives a few yards away says the fields close to where the water comes out of the pipe are unproductive compared with those in other areas. If the water from the canal is used to grow sugarcane, it has an off taste. Once, when the plant restarted operations after shutting down a length of time, the canal overflowed into his fish pond, killing all of the fish he was raising for sale. Neighbors, he claims, have lost cows or buffalos. "I am not a doctor, I am not sure how they died," he says. "But they drank that water."

The plant itself is sectioned off the highway by two gates topped with barbed wire. Unlike representatives of Coca-Cola FEMSA, who refuse to even talk about their operations, much less show off a bottling plant, the local bottler Hindustan Coca-Cola Beverages Pvt. Ltd. agrees to a tour of the interior. Leading the way is Kalyan Ranjan, Hindustan Coca-Cola's external affairs manager for Northern India. Short and nattily dressed, he wears dark sunglasses and a permanent scowl. But he is also remarkably patient with a day and a half's worth of questions about Coke's operations—which is more than can be said about any of Coke's public relations representatives in the United States or Mexico.

The first glimpses inside the plant there are underwhelming. In the stairwell just inside the entrance, a Sundblom Santa Claus smiles from an old poster, his red suit faded by the sun. Farther along, the cubicles lining the corridor upstairs are dilapidated, their walls sagging. In the conference room, the tables are covered with peeling contact paper and are surrounded by red plastic lawn furniture and, incongruously, a black leather couch.

Sitting down on the sofa, Ranjan sighs and says the allegations against the company have been blown out of proportion. Yes, water levels in the area have fallen, but the problem is the persistent drought, not the extraction from the plant. "If the question is groundwater depletion, the answer is yes. If the question is whether it's the responsibility of Coke, the answer is no," he says. "The simple reason is we are the smallest user, so in that sense, we are the smallest contributor to the problem." Sticking to the corporate playbook of diffusing responsibility for the problem, he says Coke uses only 3 percent of the area's groundwater, while agriculture accounts for more than 80 percent.

As for solid waste, he says the company disposes of it at a government-designated facility, and has never distributed it for fertilizer. "We have never dispensed biosolids to farmers," he says. "Not an ounce, never ever, not here, not anywhere." That vehemence is surprising, since Hindustan Coca-Cola's own vice president said as recently as 2003 that the sludge was "supplied to farmers free of cost, as it was found to be a good soil conditioner." Another statement on Coke's website asserts that "since 2003, we no longer distribute biosolids to any area farmers for agricultural use," implying that up until 2003 it did, in fact, distribute sludge.

Ranjan does admit that the company had a problem with wastewater flowing from the plant, but says it lasted only three or four days, despite contemporary media accounts that say the problem persisted for months. Furthermore, he says, the water that flowed from the plant was treated wastewater, which should have been completely harmless—a fact that Ranjan says he will demonstrate after the plant manager, Sanjay Bansal, arrives to lead a tour.

Bansal shows the way to the pump house, where the plant has two bore wells—one with a capacity of 50,000 liters per hour, and a backup of 30,000 liters—for a total extraction of some 15 million liters during June, its busiest month. From there, a pipeline leads to the water treatment facility, where Bansal explains a seven-step process of purification, starting with the application of lime and bleach, continuing through a carbon filter to remove chemicals, then ultraviolet light to kill bacteria, and then successively smaller filters that remove any particles left in the water. From there, the water passes into the bottling facility. "German," Bansal nods approvingly at the Krones automatic electronic bottling machine on the way past a blur of glass bottles—the one part of the plant that looks identical to the Coca-Cola Enterprises plant in Massachusetts.

Finally, to complete the cycle, the water passes to the wastewater treatment plant, which looks surprisingly rudimentary compared with the shiny and complex intake treatment room. A catwalk leads over several open tanks where water is sprayed with ammonia to reduce the pH level and aerated in a froth to reduce the oxygen bacteria need to survive. The water is then filtered through tanks where chemicals and bacteria dry as sludge, while the rest of the water is pumped into holding tanks to be flushed out as waste.

A small laboratory full of test tubes and beakers checks the wastewater for pH as well as dissolved solids and biological oxygen demand (BOD)—a measure of dissolved organic matter that can lead to bacterial growth. A whiteboard on the wall shows that on the day of the tour all of these measures are below the standards set by the Central Pollution Control Board of India. To prove that the water can support life, Bansal shows off a small tank containing two ground fish, which he says are swimming in the same treated wastewater that will be flushed from the plant. "That is the ultimate test," he says.

Leading the way into the manager's office, he introduces a local farmer from the nearby village of Karipur named Dudh Nath Yadav. The bottling company has done a lot of good for his village, he says, giving young people employment at the plant. While he says the groundwater has receded in the past four or five years, the farmers protesting Coke have exaggerated the amount, which he puts at only fifteen feet. "They don't have too much support," he says of the protesters. Ranjan chimes in, insisting that he has never seen more than 150 people protesting in front of the plant, half of them from the Lok Samiti school.

Of all of the claims that Ranjan makes, the idea that protesters have very little support is the most easily contradicted. Photos, eyewitness accounts, and independent news reports have documented thousands of people at a time protesting in front of the plant in Mehdiganj. And that is neither the first nor the only place that Coke has met opposition in the country. In fact, not since France after World War II has any country shown such vehement opposition to Coke on so many fronts, part of a rocky history that has beset the company for decades.

Coke first entered India in 1958—back when the recently independent country was openly welcoming the investment of foreign corporations. In short order, Coke became the dominant soft drink in the market. The mood of the country changed in the 1970s, however, when a lingering mistrust of foreign powers led to a backlash against multinationals. Then Parliament passed a law requiring companies to divest at least 60 percent of their shares to local investors. Despite the fact that some twenty-two bottling plants were already majority-owned by Indians, the

Coca-Cola Export Company that supplied them with syrup was not. Not only did the government demand divestment from the syrup plant, it also required Coke to divulge the recipe for the secret formula, an obvious deal-breaker for the company. Coke's executives from John Pemberton to Robert Woodruff hadn't spent so much time imbuing the secret formula with such totemlike secrecy only to throw all of that away for the sake of one country. Reluctantly, Coke packed up and left in 1977.

Into the breach came Thums Up, a drier and fruitier cola made by the Indian company Parle that quickly snatched up the market Coke had left behind. The tide turned back in the 1990s, however; with the new globalization fostered by the WTO and IMF, countries were told that the key to prosperity was privatizing industry and reducing barriers to foreign investment. India relaxed its ownership guidelines, and Coke began exploring a return to the country—which it did in a big way in 1993. Facing opposition from Parle, however, Coke simply bought up the company, along with its brands.

Initially, Coke set out to create an anchor bottler similar to other parts of the world—but it ran into resistance from the bottlers already existing in the country, which refused to sell out or merge. By 1997, Coke shifted tack to build its own bottling system under a new entity called Hindustan Coca-Cola Beverages Pvt. Ltd., which now directly runs approximately half of the bottling plants in the country. The Indian government allowed the company under the stipulation that at least 49 percent of shares would be sold to Indian shareholders by July 2002.

Almost from the beginning, Coke's return to India was a disaster. Soft drinks had never caught on much in India outside an urban middle class that made up only 10 percent of the population. In the rural areas, people still drank traditional beverages such as coconut water, tea, and yogurt-based lassi. By 2002, per-caps in India were dismal, at just 6 bottles per person per year, compared with 17 in Pakistan, 73 in Thailand, and 173 in the Philippines. Making matters worse, Coke made the poor decision to kill the popular Thums Up brand and substitute Coke instead. The push failed, opening up more room for the ascension of Pepsi. Now Thums

Up and Pepsi both command 20 percent of the market, while Coke languishes in third place with 11 percent, despite lavish ad campaigns featuring Bollywood film stars.

Pleading poverty, Coca-Cola India asked the government for a stay of execution in divesting its shares in Hindustan Beverages, arguing it would lead to a fire sale in shares that would hurt the company's all-important brand image. The government granted it, even as the national and foreign press slammed Coke for reneging on its promise. Now, seven years after the deadline, only 10 percent of the company is Indian-owned.

Already in 2001, however, Coke's fortunes were beginning to change, first with a new strategy to divide the market into two separate parts. Sophisticated urbanites were sold an aspirational campaign invoking an upscale American way of life, with the tagline "life as it should be." Meanwhile in the rural market, the company pushed the simpler slogan "Coke means cold" to appeal to a generic love of cold drinks in the steamy backwaters of the country. Akin to its strategy in Mexico, Coke also marketed a smaller bottle for half the price in rural areas. The gambit began to show promise. Volume grew by nearly 40 percent in 2002, with the company breaking even for the first time since reentry. Business, it seemed, had finally turned a corner. Then all hell broke loose.

The first rumblings of what would grow into a national condemnation of Coca-Cola began not in Mehdiganj but in a sleepy village in the southern state of Kerala. Once known as the Malabar Coast, Kerala is a sliver of land in southwestern India, just seventy-five miles across at its widest, sandwiched between the ocean and a craggy mountain chain known as the Western Ghats.

Thanks to the wall of mountains, the state gets more rain than any other in India. Compared with the heat and frenzy of Varanasi, the air here is fresh and cool by late June after the monsoons have hit. Everything is lush and green, framed by picturesque mountain peaks with mist curling around their middles. As in Chiapas, however, all of the abundance can be misleading. Water is unevenly distributed in the state, with some areas in a "rain shadow" behind a mountain peak getting half of the rainfall of a village just a few miles away.

That is the case in Plachimada, where Hindustan Coca-Cola decided to build a bottling plant that began operation in March 2000. The company sank six bore wells to take advantage of the village's seemingly ample groundwater. Excited by the possibility of jobs, both the state and the local village council, the Perumatty Panchayat, fast-tracked approval.

"When Coca-Cola first started, people were very happy," says Ajayan, convener of the Plachimada Solidarity Committee, who grew up a few miles from here but now lives in the southern city of Trivandrum. (Like many Indians, he goes by only one name.) As in Mehdiganj, however, the villagers very quickly changed their tune, when their wells started drying up and their water started being polluted. Driving past palm trees and rice paddies, Ajayan slows the car slightly to point out the gates of the plant. Rising thirty feet above the green undergrowth, a twisted metal frame is now all that remains of the sign where Hindustan Coca-Cola once hung. "Many villages have boycotted Coca-Cola, [but] nowhere in the world has a Coca-Cola unit but Plachimada," Ajayan says proudly.

The resistance that led to that closing started in earnest in 2002, led by a shrunken sexagenarian named Mailamma, who passed away a few years ago. Ajayan pulls off the road and leads the way down a path of red earth lined with brick walls to Mailamma's home. In what is becoming a familiar ritual, he shows off the well in her front yard, empty except for a few feet of brackish water. Along with the lack of water, Mailamma and others started noticing a bitter taste to the water they did have. A teacher at a nearby school found that her students were increasingly absent because of stomach ailments and skin rashes, or late because they were sent farther and farther away to fetch drinkable water. Others discovered that the water turned rice brown when used for cooking, or that baths caused itching that lasted for days. As in Mehdiganj, the villagers also allege that the company distributed sludge for use as fertilizer, causing coconuts to shrink and turn yellow.

The problems with the water continue to this day—as evidenced by clusters of bright plastic jugs sitting by the roadside, which are filled every week by trucks the government has forced Coke to provide to bring in clean water. Even so, say residents, there is never enough water to get through the week, so they are forced to continue to use well water—when that is available. A well in the center of the village, just a few feet from the plant, is almost dry, despite the fact that the plant closed more than four years ago. The hand pumps nearby have only recently started to work again, but the water is still polluted. "You taste the water, you'll see," Ajayan urges, pumping the handle a dozen times before water comes out in a trickle. Sure enough, it tastes clean enough at first, but within a few seconds it leaves a bitter aftertaste difficult to describe—like lime with a slightly metallic or sulfurous undertone that clings to the back of the tongue for hours. According to Ajayan, this is a vast improvement from how the water used to taste, back when the community was spurred to action.

Coke hardly could have picked a worse place in India to set up shop than Plachimada. Like Chiapas in Mexico, Kerala has long been a state apart in India, setting up a socialist government in the 1950s and now trading political power between two left-leaning coalitions. The state's social consciousness has led to a literacy rate of over 90 percent, and health stats far above the national average. On the other hand, the antibusiness climate had led to high unemployment, and given Kerala a reputation of little more than a haven for restless trade unions and righteous NGOs.

Coinciding with Coke's arrival, Kerala had also seen a surge in political consciousness of India's indigenous people, the Adivasis, who had won a huge victory in October 2001, when the state returned a portion of their ancestral lands. Emboldened by their newfound political muscle, some Adivasis from Plachimada turned their attentions to the Coke plant. After the problems with water started emerging, some urged to shut the plant down by force. A leftist intellectual who had advised the community in the land campaign, however, urged patience, worried the village would face a backlash if it resorted to violence. "I told them their strength was in the local, but their weakness was in not being able to reach out of the local," says C. R. Bijoy. "We had to make the local space a space of struggle."

Under the leadership of Mailamma and an Adivasi tribal chief, Veloor Swaminathan, that is exactly what they did, constructing a forty-foot thatched-roof hut directly across from the plant, which still exists in perfect repair, hung with framed pictures of Gandhi at his spinning wheel among propaganda posters. There they settled in for an around-the-clock sit-in that eventually lasted more than four years and has since been used as a textbook study for how a small group of citizens with limited resources can take down a rich multinational.

At each stage of the protest, the villagers worked with what they had, to gather first evidence, and then support, and gradually expand locally, nationally, and even internationally. From the beginning they sought to legitimize their experience with hard evidence. Sending the water out to a local lab, they were validated to find levels of dissolved minerals so high it was "unfit for human consumption, domestic use (bathing and washing), and for irrigation."

Armed with that science, the villagers demanded that the local council, the Perumatty Panchayat, cancel the plant's license to operate. But the council dragged its feet in the face of Coke's own tests contradicting the villagers' claims of water depletion and pollution. "In the beginning we were not against the plant, because so many people were getting employment," admits former village council president A. Krishnan. "We told them we cannot take any action without investigating."

By now, protests in front of the plant attracted hundreds—and on some days, thousands—of people. As word spread, outside groups such as the Indian branch of Greenpeace used the situation to decry the liberalization of the Indian economy as a cautionary tale of the evils of globalization, adding their own foot soldiers to the protest. The village was fast becoming an activist carnival. For each outside group, villagers would show off their depleted wells, let them taste the water, show them the failed attempts to boil rice. Sympathetic stories in the media followed, emphasizing the David versus Goliath aspects of the story, and day by day political pressure grew.

Eventually, both of the state's two communist parties declared their support for the villagers. Coke maintained the support of the mainstream Congress Party, which then controlled Kerala's parliament, and the left-of-center Janata Dal (Secular) Party, which controlled the local village council. But the *panchayat* was wavering in the face of the activist occupation of the village—and Coke itself pushed it over the edge when they rebuffed the council's request for information to dispute the activists' claims. "They were just too arrogant," says Krishnan. "They said we've already talked to the big guys, we don't need to talk to you guys."

Stung by the response, the *panchayat* reversed itself, revoking the plant's operating license on April 9, 2003, a year after the protest had begun. The stage was set for a showdown with the state government, which still supported the company. Just at that moment, in July 2003, a BBC radio crew appeared on the scene and dramatically changed the game. Told by farmers that Coke had distributed solid waste as fertilizer, the crew took a sample back to analyze its nutrient content to see if it actually could be used to help grow crops.

No one expected the results they found. The tests from the University of Exeter revealed not only that the sludge was useless as fertilizer, but also that it contained dangerous levels of the toxic heavy metals lead and cadmium. Samples taken from a nearby well also found toxic levels of lead and cadmium, which is known to cause prostate and kidney cancer with prolonged exposure.

The news report rocked the country, from Plachimada to Mehdiganj. After years of anecdotal reports that the sludge was harmful to livestock and crop production, here at last was proof from an internationally respected news agency. India has long had a double standard about Western foreign countries. On one hand, the long shame of colonialism has created a fierce animosity toward foreign influences—evidenced by the early backlash against Coke. On the other hand, the long period of British rule has created an almost reflexive deference to foreigners. While the tests by the Indian company hadn't resonated, the evidence from a respected British university couldn't be ignored.

Shamed before the international press, the Kerala Pollution Control Board did its own tests, concluding within a week that Coke's sludge contained levels of cadmium four times the tolerable limit of 50 milligrams per kilogram. The following day, the Janata Dal Party held a joint press conference with the *panchayat.* Not only did it support the local government in revoking the license, party officials said, but it also vowed to pursue legal action to close down the plant.

In the midst of this controversy, Coke was blindsided by the release of another report that helped turn the growing local backlash into a national movement. A month after the BBC report, on August 5, 2003, a Delhi-based environmental group called the Centre for Science and Environment (CSE) called a press conference on a sweltering day in the nation's capital to announce to a crowded room of journalists that soft drinks around the country contained dangerous levels of pesticides. Coca-Cola, it reported, contained residues of DDT and malathion forty-five times the European standards. (Pepsi, too, was called out, for containing pesticides at thirty-seven times the European standards.)

The issue struck directly at the heart of urban India, where the majority of soft drinks were consumed. No longer was this a question of stealing water from poor farmers, this was a company poisoning everyone. Indian consumers, the findings implied, were not worth the same care that companies lavished on consumers in the United States and Europe where Coke was pesticide-free. Coke's famous promise that its products were the same everywhere in the world had been exposed as a lie.

The day after the announcement, national pride kicked in. India's right-wing Parliament immediately banned the sale of soft drinks in its cafeteria, while protesters in Mumbai (Bombay) symbolically broke Coke bottles and trampled on logo-bearing cups. Elsewhere, angry Indians tore down posters of Bollywood film stars Aamir Khan and Kareena Kapoor, who'd just signed endorsement deals with the company. The reaction from the industry was swift, if cynical. "Within days, Coke's men from the Hong Kong group office were in Delhi to personally assess the situation," wrote Nantoo Banerjee, Coke's former head of public relations, in a scathing tell-all about his former company. "The key message was: manage Parliament, manage ministers, and manage media. . . . To them, everything in India appeared to be 'manageable' with money and connections." Led by Coca-Cola India, the soft drink industry published a full-page ad in India's English-language newspapers stating on the basis of its own tests "we can safely assert that there is no contamination or toxicity whatsoever in our brand of beverages." The facility CSE used to measure its own tests, the company went on to say, was not accredited highly enough, causing the tests to be hopelessly flawed.

The PR campaign did nothing to dim the public fury—sales of Coke plummeted more than 30 percent in just two weeks. The final blow came when a Joint Parliamentary Committee backed up CSE's findings, saying its study was "correct on the presence of pesticide residues in . . . branded products of Coca-Cola." The company changed courses to diffuse blame. Rather than claiming its drinks did not contain pesticides, it now argued it wasn't their fault if they *did*, since hazardous chemicals were endemic to the Indian food and water supply. If the government didn't enforce its environmental regulations, then how could the company be expected to abide by them? Coke, they argued, has just been singled out to further CSE's own political agenda, exploiting the fact they were a foreign company to sway public opinion.

CSE's Kushal Yadav, however, disputes Coke's contention that "everything has pesticides." In fact, he says, tests on fruits, vegetables, and sugar found relatively few cases of pesticide contamination. If soft drinks were contaminated, he concluded, it was from the groundwater that Coke was not cleaning—despite the state-of-the-art water-intake treatment system that the company now shows off at its plant in Mehdiganj.

Whatever the cause, the pesticide story garnered more anti-Coke press in a week than the struggles around groundwater depletion and contamination had in over a year. Coke's most valuable asset—its brand—had been tarnished, and its reputation called into question. A public that had mostly ignored a problem affecting the very livelihood of some of the world's most desperate people had been galvanized by contamination of a daily treat for the middle class. On the other hand, if it weren't for the pesticide situation, the overmatched villagers fighting Coke plants in Kerala may never have achieved the opening for national—and international—recognition.

"On the contrary," says Yadav. The pesticide issue "brought out in the open the other issues. Groundwater depletion, groundwater pollution, all of these issues came to the fore." And in the summer of 2003, they began emerging in Coke's home country as well, as the situation in India garnered more and more press in the United States—mostly through the work of one Indian-American activist who worked tirelessly to raise the issue.

Amit Srivastava was born in the United States, when his father, a business management professor, was on a sabbatical at the University of Illinois. His parents were originally from the Indian state of Bihar, a few hundred miles east of Varanasi. He spent his childhood in Tanzania and India, getting a crash course in poverty before going back to Illinois for high school. Originally, he entered the University of Illinois for computer engineering but felt increasingly under pressure to *do*, not to learn. "I realized very quickly I was never cut out for college work," he says in a taxi, speeding through the agricultural fields outside Varanasi. After his nontraditional upbringing, he never lost a sense of outrage wherever he saw exploitation in his adopted homeland. He dropped out of college and began traveling around the country to organize college students to fight for environmental justice in their communities—frequently involving big corporations he accused of polluting the environment and exploiting people.

Now sporting a ponytail and baseball cap, he looks like he is hardly out of college, despite his forty-four years of age. Back in the 1980s and 1990s, he was frustrated by a lack of awareness of the environmental justice issues he was pushing. Environmentalism then was about saving whales and rain forests, not exposing cancer clusters around Baton Rouge. But he continued fighting, traveling overseas to Norway and Japan to tackle issues in those countries as well. When India began liberalizing its economy in the 1990s, he was naturally drawn home.

"At the time, the entry of corporations into India was a new thing," he says. "I realized the movement in India could stand to benefit from an active movement in some of these countries like the United States where decisions were being made." He launched the India Resource Center in 2002 with a budget of $60,000 a year, much of it originally provided by Body Shop founder Anita Roddick—a true believer in the spirit of corporate social responsibility who had recently traveled to Plachimada and decried Coke's insensitivity there. After traveling there himself the following year, Srivastava knew he'd found a nemesis worthy of his time. "I'll spend my whole life on Coca-Cola if I have to, why not?" he asks.

Despite the growing attention Plachimada was receiving in the international press, the local activists in Kerala were skeptical of being co-opted by international nonprofits who wanted to use the fight to push their own issues. Srivastava came to them with the proposal not to support their struggle from afar but to take the issue to the home of Coke itself—the United States. "The whole point is not to support the struggle, it is to join the struggle," says C. R. Bijoy. "One of the people who picked up on this was Amit."

Like Ray Rogers, Srivastava realized early on that the vulnerability of Coke lay in its brand image. In fact, he hooked up with Rogers in New York in spring 2004 "walking out with two boxes full of propaganda" to begin organizing on college campuses. From then on, anytime SINALTRAINAL raised its own issues on campus, it also mentioned India; when Srivastava made his own visits to campuses, he brought up anti-union violence in Colombia. While Srivastava admits that the Indian situation isn't as dramatic as the murders that took place in Colombia, he argues that in some ways it is more compelling, since the bottling plants there were actually owned by the company in Atlanta, not contracted out to a separate franchisee, making Coke's alleged infractions more direct. And while the violent civil war in Colombia is unique, Coke's water use is an issue all over the world.

An increasingly militant movement in both Plachimada and Mehdiganj began using more direct tactics to put pressure on Coke. Word of the BBC report about Coke's toxic sludge gave new fire to the community in Mehdiganj, which demanded its local pollution control board carry out tests. But Uttar Pradesh (UP), the state in which Varanasi is located, is not Kerala. Both culturally and politically, the state is strictly ordered along caste lines, with the Shudra and Dalit castes populating the rural villages strictly separated from the Brahmin and Kshatriya castes populating finance and industry. It also has a reputation for being one of the more corrupt states in the country. In 2009, a few months before the Lok Samiti graduation ceremony, police arrested the regional head of the state pollution control board in Varanasi—the person responsible for overseeing the Mehdiganj Coke plant. They charged him with taking a bribe from another business in exchange for a "no objection" certificate allowing it to operate.

Years earlier, however, the pollution control board not only declined to test Coke's sludge, but also denied Coke was even distributing it to farmers. "The pollution control board said, 'We have visited the village and they are not doing this,' " says Nandlal. " 'If you have seen this, show it to us.' " Exasperated, he and his fellow activists appeared at the board's offices one day with a sack full of sludge and dumped it on the desk of the clerk: "We kind of took him hostage." Several dozen protesters blocked the main entrance until officials agreed to investigate.

By this time, the establishments in Mehdiganj and Plachimada weren't the only bottling plants facing controversy. A study by the state pollution board in West Bengal found toxic levels of cadmium in the effluent of three plants around Kolkata. And in 2003, the Central Pollution Control Board conducted tests of sludge from sixteen Coke and Pepsi plants—and found eight Coke plants to have excessive levels of lead and cadmium. And it added a third toxin: chromium, a heavy metal that causes skin rashes and dermatitis on contact and is a suspected carcinogen with repeated ingestion. The agency henceforth ordered Coca-Cola to treat its waste as hazardous, requiring disposal in specially lined concrete landfills.

More recently, the nonprofit Hazards Centre has continued to confirm the presence of toxic heavy metals around Coke plants. Located on Delhi's southern fringes in a cramped concrete apartment building, the office is a buzzing hive of young researchers sitting around computers. In the middle sits director Dunu Roy, sporting a white ponytail and balding slightly on top.

Roy's group first did an assessment of Plachimada's groundwater back in 2006; since then it has done assessments of water conditions at five other Coke plants around India, publishing a report in 2010. In each location, the scientists measured the presence of lead, cadmium, and chromium in both the groundwater and the effluent coming directly out of the plant. All five plants contained chromium, some in levels of up to eleven times government limits. In addition, cadmium was found at two plants, including Mehdiganj, and lead at one. In summary, says Roy, "two things are incontrovertible." One: that the water draining directly out of the plant contains heavy metals. And two: that contamination in the groundwater decreases as one gets farther away from the plants.

So what about the wastewater treatment plant that Ranjan so proudly showed off at the Mehdiganj plant? Roy takes one look at the data showing limits on pH, dissolved solids, and oxygen demand, and immediately says that Coke is tracking the wrong numbers. That data, he says, will tell you only if the water is potable, not that it is free from chemical contamination. None of the aeration or filtering that Hindustan Coke does will remove heavy metals, he says, which need to be percolated out using salts. Not only is that process expensive, but then you are left with hazardous solid waste that needs to be disposed of. The bioassay with the two fish, he adds, is completely laughable, completely failing the scientific protocol for such a test. "To do this bioassay, you need to have six tanks with different concentrations in the water, with twenty fish in each tank," he says. "So you'd need 120 fish in all."

Increasingly armed with countrywide data, the various campaigns against Coca-Cola began coordinating their activities. Ajayan and Nandlal met for the first time in January 2004, along with Srivastava and other international activists, at the World Social Forum, an annual progressive strategy session–cum–spring break for lefties that coincides with the meeting of the world's political and financial masters at the World Economic Forum in Davos, Switzerland. Held in Mumbai, the forum featured a march of some five hundred people to protest Coke, led by Indian environmentalist Medha Patkar; SINALTRAINAL president Javier Correa was marching right alongside.

Immediately afterward, several dozen environmental activists came to Plachimada for a somewhat grandiosely named World Water Conference, a three-day who's who of lefties, including Canadian water activists Tony Clarke and Maude Barlow, French antiglobalist farmer José Bové, and Bolivian peasant leader Oscar Olivera, who had organized a successful peasant movement against water privatization by Bechtel in Cochabamba. There the activists struck a militant tone, calling on Coke to "Quit India"—the same slogan Gandhi used in his long fight against British occupation.

Nandlal and his fellow activists evoked Gandhi's spirit more confrontationally in Mehdiganj, where they began a hunger strike in front of the plant in January 2004. Coke obtained a restraining order prohibiting protests within three hundred meters (despite the fact that some of the protesters actually *lived* within that radius), which was violated in late 2004 with a ten-day march of some one thousand villagers, some carrying "Quit India" signs in a direct evocation of Gandhi's March to the Sea.

By the time they arrived at the plant in Mehdiganj, a cordon of police was waiting, blocking the entrance. In a group, the villagers surged past the three-hundred-meter line, as police began striking them with batons. Even as the protesters dropped to the ground in pain, heads and arms bleeding, they say, they held to a vow of nonviolence (with one well-marked apparent exception of an elderly woman who took off her slipper and began hitting a policeman with it).

In all, says Nandlal, police arrested more than 350 people, including more than forty women. He himself spent fifteen days in jail, shaken by the violence—especially seeing police beating women from his village. "It was really painful," he says. "I thought about giving up. But the community had not given up." In fact, it was the women who pushed to continue the protests. "Women are most in need of water," says Vishwakarma, "to clean, cook, bathe—their whole lives are dependent on water. Men have a limit, but when women are angry, they will never stop." A few weeks after the violence, some five hundred marchers wearing black ribbons over their mouths marched up to the three-hundred-meter line, standing silently in protest. A year later, in 2005, police stood aside as eight hundred people marched right up to the gates.

At the same time, the battle lines had been drawn more metaphorically in Kerala, now with the state's opposition political parties and the village council on one side, and the state government and Coca-Cola on the other. When the case to decide Coke's fate finally went to court, Kerala's high court returned two conflicting decisions—first declaring in December 2003 that the company's groundwater extraction was "illegal" and the *panchayat* was justified in canceling the license; and then on appeal, saying the council had acted without sufficient information, and needed to do a groundwater study first.

In light of a crippling drought that year, however, the state's chief minister declared in February 2004 the plant would be banned from extracting groundwater until the government's study was completed. The pickets at the hut went on for another year as the two sides waited for the results, which eventually came as a victory for Coke in February 2005, ruling that the company could extract up to half a million liters a day without affecting groundwater.

Asked about the ruling, the former village council president Krishnan discounts the study, contending that the company must have bribed the government officials who conducted it. "The thing is very simple, because they tried to bribe me," he says impatiently, contending that he was approached by Coke officials offering money for "community or personal development." While Krishnan declines to say how much, another source says the offer was as high as $200,000—a small fortune in India.

Still defiant, the *panchayat* appeared to follow the court order to renew the license in June 2005—but only if the company would agree to certain conditions, among them that Coke "divulge all of its ingredients." In other words, the *panchayat* of a tiny village in southern India was asking Coke to provide it with the vaunted secret formula that the company had guarded for decades in an Atlanta safe-deposit box—a formula that the company had refused to give up years earlier in favor of leaving the entire country. The village council must have known that Coke would never comply.

Meanwhile, whatever influence Gandhi's spirit of nonviolence had on the village activists, they made it clear they would resist the reopening of the plant by any means necessary. Sure enough, in August the protest turned ugly, with police charging a line of protesters and injuring six while arresting seventy. Into the breach stepped the state pollution control board, which declared a few days later that the plant couldn't reopen because its application was incomplete. The company had not mentioned cadmium in its raw materials, it charged, despite the heavy metal's presence in the wastewater sludge—therefore it must provide a new application explaining how the chemical was used in the production process.

The announcement was essentially checkmate for the company, which declined to submit a new application. In fact, the plant hasn't extracted a single liter of water since it closed in March 2004. Even as the activists celebrated the outcome, however, the result was in some small way a victory for the company as well. Faced with the real possibility of violence—even deaths—Coke had everything to lose in forcing a reopening, especially now that the eye of the world had been turned on the situation in India.

Now, at least, the company saved face by arguing it was prevented from operating by a capricious state with a known communist past, with which it refused to do business.

As Coke's former public relations head, Banerjee, says, Coke "would at least win public sympathy from other parts of India, and Kerala would once against be damned as an 'investors' graveyard' by the media and the public." That refrain was taken up not only by the company, but also by the U.S. government when a new study by CSE found even more pesticides in Coke and Pepsi in 2006 and the Kerala state government, now eager to align itself with the Plachimada movement, banned the sale of Coke and Pepsi in the entire state. (At least six other states pushed through more limited soft-drink bans, prohibiting sales in hospitals and educational institutions.)

"This kind of action is a setback for the Indian economy," said U.S. undersecretary of international trade, Franklin Lavin, his comment reminiscent of the outcry fifty years earlier when France banned Coke. "In a time when India is working hard to attract and retain foreign investment, it would be unfortunate if the discussion were dominated by those who did not want to treat foreign companies fairly." The bans were soon struck down by courts on the grounds that state government had no authority to ban imported products.

Even so, the plant closure in Plachimada continued to resonate across India—and the world—showing the power and political pressure that could be mobilized by a determined group of citizens. "Whatever the technical reasons for the closure of the plant, it was really done because of the community resistance," boasts Ajayan. And that included not only local resistance, but also the international pressure. "So far as their brand image is concerned," says Bijoy, "the campaign in India didn't seem to bother them that much. The campaign in the U.S. seemed to worry them."

Closing one plant, however, didn't necessarily make it easier to close any more. Coke knew that brand image cut both ways. When Neville Isdell took charge in the summer of 2004, he moved to neutralize the Indian situation as quickly as he had moved to still the controversy around childhood obesity in the United States. Within weeks, he'd flown to India personally to assess the situation, even toying with the idea of spinning off Hindustan Coca-Cola to become a franchise bottler, providing a buffer to insulate the company from criticism. In the end, however, Coca-Cola India took a course more similar to the one taken in the United States than that taken in Colombia: remaking itself from an environmental pariah to an environmental leader.

The village of Kala Dera is located some twenty-five miles from Jaipur, the capital of the northwestern state of Rajasthan and one of India's top tourist attractions. Known as the pink city for the rose color of its ancient walls, Jaipur is chock-full of temples and maharaja palaces. The opulence quickly fades, however, on the dusty road out to Kala Dera, a screaming tumult of roadside cafés and brightly colored shops spilling sacks of grain and farming equipment.

Past the commercial areas, green shoots sprout from earth where farmers have planted wheat in advance of the monsoon. Few people are out to tend them, however, on this mid-June day, when it's 110 degrees and there is little shade to break up the sun's heat aside from the spiky khejri trees that provide fodder for camels. This is a transitional zone; half of Rajasthan is fed by rivers, the other is arid desert completely dependent on groundwater.

Few areas are less ideal for a water-intensive industry like bottling soft drinks. Then again, the same aridity that makes the land thirsty also parches the throats of the populace. To cut transportation costs to serve the area, Hindustan Coca-Coca built a bottling plant here in 1999 in an industrial park set up by the state government. "Rajasthan is an important market," says northern India public affairs head Ranjan. "There was market potential—that is the only reason we sited it here."

Today Ranjan has brought with him a colleague, whom he identifies as a public relations consultant named Sunil Sharma, who is dressed in a dark blue long-sleeve shirt and is as gregarious as Ranjan is taciturn. "I have been on roads all over the world, to Holland, Belgium, Paris," he says as he pulls into honking traffic on the way from Jaipur. "And I come back to India and the air is stinky, but it's great. I breathe it in, and it's a perfect democracy, I think. Anyone can drive anywhere, anyone can do anything."

He seems to realize what he's said the moment it's out of his mouth. After all, it wasn't long before Coke was accused of doing anything it wanted in Kala Dera—especially depleting the aquifer without regard to community water needs. As in Mehdiganj, Ranjan denies the charge. While here he concedes the water level is dropping, he cites studies showing that industry accounts for less than 1 percent of water use, while farmers use 85 percent. "Having said that," he adds, "we also need to look at what water users are doing to replenish the water they are taking."

That is Ranjan's goal today. Learning from the controversy elsewhere in the country, Coca-Cola India has moved aggressively in the name of corporate social responsibility to actually replace the water they have taken from the desert here. To do that, they use a process developed by local farmers for centuries in India called "rainwater harvesting," through which the company claims it has recharged seventeen times the amount of water it has extracted in Rajasthan.

Before leaving Jaipur, Ranjan and Sharma drive up to a school where Sharma points out pipes attached to the walls. They funnel rain collected on the rooftop to an open rectangular tank. At one end is a concrete circle a foot or two across filled in with sand and gravel. That's just the top of the "recharge shaft," says Sharma, a two-hundred-foot bore well that filters water directly down into the aquifer.

The system can recharge 1.3 million liters of water annually "if the rainfall is average," says Sharma, meaning 560 millimeters of rain over the four rainy months between June and September. Asked about the actual recharge of the shaft, Ranjan replies that the company hasn't yet instituted a means for measuring that, though they are working on it. A school official leading the tour says the system has fixed previous problems with water scarcity, even though "we still have a problem in summer." Sharma immediately corrects him: "No, you have no problems." Looking a bit flustered, the official clarifies, "In the summer months, we had problems. Now we have no problems."

While Coca-Cola admits that rainwater harvesting in Jaipur does nothing to recharge the aquifer in Kala Dera, Ranjan says the company has installed some 150 projects within three kilometers of the plant, constructed atop other buildings or positioned in riverbeds to catch runoff. And that's not all the company has done to help local farmers. In 2005, the company upgraded Kala Dera's general hospital, its women's hospital, and even its veterinary hospital. And along the road to the village, it has partnered to create a "farm education center" to teach farmers new "drip irrigation" methods that use 70 percent less water than flood irrigation traditionally used by farmers.

Those corporate social responsibility efforts have earned the company goodwill among at least some in the village, including a farmer with scraggly salt-and-pepper hair and a long white kurta whom Ranjan introduces. The water level has stabilized at around ninety feet below the ground, says the man, who works as a building contractor in addition to growing wheat and spinach on seven acres of land. Those who have protested the plant, he continued, are outsiders from other villages jealous of the improvements Coke has made there. The principal of another school where Coke has instituted rainwater harvesting goes further, saying that the protesters are "day laborers" from another village paid to swell the ranks at protests.

There's no question in their minds who did the hiring—Amit Srivastava and his local representative, a Jaipur-based activist named Sawai Singh. According to Sharma, Srivastava shows up a day before or a day after the protests, hiring laborers from the neighboring village of Chamu to take part in the demonstrations at 100 rupees ($2) a pop. Local organizers, he says, Srivastava hires for 2,000 rupees ($100) a month.

Srivastava himself arrives in Kala Dera's marketplace an hour later, baseball cap covering his eyes, and accompanied by several of those local organizers he's been accused of hiring for money. When told of Coke's contention that he's paying off the village, he laughs. Far from orchestrating a protest movement from eight thousand miles away, Srivastava contends that it's Coca-Cola India that is manipulating public opinion in the area. "This is a big corporate scam," he says, "we'll show you all of it."

Together, they lead the way to a school just behind the marketplace, quite a different scene from the ones Ranjan and Sharma have shown off. Here, the pipes that run down from the roof are rusting and broken, and in at least one case taped together with packing tape. Behind the school, the concrete basin to collect the water is cracked in several places. No matter the condition of the structures, however, the local head of the resistance, Mahesh Yogi, says that it doesn't matter since they don't work without rain. And Rajasthan has experienced intense drought for the past few years, with just three or four annual days of rain at most. Yogi farms two and a half acres of land, he says, but is able to grow crops on only one acre because of a shortage of water. Since his wells dried up, he says he's had to take a loan of 150,000 rupees ($3,000) for a new 225-foot bore well, taking a second job selling cell phone minutes to support his three small children.

As in other communities, the farmers here accuse Coke of polluting the land as well; since the factory is set within a dense industrial park, however, it's impossible to prove it. In the industrial park on the edge of town, a haze of foul-smelling smoke hangs over the cluster of factories, while behind them, burning piles of white slag fill a wide trench with a stream running down the middle. "This is not all Coca-Cola," says Srivastava, "but this is the kind of enforcement you see. This is the unfortunate story of the Third World." (Ranjan repeats the assertion from Mehdiganj that all solid waste is disposed of at a government-registered facility.) Downstream from the plant, the water itself is obviously polluted, with a green scum floating on top. Passing farmers repeat the same story—if cattle stand in it too long, they get rashes on their legs, and some have even died from drinking it. Whether it's justified or not, there's no question whom villagers blame for all of these problems: Coca-Cola. In fact, in direct contradiction of Ranjan and Sharma's contention that the protesters are hired from outside, a random cross-section of farmers milling around the marketplace mention the company when asked about the water shortages and pollution.

Typical is a farmer named Lakshmi Narayan, who grows groundnut, wheat, and mustard on seven acres of land—but is now able to farm only less than an acre. "Coca-Cola," he answers simply when asked why he thinks the water level has gone down. "Other factories do use water, but it's far less than Coke." As a crowd gathers around him, several other farmers all agree that Coca-Cola is to blame for their distress. Asked how many of them have taken part in protests against the company, every one of them raises a hand.

The extent to which the company is downplaying opposition becomes even clearer after driving a few miles out of town to the home of Rameshwar Prasad Kuri, a prosperous farmer everyone calls by the honorific "Kuriji." Today happens to be the day before the wedding of one of his sons, and his well-kept house is full of men and small children running underfoot. Kuriji's family has owned this farm for five generations; when he was a young man, however, he left to enter the civil service, eventually becoming assistant director of the state agricultural department.

With a civil servant's meticulous love for detail, he has kept track of the water level in his well, which he says was twenty-five to thirty feet below the surface when he retired in 2002. After Coke opened its bottling plant three kilometers away, however, he says the water level has gone down eight to ten feet a year. As in the other villages, Kuriji's open well is dry, and he has had to buy a more powerful motor to get any water out of his bore well. As a result, he is able to irrigate only half of his seventeen acres. The loss of income has forced his family to take their children out of private school and put off buying a car to make the seven-kilometer trip to market. "The only positive effect is that I don't smoke anymore," he laughs. "I don't even drink tea because we can't afford it."

Kuriji's face is a relief map as expressive as any desert landscape, set with small watchful eyes. He sits cross-legged on a cot wearing a white kurta and gray slacks, periodically letting forth unself-conscious burps that perfume the air slightly with curry. One of the first farmers in the area to organize against the company, Kuriji took the lead from the successful protests in Kerala and Mehdiganj, and he helped organize protests here in 2004, leading marches and rallies around the plant. "Coca-Cola is snatching away our livelihoods," he says, shaking his head. "We invite Coca-Cola as a guest, and they pick our pockets."

When told of Sharma's contention that the group hires day laborers to swell its numbers, Kuriji's face crinkles with laughter. "Who has that kind of money?" he asks, incredulous. Ever the civil servant, he pulls out a photo album full of pictures of protests. "Do these look like hundred-rupees-a-day day laborers?" he asks, pointing to the faces of men much like those around his home for the wedding, simply dressed but not poor. Next, he opens a ledger book in which he's written captions for each photo with name after name of participants, some with signatures beside them. "This is ample proof they are not day laborers," he concludes.

Even so, the movement here has struggled to achieve the critical mass seen in Plachimada, or even Mehdiganj. The largest protest was in May 2004, when, a news report says, some two thousand people came to see Indian environmentalist Medha Patkar and local Gandhian social activist Sawai Singh. As in Kerala, Singh has helped bring a petition against the company, arguing that local people had the right to groundwater before a multinational corporation, but it was denied by the local court. Recently, however, Rajasthan has seen a change of government from the more conservative Bharatiya Janata Party (BJP) to the socialist-leaning Congress party, giving the community members hope that the issue will be revisited. "We are not ready for defeat," says Kuriji. "We will carry on this agitation and Coke will get tired. We will certainly shut down the plant."

Kala Dera isn't the only place where Coke has pursued corporate social responsibility in India. By 2008, the company claimed to have more than three hundred rainwater-harvesting structures around the country.

With the twenty-three projects around Mehdiganj, Coke India says it is able to recharge 46,933 cubic meters per year, versus the plant's consumption of 38,191. In 2008, in fact, the company declared the plant to be "water neutral"—that is, it recharges more water than it extracts. According to Ranjan, the water levels in the area of the plant actually rose between 2007 and 2008, from twenty-eight feet to nineteen feet belowground. In order to make that claim, however, the company relies on the closest government monitoring site, three miles southwest of the plant. In an official document the company submitted to the local groundwater board, meanwhile, it admitted the level at the plant was eighty feet belowground.

The community also tells a different story about Coke's rainwater harvesting. The figures for Coke's recharge potential rely on an average rainfall of 1,000 millimeters a year, but in many of the past few years, it's been only half that. What's more, in 2008, activists say half of the rain fell on one day—overflowing the capacity of the rainwater storage tanks. As in Kala Dera, several rainwater harvesting structures are in dilapidated condition. On one, built on the rooftop of the local police station, the main pipe coming from the roof isn't even connected to the underground tank. "No one has ever come here after the management first installed it," says one police officer. "The pipes are all blocked and the water overflows."

Ranjan dismisses the activists' rainwater-harvesting tours as publicity tours. "They always take you to a place with a broken pipe," he says, insisting that the company does an annual maintenance before the monsoons. Whether or not the structures are in working order, however, there is truth to back up the activists' claims that there is simply not enough rain to make them work. Despite Coke's claims that it recharged the water it took out in Kala Dera, government figures show that water levels still declined in Kala Dera by more than ten feet between 2007 and 2008. Rainfall levels for 2009, meanwhile, were only half of the prior year's total.

India has been experiencing droughts all over the country the last few years, says M. S. Rathore, head of the Jaipur-based nonprofit Centre for

Environment and Development Studies. He actually agrees with Coke that farmers are responsible for most of the water depletion, overexploiting the carrying capacity of the land in an effort to grow as much as possible. That doesn't mean Coke's contention that industry uses only 1 percent of the water is accurate. While that may be a statewide average, in certain districts industry uses up to 50 percent. And the same goes for the rainfall averages, which are drawn from one hundred years, despite the fact that Rajasthan, at least, gets only one year of good rain in every seven or eight years. Of the remaining years, half of them may see just two or three rainy days total.

So what about Coke's claims that it is recharging seventeen times what it takes out in Kala Dera? He shakes his head immediately. "It's not possible. I don't believe them." Is it possible even to recharge half that, a quarter of that? "If they are recharging even five times, then the water level should come up—did it?" he shoots back. "No. Contrary to that, the water level is coming down in that area, it's not coming up. The calculation may be right, but what is actually happening? Did they get it?"

Ranjan repeats his assertion that Coke can't accurately measure the actual recharge of its rainwater wells. While they could put in a groundwater gauge called a piezometer to measure water levels, he says, it would require sending someone manually to check it after each rainfall. "It will not work in auto-mode," he says. "There has to be someone there to take the reading."

Merely a little bit of research online, however, turns up a company called Integrated Geo Instruments and Services in Hyderabad, India, that not only produces a line of groundwater monitoring equipment, but also lists Hindustan Coca-Cola among its clients. Contacted via e-mail, a representative confirms that it offers something called an "automatic water level indicator"—a computer attached to a length of cable that registers groundwater levels in a well "continuously and without human intervention." In fact, the representative says, Coke uses these very devices throughout India to monitor water levels in its bore wells. The cost: $1,800 each, meaning that Coke could outfit every one of its rainwater structures with a probe for just $540,000, a fraction of the $10 million it recently bequeathed to the Coca-Cola India Foundation to spend on community CSR projects throughout the country.

Reached at the company's headquarters, the representative confirms that the logger can automatically monitor groundwater levels, and also says that Hindustan Coca-Cola has bought loggers in the past from the company to monitor its intake wells. Ranjan doesn't respond to e-mails asking if Hindustan Coca-Cola has considered using such a device to monitor rainwater harvesting.

Leaving Jaipur for the railway station, it miraculously begins to rain. Within moments, it's a hard rain, washing over the pavement and soaking into the dirt on both sides of the road. It tapers off quickly, however, and in five minutes, it's all but over. Srivastava's cell phone rings, and it's Professor Rathore, speaking excitedly on the other end. Srivastava nods and thanks him before hanging up. "He says that accounts for one rainy day."

TEN

The Case Against "Killer Coke"

Despite activists' successes holding Coke accountable in India, the real fight over operations in that country—as well as in Colombia—would be fought in the United States.

A week after being wrestled to the ground and ejected from Coke's 2004 annual meeting, Ray Rogers was back on the campaign trail, looking for one big campus to serve as a poster child for his campaign. In late April 2004, he stood in front of the unsubtly named Radical Student Union at the University of Massachusetts, trying to fire up students to break their exclusive pouring-rights contract expiring in August. "The Coca-Cola Company is an enterprise rife with immorality, corruption, and complicity in gross human rights violations," he boomed. He then introduced his fellow speakers: Dan Kovalik, who talked softly but no less passionately about the Colombia murders and the stalled ATCA case, and Amit Srivastava, who ran down the outrages of water depletion, pollution, and pesticides in India.

After first making common cause at the World Social Forum in Mumbai, the Colombia and India campaigns had joined in a kind of global version of the Teamster and Turtles alliance to tie together Coke's international labor and environmental sins. In doing so, the new Campaign to Stop Killer Coke became, in effect, the first truly globalized campaign since the word "globalization" was coined. Unlike previous campaigns focusing on a single issue—sweatshops (Nike) or baby formula (Nestlé)—this would combine disparate offenses in an all-encompassing critique on corporate capitalism. And what better corporation to make the critique through than "the essence of capitalism," Coke.

Rogers and Srivastava began gathering other stories of the company's alleged misdeeds, from child labor in sugarcane plantations in El Salvador to strike-busting in Russia and the Philippines. Colombia and India, however, would be the focus. By now, more than one hundred schools had campaigns to cut their contracts with Coke based on allegations in the two countries, and the Coca-Cola Company was beginning to respond to prevent it from snowballing any further. After the shareholder meeting, Coke bought the domain killercoke.com (as opposed to Rogers's killercoke.org) and pointed it back to a new website, cokefacts.org, in an effort to set the story straight.* Despite the allegations from the student campaigns, it assured visitors, Coke had nothing to do with the murders in Colombia, for which it had been cleared in court cases in both the United States and Colombia. And it added new proof of its support of union rights, including the fact that 31 percent of Coke workers in Colombia were unionized, versus a national rate of 4 percent. It failed to note, however, that that rate applied only to official employees—not the increasing number of contract workers in the bottling plants, a fact the Killer Coke campaign soon pointed out.

The feeble PR push did little to blunt the student campaign, which came roaring back to campus in the fall with the help of a new ally: the group that led the last great student activist campaign against Nike, United Students Against Sweatshops (USAS). Together Killer Coke and USAS

*The killercoke.com site has since been taken down.

would mount a challenge to Coke's brand on international issues every bit as dangerous as the childhood obesity campaign on the domestic scene, and almost at the exact same time. To counter them, Coke would have to move strategically to take the fight from the courtroom and campuses to the back rooms where it could sap the energy of the campaign and exploit philosophical differences among the activists themselves to prevent it from going mainstream.

The rally against Coke fit well into USAS's goals. Even after the Nike campaign had ended with the apparel makers' announcement of new factory policies through the Clinton-backed Fair Labor Association, USAS had not given up their fight against what they saw as global abuses by corporations overseas. Dismissing the Clinton standards as mere "corporate cover-up," the students had created their own group, the Worker Rights Consortium (WRC), signing up some two hundred member colleges from Harvard to the University of California who agreed to adhere to binding decisions on what companies they could do business with based on their labor policies.

By the fall of 2004, it was looking for new ways to broaden focus beyond just sweatshops—and it found one with the help of a Colombian-American student activist at UC Berkeley named Camilo Romero. Born in the United States, Romero had always acutely felt the discrepancy in privileges between himself and his Colombia-born family members. When one of the leaders of SINALTRAINAL came to Berkeley to talk about the Coke boycott, he saw a chance to directly affect a situation in his family's country by advocating for it in his own.

Joining with two Latin American friends, Romero sought to use Coke as a way to show U.S. businesses exploited workers in Latin American countries. Soon after forming a group to advocate cutting Berkeley's contract, he was approached by an organizer from USAS to take the campaign national.

He accepted—with some reservations. Looking around at the student group's membership, he saw a lot of well-meaning but "privileged white kids." From the beginning, he vowed the campaign would draw in students from a more diverse range of backgrounds, to present a more nuanced critique of the situation in Latin America. As part of a new generation of activists, he didn't necessarily agree with Saul Alinsky's tactics of "polarizing" a target no matter what the cost. As he began reaching out to campuses farther east, however, he quickly found out about Rogers's campaign—which was making headway at some of the largest and most influential campuses in the country, though with a very different message.

Rogers was still on the hunt for a school where he could fire a meaningful shot across Coke's bow. After UMass renewed its contract over the summer, he moved on to a new target: Rutgers University in New Jersey, vowing the same thing wouldn't happen here. It was the perfect place to set an example. Not only was the campus big—with 50,000 students—and close to Rogers's headquarters in New York, but the contract was also particularly egregious. In exchange for $10 million over the course of ten years, the school agreed to Coke advertising all over campus, to the point of sanctioning the cheer "Always Rutgers, Always Coca-Cola" over the loudspeaker during athletic events.

With the help of a labor studies professor, Rogers plastered the campus with Killer Coke posters and organized students to demand the administration go with a different vendor. To his surprise, the university agreed to delay its decision until May 2005 to solicit bids. That spring, Rogers and Srivastava appeared together on campus with a giant inflatable Coke bottle on the steps of the student center with the logo "College Control," while the campus USAS chapter supplied shock troops behind the scenes.

Tensions were rising, however, between the tactics of Rogers and the USAS students. Romero especially took issue with the gory posters like the Colombian Coke Float that sensationalized the issue with the bodies floating in the Coke glass. "It certainly catches your eye," says Romero. "But people don't necessarily feel welcome to it. It's this particular kind of activism—the chest-pounding, look at me, this corporation is the devil." Romero felt the macabre imagery trivialized the complexity of the situation in Colombia. Worse, he thought they risked the message being dismissed as the ravings of a "crazy, loudmouth guy"—Rogers.

Rogers would have none of it. When he caught wind of the criticism of the way he ran the campaign, he took Romero aside to address it. "Maybe you don't like it, but boy, is it having an impact," he argued, reminding him he'd knocked off four colleges before USAS had even joined. The Colombian Coke Float and the other lurid posters, he announced, would stay.

By May, the fight for Rutgers was over. The school announced that it would sign a ten-year, $17 million contract with Pepsi, effective immediately. Even though the school insisted it went with the company that offered the better proposal financially, Rogers declared victory, counting the decision a "big blow to the company." If there was any question about why Rutgers dumped Coke, the campaign sought to remove it with more direct appeals at two other universities: the University of Michigan and New York University (NYU).

The country's largest private university with 50,000 students, NYU didn't have an exclusive contract with Coke, but it did have about a hundred vending machines and retail operations in dozens of campus stores. This time, USAS led the way, demanding Coke submit to an independent investigation by the Worker Rights Consortium (WRC) if it wanted to stay on campus. Students wrapped vending machines in crime-scene tape and staged a "die-in" on the steps of the library with the names of the slain Colombian workers. Their campaigning paid off when, in November 2004, the student senate voted sixteen to four to ban Coke from campus if the company didn't agree to an investigation by the WRC. The resolution was weakened by the all-university senate to demand only that Coke participate in a university-sponsored forum with the WRC. Even so, Coke apparently decided that giving any legitimacy to the organization with a binding power to censure sales was too much, refusing to participate. The issue was tabled, to be taken up in the fall.

Meanwhile, activists at the 40,000-student University of Michigan demanded that the school reconsider Coke's nine contracts—worth a collective $1.3 million a year—on the grounds that they violated the university's new vendor "code of conduct." In a petition to the school's "dispute review board," students demanded the company agree to an independent investigation not only in Colombia but in India as well. After a hearing in March 2005, the board ruled in the students' favor, requiring investigations by the end of the year. "If they don't step up and participate in corrective actions . . . in a big way," said the board chair, "it would be cause to terminate the contract."

New Coke CEO Neville Isdell watched the spread of the Killer Coke campaign on campus with mounting anxiety. Going into the annual shareholder meeting in April 2005, he was already several months into his eighteen-month plan to turn around the company. He'd reversed Coke's slide in profits, begun to get a handle on the childhood obesity situation, and set in motion Coke's new environmental thrust in India. And almost as soon as he took control, he hired Ed Potter to defuse the Colombia situation and protect the company from future problems with the overseas labor force.

Ed Potter had represented companies as an international labor lawyer in D.C. for more than two decades, even serving as the employer representative to the United Nations' International Labour Organization (ILO). Recently, he'd helped Coke put into place a Workplace Rights Policy, which went even further in spelling out the protections for workers. Soon after, Isdell hired him on staff as the company's new director of global relations. Quickly, he moved to get in front of the "Killer Coke" situation by declaring a new corporate code of conduct on labor and environmental issues. Like previous codes, however, it applied only to direct employees of the Coca-Cola Company and subsidiaries in which Coke owned at least a 50 percent interest. As for bottlers, Coke was "committed to working with and encouraging" them "to uphold the values and practices that our Policy encompasses."

At the same time, Isdell attempted to take away one of the campaign's main issues by commissioning an investigation into Colombian working conditions by a supposedly independent group, the Cal Safety Compliance Corporation. Standing up at the 2005 annual meeting, Isdell was able to report the study's conclusions: that workers were allowed collective bargaining rights free of intimidation.

He continued with a page out of the obesity playbook, simultaneously denying responsibility for the violence in Colombia and positioning the company as part of the solution with the announcement of a new $10 million foundation to aid victims in the country. Likewise for India, he denied the company was responsible for water shortages, at the same time touting the company's rainwater-harvesting initiative. All in all, it was an impressive presentation, countering the main allegations against the company head-on with a mix of defiance and compassion.

Opening the floor to questions, Isdell never knew what hit him. Immediately, activists jumped up to form two long lines. Rogers was first to speak, of course, dismissing Cal Safety as nothing but the "fox guarding the henhouse," since the group had interviewed workers handpicked by management and didn't even investigate links to paramilitaries. That was just the beginning of a ninety-minute slugfest the *Financial Times* later said "felt more like a student protest rally" than a stockholder meeting as Srivastava, CAI's Gigi Kellett, a nun, a Teamster, and several students all piled on the criticism.

Despite the finely orchestrated display, the real negotiations began after the meeting, when Potter requested to meet with college administrators to see if they might come to an agreement. USAS's Romero was tentatively hopeful when Potter suggested a commission with students and administrators that would set the ground rules for a new, truly independent investigation. Whatever good faith Potter may have had going into the negotiations, however, Coke was soon setting its own rules, insisting nothing in the investigation could look back more than five years (falling short of both the Gil case and the detentions in Bucaramanga), and nothing could be admissible in court. The students dismissed those demands out of hand; by October, five out of six of them had dropped out of negotiations.

By that time, the day of reckoning was approaching at both NYU and the University of Michigan. As NYU's senate reconvened to consider the vending machine ban, Coke continued in its refusal to meet with the WRC. The university issued an ultimatum—either Coke agree by December, or the Coke machines would go. When the deadline passed, NYU announced it would begin removing Coke from campus, effective immediately. But that wasn't all. When the University of Michigan's December 31 deadline passed three weeks later, it, too, declared it would be severing its ties with Coke. This decision was even more significant, since unlike both NYU and Rutgers, the university was breaking an exclusive contract and it was doing so specifically because of the company's human rights violations—and not only in Colombia but in India as well. Whatever Potter and Isdell were doing, it clearly wasn't working—at least not yet. By this time, the Killer Coke campaign could claim about two dozen universities around the world that had dumped Coke. Even the student newspaper at Emory—the university started with money from Asa Candler himself and known as "Coca-Cola University"—had written editorials supporting the campaign. "Certainly if there was any wrongdoing in the past," Emory's president announced approvingly, "Coke needs to be held responsible for it."

Around the same time Coke was suffering these defeats, allegations of anti-union violence emerged in a new country: Turkey. In April 2005, a group of drivers who transported Coke for a contractor were fired after they tried to unionize. When, along with family members, they occupied the local Coca-Cola headquarters in a nonviolent protest, members of Turkey's secret police attacked them with tear gas and clubs, sending dozens to the hospital. The union accused the company—which owns 40 percent of the bottler—of instigating the violence by calling in the police. After hearing about the Colombia situation, union members contacted Terry Collingsworth, who filed an ATCA case in New York, arguing that the police violence amounted to torture under international law.

While Coke didn't deny that protesters were attacked, the company claimed that police acted of their own accord, despite requests from Coke to hold off attacking. Even so, the company insisted, the dispute was between the union and the contractor; Coke had nothing to do with it. Coke spokesperson Kari Bjorhus brushed off such attacks as "the flipside of being a big brand," as she told *Brandweek* in December 2005. "You become a focal point for many issues because of the visibility of your trademark." (The case was eventually dismissed upon a finding that the union hadn't first exhausted its remedies in Turkey; it was promptly appealed.)

Behind the scenes, however, the Coca-Cola Company was still maneuvering to stop the Campaign Against Killer Coke before it spawned opportunistic attacks from any other countries. Just as it rolled out increasingly stringent policies on soda in schools until it found one the public would accept, Coke now announced a new independent investigation to take the place of the discredited Cal Safety report. This time, it called upon one of the most respected brands in the world: the United Nations. In advance of the 2006 shareholder meeting, the company announced that the International Union of Food and Allied Workers (IUF) had asked the United Nations' International Labour Organization (ILO) to "investigate and evaluate past and present labor relations and workers' right practices of the Coca-Cola bottling operations in Colombia," as Coca-Cola North America president Don Knauss wrote in a letter to the University of Michigan.*

The anti-Coke campaign immediately cried foul, pointing out that Ed

---

*While the IUF was the main union opposing Coke during the violence in Guatemala in the 1970s and 1980s, it had recently taken a more conciliatory approach to negotiating with the company. In fact, it was an IUF affiliate that had replaced SINALTRAINAL at the Carepa plant in Colombia. Despite ostensibly supporting SINALTRAINAL in its case against Coke, the IUF continued to throw cold water on its allegations by publicly insisting there was no evidence linking Coke to the violence.

Potter had been the U.S. employer representative to the ILO for the past fifteen years. "There are 640 people who have a final vote in the ILO conference's legislative process," responded Potter. "To suggest there is any undue influence is preposterous." He had less of an explanation for why the company was willing to admit the results of this investigation in court, when that was such a nonstarter in a student-led commission.

Rogers thought that he saw one: Despite Coke's assurances that the UN agency would investigate "past and present" practices, an ILO official told him on the phone that the agency would be doing only an "assessment of current working conditions." At the 2006 meeting, Rogers decried the ILO investigation as just "a new scam" that would do nothing to explore bottling plant managers' ties to paramilitary violence. "I can't think that engaging the ILO is a publicity stunt," replied Isdell coolly. "We have a document. We have an agreement, and they are going to investigate past and prior practices."

That wasn't the only investigation the company would be allowing, Isdell told the crowd. The Energy and Resources Institute (TERI), a respected NGO based in New Delhi, would also be conducting an audit of the company's water use. "My message to you today is that the transition is complete," said Isdell. "We are well on our way to becoming the company you expect us to be." As with the ILO, activists raised red flags against TERI—with Srivastava pointing out that the organization listed Coca-Cola as a sponsor on its website, had been paid by Coke to do environmental assessments in the past, and had publicly declared Coke one of the most responsible companies in India, and thus was hopelessly biased.

But the two proposed investigations were good enough to buy the company time. The University of Michigan reinstated its contract just three months after cutting it, pending the outcomes of the ILO and TERI reports. The campaigns at other colleges, meanwhile, lost momentum as administrators adopted a wait-and-see attitude. By August 2006, Potter insisted that the student campaign had "stalled," something virtually inconceivable when NYU and Michigan had dumped Coke months earlier. Now he and Isdell sought to press the advantage to get rid of Killer Coke back where the fight began—in court.

The three years since Judge Martínez had dismissed Coke from the ATCA case in 2003 had not been kind to Terry Collingsworth and Dan Kovalik. Martínez's indifference, if not contempt, for the case was apparent from the get-go. He seemed to take pride in getting details wrong, at points referring to Urabá as "Bogotá or Medellín or wherever the heck it was" and to Isidro Gil as "Joe Blow." His spontaneous style might seem refreshing to someone without a case before him, but to SINALTRAINAL's lawyers it was downright infuriating. Each June, he dismissed all pending motions, allowing them to be resubmitted the following year. Finally at a hearing in June 2006, Panamco's lawyer was reciting the judge's history of dismissals when Martínez broke in. "If you didn't know any better," he said, "you would think that I didn't want to have anything to do with this case, wouldn't you?"

Collingsworth and Kovalik were flabbergasted to hear such disdain expressed openly by a United States judge. A few months later, Martínez proved the point in a ruling that finally dismissed all the bottlers from the case as well. The evidence provided by Collingsworth and Kovalik was just too vague to link plant managers to the paramilitaries, wrote Martínez, adding that it was the duty of the courts to guard against "unwarranted international fishing expeditions against corporate entities." Coca-Cola Company spokeswoman Kerry Kerr swiftly responded, saying, "We hope this decision will now enable us to put this case behind us." It wouldn't, of course. Collingsworth and Kovalik filed a right to appeal, arguing that the case was wrongly decided when the judge allowed the sample bottling agreement rather than the actual one, thereby denying the union proper discovery to prove its case. "Put aside Colombia, Coca-Cola, murders, anything. This appeal is about fundamental, inflexible, never can violate legal procedures," says Collingsworth.

Before the lawyers could file, Collingsworth received a call from Ed Potter, whom he knew through D.C. labor law circles. Now just a year into his position, Potter asked if perhaps there was a way they could work out a settlement. At his insistence, the two sides engaged a retired judge in San Francisco, Daniel Weinstein, to act as a formal mediator in their talks. The two sides drew up a "term sheet" on August 17, 2006, agreeing they would use their "best efforts" to finalize a settlement within six weeks. In broad terms, the settlement would include cash compensation for the victims in Colombia along with a new workers' rights policy by the company to prevent future violations. In exchange, the lawyers would call off the dogs, including Ray Rogers's campaign maligning Coke.

Collingsworth told Potter that while he wouldn't be able to curtail campaigning by Rogers while negotiations ensued—or USAS or Srivastava for that matter—he could promise that as an act of good faith SINALTRAINAL would suspend its campaign and refrain from publicly criticizing Coke as they talked out a settlement. That promise was a hasty one—and in the end, a fatal one for the union's case.

Instead of the promised six weeks, the negotiations dragged on for the next eighteen months. And once the union's biggest weapon—its voice in the campaign—was taken away, it lost the leverage to make strong demands of the company. The negotiations unfolded under a strict cloak of confidentiality, and both sides' lawyers are still prohibited from revealing what was discussed. Documents from the settlement talks, however, reveal the extent of the gap between the union's and Coke's goals—and how aggressively Coke was willing to protect its image.

Whether through misunderstanding or willful disregard for the agreement, SINALTRAINAL resumed criticizing Coke on its website. After all, Coke was destroying the union with its increasing use of contract workers, union leaders reasoned, and the death threats continued to appear at their union halls. If Coke wasn't going to stop the paramilitaries from threatening them, why should they keep their mouths shut? Immediately, Coke's lawyers protested to Judge Weinstein, who blasted back from his BlackBerry that both sides refrain from public statements until he had a draft of the settlement on his desk by the first week of October 2006. Despite a flurry of conference calls and e-mails among Collingsworth, Kovalik, and Coke's lawyers, SINALTRAINAL continued to distribute flyers and post messages to its site about its ongoing campaign, and Coke trolled Web and newspaper reports for even the slightest notice of disparagement that it could use to hold over the union's head with the judge.

As the two sides pushed closer to agreement in October, Coke made clear its goal was to stop the bad publicity against the company, refusing any admission of liability in the torture or murder cases. Furthermore, it insisted SINALTRAINAL agree to never campaign internationally against Coke again. In fact, in a draft of the settlement, it required that the union scrub Internet search engines and archives to get rid of any mention of Killer Coke—as if the campaign never existed. For its part, Coke would pay just over $12 million to the union, including $1 million for Isidro Gil's heirs, and $4 million to be divided among Correa, Galvis, Flores, Garcia, and González. The bulk of the rest would go into a $6 million fund for victims of trade union violence, jointly administered by Coke's foundation and the union representatives; Collingsworth and Kovalik would receive $2 million in escrow to cover "administrative fees" for their part in managing the fund. Finally, the company would agree to a new workers' rights policy—but only for full-time workers, not contract workers—and a confidential "global forum" four times a year in which Coke would meet to discuss ongoing labor issues.

And then there was one more thing, added by Coke's lawyers: In order for the employees to get their money, they would have to resign from the union.

When the agreement arrived in Colombia, it was met with disbelief by Javier Correa and the rest of SINALTRAINAL's leadership. If Coke wanted them to stop talking about past cases such as Gil's murder, that was fine, but how could they refrain from criticizing the company for abuses that hadn't occurred yet? And resigning from the union? In their minds, the court case, the campaign, the negotiations—all of it—was an attempt to *save* the union. That requirement would defeat the entire purpose of the agreement.

Frustrated with the stalled talks, SINALTRAINAL went on the offensive, sending representatives to participate in a tour in Germany called, without subtlety, "Coke Kills." Coke's lawyers hit the roof. "Every request we made for . . . the immediate cessation of anti-Coke hostilities—was met with an attitude that borders on 'who cares,'" Coke's outside lawyer Faith Gay wrote to Collingsworth in November. "Obviously this is the primary issue that *we do* care about. Non-disparagement is why we are paying money to your clients." As far as the company was concerned, she accused the union of not negotiating in good faith. "To be frank, we believe that plaintiffs are unwilling to disarm for internal political reasons and because they know no other means of interacting with their employer(s)."

To prove they meant business, Coke's lawyers filed a motion with Weinstein demanding he fine SINALTRAINAL $150,000 for breach of the term sheet. Furthermore, it demanded he force Rogers to end his campaign as well. Weinstein didn't go for it, but he did order the union to pay $120,000 in penalties. As frustrated as Coke was getting with the union, Collingsworth was getting just as frustrated. "Look, don't waste my time," he told his clients. "If there is an internal political reason why there's not ever going to be a deal, tell me now." Correa responded that the union was willing to negotiate—if Coke would give it some assurances that it could stop eroding the union both through use of contract workers and through threats by paramilitaries.

In April 2007, the negotiating team headed to Atlanta to try one last time to strike an agreement. Serving as a translator for the group, Camilo Romero admits to feeling intimidated as he headed down with Collingsworth and Kovalik into the "lions' den": the penthouse suite of Atlanta's King & Spalding Building. Accompanying them was the union's team of negotiators: president Javier Correa, international relations head Edgar Paez, and secretary/treasurer Duban Velez. And also along for the ride was Ray Rogers.

Even as the union had begun its protracted talks with Coke, Rogers had not been idle. He was hot on the trail of a contract at the 35,000-student University of Alberta when Collingsworth called to tell him he'd eventually have to end his campaign if negotiations went according to plan. Rogers was fine with that, he said. "But first, tell me, what did we win?" As he caught wind of the details, he, too, was incredulous. No admission of guilt, no assurances the union would continue, no promise of dealing with subcontracting, and a comparatively minuscule dollar amount by corporate standards. (By comparison, Exxon agreed to pay $5 billion for the *Valdez* spill.) Rogers told the lawyer he'd go along with whatever the union leaders decided—but he wanted a chance to talk with them first.

The night before negotiations started in Atlanta, Romero was put in the awkward position of translating for Rogers as he addressed the Colombians in their hotel room. Coke spent $20 million for a few minutes of advertising during the Super Bowl, he told them. Surely they could afford more than that to compensate victims of torture and murder. "We don't intend to give up our fight against the company," answered Correa. "Nor will we accept that people make money on us as victims"—implying that Rogers was looking for his own cut. Privately, Romero also interpreted Rogers's plea as a personal money grab.

Despite their past clashes over Rogers's campaign tactics, Romero was on the same page in thinking Coke was offering a bum deal that didn't ultimately address any of SINALTRAINAL's key demands. Sitting around the heavy wood conference table overlooking downtown Atlanta, the two groups went over the main points of contention without progress—Coke holding fast to the basic agreement—that SINALTRAINAL and Killer Coke be muzzled in exchange for money, with no other enforceable obligations. Finally Kovalik walked out, followed soon by the Colombian team.

But Collingsworth proposed that he try one last time to personally negotiate with Ed Potter. Early the next morning, Collingsworth called to say he'd had a breakthrough—the company would pay settlement money to end the lawsuit and Rogers's campaign, but SINALTRAINAL would be free to say whatever it wanted in the future.

The Colombians delayed their flight home to meet with Coke's representatives for a handshake, even taking pictures with the Atlanta skyline in the background. They flew back to Bogotá thrilled about bringing the arrogant multinational to its knees, even as the union lived to fight another day. When the translation of the agreement finally arrived, their elation turned to dismay as they saw that all of the old language forbidding the union from denouncing the company had remained.

The union went back on the attack, with renewed calls for a boycott, and Coke again protested the breach in the cease-fire. A frustrated Potter wrote Collingsworth to say, "It may be time to move on and conclude no agreement is possible and that we were just wasting our time for the last fourteen months." Twisting the knife, he added: "We are in a much better position to deal with this dissipating campaign than we were in 2005." As reluctant as the lawyers were to admit it, Potter was right. Despite continued campaigning by Rogers and Srivastava, the student campaign had peaked with the victories at NYU and Michigan. Since then, the lack of active campaigning by the Colombian workers had thrown the campaign into disarray. For all of Coke's complaints about SINALTRAINAL breaking their agreement, in fact, the union had substantially reduced its public comments and appearances, especially at the schools that formed the backbone of the campaign. When Srivastava went up against the largest Coca-Cola contract in the country—a ten-year, $38 million contract at the University of Minnesota—he learned too late that SINALTRAINAL wouldn't appear to make its case to the administration. Coke, of course, did show up, and the contract was renewed.

The more he saw the campaign slip away, the more livid Rogers became about the botch that the lawyers had made of the negotiations. In the same way the anti-obesity lawyers had given Coke the upper hand when it agreed to hold off bringing a lawsuit, SINALTRAINAL's agreement to suspend campaigning had taken all the fire out of Killer Coke. "When you do something like that, you're playing into their hands and undermining your own power," says Rogers. "When they are feeling the heat, that's when you need to pick up a bigger club."

It's that attitude that made Rogers the biggest threat to Coke—and the company knew it. In the last draft of the settlement agreement from October 2007, "Killer Coke" is mentioned repeatedly throughout the text, which spells out in heartless detail exactly what issues can be raised by whom and when. In return for the leniency granted the union in the face of their breach of negotiation terms, SINALTRAINAL was offered even less money—$8 million. And of that, $3 million would go to the lawyers for a "discretionary fund" to cover their fees and "ensur[e] that the Killer Coke Campaign is dismantled." In other words, Coke would get rid of its biggest adversary, all for less money than the $10 million it had paid a year before to establish its Colombian foundation.

Even before the final draft was inked, Correa and his colleagues in Bogotá had made up their minds not to go along with it. "Ladies and Gentlemen of The Coca-Cola Company," Correa began in a letter sent in September. "It is not right that . . . SINALTRAINAL remains unprotected and silent, while the company has no restrictions, deactivates the campaign and does not adopt policies which respect the rights of its workers. . . . Given this situation, we have decided to tie ourselves again to the campaign."

The union demonstrated that in a big way with its next move: filing a complaint with the International Labour Organization alleging paramilitaries were carrying out violent attacks against workers at the same time the company was implementing policies to suppress union representation. Coke demanded the complaint be withdrawn, saying it would "cause irreparable damage both to [the Coca-Cola Company] itself and to the chances of successfully negotiating an end to the KillerCoke [*sic*] campaign." It was a strange attitude to take from a company that had already committed itself to an independent investigation of the very same claims by the very same agency. When the union refused to withdraw it, Coke again appealed to Weinstein for another fine. Collingsworth gave up—faced with a client who had already pulled out of negotiations, in action if not in word, and an adversary ready to pounce on any infraction, he made it official and told Weinstein that the union was pulling out of negotiations and canceling its obligations under the term sheet.

A year and a half after entering negotiations, he and Kovalik had to admit they had little to show for the effort. All the union stood to gain was money—and without promises of protection, even that was a double-edged sword in Colombia, opening them up to the possibility of heightened violence. Meanwhile, whether or not Coke was bargaining in good faith, the delay only helped the company.

Even as the negotiations failed, Rogers was ready to go back on the attack at the many universities ripe for the picking. At most of them, however, the key student activists who had started the campaigns had graduated. And now, Coke was about to unveil a one-two punch to ensure that no new activists would take their places.

While Colombia and the negotiations with SINALTRAINAL occupied the forefront of Coke's attention, the villagers in India had pressed on with their battle against the company. In Uttar Pradesh, Nandlal and Srivastava released a devastating report about pollution at a second bottling plant one hundred miles from Mehdiganj, complete with pictures of bags of sludge strewn around the property. Three months later, the franchisee Brindavan Brothers announced it was shuttering its doors because of "unbearable financial losses."

While Coca-Cola was seemingly losing ground, it was planning to outflank activists with the TERI report—the investigation done at the behest of the University of Michigan—which it finally released in January 2008. Surprisingly, given TERI's ties to Coke, the environmental group appeared to support the campaign's demand to close the plant at Kala Dera, saying that "it is obvious that the area is overexploited and it is highly unlikely that the water situation would improve." Unless the company could transport water from another location or store it during the rainy season, TERI wrote, the company should shut it down. The report went on to contradict Coke's claims of water neutrality by finding that "water tables have been depleting in Mehdiganj," even while it stopped short of recommending that the plant there close.

By contrast, on the issue of pollution, the report supported Coke, saying it "generally meets the government regulatory standards," even while it occasionally fell short of the company's own, more stringent, standards. TERI declined to offer an opinion, however, on whether Coke was responsible for groundwater contamination around the plants, saying it was beyond the scope of the report. Finally, on the issue of pesticides, the report concluded they were totally absent in the water used for production, even as it declined to test the actual beverages Coke produced.

Both sides rushed to spin it in a favorable light. "Enough is enough. Now even Coca-Cola's ally in India has found the company to not be up to the mark," said Srivastava. Coke soft-pedaled, promising in a letter to the University of Michigan to use the findings to create a new "community engagement framework" to "engage with stakeholders" and institute new "global guidelines for operating plants" by early 2008. As for Kala Dera, the company announced it wouldn't be shutting the plant—but would instead step up its rainwater harvesting to help the surrounding community. "The easiest thing would be to shut down, but the solution is not to run away," said Atul Singh, CEO of Coca-Cola India. "If we shut down, Rajasthan is still going to have a water problem." Even TERI, however, expressed skepticism about the efficacy of rainwater harvesting, upholding the activists' claims that many of the rainwater-harvesting structures were in "dilapidated condition."

When the report landed on the desk of administrators in Michigan, however, virtually none of that mattered. It took university vice president Tim Slottow only three days to declare that the university would retain its contract with Coke, for the surprising reason that TERI found no pesticides in the water Coke used for production. Incredibly, that's what the fine print of the Michigan's dispute resolution board had declared would be the standard for decision-making. Groundwater depletion and pollution would be too difficult to accurately measure, the board concluded, despite being the main points of contention in the student activist campaign. And yet TERI didn't even measure whether pesticides were present in Coke beverages.

Even as Coke was able to use the TERI report to blunt the attack from

India, the full brilliance of its strategy wasn't revealed until another report landed on a desk at another university.

After the breakdown in negotiations on Colombia, Collingsworth and Kovalik filed their appeal of the ATCA case on March 31, 2008. As they waited for their day in court, everyone else was waiting, too—for the release of Coke's much-vaunted ILO report into the Colombian bottling plants. In fact, the UN agency had slowly made good on its promise to investigate, with six "senior officials" from Geneva setting up shop in Bogotá over the summer of 2008 and meeting with company managers, touring plants, and interviewing workers. In all, they were there twelve days.

The ILO finally released its report on October 3, 2008, and like the TERI report it was a mixed bag for Coke. The agency criticized the bottler for hostility toward unionization, with managers threatening workers against joining unions, and punishing them with withheld pay, repeated dismissals, and even assaults if they did. The ILO reserved its highest criticism for the practice of subcontracting, noting that at some plants up to 75 or 80 percent of workers now worked on a temporary or contract basis. Those workers, it found, received lower wages and worked far longer hours than the full-time workers—in some cases even required to work twenty-four-hour shifts.

Despite the harsh assessment, at no point did the ILO investigate the company's alleged past contact with paramilitaries, or their history of murder, threats, and intimidation. The Killer Coke campaign pounced, throwing back Neville Isdell's comments from the shareholder meetings in which he promised to investigate "past practices." But sure enough, that was never what the IUF had asked Coke to do, says Ron Oswald, the general secretary of the international union that formally requested the assessment. He confirms all along that the assessment was intended to look only into current working conditions, despite Coke's clearly positioning the report as a response to the student protests at NYU and Michigan. "We told them very clearly they should not do that," he says. "It was never intended to be the response that a number of people continue to ask for and what I think is a legitimate request."

In fact, such an investigation was beyond the scope of the ILO committee that led the inquiry, says Kari Tapiola, the head of the ILO's Committee on Standards and Fundamental Principles and Rights at Work. "We said right from the beginning that we can only look into what the situation is currently," he says, "we would not start going into an area that is covered by the complaint section of the freedom of association." The what? "A separate committee to which trade unions or employers can complain." As it happens, that's the very ILO committee to which SINALTRAINAL filed its complaint after ending negotiations with Coke, sending the company immediately running to Judge Weinstein for sanctions.

Virtually the only interview granted by the Coca-Cola Company for this book was a forty-minute phone interview with Ed Potter. Asked when the company first discovered that the ILO wouldn't be looking into past practices, Potter equivocates. "I think there is a little dancing on the head of a pin here," he says, "because when you are looking into the present presumptively you are also looking into the past." But clearly the company "would never have agreed" to looking into acts of violence that were already subject to court proceedings, he says. "It was never going to happen." As with the TERI report, the scope of the report had been seemingly predetermined to support Coke; in no case would it answer the question that NYU had presumably asked it to—whether the company had colluded with paramilitaries to perpetrate violence against its workers.

The question now was whether the university would accept the ILO assessment as fulfillment of its call for an independent investigation. The university senate held off the vote until February 5, 2009—by coincidence the day after SINALTRAINAL was finally scheduled to get its hearing in Miami on the appeal of the ATCA case. That morning, Collingsworth headed to the twentieth floor of Miami's federal building. Waiting there for him was a panel of three judges, each with a scowl deeper than the last. Collingsworth launched into an argument he'd been rehearsing for the better part of three years—that the case had been wrongly decided when Judge Martínez allowed the sample bottling agreement as the sole item of discovery.

"Who at Coca-Cola wanted Gil murdered—who?" interrupted Judge Bernard Tjoflat. Collingsworth began to answer, "On an aiding-and-abetting theory . . ."

"Who?" barked Tjoflat.

"We don't know that information yet," Collingsworth admitted. But the names of plant managers listed in the complaint, he continues, should at least be enough to get them a copy of the actual bottler agreement and a list of those responsible for implementing it.

"Here is the fishing in this area of the law," said Tjoflat, referring to Judge Martínez's earlier warning against "international fishing expeditions."

If there was any doubt the hearing was turning into a disaster, the relatively easy reception given to Coke's lawyer Faith Gay clinched it. After the hearing, Collingsworth walked down to the courthouse cafeteria with Bill Scherer, a well-known Republican lawyer in Florida whom he'd brought with him to help make his case. Scherer reassured him, "I thought you did great." After all, he said, isn't Coke dealing in contradiction? In its public announcements, the company touts its workplace policies for bottlers, and yet in court it argues it has no control over them. "So which is it?" he asks. "How is Coca-Cola going to enforce their rights policy if they don't have control. Ask Ed Potter about that."

Posed exactly that question, Potter responds in great detail about the series of audits and worker complaint mechanisms that have been put in place to enforce Coke's new workplace policies, including its "guiding principles" for bottlers since 2006. For the big bottlers, he says, the Coca-Cola Company gets directly involved when violations of labor or environmental policies occur. "We really do not let go of these conversations until there is a resolution," he says. "Believe me, in my whole time here, I have never had a bottler that said we are not going to play here. It's never happened."

In other words, Potter is saying the company does have control over its bottlers—if nothing else, through the power of influence. So does that mean the bottling agreements have changed since the days of Gil's murder? "My sense is the language of the franchise agreements hasn't changed for a long, long time," he says. "But the understanding of what people need to be responsible for, accountable for, has evolved over time." If the Gil case had happened today, he says, "It's not something that would linger and fester. There would be people on the ground, and it would be a different degree of attention to the issues that were raised." It's hard to believe Potter is actually saying this, basically admitting that Coke had everything it needed to deal with the violence at bottlers in Colombia from the moment it happened, as early as the first murder in Carepa in 1994. And yet Coke failed in its responsibility to stop or investigate the crimes.

Now, more than twelve years later, the company was still shirking that responsibility. The night of the Miami hearing, Adolfo "El Diablo" Cardona stood in front of a blackboard in a small room in NYU's Vanderbilt Hall. With Romero translating, he retold for perhaps the hundredth time the story of Gil's murder, his attempted abduction, the destruction of the union. The next day, Romero sat in the hearing room of the NYU senate as its members deliberated their ban on Coke. The chair, Arthur Tannenbaum, began the meeting arguing that the ILO assessment, while not perfect, is the best the university could hope to achieve. At this point, an investigation into the murders would be impossible. Hearing those words, Romero felt his heart sink. When the vote came down, it was a close defeat, twenty-eight to twenty-two, in favor of lifting the ban. The last bright spot of the Campaign to Stop Killer Coke had dimmed.

Even as the campaign watched its two biggest victories snatched away, one would think they could take solace in the new framework the company had put in place to control its bottlers. After all, Ed Potter himself promised that if a situation similar to the violence in Colombia occurred today it would be handled much differently. That hasn't necessarily been borne out, however. In fact, a similar case *did* occur. It happened in Guatemala, and it happened on Potter's watch.

José Armando Palacios was spared the violence that infected Coke's bottling plants in Guatemala in the late 1970s and early 1980s. Though he began to work for Coke in 1979, it was at a separate plant not owned by anti-union John Trotter, but by another company named INCASA. He joined the union early, soon becoming a leader. In 1991, he took a job as an in-house security guard, a position that had been forbidden by management to unionize. Palacios had a secret plan to organize the security guards anyway—arguing that they would be a valuable asset to the union, able to tip off union leaders to visits by authorities when they engaged in work stoppages or slowdowns.

He quickly succeeded in persuading the other five guards to join. But at the time, union leaders thought the idea too risky, so Palacios bided his time for more than a decade until 2004 when new leaders were willing to risk it. As soon as they made their intentions clear, though, Palacios says he started receiving threats from the plant's personnel manager, Eduardo García, who allegedly told him he'd have to abandon the effort, or else he'd use his connections in the army to have him disappeared. (Palacios reported the incident to the Public Prosecutor's Office, which set up a meeting with García, in which he denied making any threats but did sign a statement with Palacios promising to continue woking with "mutual respect" in the future.) A few months later, in June 2004, Palacios was working the graveyard shift when he heard shouts at one-thirty in the morning saying, "You are going to die, you son-of-a-bitch unionist!" Palacios threw himself to the ground just as shots rang out. He crawled under a truck, heart pounding and breathing heavily as he waited to be killed.

He survived, as several private security guards arrived to rescue him and his assailants fled. Those same guards later showed him a copy of a memo they had received from García to the head of their company, a retired army colonel, saying Palacios was "totally damaging" to the company, and listing the hours he worked at night. If anything, the shooting strengthened Palacios's resolve to unionize, with memories of the bravery of the bottling plant leaders in the 1980s still in his mind. "If our movement didn't have martyrs, capitalism would have swallowed us long ago," he says.

After the shooting, the bottler offered to pay him severance and fly him to the United States if he resigned. Soon after he refused, men burst into his house while he was out shopping, threatening his wife and son at gunpoint before leaving—an incident Palacios sees as a direct reprisal for his intransigence. Finally, in May 2005, the bottler fired him, just two months after Ed Potter had arrived at Coke, and even as he was promoting Coke's new zero-tolerance policy for anti-union violence. The union protested the firing as illegal, and fought to reinstate him at the company. After several more attempts on his life, however, Palacios went into hiding, eventually reaching out through a nonprofit to the Coca-Cola Company in Atlanta.

In December, he received an e-mail from Ron Oswald, head of the IUF—the international union that had supported the organizing effort in Guatemala in the 1980s, but had more recently been critical of SINALTRAINAL's fight in Colombia. Oswald told him that he'd been in contact with Ed Potter, and the Coca-Cola Company was offering to "make resources available to improve security" for him—if he agreed to leave the bottling company. "They recognize that this cannot be done through the bottler since there is at least some ground for our suspicions that the threats are instigated by the local bottler," he wrote. (In an interview, Oswald says that he was not involved in the details of the negotiations with Coke, though he does feel that the bottling company in Guatemala has long been hostile to union organizing.)

But Palacios didn't want to leave the bottler, he told Oswald, as e-mails flew between intermediaries with the company. In January 2006, he received another offer from a Coke representative, repeating the offer that Coke Atlanta would fund a hefty "protection package" if Palacios would only leave the bottling company. Once again, Palacios refused. The very next day, he headed home briefly to pick up a few things, parking his red pickup truck on the street. As he got out of the car, another man in a red car pulled up on the same street and got out at virtually the same time. A man standing on the corner pulled out a revolver and shot that man three times in the chest, killing him right in front of Palacios, who believes the shots were actually intended for him.

From that point on, Palacios lost faith in talking with Coke. Oswald still wrote e-mails assuring him he was in "almost daily contact" with Potter about the case, but there might be a complication should Palacios happen to be "approached by a certain D.C.-based lawyer with promises of significant sums of 'settlement' money"—a clear allusion to Collingsworth and the Colombia ATCA case. Around the same time, a Costa Rican lawyer for the Coca-Cola Company named Rodrigo Romero arranged a meeting at a hotel in Guatemala City. According to Palacios, he offered him $15,000 and a plane ticket to the United States, if only he would sign a blank piece of paper, which he was told was a confidentiality agreement requiring him never to badmouth INCASA or Coca-Cola again. Palacios's struggled to control his anger. Thinking of his family, he told the lawyer calmly that he'd consider the offer. A few days later, Romero sent Palacios an e-mail, cc'ing Potter, to confirm he offered money to Palacios, whom he says "agreed to let me know the sum over the weekend."

Palacios intended nothing of the sort. "He thought I was some fool," says Palacios, "to sign some document I would later regret for the rest of his life." Finally after realizing that neither the bottling company nor the Coca-Cola Company would protect him, he reluctantly took a severance package (without a confidentiality agreement) and fled to the United States. It took another two years for his family to be able to join him on asylum there. Now living in Detroit, Palacios started talking with "a certain D.C.-based lawyer" about bringing a lawsuit, which Collingsworth eventually filed in New York Supreme Court in February 2010.

On the face of it, the case for Coke's culpability was even stronger than the SINALTRAINAL case in Colombia. After all, Potter and Coke's lawyer had directly inserted themselves into the situation, telling Palacios they could assure his security in exchange for his resignation and his silence. When he refused, they left him and his family unprotected from attack. "I think Coca-Cola could have stopped INCASA from doing what it was doing at any time," says Palacios. "If they didn't stop it, it's because they didn't want to."

The parallels between Colombia and Guatemala are too strong to ignore. In one sense at least, Potter is right: The company was all over the case from the beginning. But it was not to protect the workers, but to protect the company. In fact, at the very same time Coke was negotiating with SINALTRAINAL's leaders to make them leave the union and stop disparaging Coke, it was following the same script with Palacios. To be fair, in both cases the company was dealing with avowed troublemakers with an active anticorporate, even anticapitalist mind-set. Asked what he thinks is really going on with the Colombia case, Potter answers indirectly, but his response speaks volumes.

A few years ago, he says, he read a book about the investigation of the murder of a Catholic priest in Guatemala. "The author describes how trade unionists have learned to protect themselves by making themselves martyrs," he says. "By drawing attention to themselves, they protect themselves." In that view, Coke is the scapegoat, exploited by workers for their own self-preservation. In such a scenario, it makes sense that the company should fight tooth and nail against making concessions. No matter how lamentable the violence in some Third World country, it doesn't justify ransoming the company's brand.

"I've had lots of discussions with some of the oil companies we've sued," says Collingsworth. "Basically the way they put it is: 'Look, Colombia or Indonesia or Burma, that's a rough country. We're there to create jobs and to make the best of a bad situation, but we didn't start that war. We're not going to end that war.' But you can't say you are an innocent bystander if you are part of the support network for one of the actors in a violent exchange."

It's hard to believe that a company like Coca-Cola doesn't care about the safety of its workers or the health of its customers or the environment at least on some level. If there is a larger lesson to be drawn from the various attempts to hold Coke accountable, it's that a corporation will never willingly box itself into a corner with any legally binding ties that force it to improve the lot of the communities where it operates—at least not when they cut into its ability to make a profit. That includes binding collective bargaining agreements with unions as much as binding regulations on water use or on how it can advertise and sell it products.

Just as Asa Candler and Robert Woodruff were happy to give millions for philanthropic causes but resented paying thousands in taxes, today's generation of leaders at Coke have done real good in the world—building schools, sponsoring physical education, spurring recycling, stewarding water—when their programs are both voluntary and in support of the larger goals of the company. In a perfect world, the free market would ensure it more broadly took health and environmental issues through pressure from consumers in buying products that supported their moral viewpoint. The amount of money and advertising Coke has put into creating its brand, however, distorts the ability of consumer actions to hold it accountable.

The actions against Coke show that changing a corporation against its will requires two things: binding legal consequences that threaten its bottom line and a sustained public campaign that threatens its brand image. In places where activists have been most successful against Coke—for example, in the closure of the Hindustan Coca-Cola plant in Kerala—both elements have been present. In places where neither is there—look no farther than Chiapas—a campaign can barely get off the ground. And of the two elements, it is ultimately the threat to brand image that has proved more important in Coke's case—that's why the campaigners against soda in schools were able to eke out an agreement without the threat of a lawsuit, while the Colombian union leaders foundered once they took away the public pressure of a campaign.

In each of these cases, the tactics by the company have been the same—to remove the threat to its brand without agreeing to any enforceable requirements that might hold it accountable down the line. To fight back the various threats, the company has allayed public pressure by promising increasingly strict but still voluntary solutions—guidelines on soda sales it could oversee, workplace policies that applied only to direct employees, independent investigations that didn't actually investigate the most controversial accusations—until it found ones that the general public would accept.

In the case of the murder of Isidro Gil and the other Colombian union members, that was enough. When the decision came down on the ATCA appeal on August 11, 2009, it surprised no one. In a thirty-page opinion, the three-judge panel essentially called the allegations "too vague and conclusory" to warrant further discovery. Barring some sensational testimony from a demobilized paramilitary commander, it's unlikely we'll ever know what connections, if any, Coke's Colombian bottlers—much less Coke Atlanta—had to the murders. In point of fact, though, we'll also never know with any certainty whether Coke is innocent. After all, if the company honestly had no involvement in the violence, then why have company executives so long resisted an investigation into the murders, as their own general counsel urged them to conduct more than five years ago?

In at least one regard, Potter and Collingsworth agree—the union members do look to the lawsuit and the Killer Coke campaign as the reason they are still alive. Despite its missteps during negotiations, the campaign did show how an activist campaign could support a court case and lead a company to change its policies, if not its practices. And however confident the Coca-Cola Company may be that Neville Isdell's combination of socially responsible marketing, penthouse negotiations, and predetermined investigations has dispensed with the activist campaign, his final appearance as CEO of the Coca-Cola Company showed the activists against Coke are not through yet.

It was a diminished crew that arrived for Coke's annual shareholder meeting in April 2009. Unlike past years when the meeting had been held in Wilmington, this year Coke had called it home to Atlanta, ostensibly as a tribute to outgoing CEO Neville Isdell. But the company must surely have considered the fact that Atlanta is much farther to travel for activists from Boston, New York, and San Francisco. The dozen or so who did make the trip included Ray Rogers, of course, as well as Camilo Romero,

Amit Srivastava, and CAI's Gigi Kellett. Hoping to still make a splash in spite of the low numbers, Rogers brought what he called his "secret weapon," a giant mobile billboard attached to a truck cab with the slogan, "Don't Drink Killer Coke Zero—Zero Ethics! Zero Justice! Zero Health!" on the side and pictures of murdered union workers Isidro Gil and Adolfo de Jesús Múnera on the back.

A warm, southern breeze was blowing as shareholders walked up the ramp to the Gwinnett Convention Center, a half-hour north of the city where Coke was born. By coincidence, the day chosen for the meeting happened to be Earth Day, a fact underscored by the environmental showcase Coke set up in the lobby with displays touting new soda bottles and T-shirts made from recycled PET and a video loop of the Spartanburg recycling plant.

Inside the convention hall, a high ceiling full of metal panels in geometrical shapes created the feeling of being inside a giant erector set. "We'd like to start with a little bit of happiness from Coca-Cola," began Isdell, taking the stage to launch Coke's newest advertising campaign, "Open Happiness," with a new music video. "I think the song really captures the positivity, the optimism, and the real fun of Brand Coke," he said. "This is a business about people, a business about belief. If we want to have a sustainable business, then the communities we serve need to be sustainable in and of themselves."

Standing before the crowd, Isdell had a lot to be happy about. He was handing over a stronger and more secure company than the one he'd inherited, having navigated Coke over the rocky shoals of childhood obesity and Colombian murder trials, the bottled water backlash and controversy over water pollution and depletion in India. He turned over the meeting to Muhtar Kent, a Turkish businessman who rose from head of international relations to become Coke's newly minted CEO. Immediately, Kent dispensed with the happiness talk to address what mattered most: growth. Every day, he said, the world had "multiple hydration occasions," and the increasing trends of urbanization and a growing middle class around the world perfectly positioned Coke to take advantage of them. Putting up a

PowerPoint chart, he showed that Mexico consumed some six hundred cups of Coke products per person per year, and the United States had four hundred, while the global average languished at one hundred. "What an amazing opportunity!" he concluded.

Kent handed the meeting back to Isdell for questions. True to form, Rogers was first out of his seat, launching into a rant about the illegitimacy of the ILO and TERI investigations into Colombia and India. "I wish you had updated your facts from the last time you were here," said Isdell, before turning to another questioner, who asked a more innocuous question about the old age of the board of directors. "I want to start a youth movement," the questioner said.

Suddenly a student with the Killer Coke campaign leaped up, yelling, "I am part of the youth movement, and we are not on your side."

"If you want to ask your question, I must ask you return to your seat," responded Isdell. "If not you'll be evicted." The youth kept yelling, red-faced, as security guards in black jackets came up and put their hands on his shoulders, leading him out of the room in a reminder of Rogers's own ejection five years earlier.

It was pure political theater—but it started a roll for the activists in the crowd. With floodlights in Isdell's eyes, he had no control over whom he called on, and one by one the forces of Killer Coke took the mic. Srivastava stood up to blast operations in India, warning investors that Coke may be forced to pay hefty fines in India. Next Camilo Romero blamed Coke for failing to bargain in good faith with the Colombians. Then it was Kellett, describing Coke's newly announced global "water neutrality" policy as just a big Ponzi scheme, sucking down water in one part of the world while conserving it in another.

And so it went. Emerging into the bright Georgia sunshine, Rogers was elated. "If Neville Isdell thought it was his swan song, that he was going to end on a high note, then he was wrong," he said. In real terms, of course, the meeting achieved nothing. But symbolically, it put Coke on notice that however hobbled, the campaign against it wasn't finished.

After the meeting, Rogers's mobile billboard led an activist caravan back down the highway to Atlanta as cars honked and people waved. Like bees drawn to an open bottle of pop, the caravan ended up arriving downtown at the World of Coca-Cola. Few people were in Pemberton Park to see the billboard truck as it drove around blaring an original folk song called "Coke Is the Drink of the Death Squads." But Rogers would never miss an opportunity to educate one more person about Coke's misdeeds. Jumping out with a clutch of "Drink That Represses" flyers in his hand, he ran up to a bus of schoolkids on a field trip to the Georgia Aquarium.

"Hey, kids, look here!" he shouted, jumping aboard the bus and gesticulating wildly at the billboard as it drove past. Before the chaperone could react, he jumped back out, while the billboard truck circled back around the World of Coca-Cola. For a moment a snatch of muzak floated across the park from the entrance to the museum. It took a second to place the tune before it became clear: "I'd like to teach the world to sing, in perfect harmony . . ."

Acknowledgments

Obviously, to write a book of this scope, I have a great many people to thank. First and foremost, I want to thank my agent, Elisabeth Weed, who believed in this book from the beginning, encouraged me through two years of proposal revisions and pitch meetings before it had become a reality, and then through another two years of writing after it had. A huge thanks, as well, to my incredible editor, Rachel Holtzman, who was a calm in the storm throughout the writing and editing process, and offered just the right combination of prodding and trust to see me through multiple stages of rewriting, cutting, and framing the manuscript. Thanks, as well, to her assistant, Travers Johnson, and the excellent team at Avery for the behind-the-scenes work they did in making the book the best it could be.

I'd also like to express a measure of debt to the authors who have previously tackled the rich subject of Coca-Cola, on whose work I drew from heavily (and in some cases, shamelessly) in order to tell various aspects of the history and current practices of the company. For the first chapters dealing with the history of the company, Mark Pendergrast's *For God, Country, and Coca-Cola* was enormously helpful, as was *Secret Formula* by Fred Allen. I was also helped immensely by the collections of documents that Pendergrast and Allen left at the rare book library at Emory University, as well as other collections there, from which most of the historical documents I relied on are drawn. For the later history of the company, I relied on Constance Hays's *The Real Thing* and Thomas Oliver's *The Real Coke, The Real Story*. In the chapter detailing the fight to get soda out of schools, I was greatly assisted by Michele Simon's *Appetite for Profit* (and by Simon herself, who freely shared information with me from the beginning stages of the manuscript). And on international affairs, I relied on Laura Jordan's excellent thesis on Coke in Mexico, and on Nantoo Banerjee's book—also called *The Real Thing*—to elucidate Coke's problems in India.

In addition to those written sources, I'd like to acknowledge all of the patient time and effort granted to me by those struggling to keep Coke accountable, including: Ray Rogers, Lew Friedman, Terry Collingsworth, Dan Kovalik, Camilo Romero, Amit Srivastava, Jackie Domac, Ross Getman, Michael Jacobson, Stephen Gardner, Dick Daynard, Gigi Kellett, and Javier Correa and all of the other union leaders in Colombia. On the other side, I'd like to thank the executives of Coca-Cola India, especially Kalyan Ranjan, who, quite unlike their counterparts in the United States or Mexico, granted me the access I asked for and shared with me their perspective; their openness and candor have made this a better book.

I'd also like to acknowledge the Herculean efforts of my research assistants, David Mashburn, Tony D'Ovidio, Alexis Hauk, Hannah Martin, and Maddy Schricker, without whom I quite literally could not have written this book (especially David and Tony, who helped draft some early sections of Chapters 3 and 4); and the translators who helped me understand foreign perspectives along with foreign words, including Arup Chanda and Nandan Upadhyay in India; Paco Vasquez and Erin Araujo in Mexico; and my translator in Colombia, whose name I must unfortunately withhold for safety reasons. Many thanks to Laura Bravo Melguizo, who spent countless hours translating Spanish-language documents with me and correcting multiple facts and translations in the text. I'd be remiss, as well, if I didn't give a shout-out to Ula Café, whose strong coffee and friendly baristas sustained me through many long hours of writing.

Last but absolutely not least, I must thank my wife, Alexandra, who not only came up with the title for this book, but also suffered through interminable conversations about soft drinks and corporate accountability, working "vacations" in Atlanta and Chiapas, and babysitting two unruly toddlers during my long nights of writing and revising at the office. I can't thank you enough, *sangsai*, and only hope I can do the same for you with your next book.

Notes

INTRODUCTION

Page 1 On the morning of December 5, 1996: The description of Gil's murder relies on eyewitness accounts by Luis Hernán Manco Monroy, Oscar Alberto Giraldo Arango, and Luis Adolfo Cardona Usma, interviews by the author.

Page 2 twenty-eight-year-old was a natural leader: Martín Gil, interview by the author.

Page 3 union submitted its final proposal: Complaint (Docket Entry 1), *SINALTRAINAL, et al. v. The Coca-Cola Company, et al.*, United States District Court for the Southern District of Florida, 1:2001-cv-03208 (hereafter *SINALTRAINAL v. Coke*), 23.

Page 3 .38 Special: Ballistics report, December 2, 1998, Isidro Gil investigation, Fiscalía de la Nación, Unidad de Derechos Humanos, Radicado Preliminar No. 164, Republica de Colombia (hereafter Gil), vol. 2, pp. 72–76.

Page 3 shot him between the eyes: Gil autopsy report, December 10, 1996 (Diligencia de Necropsia, No. UCH-NC-96-412), *Gil* 1:87.

Page 3 more than 2,500 union members: Human Rights Watch, *World Report 2009—Colombia*, January 14, 2009.

CHAPTER 1. A BRIEF HISTORY OF COKE

Page 9 One million visitors: The World of Coca-Cola®—Atlanta, http://www.worldofcoca-cola.com.

Page 11 "patents of royal favor": Gerald Carson, *One for a Man, Two for a Horse: A Pictorial History, Grave and Comic, of Patent Medicines* (Garden City, NY: Doubleday, 1961), 9.

Page 11 Hooper's Pills . . . "Rivals might detect": James Harvey Young, *The Toadstool Millionaires: A Social History of Patent Medicines in America Before Federal Regulations* (Princeton, NJ: Princeton University Press, 1961), 13.

Page 11 bleeding . . . and "purging": Mary Calhoun, *Medicine Show: Conning People and Making Them Like It* (New York: Harper & Row, 1976), 24–25, 65–67; David Armstrong and Elizabeth Metzger Armstrong, *The Great American Medicine Show* (New York: Prentice Hall, 1991), 1–10; Alyn Brodsky, *Benjamin Rush: Patriot and Physician* (New York: Truman Talley, 2004), 29.

Page 12 practice grew into a fad: Young, 44–45; Armstrong and Armstrong, 23–25; A. Walker Bingham, *The Snake Oil Syndrome: Patent Medicine Advertising* (Hanover, MA: Christopher, 1994), 13.

Page 12 Connecticut physician Samuel Lee, Jr.: Bingham; Young, 32–34.

Page 12 Thomas W. Dyott amassed: Young, 34–35.

Page 12 The Civil War brought new patients: Young, 97.

Page 12 little more than laxatives or emetics: Young, 98–99; Carson, 30; Armstrong and Armstrong, 178.

Page 12 between 20,000 and 50,000 . . . concoctions: Young, 109.

Page 12 total sales of $80 million: Calhoun, 70.

Page 12 The winners were . . . rescuing his son from a bear: Bingham, 91–92.

Page 12 "medicine shows": Calhoun, 1–8.

Page 13 notorious showmen, Clark Stanley: Carson, 41.

Page 13 As one 1930s-era pitch doctor . . . sold themselves: Calhoun, 45, 58.

Page 13 early devotee of Samuel Thomson's . . . Extract of Stillingia: James Harvey Young, "Three Atlanta Pharmacists," *Pharmacy in History* 31, no. 1 (1989), 16–22.

Page 13 later named him an addict: A. O. Murphy testimony, *Coca-Cola Co. v. Koke Co.*, 254 U.S. 143 (1920) (hereafter *Koke*), 392; J. C. Mayfield testimony, *Koke*, 776; "The Original Coca-Cola Woman: Mrs. Diva Brown," *The Southern Carbonator*, September 1907; Hugh Merrill, "The Formula and Diva Brown: 'The Original Coca-Cola Woman,'" *Atlanta Business Chronicle*, January 7, 1991.

Page 14 "I am convinced from actual experiments": "A Wonderful Medicine," *Atlanta Journal*, March 10, 1885.

Page 14 Cocaine Toothache Drops: Armstrong and Armstrong, 160–161.

Page 14 concoction called Vin Mariani: Mark Pendergrast, *For God, Country, and Coca-Cola: The Definitive History of the Great American Soft Drink and the Company That Makes It* (New York: Basic Books, 2000 [orig. pub. 1993]), 22–23; Frederick Allen, *Secret Formula: How Brilliant Marketing and Relentless Salesmanship Made Coca-Cola the Best-Known Product in the World* (New York: HarperBusiness, 1994), 23–24.

Page 14 French Wine Coca . . . kola nut: J. C. Louis and Harvey Yazijian, *The Cola Wars: The Story of the Global Corporate Battle Between the Coca-Cola Company and PepsiCo, Inc.* (New York: Everest House, 1980), 15.

Page 15 beer was one of the first luxuries . . . cheapest form of water purification: Armstrong and Armstrong, 39, 5.

Page 15 Soon enterprising drunkards . . . "beverige": John Hull Brown, *Early American Beverages* (Rutland, VT: C. E. Tuttle, 1966), 13–16.

Page 15 mineral springs such as those at Saratoga Springs: Stephen N. Tchudi, *Soda Poppery: The History of Soft Drinks in America* (New York: Charles Scribner's Sons, 1986), 6.

Page 15 Joseph Priestley discovered how to produce: Robert E. Schofield, *The Enlightenment of Joseph Priestley: A Study of His Life and Work from 1733 to 1773* (Philadelphia: Pennsylvania State University Press, 1997), 256–258.

Page 15 movement against alcohol led by Benjamin Rush: Brodsky, 95–97, 100; Armstrong and Armstrong, 41–42.

Page 15 Alcoholics Anonymous . . . statewide prohibition laws: Brown, 78.

Page 15 many were repealed: Armstrong and Armstrong, 44.

Page 15 creating the world's first "soda fountain": H. B. Nicholson, "Host to Thirsty Main Street" (New York: Newcomen Society, December 18, 1953), 9; Franklin M. Garrett, "The Development of the Soda Fountain in Drug Stores for the Past 50 Years" (The Coco-Cola Company, n.d.); Joseph L. Morrison, "The Soda Fountain," *American Heritage* 13, no. 5 (August 1962).

Page 15 Lemon's Superior Sparkling Ginger Ale: Lawrence Dietz, *Soda Pop: The History, Advertising, Art and Memorabilia of Soft Drinks in America* (New York: Simon & Schuster, 1973), 83.

Page 16 Hires Root Beer: Tchudi, 21–22.

Page 16 Dr Pepper . . . Moxie: Dietz, 82–84.

Page 16 the South suffered a complete disruption: Louis and Yazijian, 14–15.

Page 16 Atlanta . . . known as the "Phoenix City": Pendergrast, 20.

Page 16 dozens of reformulations . . . bitter orange and cassia: Frederick Allen, *Secret Formula: How Brilliant Marketing and Relentless Salesmanship Made Coca-Cola the Best-Known Product in the World* (New York: HarperBusiness, 1994), 28.

Page 17 "three-legged iron pot": E. J. Kahn, *The Big Drink: An Unofficial History of Coca-Cola* (London: Max Reinhardt, 1960), 56–57.

Page 17 "brass kettle heated over an open fire": Pat Watters, *Coca-Cola: An Illustrated History* (Garden City, NY: Doubleday, 1978), 5, 9; see also Wilbur Kurtz, "Dr. John S. Pemberton: Originator of the Formula for Coca-Cola, A Short Biographical Sketch," January 1954.

Page 17 pharmacy owner Willis Venable himself: Watters, 16; Allen, 28.

Page 17 John G. Wilkes, who came: Elizabeth Candler Graham and Ralph Roberts, *The Real Ones: Four Generations of the First Family of Coca-Cola* (Fort Lee, NJ: Barricade, 1992), 6.

Page 17 Pemberton's pharmacy laboratory as state-of-the-art: Pendergrast, 28–29; Allen, 27–28.

Page 17 fountain drinks containing kola nut: Tchudi, 25.

Page 18 company's more recent official histories: The Coca-Cola Company, *The Chronicle of Coca-Cola Since 1886* (Atlanta: The Coca-Cola Company, 1993); Coca-Cola Heritage, www.coca-cola.com/heritage.

Page 18 coined by one of Pemberton's partners: Watters, 15; Pendergrast, 29; Allen, 28.

Page 18 label for the syrup: Charles Howard Candler, *Asa Griggs Candler, Coca-Cola & Emory College* (Atlanta: Higgins-McArthur, 1953), 10.

Page 18 just twenty-five gallons the first year: Robinson testimony, *Koke*; The Coca-Cola Company, Annual Report to the Stockholders, 1923.

Page 18 took to his bed with illness: Pendergrast, 34.

Page 19 neither drank nor smoked . . . scrap paper: Kahn, 59.

Page 19 mix up a single gallon: Graham and Roberts, 55.

Page 19 "more money to be made as a druggist": Graham and Roberts, 39.

Page 19 Candler knew the real money . . . mysterious circumstances: Pendergrast, 44–46.

Page 19 the earliest records of the company burned: "The Beginning of Bottled Coca-Cola as Told by Mr. S. C. Dobbs," October 13, 1913.

Page 20 handing out tickets for free Cokes: Allen, 29.

Page 20 Each soda fountain operator got: Asa G. Candler to Warren Candler, Atlanta, April 10, 1888, reprinted in Candler, *Asa Griggs Candler, Coca-Cola & Emory College.*

Page 20 more than 100,000 drinks a year: Pendergrast, 60.

Page 20 Sales took off . . . 50,000 gallons: The Coca-Cola Company, Annual Report, 1895.

Page 20 posting on Coke's corporate website: Phil Mooney, January 30, 2008, Coca-Cola Conversations: Did you know? 1886 vs. today, http://www.coca-colaconversations.com/my_weblog/2008/01/did-you-know-18.html.

Page 20 early copy of the formula: Pendergrast, 56; Mark Pendergrast, "Cocaine Information, Amount in Vin Mariani, French Wine Coca, Coca-Cola," Pendergrast collection, Emory University.

Page 20 Georgia Pharmaceutical Association in 1891: "Analysis of Coca-Cola, Analysis No. 7265, Office of H. R. Slack, M.D., Ph.G.," reprinted in *Coca-Cola, What Is It? What It Is* (The Coca-Cola Company, 1901).

Page 21 narcotic kick on his letterhead: Constance L. Hays, *The Real Thing: Truth and Power at the Coca-Cola Company* (New York: Random House, 2004), 102.

Page 21 Pamphlets he handed out to retailers: *Atlanta Constitution*, June 19, 1891.

Page 21 "a very small proportion": Asa G. Candler testimony, *Henry A. Rucker v. The Coca-Cola Company*, U.S. Circuit Court, District of Georgia, 52.

Page 21 wasn't entirely removed: Graham and Roberts, 19.

Page 21 needed to raise at least $50,000: Allen, 38.

Page 21 One of the very first corporations: Joel Bakan, *The Corporation: The Pathological Pursuit of Profit and Power* (New York: Simon & Schuster, 2004), 8.

Page 21 Despite initial promises to arrange interviews with Coca-Cola Company executives, corporate spokeswoman Kerry Kerr ultimately declined cooperation with this book. The only interview the company provided was a forty-minute conversation with director of global labor relations Ed Potter, which appears in the final chapter. After that interview, the company asked that further questions be provided in writing. Several dozen questions were submitted to Kerr, and she responded in an e-mail: "Much of the information you are requesting is proprietary in nature and we are unable to comment. The remaining questions are about topics to which we have responded over the years multiple times. Given the fact that this information is widely available, coupled with the decidedly subjective slant in which your questions were framed, we are declining further comment. . . . The Coca-Cola Company's practice continues to be one of engagement in conversations with all stakeholders—including supporters and critics—as long those discussions can be fair and objective."

Page 22 "directors of such companies": Adam Smith, *An Inquiry into the Nature and Causes of the Wealth of Nations* (London: T. Nelson & Sons, 1895), 311.

Page 22 The corporation took off: Bakan, 7.

Page 22 more than three hundred: Jack Beatty, ed., *Colossus: How the Corporation Changed America* (New York: Broadway Books, 2001), 5.

Page 22 And unlike their British counterparts . . . beginning in the 1830s: Beatty, 45–46.

Page 22 No corporations were as successful: Beatty, 103–112.

Page 22 corporations were chartered by states . . . any purpose they desired: Richard L. Grossman and Frank T. Adams, "Taking Care of Business: Citizenship and the Charter of Incorporation," in Dean Ritz, ed., *Defying Corporations, Defining Democracy* (New York: The Apex Press, 2001), 59–72.

Page 23 concept of "limited liability": Bakan, 11–13.

Page 23 declared corporations to be virtual "persons": David C. Korten, *The Post-Corporate World: Life After Capitalism* (West Hartford, CT, and San Francisco: Kumarian Press and Berrett-Koehler, 1999), 184–186.

Page 23 And in 1880, the federal government . . . "as well as financially": Humphrey McQueen, *The Essence of Capitalism: The Origins of Our Future* (Montreal: Black Rose Books, 2003), 29.

Page 23 few "national" products: Juliann Sivulka, *Soap, Sex, and Cigarettes: A Cultural History of American Advertising* (Belmont, CA: Wadsworth, 1998), 18–19.

Page 23 new markets in city department stores: Sivulka, 93.

Page 23 power of corporations was made complete: Bakan, 13–14.

Page 23 falling from 2,653 to 269: Sivulka, 93.

Page 23 companies that succeeded . . . quintessential example: Richard Tedlow, *New and Improved: The Story of Mass Marketing in America* (New York: Basic Books, 1990), 4–6.

Page 23 incorporated the Coca-Cola Company: Allen, 38–39; Pendergrast, 57–58.

Page 23 selling syrup wholesale . . . 400 percent profit: Charles Howard Candler, "Thirty-three Years with Coca-Cola 1890–1923" (unpublished manuscript, 1929), 20.

Page 24 legions of salesmen: Candler, "Thirty-three Years," 16–19.

Page 24 made only $12.50 a week: Candler, "Thirty-three Years," 33.

Page 24 sold in all forty-four states . . . soon to follow: Pendergrast, 61, 93.

Page 24 sleeping on a cot: Allen, 67.

Page 24 drum up clients . . . solely on advertising: Candler, "Thirty-three Years," 139.

Page 24 one-man pep squad: Allen, 71–72.

Page 24 more than 250,000 gallons . . . over a million: The Coca-Cola Company, Annual Report, 1923; Tedlow, p. 29.

Page 24 $1.5 million in sales: Tedlow, 29.

Page 24 In 1899, a Chattanooga lawyer . . . worked their territory: Allen, 106–107, 109; Pendergrast, 69–71.

Page 25 Sam Dobbs had been urging: Allen, 68.

Page 25 Chero-Cola . . . Coca & Cola: Roy W. Johnson, "Why 7,000 Imitations of Coca-Cola Are in the Copy Cat's Graveyard," *Sales Management*, January 9, 1926.

Page 25 "Unscrupulous pirates": Tchudi, 34–35.

Page 25 "gourd vines in wheat fields": Charles Howard Candler, *Asa Griggs Candler* (Atlanta: Emory University, 1950), 144.

Page 25 "the most beautiful sight we see". . . "a political parasite": Pendergrast, 96, 125.

Page 25 nascent Progressive movement: Beatty, 141–168.

Page 26 "I have spent my nights and my days": Harold Hirsch, "The Product Coca-Cola and a Method of Carrying on Business from a Legal Point of View," speech at 1923 bottlers' convention.

Page 26 J. C. Mayfield . . . Koke: Pendergrast, 43.

Page 26 Hirsch brought suit . . . when it didn't: Elton J. Buckley, "A Bottling Trade as well as a Trade Mark Decision of Great Importance," *National Bottlers Gazette*, July 5, 1919, 83; Iver P. Cooper, "Unclean Hands and Unlawful Use in Commerce," *Trademark Reporter* 71 (1981), 38–58.

Page 26 In a December 1920 ruling: Opinion, December 6, 1920, *Koke.*

Page 27 tens of millions of gallons . . . $4 million: The Coca-Cola Company Annual Report, 1922; Tedlow, 29.

Page 27 Candler bought up skyscrapers: Candler, *Asa Griggs Candler*, 262–263.

Page 27 depression got the best of him: Pendergrast, 93–95.

Page 27 eccentric drunk, who kept a menagerie: Kahn, 60.

Page 27 lacked his father's vision: Allen, 79–80.

Page 27 suffered a nervous breakdown: Pendergrast, 97.

Page 28 treated Coca-Cola as his personal piggybank: Candler, *Asa Griggs Candler*, 145.

Page 28 Progressive changes . . . profits to investors: Candler, *Asa Griggs Candler*, 266.

Page 28 "forced liquidation" . . . "he was ready": Candler, *Asa Griggs Candler*, 146.

Page 28 contribution of $1 million: Asa Candler to Warren Candler, July 16, 1914, reprinted in Candler, *Asa Griggs Candler*, 398.

Page 28 first of an eventual $8 million: *The Emory Alumnus* 27, no. 10 (December 1951), 3.

Page 28 mortgaged his own fortune: Candler, *Asa Griggs Candler*, 309–320.

Page 29 raising water rates . . . urged rich citizens: Pendergrast, 125–126.

Page 29 Howard was a lackluster president: Pendergrast, 126–127.

Page 29 head of the Atlanta Chamber . . . take over the company now: Allen, 91.

Page 29 His occupation was to make money: Tedlow, 56.

Page 29 breaking into a rival's office: Allen, 92–94.

Page 29 strapping $2 million in bonds to himself: Dietz, 97.

Page 29 secured signatures . . . $10 million in stock: Allen, 95–97; Pendergrast, 130.

Page 29 largest financial transaction: Kahn, 61.

Page 29 Not one of the children said a word: Candler, *Asa Griggs Candler*, 184.

Page 29 syndicate of three banks . . . three-man Voting Trust: Allen, 97–99; Pendergrast, 131.

Page 30 nearly 250 bottling plants . . . more than 1,000: The Coca-Cola Company, "Bottling Plants, 1886–1940," Records of The Coca-Cola Co.; Tedlow, p. 44.

Page 30 price of sugar, which skyrocketed: Allen 104; Pendergrast, 127, 139.

Page 30 "parent bottlers" . . . $1.20 a gallon: Allen, 107–109.

Page 30 "contracts at will": Pendergrast, 136.

Page 31 bottlers countered with a sliding scale: Allen, 114.

Page 31 The bottlers sued: Allen, 116.

Page 31 leeches . . . pocketed $5 million: Pendergrast, 138; Allen, 117.

Page 31 forced Dobbs to resign: Pendergrast, 139; Allen, 119–120.

Page 31 verdict in the bottler case: Pendergrast, 140–141.

Page 31 offered a compromise: Bottler agreement amendment, January 6, 1920, exhibit, *The Coca-Cola Bottling Co. v. The Coca-Cola Company*, U.S. District Court for the District of Delaware, 1920.

Page 31 take another sixty-five years: Hays, 24.

Page 31 back above $40: Allen, 138.

Page 31 to $24 million by 1923: The Coca-Cola Company, Annual Report, 1924.

Page 32 "They sold out a big share": Candler, *Asa Griggs Candler*, 185.

Page 32 "I sometimes think that once": Pendergrast, 132.

Page 32 "The syrup of life by now": Watters, 109.

Page 32 scandalized Atlanta society: Pendergrast, 132; Allen, 152.

Page 32 "Everybody is dead but me": Asa Candler testimony, *My-Coca Company v. Baltimore Process Company*, 1924.

Page 32 dying alone in a New York City hotel room: Pendergrast, 133.

Page 32 millions of dollars a year: The Coca-Cola Company, Annual Report, 1929.

CHAPTER 2. BUILDING THE BRAND

Page 36 "a woman with three breasts": E. S. Turner, *The Shocking History of Advertising!* (New York: E. P. Dutton, 1953), 21–23.

Page 36 the first serious ads . . . runaway slaves: Sivulka, 7, 12.

Page 36 wine, wigs, and perfumes: Turner, 70–71.

Page 36 first advertising agency . . . succeed on its own merit: Stephen Fox, *Mirror Makers: A History of American Advertising and Its Creators* (Urbana and Chicago: University of Illinois Press, 1997), 14–15.

Page 36 first industry to throw good taste . . . collectible trade cards: Bingham, 117–124, 129–132.

Page 36 "step a mile into the open country": Young, 122.

Page 36 One enterprising laxative maker . . . U.S. Government turned him down: David W. Dunlap, "Miss Liberty's Scrapbook," *New York Times*, May 18, 1986; Zach Nauth, "Some Trying to Cash In on Lady Liberty," *Los Angeles Times*, March 30, 1985.

Page 37 new way to reach the masses: Young, 38–39.

Page 37 11 million medicine ads . . . name of a tablet or salve: Bingham, 113–114.

Page 37 "I can advertise dish water": Young, 101.

Page 37 "The Army protects our country": Carson, 100.

Page 37 Hembold's Extract of Buchu: Sivulka, 39–40.

Page 37 half-robed girl entering or exiting a bath: Carson, 15, 25, 33, 103; Bingham, 107, color insert 39–40.

Page 37 "The greatest advertising men of my day": Turner, 138–139.

Page 37 necessity for products sold nationally: Turner, 170–171; Jeffrey Schrank, *Snap, Crackle, and Popular Taste: The Illusion of Free Choice in America* (New York: Dell, 1997), 109–110.

Page 37 concept of a "brand": Sivulka, 48.

Page 37 from mere middlemen to full-stop shops: Fox, 13.

Page 38 developing cloying catchphrases: Turner, 110–111.

Page 38 "How really different was this product": Tedlow, 27.

Page 38 spent more than $70 . . . earning less than $50: Pendergrast, 31, 475; Allen, 29.

Page 38 Coke's Spencerian script . . . advertising accrual: Watters, 50.

Page 38 advertising budget had swollen to more than $11,000: Louis and Yazijian, 23.

Page 38 Coke's very first ad: *Atlanta Journal,* May 26, 1886.

Page 39 touting the drink as refreshment and "nerve tonic": Pendergrast, 30; Allen, 36.

Page 39 "satisfies the thirsty": Louis and Yazijian, 95.

Page 39 Alfred Lasker . . . "We Do the Rest": Fox, 50.

Page 39 "Instead of advertising to one man": Robinson testimony, *Rucker,* 86.

Page 39 total of $29,500 . . . almost entirely removed: Allen, 43–45.

Page 39 E. W. Kemble and especially Samuel Hopkins Adams: Young, 215–217.

Page 40 procession of smiling, fancily dressed Victorian women: Dietz, 50; Goodrum, 90.

Page 40 convulsive demographic changes: Mady Schutzman, *The Real Thing: Performance, Hysteria, & Advertising* (Hanover, NH, and London: Wesleyan University Press, 1999), 36.

Page 40 "evidence of leisure": Thorstein Veblen, *The Theory of the Leisure Class* (Amherst, NY: Prometheus, 1998 [orig. pub. 1899]), 265, 171; see also Rob Walker, *Buying In: The Secret Dialogue Between What We Buy and Who We Are,* (New York: Random House, 2008), 64–65.

Page 40 "The President drinks Coke": Paul Richard, "Andy Warhol, the Ghostly Icon: At the N.Y. Show, Summoning Images of the Pop Legend," *Washington Post,* February 6, 1989.

Page 40 "the effect of modern advertising": Fox, 70.

Page 41 subconscious desires: Turner, 146.

Page 41 especially adopted by makers of luxury items: Sivulka, 117.

Page 41 took over advertising from the older Frank Robinson: Candler, *Asa Griggs Candler,* 139.

Page 41 Dobbs dumped Massengale . . . baseball legend Ty Cobb: Dietz, 50–52.

Page 41 circuses, cigarettes . . . soft drink companies . . . "Interestingly enough": Tom Reichert, *The Erotic History of Advertising* (Amherst, NY: Prometheus Books, 2003), 29, 46, 88.

Page 42 One 1910 ad . . . no "hint of impurity": Watters, 218.

Page 42 "clean, truthful, honest publicity": Allen, 79.

Page 42 "claiming nothing for Coca-Cola": Watters, 98.

Page 42 half a million dollars a year: Watters, 98.

Page 42 more than $750,000: Dietz, 52.

Page 42 "best advertised article in America": Graham and Roberts, 62.

Page 42 spent $1.4 million . . . just one year: Dietz, 55.

Page 43 Coke's sales declined: Pendergrast, 128.

Page 43 frequent trips to Washington . . . limited syrup producers: Allen, 89.

Page 43 "Making a Soldier of Sugar": Martin Shartar and Norman Shavin, *The Wonderful World of Coca-Cola* (Atlanta: Perry Communications, 1978), 39.

Page 43 "Lobby furiously behind the scenes": Allen, 89.

Page 43 "the very joy of living to Our Boys": Sivulka, 134.

Page 44 A lackluster student . . . manual laborer: Charles Elliott, *"Mr. Anonymous": Robert W. Woodruff of Coca-Cola* (Atlanta: Cherokee, 1982), 87–91.

Page 44 born salesman: Elliott, 93–96.

Page 44 By 1922, he was: Elliott, 97.

Page 44 Ernest Woodruff both resented and admired: Allen, 154.

Page 44 established itself as *the* national brand: Tedlow, 55; Kahn, 123.

Page 44 "The chief economic problem" . . . anxieties of *not* owning: Fox, 94–95.

Page 45 brief attempt to increase rural sales: Dietz, 44; Waters, 149.

Page 45 "within an arm's reach of desire": Allen, 158.

Page 45 newspaper reporter in North Carolina: Watters, 147.

Page 45 "A man who can see life": Dietz, 101–102.

Page 45 writing the entire Coca-Cola campaign: Dietz, 104.

Page 45 some of the best artists of the day: Pendergrast, 160.

Page 45 most memorable slogans: Louis and Yazijian, 44; Gyvel Young-Witzel and Michael Karl Witzel, *The Sparkling History of Coca-Cola* (Stillwater, MN: Voyageur Press, 2002), 95.

Page 46 Woodruff created a Statistical Department: Pendergrast, 161–163.

Page 46 "Salesmen should keep calling" . . . "We can count": Tedlow, 33–35.

Page 46 quadrupling from $40 to $160: Allen, 176.

Page 47 $4 million . . . a cool million: Allen, 177.

Page 47 celebrity endorsements: Pendergrast, 175.

Page 47 an extra $1 million: Allen, 204.

Page 47 top twenty-five advertisers: Tedlow, 86.

Page 47 gradually following the lead: Barbara Fahs Charles and Robert Staples, *Dream of Santa: Haddon Sundblom's Vision* (Washington, DC: Staples & Charles, 1992), 14.

Page 47 children leaving a Coke: V. Dennis Wrynn, *Coke Goes to War* (Missoula, MT: Pictorial Histories, 1996), 23.

Page 48 Profits of $14 million . . . $29 million: The Coca-Cola Company Annual Reports 1934 and 1939.

Page 48 "the essence of capitalism": Robert Woodruff, interview by E. J. Kahn, 1.

Page 48 personally transferred it by train: Dietz, 97.

Page 48 "Robert Woodruff could still look": Louis and Yazijian, 45.

Page 48 a backlash against the greed of corporations: Beatty, 263–272.

Page 48 he up and moved to Wilmington: Wells, 115.

Page 48 available everywhere . . . available for a nickel: Louis and Yazijian, 56.

Page 48 "The opening of foreign markets is a costly undertaking": The Coca-Cola Company, Annual Report, 1928, 63.

Page 49 "His reward was a bottle of Coca-Cola": Camilia Ascher Restrepo, "War in the Times of Coke," Cokeheads: Exploring the New World of Coke, group project of English 752: Historical Tourism, Emory University (2008).

Page 49 twenty-four-page pamphlet . . . "A nation at war": The Coca-Cola Company, "Importance of the Rest-Pause in Maximum War Effort" (1942).

Page 49 One of Coke's own . . . offered an exemption: Pendergrast, 196–197.

Page 50 reportedly had been in talks with the government: Louis and Yazijian, 67.

Page 50 order signed by General George C. Marshall . . . North Africa campaign: Pendergrast, 198–201; Allen, 255.

Page 50 "You don't fuck with Coca-Cola!": Howard Fast, *Being Red* (Boston: Houghton Mifflin, 1990), 10.

Page 50 "If anyone were to ask us": Pendergrast, 206.

Page 50 "To my mind, I am": Kahn, 12.

Page 50 full-color ads: Wrynn, 37–78.

Page 50 One ad in 1946 . . . A sign at Coke's own: Louis and Yazijian, 78.

Page 51 Ray Powers . . . ending "Heil Hitler": Pendergrast, 214.

Page 51 Max Keith . . . mustache: Pendergrast, 217–219.

Page 51 Nazi Youth rallies . . . bottler conventions: Pendergrast, 220–221.

Page 51 Keith wangled an appointment . . . Nazi general: Pendergrast, 221–223.

Page 51 Coca-Cola investigators . . . modest amount of profit: Allen, 264.

Page 52 sixty-three overseas bottling plants, financed for $5.5 million: Allen, 265.

Page 52 just 20 percent of one year's net profits: The Coca-Cola Company, Annual Report, 1945.

Page 52 In 1950, *Time* magazine: *Time*, May 15, 1950.

Page 52 shifting from D'Arcy to a new agency: Dietz, 167; Sivulka, 265.

Page 52 the company was unexpectedly rudderless: Allen, 297.

Page 52 falling flat in the messier conflict with Korea: Watters, 224.

Page 53 Madison Avenue again turned . . . attribute that sets a product apart: Mark Tungate, *Ad Land: A Global History of Advertising* (London: Kogan Page, 2007), 44.

Page 53 North Carolina pharmacist . . . stomachache: Milward W. Martin, *Twelve Full Ounces: The Story of Pepsi-Cola* (New York: Holt, Rinehart and Winston, 1962), 5–7.

Page 53 three hundred bottlers in twenty-four states: Martin, 28–31.

Page 53 spike in sugar prices all but put it out of business: Martin, 33–45.

Page 53 The company probably would have died . . . $50,000 in 1933: Pendergrast, 188–190.

Page 53 12-ounce beer bottles . . . $4 million in 1938: Martin, 60–61.

Page 53 infectious jingle: Martin, 103–104.

Page 54 went straight to the government . . . any company could use: Allen, 243–244.

Page 54 Coke sued for peace: Allen, 191–192.

Page 54 "Stay young and fair" . . . $14 million by 1955: Martin, 133.

Page 54 Coke's market share began slipping . . . "Coke can hardly": Pendergrast, 256.

Page 54 "For those who think young": Sivulka, 261.

Page 54 In 1956 . . . $53 million a year: Vance Packard, *The Hidden Persuaders* (New York: Simon & Schuster, 1953), 95.

Page 55 surveying customers in all of 1.6 million retail outlets: Kahn, 153.

Page 55 newfangled approach of "motivational research": Packard, 23, 215.

Page 55 Maidenform . . . exploited: Sivulka, 267.

Page 55 "possible symbolic mistress": Packard, 82.

Page 55 "The greater the similarity": Packard, 17.

Page 55 Vance Packard exposed the "depth boys": Packard, 24–25.

Page 55 researcher named James Vicary . . . made the whole thing up: August Bullock, *The Secret Sales Pitch: An Overview of Subliminal Advertising* (San Jose, CA: Norwich, 2004), 8–10; Stuart Rogers, "How a Publicity Blitz Created the Myth of Subliminal Advertising," *Public Relations Quarterly* 37, no. 4 (Winter 1992/1993), 12–17.

Page 55 Advertisers further denounced: Max Sutherland and Alice K. Sylvester, *Advertising and the Mind of the Consumer: What Works, What Doesn't, and Why* (St. Leonard's, Australia: Allen & Unwin, 2000 [orig. pub. 1993]), 35.

Page 56 "You'd have to be an idiot" . . . "it's precisely because we don't": Rob Walker, *Buying In: The Secret Dialogue Between What We Buy and Who We Are* (New York: Random House, 2008), 111, 68.

Page 56 Coke redoubled its efforts . . . to fill in the blank: Allen, 323; Pendergrast, 273; Louis and Yazijian, 233–234.

Page 56 both companies had an advertising style: Pendergrast, 274.

Page 56 Between 1954 and 1964 . . . 227 in 1964: Allen, 322.

Page 56 got over its single-product fetish: Allen, 330; Pendergrast, 272, 277–278.

Page 57 confronted the changing reality of America: Fox, 272.

Page 57 company stayed on the sidelines: Pendergrast, 266; Louis and Yazijian, 87.

Page 57 "I've heard the phrase": Kahn, 158.

Page 57 Woodruff personally risked . . . company dragged its feet: Allen, 338–339; Pendergrast, 280–282.

Page 57 no soldier made of sugar in Danang: Allen, 349; Pendergrast, 286–287.

Page 57 Pepsi filled the gap: Pendergrast, 288.

Page 57 reached into the World War II archive to pull out: Pendergrast, 288.

Page 57 campaign protesting the deplorable conditions: Pendergrast, 293–295.

Page 58 effectively ended union representation: Jerry Jackson, "Grove Sale Deals Blow to Labor: Coca-Cola Transaction Cancels State's Only Field Worker Contract," *Orlando Sentinel*, February 14, 1994.

Page 58 company launched new initiatives: Pendergrast, 291, 296; Allen, 356.

Page 58 plane was fogged in . . . "a tiny bit of commonality": Coca-Cola Heritage, "'I'd Like to Buy the World a Coke'—The Hilltop Story," http://www.thecoca-colacompany.com/heritage/cokelore_hilltop.html.

Page 58 the shoot was a nightmare: Pendergrast, 300.

Page 58 "sure-fire form of subliminal advertising": "Have a Coke, World," *Newsweek*, January 3, 1972.

Page 58 "Look Up, America!": Pendergrast, 305–306.

Page 58 sales of soft drinks continued to soar: William Moore and Peter Buzzanell, *Trends in U.S. Soft Drink Consumption. Demand Implications for Low-Calorie and Other Sweeteners, Sugar and Sweeteners: Situation and Outlook Report.* U.S. Department of Agriculture, Economic Research Service, September 1991.

Page 59 "At Pepsi, we *like* the Cola Wars": Tedlow, 104.

Page 59 new regional manager decided . . . liked Pepsi better: Thomas Oliver, *The Real Coke, the Real Story* (New York: Penguin, 1987), 49–53.

Page 59 The campaign doubled market share: Oliver, *The Real Coke, the Real Story*, 56–58.

Page 59 realized the scorched-earth tactics . . . "The Pepsi Challenge": Tedlow, 106.

Page 59 more traditional forms of advertising: Al Reis and Jack Trout, *The 22 Immutable Laws of Marketing* (New York: HarperBusiness, 1993), 81.

Page 60 high of 60 percent after World War II: Allen, 402.

Page 60 just 22 percent . . . "advertising alone couldn't": Oliver, *The Real Coke, the Real Story*, 118.

Page 60 fled the island . . . learned the secret formula: Hays, 68–77.

Page 60 rise to the top . . . hotly contested top slot: Hays, 77–79, 89.

Page 60 "There are no sacred cows": Oliver, *The Real Coke, the Real Story*, 74.

Page 61 The company should have known better: Oliver, *The Real Coke, the Real Story*, 127.

Page 61 The project was so secret: Oliver, *The Real Coke, the Real Story*, 138.

Page 61 Company executives stood: Oliver, *The Real Coke, the Real Story*, 155.

Page 61 montage of cowboys: Allen, 411.

Page 61 press corps leaped . . . Pepsi had nothing to do with it: Oliver, *The Real Coke, the Real Story*, 159–167.

Page 61 more than 400,000: Roger Enrico and Jesse Kornbluth, *The Other Guy Blinked: How Pepsi Won the Cola Wars* (Toronto: Bantam, 1986), 14.

Page 61 "You've taken away my childhood": Hays, 118–119.

Page 61 "Changing Coke is like": Allen, 414.

Page 61 "We have heard you" . . . "I think, by the end": Matt Haig, *Brand Failures: The Truth About the Biggest Branding Mistakes of All Time* (London: Kogan Page, 2003), 17; Enrico and Kornbluth, 238.

Page 62 again topped Pepsi in market share: Reis and Trout, 23.

Page 62 "A lot of people said": Sergio Zyman, *The End of Marketing As We Know It* (New York: HarperBusiness, 1999), 49.

CHAPTER 3. BIGGERING AND BIGGERING

Page 63 hundredth-anniversary celebration: Ron Taylor, "Coke Bills Party as Biggest Ever in Atlanta," *Atlanta Journal-Constitution,* May 10, 1986; Howard Pousher, "Epic Feast for 14,000," *Atlanta Journal-Constitution,* May 10, 1986.

Page 64 focusing everything on their quarterly earnings: John D. Martin and J. William Petty, *Value Based Management: The Corporate Response to the Shareholder Movement* (Boston: Harvard Business School Press), 13–28.

Page 64 "shareholder value movement": Marion Nestle, email to author, August 23, 2010.

Page 64 cutting waste and inefficiency: Allan A. Kennedy, *The End of Shareholder Value* (Cambridge, MA: Perseus, 2002), 49–61.

Page 64 rushed to please Wall Street: Betsy Morris, "Tearing Up Jack Welch's Playbook," *Fortune,* July 11, 2006; Kennedy, 164–166.

Page 64 hurt the long-term success of their companies: Kennedy, xi, 63–66; "Buy Now, While Stocks Last," *The Economist,* July 17, 1999; John Cassidy, "The Greed Cycle: How the Financial System Encouraged Corporations to Go Crazy," *The New Yorker,* September 23, 2002.

Page 64 no CEO was associated: Hays, 90.

Page 64 "I wrestle over how to build": Faye Rice et al., "Leaders of the Most Admired," *Fortune,* January 29, 1990.

Page 64 had a computer screen installed: Hays, 67.

Page 64 another screen at the main entrance: Betsy Morris, "Roberto Goizueta and Jack Welch: The Wealth Builders," *Fortune,* December 11, 1995.

Page 64 sloughed off divisions . . . *The Karate Kid:* Pendergrast, 340–342, 346.

Page 65 "a most unique company": Morris, "Roberto Goizueta and Jack Welch: The Wealth Builders."

Page 65 increasing per capita consumption: Hays, 92–93.

Page 65 "If we take full advantage": Pendergrast, 367.

Page 65 C on the kitchen faucet: "A Conversation with Roberto Goizueta and Jack Welch," *Fortune,* December 11, 1995.

Page 65 "biggering and biggering": Dr. Seuss, *The Lorax* (New York: Random House, 1971).

Page 65 As the 1990s dawned . . . annual growth in earnings: Hays, 41.

Page 65 Goizueta personally called the Wall Street analysts: Hays, 128–129.

Page 65 "If you weren't owning Coke": Hays, 138.

Page 65 "the closest thing we know of": "CEO of the Year 1996," *Chief Executive,* July 1, 1996.

Page 65 Stock prices rose: Hays, 129–131.

Page 66 Goizueta profited handsomely: Ira T. Kay, *CEO Pay and Shareholder Value: Helping the U.S. Win the Global Economic War* (Boca Raton, FL: St. Lucie Press, 1998), 113; Stacy Perman, "The Man Who Knew the Formula," *Time,* June 24, 2001.

Page 66 largest single payout: Hays, 136.

Page 66 "King Size". . . "Family Size" bottles: Pendergrast, 256–257.

Page 66 "Cheap corn, transformed": Michael Pollan, "The Agricultural Contradictions of Obesity," *New York Times Magazine,* October 12, 2003.

Page 67 rolled out a 50 percent . . . 100 percent HFCS version: "Sugar: A Sticky Boom," *The Economist,* October 18, 1980; Rosalind Resnick, "Bad News for Latin Sugar," *Miami Herald,* March 16, 1986.

Page 67 concept of "supersizing" really caught on: Melanie Warner, "Does This Goo Make You Groan?" *New York Times,* July 2, 2006.

Page 67 in the 1990s a 21-ounce medium soda: Eric Schlosser, *Fast Food Nation: The Dark Side of the All-American Meal* (New York: Houghton Mifflin, 2002 [orig. pub. 2001]), 54.

Page 67 customers could request . . . a quarter of soft drink sales: Greg Critser, *Fat Land: How Americans Became the Fattest People in the World* (Boston: Houghton Mifflin, 2003), 20–28.

Page 67 It was the same story at the 7-Eleven: Warner, "Does This Goo Make You Groan?"; Francine R. Kaufman, *Diabesity: The Obesity-Diabetes Epidemic That Threatens America—And What We Must Do to Stop It* (New York: Bantam, 2005), 152.

Page 67 "The Beast": Ellen Ruppel Shell, *The Hungry Gene: The Inside Story of the Obesity Industry* (New York: Grove Press, 2002), 205.

Page 67 With two-thirds of the fountain sales: Scott Leith, "Fountain Sales Are a Weak Point for Coca-Cola," *Atlanta Journal-Constitution,* December 31, 2002.

Page 68 "Bigger is better": Hank Cardello, *Stuffed: An Insider's Look at Who's (Really) Making America Fat* (New York: HarperCollins, 2009), 18–19.

Page 68 new 20-ounce bottle: Martha T. Moore, "Coke's Curvy Shape Is Back," *USA Today,* March 28, 1994.

Page 68 reversing years of discounts: Kent Phillips, "Re-Profitizing the Industry," *Beverage World,* September 1996.

Page 68 "Our goal was to make Coca-Cola ubiquitous": Cardello, 134.

Page 68 "We're putting ice-cold": The Coca-Cola Company, Annual Report, 1997.

Page 68 "the most important meal of the day": Chris Warren, "Start the Day Right: Harness the Profit Potential of Breakfast," *Refreshing News,* Spring/Summer 2006, Coca-Cola Food Service.

Page 68 56.1 gallons . . . been in 1970: Marc Kaufman, "Fighting the Cola Wars in Schools," *Washington Post,* March 23, 1999; Michael Jacobson, *Liquid Candy: How Soft Drinks Are Harming Americans' Health,* Center for Science in the Public Interest, 2005 (rev. ed.); Bill Lohmann, "Soft Drinks Vie for Top Position," United Press International, April 14, 1985.

Page 68 reclaimed 45 percent of the market: Frank Gibney, Jr., "Pepsi Gets Back in the Game: The Company Is on the Rebound with a New Vision, and an Old Problem: Coke," *Time*, April 26, 1999.

Page 69 more than $4 billion in net income: Associated Press, "Coke CEO Aims at 2B Servings Daily," March 3, 1998.

Page 69 3,500 percent increase . . . $88 a share by 1998: Dean Foust, "Coke's Man on the Spot," *BusinessWeek*, May 3, 1999.

Page 69 "We don't know how": Morris, "Roberto Goizueta and Jack Welch: The Wealth Builders."

Page 69 Coke's annual spending on advertising: Naomi Klein, *No Logo: Taking Aim at the Brand Bullies* (New York: Picador, 1999), 471.

Page 69 alienating many: Hays, 123–124; Pendergrast, 400.

Page 69 "move the needle": Zyman, 3–5, 118, 172.

Page 69 "The sole purpose of marketing": Zyman, 11.

Page 69 "spending to sell" . . . "we poured on more": Zyman, 15.

Page 69 The domestic ad budget rose: Klein, *No Logo*, 471.

Page 70 It was Zyman's job: Zyman, 138.

Page 70 "These are the consumers": Zyman, 125.

Page 70 "dimensionalizing" . . . at every occasion: Zyman, 124, 129.

Page 70 compete for Coke's vast advertising war chest: Zyman, 207.

Page 71 Hollywood powerhouse Creative Artists Agency: Naomi Klein, *No Logo*, 59.

Page 71 computer-generated family of polar bears: Matthew Grimm, "Coke Plans to Put Its Polar Bears to Work," *Adweek*, June 21, 1993; Dottie Enrico, "Coke's Polar Bear Is a Papa Bear," *USA Today*, December 8, 1994.

Page 71 Philip Morris cut the price . . . death knell for the brand: Klein, *No Logo*, 12–13.

Page 71 "We are getting a bum rap": John Huey, "The World's Best Brand CEO," *Fortune*, May 31, 1993.

Page 71 companies that succeeded . . . top of her list: Klein, *No Logo*, 21.

Page 71 original World of Coca-Cola: Klein, *No Logo*, 29.

Page 72 worth more than a billion dollars: Hays, 170.

Page 72 able to avoid paying: David Cay Johnston, *Perfectly Legal: The Covert Campaign to Rig Our Tax System to Benefit the Super Rich—and Cheat Everybody Else* (New York: Portfolio, 2003), 51.

Page 72 if anything, more relentless . . . "From his earliest": Hays, 31–34.

Page 72 buying up any bottlers that were for sale: Oliver, *The Real Coke, the Real Story*, 31–42.

Page 72 own 49 percent: Hays, 42.

Page 72 forced the new bottling company: Hays, 52–53.

Page 73 "anchor bottlers": Roberto C. Goizueta, "The Emerging Post-Conglomerate Era: Changing the Shape of Corporate America," January 1988.

Page 73 rolled right off Coke's books: Hays, 62.

Page 73 "new era in American capitalism": Goizueta, "The Emerging Post-Conglomerate Era."

Page 73 force bottlers to buy syrup: Hays, 151.

Page 73 "marketing support": Hays, 154.

Page 73 enormous amounts of debt: Hays, 157.

Page 73 "iceman" . . . phones were tapped: Hays, 174–176.

Page 73 "360-degree landscape of Coke": Hays, 7.

Page 73 "What I always wonder": Hays, 175.

Page 74 all but howling along: Hays, 35.

Page 74 Coke showed no quarter: Hays, 190.

Page 74 restrictive advertising agreements: Hays, 242–243.

Page 74 Royal Crown Cola sued: Hays, 245.

Page 74 difficulty meeting its high earnings expectations: Huey, "The World's Best Brand CEO."

Page 74 less than 20 percent of Pepsi's business: "Coca-Cola Boosts Water Sales, Still Trailing Pepsi," Bloomberg News, August 20, 2006.

Page 74 more than 80 percent of its sales: Joe Guy Collier, "Worldwide Sales a Tonic for Coke," *Atlanta Journal-Constitution*, November 16, 2008.

Page 75 "Coke fiends" . . . overtly racist coverage: Allen, 46–47.

Page 76 "increased amounts of poisonous and toxic matters": Harvey W. Wiley, *The History of a Crime Against the Food Law* (Washington, DC: Harvey W. Wiley, 1929), 29.

Page 76 "poison squad": Wiley, 57–62.

Page 76 weren't exactly scientifically rigorous: Clayton A. Coppin and Jack High, *The Politics of Purity: Harvey Washington Wiley and the Origins of Federal Food Policy* (Ann Arbor: University of Michigan Press, 1999), 55.

Page 76 went on the attack . . . self-promoter: Coppin and High, 3–5.

Page 76 nemesis, however, would be . . . railed against Coke: Pendergrast, 115.

Page 77 addition of "free caffeine" . . . neither coca leaves nor kola nut: Coppin and High, 142–145.

Page 77 couldn't be considered an additive: Coppin and High, 151.

Page 77 having left town . . . Wilson force him out: Allen, 62–64.

Page 77 all the way up to the Supreme Court . . . Coke's new formula: Pendergrast, 121–122.

Page 78 policy on Southwest Airlines: Charles Passy, "Little Wiggle Room for XXL Passengers," *New York Times*, October 15, 2006; Michelle Higgins, "Excuse Me, Is This Seat Taken?" *New York Times*, February 28, 2010.

Page 78 motorized carts Wal-Mart now offers: Michael Leahy, "The Weight," *Washington Post Magazine*, July 18, 2004.

Page 78 from 14 percent . . . to 34 percent today: Katherine M. Flegal et al., "Prevalence and Trends in Obesity Among US Adults, 1999–2008," *Journal of the American Medical Association* 303, no. 3 (January 2010), 235–241.

Page 78 some 75 million people: Calculated from U.S. Census, "Annual Estimates of the Resident Population by Sex and Five-Year Age Groups for the United States: April 1, 2000 to July 1, 2008 (NC-EST2008-01)."

Page 78 more than two-thirds of the adult U.S. population: Flegal et al., "Prevalence and Trends in Obesity Among US Adults, 1999–2008."

Page 78 increased risks for diseases: Flegal et al., "Prevalence and Trends in Obesity Among US Adults, 1999–2008"; U.S. Surgeon General, "Overweight and Obesity: Health Consequences" (Rockville, MD, 2001).

Page 79 obese teenagers . . . obese children: Cynthia L. Ogden et al., "Prevalence of High Body Mass Index in U.S. Children and Adolescents, 2007–2008," *Journal of the American Medical Association* 303, no. 3 (2010), 242–249.

Page 79 a 2006 conference in Boston: Public Health Advocacy Institute, Fourth Annual Conference on Legal Approaches to the Obesity Epidemic, Northeastern University School of Law, November 3–5, 2006.

Page 79 part of the equation is genetic: Kaufman, *Diabesity*, 225–229; Kelly D. Brownell and Katherine Battle Horgen, *Food Fight: The Inside Story of the Food Industry, America's Obesity Crisis, and What We Can Do About It* (New York: McGraw-Hill, 2003), 23; G. S. Barsh et al., "Genetics of Body Weight Regulation," *Nature* 404 (2000), 644–651; J. Eric Oliver, *Fat Politics: The Real Story Behind America's Obesity Epidemic* (New York: Oxford University Press, 2006), 105.

Page 79 increased prevalence of air-conditioning: David B. Allison et al., "Putative Contributors to the Secular Increase in Obesity: Exploring the Roads Less Traveled," *International Journal of Obesity* 30 (2006), 1585–1594.

Page 79 nearly half the increase in calories: Centers for Disease Control, "Trends in Intake of Energy and Macronutrients—United States, 1971–2000," February 4, 2004.

Page 79 largest *single* source of calories: Mark Bittman, "Soda: A Sin We Sip Instead of Smoke?" *New York Times*, February 12, 2010.

Page 79 team analyzing some thirty studies: Frank B. Hu et al., "Intake of Sugar-Sweetened Beverages and Weight Gain: A Systematic Review," *American Journal of Clinical Nutrition* 84 (2006), 274–288.

Page 79 followed five hundred eleven-year-olds: David S. Ludwig et al., "Relation Between Consumption of Sugar-Sweetened Drinks and Childhood Obesity: A Prospective, Observational Analysis," *The Lancet* 357 (2001), 505–508.

Page 80 later study by Ludwig: David S. Ludwig et al., "Effects of Decreasing Sugar-Sweetened Beverage Consumption on Body Weight in Adolescents: A Randomized, Controlled Pilot

Study," *Pediatrics* 117, no. 3 (March 2006), 673–680; Melanie Warner, "Soda Sales Fall for the First Time in 20 Years," *New York Times*, March 9, 2006.

Page 80 "It's not the exceptional child": David Ludwig, interview by the author.

Page 80 Another analysis, of thousands of nurses: Matthias B. Schulze et al., "Sugar-Sweetened Beverages, Weight Gain, and Incidence of Type 2 Diabetes in Young and Middle-Aged Women," *Journal of the American Medical Association* 292, no. 8 (August 2004), 927–934.

Page 80 "might be the best single opportunity": Caroline Apovian, "Sugar-Sweetened Soft Drinks, Obesity, and Type 2 Diabetes," *Journal of the American Medical Association* 292, no. 8 (August 2004), 978–979.

Page 80 study by Purdue University nutritionist: R. D. Mattes and D. P. DiMeglio, "Liquid Versus Solid Carbohydrates: Effects on Food Intake and Body Weight," *International Journal of Obesity* 24 (2000), 794–800; Brian Wansink, *Mindless Eating: Why We Eat More Than We Think* (New York: Bantam, 2006), 239.

Page 80 fructose isn't broken down: George A. Bray, "Diobesity: A Global Problem," *International Journal of Obesity* 26 (2002), S63.

Page 80 turning directly into fat: Brownell and Horgen, 30; Shell, 214; Critser, 137–140; John P. Bantle et al., "Effects of Dietary Fructose on Plasma Lipids in Healthy Subjects," *American Journal of Clinical Nutrition* 72 (2000), 1128–1134.

Page 81 cells to become more resistant: Kaufman, *Diabesity*, 29; Sharron Dalton, *Our Overweight Children: What Parents, Schools, and Communities Can Do to Control the Fatness Epidemic* (Berkeley: University of California Press, 2004), 37.

Page 81 name was changed to simply "type-2 diabetes": Kaufman, *Diabesity*, 14.

Page 81 *one in three* will become diabetic: "Lifetime Risk for Diabetes Mellitus in United States," http://www.cdc.gov/diabetes/news/docs/lifetime.htm; K. M. Venkat Narayan et al., "Lifetime Risk for Diabetes Mellitus in the United States," *Journal of the American Medical Association* 290, no. 14 (October 2003), 1884–1890.

Page 81 continually warning Americans: Michael Pollan, *In Defense of Food: An Eater's Manifesto* (New York: The Penguin Press, 2008), 50.

Page 81 Coke wasn't the only company: Meet the Bloggers, featuring Marion Nestle, November 21, 2008, http://meetthebloggers.org/show_112108.php; Marion Nestle, interview by the author.

Page 81 from 3,200 to 3,900 per capita: USDA Economic Research Service, Nutrient Availability Data, February 27, 2009; Marion Nestle, e-mail to the author.

Page 81 "When you come in" . . . "At the time . . . your kid is ugly": Hank Cardello, interview by the author.

Page 82 to sweeten their diet beverages: "Searle Sweetener Expands Its Market," *New York Times*, September 20, 1983.

Page 82 100 percent aspartame formula: "Coke Sweetener," *New York Times*, November 30, 1984; Pamela G. Hollie, "Pepsi's Diet Soft Drinks Switched to NutraSweet," *New York Times*, November 2, 1984.

Page 82 Complaints about the chemical more than doubled: Centers for Disease Control, "Evaluation of Consumer Complaints Related to Aspartame Use," *Morbidity and Mortality Weekly Report* 33, no. 43 (November 2, 1984), 605–607.

Page 82 "unless the CBS story snowballed": Cardello, 133.

Page 82 concerns about aspartame of minor importance: Centers for Disease Control, "Evaluation of Consumer Complaints Related to Aspartame Use."

Page 82 more than seven thousand complaints: "Clearing Up the Newest Rumors About Aspartame Sweetener," *Wall Street Journal*, June 7, 1999.

Page 82 comprehensive, if controversial, study: Morando Soffritti et al., "First Experimental Demonstration of the Multipotential Carcinogenic Effects of Aspartame Administered in the Feed to Sprague-Dawley Rats," *Environmental Health Perspective* 114, no. 3 (March 2006), 384–385.

Page 82 FDA dismissed the study: Food and Drug Administration, "FDA Statement on European Aspartame Study," May 8, 2006.

Page 82 sending representatives to lobby: "Banning Aspartame in New Mexico," *Carlsbad Current-Argus*, January 31, 2007.

Page 83 discovered excessive levels of benzene: Larry Alibrandi, former chemist at Cadbury-Schweppes, interview by the author.

Page 83 reaction of . . . sodium benzoate with ascorbic acid: Lalita K. Gardner and Glen D. Lawrence, "Benzene Production from Decarboxylation of Benzoic Acid in the Presence of Ascorbic Acid and a Transition-Metal Catalyst," *Journal of Agricultural and Food Chemistry* 41, no. 5 (May 1993), 693–695.

Page 83 more than 25 parts per billion: "Project Denver" documents provided by Larry Alibrandi.

Page 83 legal limit of 5 ppb: Environmental Protection Agency, "Basic Information About Benzene in Drinking Water," http://www.epa.gov/ogwdw000/contaminants/basicinformation/benzene.html.

Page 83 met promptly with the FDA: Food and Drug Administration, Center for Food Safety and Applied Nutrition, "Benzene Residues in Soft Drinks," Memorandum of Meeting, December 7, 1980.

Page 83 let the companies quietly reformulate: Food and Drug Administration, "Questions and Answers on the Occurrence of Benzene in Soft Drinks and Other Beverages," http://www.fda.gov/Food/FoodSafety/FoodContaminantsAdulteration/ChemicalContaminants/Benzene/ucm055131.htm#q6.

Page 83 Perrier water was found contaminated: Alan Riding, "Perrier Widens Recall After Finding," *New York Times*, February 15, 1990.

Page 83 FDA's own tests: Environmental Working Group, "FDA Data Undercut Public Safety Assurances by Top Agency Official: Tests Found High Benzene Contamination of Diet Soda," April 4, 2006, http://www.ewg.org/node/8777.

Page 83 still present in some drinks: Larry Alibrandi; Laboratory Analysis Report for American Quality Beverages, Life Sciences Laboratories, Inc., November 11, 2005; for more information, see Michael Blanding, "Hard Times for Soft Drinks," *AlterNet*, March 13, 2006.

Page 83 FDA released its own tests: Food and Drug Administration, "Data on Benzene in Soft Drinks and Other Beverages," May 16, 2007, http://www.fda.gov/Food/FoodSafety/FoodContaminantsAdulteration/ChemicalContaminants/Benzene/ucm055815.htm.

Page 83 "unequivocally that our products are safe": The Coca-Cola Company, "Company Statement on Benzene," March 17, 2006.

Page 83 reformulate the drinks and pay: "Coca-Cola Reaches Settlements over Benzene Claims," Associated Press, May 14, 2007.

Page 84 "three major political waves": David Vogel, *Fluctuating Fortunes: The Political Power of Business in America* (New York: Basic Books, 1989), 93–94.

Page 84 labeled the "food police": Activist Cash, Center for Science in the Public Interest, http://activistcash.com/organization_overview.cfm/o/13-center-for-science-in-the-public-interest.

Page 84 push to ban trans fats . . . calorie counts: Center for Science in the Public Interest, Trans Fat, http://www.cspinet.org/transfat/; Stephanie Saul, "Conflict on the Menu," *New York Times*, February 16, 2008.

Page 85 even young children . . . girls . . . two cans a day: Michael F. Jacobson, *Liquid Candy: How Soft Drinks Are Harming Americans' Health,* Center for Science in the Public Interest, 1998.

Page 85 about 10 teaspoons of sugar: Jacobson, *Liquid Candy*, 2005.

Page 85 CSPI did an update: Jacobson, *Liquid Candy*, 2005.

Page 85 "Soft drinks make no": Usha Lee McFarling, "Food Police in a Fizz over Nation's Huge Thirst for Soda Pop," Knight-Ridder Newspapers, October 22, 1998.

Page 86 established the Tobacco Industry Research Committee: David Michaels, *Doubt Is Their Product: How Industry's Assault on Science Threatens Your Health* (Oxford, England: Oxford University Press, 2008), 6.

Page 86 "Industry has learned": Michaels, x.

Page 86 Knowing that it is nearly impossible: Michaels, 60.

Page 86 secondhand smoke . . . global warming: Michaels, 198.

Page 86 "creating doubt about the health charge": Michaels, 11.

Page 87 failed for the first time in years: Hays, 248.

Page 87 contamination scare in Belgium: Patricia Sellers, "Crunch Time for Coke: His Company Is Overflowing with Trouble. But CEO Doug Ivester Says He's in Firm Control of 'the Most Noble Business on Earth,'" *Fortune*, July 17, 1999.

Page 87 Albert Meyer took a closer look: Albert J. Meyer and Dwight M. Oswen, "Coca-Cola's Accounting: Is It Really the Real Thing?" *Accounting Today,* September 28–October 11, 1998; Constance L. Hays, "The Markets: Marketplace; A Once-Sweet Bottling Plan Turns Sour for Coke," *New York Times,* May 5, 1999.

Page 87 "One cannot transact with oneself": Don Russell, "New Era Sleuth Has Coke Fizzing," *Philadelphia Daily News,* October 21, 1998.

Page 87 "smoke and mirrors": Dean Foust, "Gone Flat: The Good Old Days Weren't As Good As You Thought," *BusinessWeek,* December 20, 2004.

Page 87 private meeting . . . amount overseas: Hays, 327.

Page 88 outsourced to contract workers: Hays, 328–329.

Page 88 downgraded volume targets: Hays, 338.

Page 88 voted down by the board: Hays, 340–341.

CHAPTER 4. THE BATTLE FOR SCHOOLS

Page 89 The first time Jackie Domac heard: Domac, interview by the author.

Page 89 prohibited it from selling juice . . . about $1 per student: Gayle Pollard-Terry, "Goodbye Candy, Hello Soy Bars," *Los Angeles Times,* September 2, 2002.

Page 91 sales of soda . . . strictly regulated: Marion Nestle, *Food Politics: How the Food Industry Influences Health and Nutrition* (Berkeley and Los Angeles: University of California Press, 2007 [orig. pub. 2002]), 207–210.

Page 91 National Soft Drink Association fought back . . . lost revenue: Nestle, 210–211.

Page 91 "the company puts profit": U.S. Senate Report 103-300, Better Nutrition and Health for Children Act of 1994, 103rd Congress, 2nd Session, July 1, 1994.

Page 91 so-called pouring-rights contracts . . . paid to the facility: Howard Goodman, "One-Cola Pitch Sells on Campus," *Philadelphia Inquirer,* July 31, 1994; Chris Roush, "Pepsi Deal Breaks Coca-Cola's NFL Monopoly," *Atlanta Journal-Constitution,* August 4, 1995.

Page 91 Woodland Hills, Pennsylvania, for example: "School News," *Pittsburgh Post-Gazette,* April 21, 1994.

Page 91 Sam Barlow High School: "Pepsi, Please," *Oregonian* (Portland), October 30, 1998.

Page 92 contract in DeKalb County: Elizabeth Lee, "School Lunches: Good Choices? Soft Drink Sales Provide Big Revenues, Little Nutrition," *Atlanta Journal-Constitution,* May 5, 2003.

Page 92 "Coke Dude": John Bushey, "District 11's Coke Problem," *Harper's,* February 1, 1999; Constance L. Hays, "Today's Lesson: Soda Rights," *New York Times,* May 21, 1999; Schlosser, *Fast Food Nation,* 56–57.

Page 92 Coke sweetened the pot . . . "They have become": Sherri Day, "Coke Moves with Caution to Remain in Schools," *New York Times,* September 3, 2003.

Page 92 former college athletic director: Marc Kaufman, "Health Advocates Sound Alarm As Schools Strike Deals with Coke and Pepsi," *Washington Post*, March 23, 1999.

Page 93 DeRose would agree to speak: Dan DeRose, e-mail to the author.

Page 93 "My basic philosophy": Billie Stanton, "Are Ad-Splashed Schools Selling Out Our Kids?" *Denver Post*, November 28, 1999.

Page 93 one signed by Cicero–North Syracuse High School: Ross Getman, interview by the author; Lori Duffy, "C-NS Gets a Taste of Coke-Fueled Stadium; Coca-Cola, Taxpayers Would Fund $5.5m Complex," *Post-Standard* (Syracuse, NY), July 14, 1998.

Page 93 with the help of the president of the state assembly: Michael Bragman, "Coke-School Agreement Good Deal for Taxpayers," *Post-Standard* (Syracuse, NY), August 3, 1998.

Page 93 two fully stocked Coke machines: Amber Smith, "First Impressions: Bragmans Prepare Their Home to Host a Barbecue with Hillary Clinton," *Post-Standard* (Syracuse, NY), July 8, 1999.

Page 93 2-cent-per-container soda tax . . . reelection campaigns: Kevin Sack, "How Albany Works, Lesson 1: Lobbying, the Beverage Industry Pushes Hard for a Tax Break, and Succeeds," *New York Times*, June 12, 1995; Erik Kriss, "Bragman Holds Largest Larder in the Region; Election Reports Disclose Donations to New York Candidates," *Post-Standard* (Syracuse, NY), July 24, 1998; Jacqueline Arnold and Jim Emmons, "Cola Wars Loom for CNY School Districts; Liverpool and North Syracuse Are Putting Together Million-Dollar Deals with Coca-Cola," *Post-Standard* (Syracuse, NY), April 13, 1998.

Page 93 standing next to Bragman . . . money for the stadium: Duffy, "C-NS Gets a Taste of Coke-Fueled Stadium."

Page 94 written up in Coke's hometown newspaper: Jennifer Brett, "Corporate Partnership: Cash Strapped Schools Ponder Sponsorships," *Atlanta Journal-Constitution*, January 21, 1999.

Page 94 school districts from Portland . . . to Edison: Kaufman, "Health Advocates Sound Alarm As Schools Strike Deals with Coke and Pepsi."

Page 94 92 percent of high schools . . . 43 percent of elementary schools: Elizabeth Becker and Marian Burros, "Eat Your Vegetables? Only at a Few Schools," *New York Times*, January 13, 2003; C. Miller et al., "Nutrition Services and Foods and Beverages Available at School: Results from the School Health Policies and Programs Study 2000," *Journal of School Health* 71 (2001), 313–324.

Page 94 "If a high school student drinks a Coke": Cardello, 109.

Page 94 targeted kids with special come-ons: Allen, 207; Pendergrast, 203.

Page 94 "children under 6 or 7 years old ": Dietz, 127; Watters, 229.

Page 95 babies recognize brands: Daniel S. Acuff and Robert H. Reiher, *Kidnapped: How Irresponsible Marketers Are Stealing the Minds of Your Children* (Chicago: Dearborn, 2005),

71; Susan Gregory Thomas, *Buy, Buy Baby: How Consumer Culture Manipulates Parents and Harms Young Minds* (Boston: Houghton Mifflin, 2007), 5.

Page 95 "With soft drink consumption": Steve Matthews, "Connecticut May Ban Soft Drinks in Schools on Obesity Concern," Bloomberg News, May 25, 2005.

Page 95 "collectors' items": Allan Petretti, *Petretti's Coca-Cola Collectibles Price Guide*, 10th ed. (Dubuque, IA: Antique Trader Books, 1997).

Page 95 "You take any character that is cute": Daniel Acuff, interview by the author.

Page 95 originally intended for teens or adults: Juliet B. Schor, *Born to Buy* (New York: Scribner, 2004), 40.

Page 95 helped foment the concept of "product placement": Scott Leith, "Coke Leads Push to Place Products in Movies, TV," *Atlanta Journal-Constitution*, October 29, 2000.

Page 95 "ludicrously conspicuous": Tom Shales, "'Young Americans': WB's Summer Fling," *Washington Post*, July 12, 2000.

Page 95 sponsorship of the runaway television hit . . . "35- to 64-[year-olds]": Theresa Howard, "Real Winner of 'American Idol': Coke," *USA Today*, September 9, 2002.

Page 96 brokered a $150 million deal: Olinka Koster, "Harry Potter Author's Coca-Cola Deal," *The Advertiser*, October 19, 2001.

Page 96 Coke wouldn't appear . . . Minute Maid juices, and Hi-C: "CSPI Says Coke Deal Makes 'Chamber of Secrets' More Like 'Chamber of Commerce,'" U.S. Newswire, October 24, 2002.

Page 96 "Kids love Harry Potter": Greg Hassell, "Marketing Column," *Houston Chronicle*, October 10, 2001.

Page 96 "The target is really": Scott Leith, "Analyst Criticizes Coke's Marketing Efforts," *Atlanta Journal-Constitution*, June 14, 2001.

Page 96 second-highest-grossing film at the time: Brian Fuson, "Warner Reaps More Magic from Potter: $88mil Bow," *Hollywood Reporter*, November 19, 2002.

Page 96 most successful campaign of the year: Scott Leith, "Coca-Cola Confident of 'Harry Potter' Benefits," *Atlanta Journal-Constitution*, February 1, 2002.

Page 96 eighty-five of them between 2001 and 2009 . . . *Enchanted:* BrandChannel, Movie Product Placement, http://www.brandchannel.com/brandcameo_brands.asp?all_year=all_year#brand_list.

Page 96 leap to online advertising . . . 100,000 visitors a month: Louise Story, "Coke Promotes Itself in a New Virtual World," *New York Times*, December 7, 2007; author visit to CCMetro.

Page 97 Domac and her students . . . keeps the figures: Domac, interview by the author.

Page 98 ban on soda in the entire Los Angeles: Helen Gao, "Soda Ban May Burst Bubble; LAUSD Students Could Be the un-Pepsi generation," *Daily News* (Los Angeles), August 26, 2002.

Page 98 data from a new UCLA study: Gao, "Soda Ban May Burst Bubble."

Page 99 threatening to pull its sponsorship: Gao, "Soda Ban May Burst Bubble."

Page 99 unanimously voted to cut their contract: Helen Gao, "Last Sip for Campus Sodas; School Board Bans Soft-Drink Sales," *Daily News* (Los Angeles), August 28, 2002; Erika Hayasaki, "Schools to End Soda Sales; L.A. Unified: The Soft Drinks Won't Be Allowed on Campuses Starting in 2004. They May Be Replaced by More Healthful Beverages," *Los Angeles Times*, August 28, 2002.

Page 99 spawning similar resolutions: "School Ad Backlash," *Denver Post*, October 1, 2000.

Page 99 "This is like using a squirt gun": Daniel B. Wood, "A Farewell to Fizz from LA Lunchrooms," *Christian Science Monitor*, August 30, 2002.

Page 99 "it's the couch, not the can": Sherri Williams, "More Limits Sought on Soda Sales in Schools," *Columbus Dispatch*, January 9, 2004.

Page 99 "Step with It!": "Coca-Cola: The Bottom Line," Datamonitor, July 19, 2002.

Page 100 praise from . . . Tommy Thompson: Scott Leith, "Atlanta-Based CCE Takes on Critics, Defends Soft-Drink Sales in Schools," *Atlanta Journal-Constitution*, April 6, 2003.

Page 100 Coke reportedly "donated" $200,000: Melanie Warner, "Striking Back at the Food Police," *New York Times*, June 12, 2005.

Page 100 "There is a rush": Dan Mindus, senior analyst, Center for Consumer Freedom, interview by the author.

Page 100 four to eight times more likely: David S. Ludwig, "Relationship Between Funding Source and Conclusion Among Nutrition-Related Scientific Articles," *Public Library of Science* 4, no. 1 (January 2007), e5.

Page 100 "Is that happening today": David Ludwig, interview by the author.

Page 100 The argument hits deep: See Lori Dorfman and Lawrence Wallack, "Moving Nutrition Upstream: The Case for Reframing Obesity," *Journal of Nutrition Education and Behavior* 39, no. 2S (March/April 2007), S46–50; Raj Patel, *Stuffed and Starved: Markets, Power, and the Hidden Battle for the World Food System* (Hoboken, NJ: Melville House, 2007), 276; Abigail C. Saguy and Kevin W. Riley, "Weighing Both Sides: Morality, Mortality, and Framing Contests over Obesity," *Journal of Health Politics, Policy and Law* 30, no. 5 (2005), 869–923.

Page 101 spent $2.8 billion in advertising: The Coca-Cola Company, Annual Report, 2009.

Page 101 "Certainly students should be taught": Lori Dorfman, director, Berkeley Media Studies Group, interview by the author.

Page 101 strategic retreat . . . "We just don't think": "Coke Easing Off Marketing in Schools," *Houston Chronicle*, March 15, 2001.

Page 101 nobody bothered to tell . . . ponied up a bid: Scott Leith, "Obesity Weighs Heavily on Colas; Industry Studies How to Fight Back in Health Debate," *Atlanta Journal-Constitution*, February 6, 2005.

Page 101 "What is the plan?" . . . placed on its board: Sherri Day, "Coke Moves with Caution to Remain in Schools," *New York Times*, September 3, 2003.

Page 102 "They are a win for the students": "Sodas in Schools Become an Issue," *Atlanta Journal-Constitution*, September 6, 2001.

Page 102 news articles in 2001 and 2002: Berkeley Media Studies Group, "Obesity Crisis or Soda Scapegoat? The Debate over Selling Soda in Schools," January 2005.

Page 102 average only $12 to $24 per student: Amy Hsuan, "Schools' Soda Deals Losing Fizz," *Oregonian* (Portland), November 15, 2006.

Page 102 Another analysis by CSPI: Center for Science in the Public Interest and Public Health Advocacy Institute, "Raw Deal: School Beverage Contracts Less Lucrative Than They Seem," December 2006.

Page 102 announced its own new policy . . . scoreboards stayed: "Coke Announces Policy on Soda Sales in Schools," *Washington Post*, November 18, 2003.

Page 102 industry conference in New York City: Scott Leith, "Simplistic Solutions Won't Cure Obesity, Coke CEO Says," *Atlanta Journal-Constitution*, December 9, 2003.

Page 103 2 percent overall: Scott Leith, "Sales Growth Slow, Profit Flat at Coke," *Atlanta Journal-Constitution*, February 12, 2004.

Page 103 *declined* 3 percent: Elizabeth Lee, "Cola a Day Doubles Diabetes Risk," *Atlanta Journal-Constitution*, August 25, 2004.

Page 103 Matthew Whitley, had lashed out . . . paid no fine: U.S. Securities and Exchange Commission, "In the Matter of The Coca-Cola Company, Respondent," Administrative Proceeding File No. 3-11902, April 18, 2005; William Spain, "No Fine for Coke in 'Channel-Stuffing' SEC: Beverage Behemoth to Continue 'Remedial Actions,'" MarketWatch, April 18, 2005.

Page 103 In one 2003 poll in California: California Endowment, "A Survey of Californians About the Problem of Childhood Obesity," October/November 2003.

Page 103 "a simplistic" . . . "absurd and outrageous": Leith, "Simplistic Solutions Won't Cure Obesity, Coke CEO Says."

Page 103 The first anti-soda bill . . . schools K–12: Michele Simon, *Appetite for Profit: How the Food Industry Undermines Our Health and How to Fight Back* (New York: Nation Books, 2006), 224–25.

Page 104 slip out the back door: Domac, interview by the author.

Page 104 industry-paid experts . . . high schools anyway: Simon, 226–227.

Page 104 California experience would be repeated: Simon, 234–236; Greg Winter, "States Try to Limit Sales of Junk Food in School Buildings," *New York Times*, September 9, 2001; Scott Leith, "Selling Soft Drinks to Kids: Obesity Battle Shifts to Schools," *Atlanta Journal-Constitution*, June 15, 2002.

Page 104 "When it came to the two": Michele Simon, interview by the author.

Page 104 The most notorious example . . . governor Jodi Rell: Simon, 231–233.

Page 104 selectively shared revenue data: Alison Leigh Cowan, "Food Fight," *New York Times*, May 29, 2005.

Page 104 debate in the House was the longest: Alison Leigh Cowan, "Hartford House Votes to Limit School Junk Food Sales," *New York Times*, May 18, 2005.

Page 105 times when their parents had denied them candy: Simon, 231.

Page 105 "well-stocked" cooler of Coke: Alison Leigh Cowan, "Healthy Food in the Lunchroom? First, You Need a Healthy Debate," May 16, 2005.

Page 105 support of 70 percent . . . allowing sales in high schools: Simon, 231–232.

Page 105 "undermin[ing] the control and responsibility": Alison Leigh Cowan, "Rell Vetoes Junk-Food Limit in Connecticut's Public Schools," *New York Times*, June 15, 2005.

Page 105 in France, lawmakers voted: Isabelle de Pommereau, "French Schools' New Bête Noire: Vending Machines," *Christian Science Monitor*, October 8, 2004.

Page 105 "Clearly we are playing catch up": Scott Leith, "Obesity Weighs Heavy on Colas, Industry Studies How to Fight Back in Health Debate."

Page 105 "to better reflect the expanded range": PR Newswire, November 11, 2004.

Page 106 new director, Susan Neely: "Ex–Homeland Security Official Susan Neely Takes the Helm at ABA," *Beverage Digest*, April 29, 2005; Caroline Wilber, "Beverage Industry Ads Tout New School Policy," *Atlanta Journal-Constitution*, October 13, 2005.

Page 106 "The industry thinks": Caroline Wilbert, "Bottlers Across the Country Lobby to Stay in Schools," Cox News Service, July 11, 2005.

Page 106 Beverage Institute for Health and Wellness: Dominic Mills, "Coke Calls In the Men in White Coats,"*Daily Telegraph* (London), March 16, 2004.

Page 106 conference in Mexico City: Alex Beam, "A Knack for Cooking Up Controversy," *Boston Globe*, November 4, 2004.

Page 106 rose 74 percent . . . "the glory days": Scott Leith, "U.S. Soft-Drink Industry Ruminates on How to Recharge Its Batteries," *Atlanta Journal-Constitution*, May 27, 2004.

Page 106 quietly pushed Daft out: Neil Buckley and Betty Liu, "Wall Street Is Convinced That Steven Heyer, the Company's President and Chief Operating Officer, Is the Man for the Top Job," *Financial Times*, March 10, 2004.

Page 106 to take his place was Neville Isdell: Claudia H. Deutsch, "Coca-Cola Reaches into Past for New Chief," *New York Times*, May 5, 2004.

Page 107 "help more people by working": Andrew Ward, "Coke Joins Battle for the Brand," *Financial Times* (London), November 21, 2006.

Page 107 in the core of the brand: Andrew Ward, "Coke Gets Real: The World's Most Valuable Brand Wakes Up to a Waning Thirst for Cola," *Financial Times*, September 22, 2005.

Page 107 eighteen to twenty-four months: Caroline Wilbert, "Interview: Coke CEO Neville Isdell: Boss Confident About Strategy," *Atlanta Journal-Constitution*, November 13, 2005.

Page 107 "I came back to the Coca-Cola Company": Scott Leith, "New Chairman and Chief Executive Vows to Reignite Coke's Growth," *Atlanta Journal-Constitution*, September 16, 2004.

Page 107 "Regardless of what the skeptics": Foust, "Gone Flat."

Page 107 committed an extra $400 million: Ward, "Coke Gets Real."

Page 107 "Carbonated soft drinks": Raja Mishra, "In Battle of Bulge, Soda Firms Defend Against Warning," *Boston Globe*, November 28, 2004.

Page 107 "Healthier consumers are going to be": "Coke Boss Counters Obesity Criticisms," *Toronto Star*, June 18, 2004.

Page 107 Chicago and New York had joined: Raja Mishra, "School Lunch Bill Targets Obesity: Bill Aims for Healthier School Lunches," *Boston Globe*, October 10, 2004.

Page 107 New Jersey passed the first: John Holl, "School Policy in New Jersey to Take Junk off Lunch Tray," *New York Times*, June 7, 2005.

Page 108 Arnold Schwarzenegger championed: Dorsey Griffith, "Junk Food Junked: Governor Signs Bill Strictly Limiting Sales in Public Schools," *Sacramento Bee*, September 9, 2005.

Page 108 PepsiCo had for the first time: David Teather, "Bubble Bursts for the Real Thing As PepsiCo Ousts Coke from Top Spot," *Guardian*, December 27, 2005.

Page 108 4 percent increase . . . "There is growth": Caroline Wilbert, "Coke Exceeds Profit Target," *Atlanta Journal-Constitution*, February 8, 2006.

Page 108 "intellectual godfather of tobacco litigation": Activist Cash, http://activistcash.com; Center for Consumer Freedom, http://www.consumerfreedom.com.

Page 109 $250 billion settlement: Joe Nocera, "If It's Good for Philip Morris, Can It Also Be Good for Public Health?" *New York Times*, June 18, 2007.

Page 109 global tobacco treaty: World Health Organization, "Global Tobacco Treaty Enters into Force with 57 Countries Already Committed," press release, February 24, 2005.

Page 109 "The number of analogies": Dick Daynard, interview by the author.

Page 109 percolating since a conference: Stephen Gardner, interview by the author.

Page 109 eventually backed down: Keith Ervin, "School Board Is Warned Against Coke Contract," *Seattle Times*, July 2, 2003; Tan Vinh, "Soft Drinks Limited for Middle-Schoolers; District Extends, Restricts Coca-Cola Contract," *Seattle Times*, July 18, 2003.

Page 109 "I look at Coke and Pepsi": Gardner, interview by the author.

Page 110 one study at Johns Hopkins University: "Caffeine Added to Soft Drink to Addict Consumers, Says Study," *Food & Drink Weekly*, August 21, 2000.

Page 110 "There are trial lawyers": Mindus, interview by the author.

Page 110 quietly approached Gardner: Gardner, interview by the author.

Page 110 trouble finding plaintiffs: Simon, interview by the author.

Page 111 drew up a confidential document: "Proposed School Beverage Policy, Draft Dated March 30, 2006 (2) For Discussion Only, Between the American Beverage Association and Industry Representatives, the Center for Science in the Public Interest, and Public Health Advocacy Institute."

Page 111 even Governor Rell bowed . . . passed the bill in late April 2006: Stacey Stowe, "To Some in Hartford, Coke Is a Real Evil Thing," *New York Times*, April 7, 2006.

Page 111 calling a press conference a week later: American Beverage Association, "Statement by Susan Neely, American Beverage Association President and CEO Regarding the Partnership with the Alliance for a Healthier Generation on a New School Beverage Policy," May 3, 2006.

Page 112 "I don't think there are any villains here": Bruce Mohl, "After Soda Ban, Nutritionists Say More Can Be Done," *Boston Globe*, May 4, 2006.

Page 112 announced new guidelines . . . Advertising wasn't even addressed: Caroline Wilbert, Elizabeth Lee, and David Ho, "Beverage Industry Tightens Policy," *Atlanta Journal-Constitution*, May 4, 2006.

Page 112 "I think there was considerable bad faith": Daynard, interview by the author. In an e-mail to the author, Alliance for a Healthier Generation spokesman Doug Cavarocchi declined comment on whether the organization was aware that a parallel negotiation was transpring.

Page 113 $10 million ad campaign: Scott Leith, "Soft Drink Makers Start PR Offensive; Industry Ads Focus on Kids' Health," *Atlanta Journal-Constitution*, September 7, 2006.

Page 113 One school in Wisconsin . . . Portland, Oregon, school district: Annys Shin, "Removing Schools' Soda Is Sticky Point," *Washington Post*, March 22, 2007; Arthur Gregg Sulzberger, "Threat of Fine Forces Talks on Coke Sales," *Oregonian* (Portland), February 6, 2007.

Page 113 It took six months: Krisy Obbink, director of dining services, Portland (Oregon) Public Schools, interview by the author.

Page 113 local affiliates of the American Heart Association: "Is the American Heart Association Pulling Its Troops out of State Beverage Fights?" *Corporate Crime Reporter*, June 1, 2006; Simon, e-mail to the author.

Page 113 A past president of the AHA: David Faxon, interview by the author.

Page 113 thirty-four states had some combination: Michelle M. Mello et al., "The Interplay of Public Health Law and Industry Self-Regulation: The Case of Sugar-Sweetened Beverage Sales in Schools," *American Journal of Public Health* 98, no. 4 (April 2008), 13–22.

Page 114 On a federal level: Jane Black, "Senate Drops Measure to Greatly Reduce Sugar and Fat in Food at Schools," *Washington Post*, December 15, 2007.

Page 114 study by a consultant . . . down 88 percent: American Beverage Association, Alliance School Beverage Guidelines Final Progress Report, March 8, 2010.

Page 114 "It's a brand new day": American Beverage Association, "Beverage Industry Delivers on Commitment to Remove Regular Soft Drinks in Schools, Driving 88% Decline in Calories," March 8, 2010.

Page 114 grudgingly accept the ABA report: Margo Wootan, interview by the author.

Page 114 industry-funded study with a jaundiced eye: Roberta Friedman, public policy director, Rudd Center for Food Policy and Obesity, Yale University, and Simon, interviews by the author.

Page 114 one independent study . . . never even heard of them: Lindsey Turner, research assistant professor of nutrition, Institute for Health Research and Policy, University of Illinois, Chicago, interview by the author.

Page 115 soda sales fell in the United States: Melanie Warner, "Soda Sales Fall for First Time in 20 Years," *New York Times,* March 9, 2006.

Page 115 2.3 percent . . . in 2009: Valerie Bauerlein, "U.S. Soda Sales Fell at Slower Rate Last Year," *Wall Street Journal,* March 25, 2010.

Page 116 A 2008 study in Maine: Janet E. Whatley Blum et al., "Reduced Availability of Sugar-Sweetened Beverages and Diet Soda Has a Limited Impact on Beverage Consumption Patterns in Maine High School Youth," *Journal of Nutrition Education and Behavior* 40, no. 6 (November–December 2008), 341–347.

Page 116 Another study, of 11,000 fifth-graders: Meenakshi M. Fernandes, "The Effect of Soft Drink Availability in Elementary Schools on Consumption," *Journal of the American Dietetic Association* 108, no. 9 (September 2008), 1445–1452; Elsevier company news, "New Study Assesses the Impact of Soft Drink Availability in Elementary Schools on Consumption," September 2, 2008.

Page 116 6 percent in 2007 and 5 percent in 2008: The Coca-Cola Company Annual Report 2009.

Page 116 80 percent of Coke's total sales: Joe Guy Collier, "Worldwide Sales a Tonic for Coke," *Atlanta Journal-Constitution,* November 16, 2008.

Page 116 "lost generation" for soda: Caroline Wilbert, "Teens Back Off Sugary Drinks," *Atlanta Journal-Constitution,* June 22, 2006.

Page 116 "successfully repeal Maine's . . . soda tax": Joey Peters, "Industry lobbying turns soda taxes from fizzy to flat," *Stateline,* July 7, 2010.

Page 116 "$17 million for a similar initiative": Curt Woodward, "Washington voters reject taxes on candy, gum, pop," Associated Press, November 3, 2010.

Page 116 "After a $9 million advertising campaign": Anemona Hartocollis, "Failure of state soda tax plan reflects power of an antitax message," *The New York Times,* July 2, 2010.

CHAPTER 5. THE BOTTLED WATER LIE

Page 119 Perrier had introduced . . . getting for free: Elizabeth Royte, *Bottlemania: How Water Went on Sale and Why We Bought It* (New York: Bloomsbury USA, 2008), 30; Charles Fishman, "Message in a Bottle," *Fast Company,* December 19, 2007.

Page 119 Perrier's profits from water rose: Fishman, "Message in a Bottle."

Page 119 Evian, pioneered the use of lightweight bottles: Fishman, "Message in a Bottle."

Page 120 $160 million recall: Alan Riding, *New York Times,* "Perrier Widens Recall After Finding," February 15, 1990.

Page 120 swooped in to acquire Perrier: Richard Tomlinson, "Troubled Waters at Perrier," *Fortune*, November 29, 2004.

Page 120 sales shot up from $115 million: Royte, 33; Tony Clarke, *Inside the Bottle: Exposing the Bottled Water Industry* (Ottawa: Canadian Centre for Policy Alternatives, 2007 [orig. pub. 2005]), 24.

Page 120 profit margins on water: Clarke, 83; Betsy McKay, "Coke Strays from the Real Thing—Investors Fret That Bottled Water, Other Beverages, Don't Quench Their Thirst for Soft-Drink Profit," *Wall Street Journal*, October 29, 2002.

Page 120 proprietary mix of minerals: Hays, 246–247.

Page 120 Intended to signal relaxation and refreshment: David F. Gallagher, "Just Say No to H_2O (Unless It's Coke's Own Brew)," *New York Times*, September 2, 2001.

Page 120 bought Belmont Springs . . . lackluster sales: Clarke, 30.

Page 120 $20 million campaign: "Dasani Pours on Wellness," *Brandweek*, April 23, 2001.

Page 120 Coke targeted women . . . replenished themselves with Dasani: "Dasani and *Glamour* Magazine Launch National Contest to Honor Women at Their Best," Internet Wire, July 19, 2002.

Page 121 up to $8.5 billion overall: Beverage Marketing Corporation, "Bottled Water Perseveres in a Difficult Year, New Data from Beverage Marketing Corporation Show," April 20, 2009.

Page 121 behind Pepsi's Aquafina: Hillary Chura, "Dasani: Kellam Graitcer," *Advertising Age*, October 8, 2001.

Page 121 average French person drank: Paul Simao, "Bottled Water War Cuts into Profits," *Calgary Herald*, January 31, 2004.

Page 121 £7 million: "LFH Bottles Coca-Cola Water Brand," *Design Week*, February 5, 2004.

Page 121 "The more you live"; "Prepare to get wet": "Advertising for Dasani," *Marketing Week*, February 5, 2004.

Page 122 high-divers plummeted: Martin Wainwright, "Fall Guy: Daredevil Dives Promote Bottled Water," *Guardian*, February 11, 2004.

Page 122 actually bottled in the southeast London suburb: Michael McCarthy, "Pure? Coke's Attempt to Sell Tap Water Backfires in Cancer Scare," *Independent*, March 20, 2004.

Page 122 "perfected by NASA": "Soft Drink Is Purified Tap Water," BBC News, March 1, 2004.

Page 122 "enhance the pure taste": "When You Get Headlines in the Press Like 'The Real Sting' in the Sun, 'Coke Sells Tap Water' in the Mirror and 'Eau de Sidcup: Didn't Del Boy Try That?' in the Daily Mail, You Know There's a Story to Amuse," *Eastern Daily Press* (UK), March 16, 2004.

Page 122 "as pure as water gets": McCarthy, "Pure? Coke's Attempt to Sell Tap Water Backfires in Cancer Scare."

Page 122 handed out for free: Valerie Elliott and Angela Jameson, "Coca-Cola Withdraws 'Sidcup Tap' Water," *Times* (London), March 20, 2004.

Page 123 all but blamed the British government: Alison Purdy and Rachel Williams, "Coca-Cola Orders Recall of Bottled Water," Press Association (UK), March 19, 2004.

Page 123 FDA had warned manufacturers: *Federal Register* 66, no. 60 (March 28, 2001).

Page 123 formula for how much bromate: Barbara L. Marteney and Kristin Safran, "Continually Evolving Regulations for D/DBPs," *Water Quality Products*, September 2001.

Page 123 Nestlé stopped using ozonation: Carlos David Mogollón, "Perrier Restricts Ozone Use Awaiting Better Control Options," *Water Conditioning & Purification*, August 2001.

Page 123 typical headline: Philip Henser, "Should I Really Despise Coca-Cola?" *Independent*, March 26, 2004.

Page 123 plays on Coke's own branding: John Arlidge, "Coca-Cola: Don't Drink the Water," *Observer*, April 18, 2004.

Page 124 CAI cut its teeth in the fight: Bella English, "Taking Down the Marlboro Man: Kathy Mulvey Helped Negotiate a Treaty That, If Ratified, Would Ban Tobacco Advertising, Promotion, and Sponsorship," *Boston Globe*, December 23, 2003.

Page 124 founded as the Infant Formula Action Coalition: Marion Nestle, 145–158.

Page 125 some $9 billion annually . . . almost 10 percent: Beverage Marketing Corporation, "Bottled Water Perseveres in a Difficult Year, New Data from Beverage Marketing Corporation Show," April 20, 2009.

Page 125 Gallup poll at the time: Environmental Protection Agency, "Analysis and Findings of the Gallup Organization's Drinking Water Customers Satisfaction Survey," August 6, 2003, 4.

Page 125 set a "low priority": Food and Drug Administration, Center for Food Safety and Applied Nutrition, "Bottled Water Regulations and the FDA," August–September 2002.

Page 125 standards are slightly lower . . . voluntary recalls: International Bottled Water Association, "Regulation of Bottled Water: An Overview."

Page 125 A classic study: Natural Resources Defense Council, "Bottled Water: Pure Drink or Pure Hype?" March 1999.

Page 126 the American Medical Association found: Case Western Reserve University, "Study Finds Some Bottled Water Has More Bacteria and Less Fluoride Than Tap Water," *Science Daily*, March 22, 2000.

Page 126 a 2002 study by the University of Tuskegee: Abua Ikem et al., "Chemical Quality of Bottled Waters from Three Cities in Alabama," *Science of the Total Environment* 285, nos. 1–3 (February 21, 2002), 165–175.

Page 126 A 2004 study by the FDA: Food and Drug Administration, Center for Food Safety and Applied Nutrition, Office of Food Safety, "Questions and Answers About Perchlorate," February 8, 2009.

Page 126 found thirty-eight different pollutants: Olga Naidenko et al., "Bottled Water Quality Investigation: 10 Major Brands, 38 Pollutants," Environmental Working Group, October 2008.

Page 126 traces of pharmaceutical drugs: Jeff Donn, "Pharmaceuticals Found in U.S. Drinking Water," Associated Press, March 10, 2008.

Page 126 "After learning about all the things": Royte, 135.

Page 126 just over $2 per gallon: Mintel International Group, "Bottled Water—US—2008, Executive Summary."

Page 126 one- or two-tenths of a cent per gallon: Natural Resources Defense Council; Food & Water Watch.

Page 127 idea of the Tap Water Challenge: Gigi Kellett, interview by the author.

Page 127 Newark or Philadelphia tap water: Gary Haber, "Dozens Protest Coca-Cola Outside Annual Meeting," *News Journal* (Wilmington, DE), April 20, 2006; Akweli Parker, "Taking the Water Taste Test; Actually, No One Bothered to Keep Score in This Bottled vs. Tap Challenge. Activists Felt They Made Their Point," *Philadelphia Inquirer*, March 22, 2006.

Page 127 sources its water from an underground aquifer: Lee Klein, "Bottled Water Gets the Boot," *Miami New Times*, August 14, 2008.

Page 128 17 million . . . three times that: Peter H. Gleick and Heather Cooley, "Energy Implications of Bottled Water," *Environmental Research Letters* 4 (2009), 1–6.

Page 128 33 percent in 2009: Environmental Protection Agency, "America Recycles Day," November 10, 2009.

Page 128 50 percent in 1992: Container Recycling Institute, "Water, Water Everywhere: The Growth of Non-Carbonated Beverages in the United States," February 2007.

Page 128 33 billion liters: Beverage Marketing Corporation, "Bottled Water Perseveres in a Difficult Year, New Data from Beverage Marketing Corporation Show," April 20, 2009.

Page 128 rates of less than 20 percent: Container Recycling Institute, "Water, Water Everywhere: The Growth of Non-Carbonated Beverages in the United States," February 2007.

Page 128 some 3 billion pounds: Jenny Gitlitz and Pat Franklin, "The 10¢ Incentive to Recycle," Container Recycling Institute, July 2006.

Page 129 "Consumers are making a choice": Marc Gunther, "Bottled Water: No Longer Cool? Activists Turn Up the Heat on Coca-Cola, PepsiCo and Nestle," *Fortune*, March 25, 2007.

Page 130 University of Central Florida's new stadium: Matt McKinley, "New Stadium Gets out of Hot Water," *Central Florida Future*, September 18, 2007; Luis Zaragoza and Claudia Zequeira, "UCF in Hot Water with Fans; Stadium Has No Drinking Fountains, Students Thirsty for Answers," *Orlando Sentinel*, September 18, 2007.

Page 130 led by Coke, showed up to lobby: Jennifer 8. Lee, "City Council Shuns Bottles in Favor of Water from Tap," *New York Times*, June 17, 2008.

Page 130 did approve a resolution to study: U.S. Conference of Mayors, "Bottled Water: The Impact on Municipal Waste Systems," May 1, 2008.

Page 131 passage of the earlier, tougher call: Vinnee Tong, "US Mayors Vote to Phase Out Bottled Water Consumption," Associated Press, June 23, 2008.

Page 131 nixed bottled water: Michelle Locke, "California's Chez Panisse Among Upscale Restaurants Leading Bottled Water Backlash," Associated Press, March 29, 2007.

Page 131 Mario Batali followed suit: Marian Burros, "Fighting the Tide, a Few Restaurants Tilt to Tap Water," *New York Times,* May 30, 2007.

Page 131 "one of capitalism's greatest mysteries": "Bottled Water and Snake Oil," Economist .com, July 31, 2007.

Page 131 "Think Outside the Bottle" pledge . . . raised $100,000: Melissa Knopper, "Bottled Water Backlash," *E—The Environmental Magazine,* May/June 2008.

Page 132 revealing the source of its water: 2008 Nestlé Waters North America Corporate Citizenship Report; Nestlé Waters North America, Quality Reports, http://www.nestle-watersna .com.

Page 132 "The FDA's definition": Chris Vogel and Lee Klein, "Houston Turns Back to Tap Water: That Stuff Flowing from the Faucet Is Safe, Cheap and Environmental," *Houston Press,* August 14, 2008.

Page 133 "We've set pretty aggressive goals" . . . 30 percent fewer emissions: Fred Roselli, interview by the author.

Page 133 "Business managers can more effectively contribute": William C. Frederick, *Corporation, Be Good! The Story of Social Responsibility* (Indianapolis: Dog Ear, 2006), 7–10.

Page 134 Henry Ford had found that out . . . customers' pocketbooks: Bakan, 36–37.

Page 134 "The corporation's legally defined mandate": Bakan, 1.

Page 134 second wave of corporate social responsibility: Frederick, 23–35.

Page 134 further entrenched by the Reagan administration: Frederick, 57–67.

Page 134 Goizueta sloughed off the do-gooding subsidiaries: Pendergrast, 346.

Page 134 "enhance our ability to meet the growing needs": The Coca-Cola Company, "The Coca-Cola Foundation, n.d."

Page 135 "It's not that we plan to be boastful now": David Greising, *I'd Like to Buy the World a Coke: The Life and Leadership of Roberto Goizueta* (San Francisco: John Wiley & Sons, 1998), 295.

Page 135 areas closely aligned with the goals . . . "strategic philanthropy": Greising, 296.

Page 135 corporations increasingly began tying: Craig Smith, "The New Corporate Philanthropy," *Harvard Business Review,* May–June 1994.

Page 135 Exxon investing heavily . . . Yoplait had already signed on: Philip Kotler and Nancy Lee, *Corporate Social Responsibility: Doing the Most Good for Your Company and Your Cause* (Hoboken, NJ: John Wiley & Sons, 2005), 19.

Page 135 84 percent of people would switch: Kotler and Lee, 12.

Page 135 "a cool appraisal of various costs": Kotler and Lee, 17; Rebecca Collings, "Behind the Brand: Is Business Socially Responsible?" *Consumer Policy Review*, September–October 2003.

Page 136 most notorious example is British Petroleum: Ed Crooks, "Back to Petroleum," *Financial Times*, July 7, 2009.

Page 136 more than 4 million barrels of oil: Timothy J. Crone and Maya Tolstoy, "Magnitude of the 2010 Gulf of Mexico oil leak." Science, 330, no. 6004, (19 October 2010).

Page 137 to create Coca-Cola Recycling . . . own packaging materials: The Coca-Cola Company, "Coca-Cola Expands U.S. Recycling or Reuse Goals," February 13, 2008; Joe Guy Collier, "Cause That Refreshes: Plant Boosts Coke's Plastic Recycling Effort," *Atlanta Journal-Constitution*, January 15, 2009.

Page 137 "where commercially viable": Coca-Cola Enterprises, Corporate Responsibility and Sustainability Report 2007, 1; Coca-Cola Enterprises, Corporate Responsibility and Sustainability Report 2008, 29.

Page 137 pledged back in the early 1990s: Dave Aftandilian, "Coke's Broken Promise," *Conscious Choice*, February 2000; Barnaby J. Feder, "Pepsi and Coke to Offer Recycled-Plastic Bottles," *New York Times*, December 5, 1990.

Page 138 just too expensive in the United States: Aftandilian, "Coke's Broken Promise."

Page 138 "the demand for recovered bottles": Collier, "Cause That Refreshes."

Page 138 problem with PET . . . demand for raw materials: Mike Verespej, "Coke Set to Open JV PET Recycling Plant," *Plastics News*, January 16, 2009; Tex Conley, chairman, Container Recycling Institute, interview by the author.

Page 138 driving rates above the 30 percent: Sean O'Leary, "City Pleased with RecycleBank Pilot," *Hartford Business Journal*, November 10, 2008; Keith Naughton and Daniel McGinn, "Saving the World for a Latte," *Newsweek*, September 27, 2008; Brian Lee, "Recycling Effort a Bust; Crackdown on Southbridge Trash Scofflaws," *Telegram & Gazette* (Worcester, MA), February 2, 2010.

Page 138 "It's a series of building blocks": Lisa Manley, interview by the author.

Page 139 rates average 70 percent: Gitlitz and Franklin, "The 10-Cent Incentive to Recycle."

Page 139 According to CAI's Gigi Kellett: Kellett, interview by the author.

Page 140 partnership with Nestlé: Shari Roan, "Less Than Zero?" *Los Angeles Times*, November 27, 2006.

Page 140 A study by Coke and Nestlé: Elizabeth Weise, "Drink Makers Defend Calorie-Burning Claims," *USA Today*, February 12, 2007.

Page 140 "negative calories": Beverage Partners Worldwide, "New Enviga™ Proven to Burn Calories; Sparkling Green Tea Creates a Brand New Category That Combines Great Taste and Negative Calories," PR Newswire, October 12, 2006.

Page 140 Coke had paid . . . $4.1 billion: "Coca-Cola Buys Vitamin Water Maker Glaceau for $4.1 Billion in Cash," Financial Wire, May 29, 2007.

Page 140 found its way quietly into schools: Andrew Martin, "Sugar Finds Its Way Back to the School Cafeteria," *New York Times*, September 16, 2007.

Page 141 "When I bought VitaminWater": Center for Science in the Public Interest, "Coke Sued for Fraudulent Claims on Obesity-Promoting VitaminWater," January 15, 2009.

Page 141 "opportunistic PR stunt; "grandstanding": The Coca-Cola Company, "Statement on the Glaceau VitaminWater Lawsuit," January 15, 2009.

Page 142 faced its own controversy: Bridget Murray Law, "New Sweetener Is Not So Sweet for Your Diet," msnbc.com, April 17, 2009.

CHAPTER 6. *"¡TOMA LO BUENO!"*

Page 146 healing art: Carlos Humberto Gallegos Aguilar, interview by the author.

Page 146 people are performing the same ritual: Gallegos, interview by the author.

Page 147 635 cups of Coke beverages annually: The Coca-Cola Company, Per Capita Consumption of Company Beverage Products, 2008, http://www.thecoca-colacompany.com/ourcompany/ar/pdf/perCapitaConsumption2008.pdf.

Page 147 one of the first foreign countries to sell Coke: Pendergrast, 93.

Page 147 small amounts in Cuba, the Philippines: Louis and Yazijian, 46; Allen, 170.

Page 147 from sporadic to anemic: Pendergrast, 166–167; Allen, 171.

Page 148 owned outright by Coke, as in India: Pendergrast, 184.

Page 148 forced to repeal the law: Louis and Yazijian, 64–65.

Page 148 resentment from some foreigners: Barry Rubin and Judith Colp Rubin, *Hating America: A History* (London: Oxford University Press, 2004), 125–145.

Page 148 wild rumors about the American drink: Kahn, 24.

Page 149 Nowhere was opposition stronger than in France: Richard Kuisel, *Seducing the French: The Dilemma of Americanization* (Berkeley: University of California Press, 1993); Rubin and Rubin, 132–145.

Page 149 "Coca-Colonization": Kuisel, 55; Rubin and Rubin, 146.

Page 149 "the moral landscape of France": Kahn, 28.

Page 149 "Coca-Cola was not injurious to the health": Louis and Yazijian, 77.

Page 149 "This is the decisive struggle for Europe": Allen, 4.

Page 149 trade war on French wine, cheese, and Champagne: Kahn, 30.

Page 149 1953 poll: Kuisel, 68.

Page 149 "It's because Coke is a champion": Kahn, 32.

Page 149 nationalized bottling plants: Pendergrast, 312.

Page 150 Pepsi broke into the Soviet Union: Pendergrast, 275.

Page 150 every excuse not to open . . . stayed with the Jews: Allen, 339–341; Pendergrast, 286.

Page 150 against company policy to give in to a boycott: Watters, 194.

Page 150 more than half his time flying: Pendergrast, 302.

Page 150 40 percent of consumption and 55 percent of profits: Watters, 2.

Page 150 "We're not multinational": Louis and Yazijian, 153.

Page 151 so-called halo effect: Pendergrast, 291.

Page 151 "We have our own built-in State Department": Louis and Yazijian, 285.

Page 151 State Department approved a $300 million loan: Louis and Yazijian, 285.

Page 151 polyester suits . . . the cancer of unionism: Henry J. Frundt, *Refreshing Pauses: Coca-Cola and Human Rights in Guatemala* (New York: Praeger, 1987), 4.

Page 152 twelve-hour shifts . . . firing 154 workers: Frundt, 8–9.

Page 152 to make it more difficult: Frundt, 17–27.

Page 152 Sisters of Providence . . . demand an independent investigation: Frundt, 28.

Page 152 nuns cried foul: Frundt, 36–37.

Page 152 General Romeo Lucas García . . . rout any leftist influences: Mike Gatehouse and Miguel Angel Reyes, *Soft Drink, Hard Labour* (London: Latin American Bureau, 1987), 3, 11.

Page 152 Israel Márquez was sprayed by machine-gun fire: Frundt, 61.

Page 153 ambushed by two men: Frundt, 64.

Page 153 Manuel López Balán, was also killed: Frundt, 82.

Page 153 Márquez traveled to Wilmington . . . out of order: Frundt, 84–86.

Page 153 exonerated the franchisee: Frundt, 86–90.

Page 153 call to boycott . . . work stoppages at Coke plants: Frundt, 105–107.

Page 154 buyout by two handpicked bottling executives: Frundt, 163–167.

Page 154 But Coke's stalling had left eight workers dead: Gatehouse and Reyes, 12–13.

Page 154 Per-caps in Latin America: Pendergrast, 367.

Page 154 minutiae of foreign markets: Allen, 421–422.

Page 154 "Our success": Pendergrast, 389.

Page 155 Nelson Mandela denied Coke's offers: Lawrence Jolidon, "Divestment, Sanctions, Not Always Simple," *USA Today*, June 19, 1990; Clarence Johnson, "ANC's Oakland Headquarters," *San Francisco Chronicle*, June 27, 1990.

Page 155 contributing heavily . . . corporate jets: Deborah Scroggins, "Mandela in Atlanta: Regular Folk to Coke Elite Vie to Help His Cause," *Atlanta Journal-Constitution*, July 11, 2009; Lewis Grizzard, "Respect for Mandela Went down the Drain," *Atlanta Journal-Constitution*, July 18, 1993.

Page 155 sixth most valuable company: Allen, 421–422.

Page 155 "This is a classic situation": Hays, 295.

Page 155 lambasted on late-night talk shows: Hays, 296.

Page 156 ad blitz to wallpaper the country in red and white: Laura K. Jordan, "El problema de la responsibilidad social corporativa: La empresa Coca-Cola en Los Altos de Chiapas" (thesis, San Cristóbal de las Casas, Chiapas, Centro de Investigaciones y Estudios Superiores en Antropología Social, 2008), 73.

Page 156 **"It is not uncommon":** Richard J. Barnet and Ronald E. Muller, *Global Reach: The Power of Multinational Corporations* (New York: Simon & Schuster, 1974).

Page 156 **$68 million for unfair competition:** "Mexican Shopkeeper Defeats Coke," BBC News, November 17, 2005; "Coca-Cola Fined for Anti-competitive Practices in Mexico," Datamonitor NewsWire, November 21, 2005; James Hider, "Woman Who Flattened Coca-Cola: A Tenacious Small Trader Took on the Biggest of the Big Boys and Won," *Times* (London), November 18, 2005.

Page 157 **FEMSA's stock price tripled, from $35 to more than $115:** Jordan, 65.

Page 157 **more than a 30 percent stake in Coca-Cola FEMSA:** Coca-Cola FEMSA, S.A.B. de C.V., Annual Report 2009 shows that Coke owns 31.2 percent of Coke FEMSA; in 2004, according to that year's Annual Report, Coke owned 39.6 percent.

Page 157 **brought up to Chamula by horse:** Jordan, 74.

Page 157 **pushed by the village elders . . . "There are problems":** June Nash, interview by the author; see also Beverly Bell, "Cola Wars in Mexico: Tzotzil Indians in Mexico Know the Dangers of Globalization and Soda Pop," *In These Times*, October 6, 2006.

Page 157 **concessions were granted politically:** June Nash, *In the Eyes of the Ancestors: Belief and Behavior in a Maya Community* (New Haven, CT, and London: Yale University Press, 1970), 629.

Page 158 **"[It is] part of daily life":** Jordan, 77.

Page 158 **"Indigenous people":** Cristóbal López Pérez, interview by the author.

Page 159 **"We can't blame Coca-Cola":** Juan Ignacio Domínguez, interview by the author.

Page 160 **"These three years":** Marcos Arana Cedeño and Liliana López, interviews by the author.

Page 161 **liter of Coke sells for 10 pesos:** Hermann Bellinghausen, "Aggressive Campaign of Coca-Cola from Chenalho to Acteal," *La jornada*, November 3, 2001; Arana and Domínguez, interviews by the author.

Page 161 **cheaper than its main ingredient:** Shop visit by author.

Page 161 **The rumor persists . . . does nothing to dispel:** See Rob Walker, "Cult Classic," *New York Times*, October 11, 2009.

Page 161 **began using cheaper HFCS:** José Yuste, "Activo empresarial," *Crónica*, February 10, 1997.

Page 161 **60 percent HFCS:** "Mexican Soft-Drink Bottlers to Turn to Sugar in the Wake of HFCS Tax," *Food & Drink Weekly*, January 21, 2002.

Page 161 **30 percent, but with plans:** Coca-Cola FEMSA Earnings Conference Call, Fair Disclosure Wire, July 24, 2009.

Page 161 Mexico repealed the tax: Alan Field, "Mexico Drops Sweetener Tax, Ending U.S. Trade Dispute," *Journal of Commerce*, January 5, 2007.

Page 162 dates back to the late 1980s . . . part of Oaxaca as well: Jordan, 74–75.

Page 163 1.37 million liters a day: Jordan, 129.

Page 163 the company takes no more than 2 percent: Jordan, 118, 130.

Page 163 "The water here": María de la Ascunción Gómez Carpio, interview by the author.

Page 163 "There used to be a lot of water": Rosa María Reazola Estevané, interview by the author.

Page 164 mayor of the town of Apizaco . . . "We comply with the law": Marie Kennedy and Chris Tilly, "Challenging Coke's Thirst for Water: The Apizaco Story," *Progressive Planning*, Fall 2007.

Page 164 Back in the 1970s . . . best-selling soft drink: Kate Milner, "Profile: Vicente Fox," BBC News, July 3, 2000.

Page 164 "Working at Coca-Cola": Sam Dillon, "From Moving Mexico's Cola to Shaking Its Politics," *New York Times*, May 9, 1999.

Page 164 Nicknamed "The Coca-Cola Kid" during his campaign . . . put him on top: John Ross, "Fox, Inc. Takes over Mexico," *Multinational Monitor*, March 2001; Tim McGirk, "The Moment of Truth," *Time*, December 4, 2000; Rodolfo Montes, "Amigos de Fox: Sí recaudaron recursos durante la campaña panista," *Proceso*, July 14, 2002; "Fox Team Includes Friends, Financial Reporters," *America's Insider*, October 12, 2000; "Former Fox Fund-raiser: Not All of Mexican President's Collaborators Loyal," Associated Press, August 8, 2003.

Page 165 appointed another former Coke director general: Jesús Olguín Sánchez, "Presidency of the Republic," http://fox.presidencia.gob.mx/en/cabinet/?contenido=18150.

Page 165 privatization of much of the country's water network: Nash, 632–633; P. Wester et al., "The Hydraulic Mission and the Mexican Hydrocracy: Regulating and Reforming the Flows of Water and Power," *Water Alternatives* 2, no. 3 (2009).

Page 165 eight concessions to dump waste in public waters: Gustavo Castro Soto, "La Coca-Cola en México: El agua tiembla" (part 10), *Otros mundos Chiapas*, January 7, 2005, citing data from an investigative report by the now defunct Mexican newspaper *El independiente*, July 14, 2003.

Page 165 $650 million in annual profits: "Mexico: Coca-Cola FEMSA Sales, Profits, Jump," Just-drinks.com, February 12, 2010.

Page 165 as little as three-hundredths of a cent . . . "Nothing": Jordan, 134–135.

Page 165 wearing black ski masks: Mihalis Mentinis, *Zapatistas: The Chiapas Revolt and What It Means for Radical Politics* (London: Pluto, 2006).

Page 166 Subcomandante Marcos . . . several Zapatista bases: Mentinis, 20; Worth H. Weller, *Conflict in Chiapas: Understanding the Modern Mayan World* (North Manchester, IN: DeWitt, 2000), 84.

Page 166 "We have a way": Beverly Bell, "Cola Wars in Mexico: Tzotzil Indians in Mexico Know the Dangers of Globalization and Soda Pop," *In These Times*, October 6, 2006.

Page 167 too egregious for some to ignore: John Ross, "Coca-Cola's Raid on a Sacred Mountain," *Counterpunch*, September 7, 2007.

Page 167 coalition of neighborhood groups: César Morales, interview by the author.

Page 168 spend some $50 million annually: Gustavo Castro, interview by the author.

Page 168 "The adults aren't salvageable": Teresa Zepeda, interview by the author.

Page 168 In 1999, the Coca-Cola Foundation . . . put up $155,000: Jordan, 102.

Page 169 authorization for a small bottling plant: Jordan, 110; Domínguez, interview by the author.

CHAPTER 7. "SYRUP IN THE VEINS"

Page 172 sales languished over the years: Testimony of Richard I. Kirby, Oral argument and evidentiary hearing, April 22, 2005, *SINALTRAINAL, et al. v. The Coca-Cola Company, et al.*, United States District Court, Southern District of Florida, 1:2001-cv-03208 (hereafter *SINALTRAINAL v. Coke*); William José Alberto Cruz Suarez deposition, Isidro Gil investigation, Fiscalía de la Nación, Unidad de Derechos Humanos, Radicado Preliminar No. 164, República de Colombia (hereafter *Gil*), vol. 2, pp. 191–196. (Cruz was Bebidas's lawyer in Colombia.)

Page 172 sectarian bloodletting . . . Manuel Marulanda: Robin Kirk, *More Terrible Than Death: Massacres, Drugs, and America's War in Colombia* (New York: Public Affairs, 2003), 15–41; Steven Dudley, *Walking Ghosts: Murder and Guerrilla Politics in Colombia* (New York: Routledge, 2004), 3–19.

Page 172 Fuerzas Armadas . . . Revolutionary Armed Forces of Colombia: Kirk, 47–55; Dudley, 19.

Page 173 infiltrated the unions in the banana-processing plants: Dudley, 129.

Page 173 kidnapping and holding wealthy people: Kirk, 67.

Page 173 ELN "taxed" bottling plants: "Los paras contra Coca-Cola," *Cambio*, February 8, 1999.

Page 173 rancher named Ramón Isaza: Joseph Contreras, "Paramilitary Patriarch," *Newsweek*, September 6, 1999.

Page 173 they began killing FARC and ELN "tax collectors": Kirk, 102–125; Dudley, 73.

Page 173 increasingly brutal massacres: Dudley, 19, 71–73.

Page 173 paramilitaries . . . declared illegal: Kirk, 125–128.

Page 173 Autodefensas Unidas de Colombia: Kirk, 141–177.

Page 174 the brutal Freddy Rendón Herrera: David Adams, "Colombia Shaken As Paramilitary Leaders Testify," *St. Petersburg Times*, June 18, 2007.

Page 174 ordering the deaths of three thousand: "'H.H.' se confiesa," *El spectador*, August 2, 2008; "Ex–Paramilitary Chief in Colombia Admits to Atrocities," Agence France Presse, August 3, 2008.

Page 174 decapitated a boy in front of the crowd: Kirk, 195; Joshua Hammer, "Mayor with a Mission," *Newsweek*, April 21, 1997; Tom Boswell, "Leading a City That Has Become a Battlefield," *National Catholic Reporter*, January 24, 1997.

Page 174 cut off the head of an elderly man: Adams, "Colombia Shaken As Paramilitary Leaders Testify."

Page 174 bottling plant in Carepa was struggling: Luis Hernán Manco Monroy and Oscar Giraldo Arango, interviews by the author.

Page 174 SINALTRAINAL began to organize workers: Alejandro García, lawyer for SINALTRAINAL, interview by the author; William José Alberto Cruz Suarez deposition, *Gil* 2:191–196.

Page 174 workers can be fired at will: Alejandro García, interview by the author.

Page 175 Manco simply disappeared: Manco, interview by the author.

Page 175 Two weeks later, it was Giraldo's turn: Giraldo, interview by the author.

Page 175 shot while drinking on his front stoop: Gómez death certificate, *Gil* 1:82; letter from Luz Marina Cifuentes Cataño, March 31, 1997; *Gil* 1:108–109.

Page 175 seeing Milan socializing with local paramilitaries: Complaint (1), *SINALTRAINAL v. Coke*, 20; Manco and Giraldo, interviews by the author.

Page 175 "sweep away the union": Complaint, *SINALTRAINAL v. Coke* (1), 19; Luís Adolfo Cardona Usma deposition, *Gil* 2:181–187.

Page 175 "hasn't been destroyed": Hernán Manco, amplification of deposition, *Gil* 1: 283–291; Manco, interview by the author.

Page 176 protesting Milan's associations: Letter from Javier Correa to Bebidas y Alimientos de Urabá, September 27, 1995, included as exhibit B to original complaint (1), *SINALTRAINAL v. Coke.*

Page 176 negotiating a new labor contract: List of worker demands, November 22, 1996, *Gil* 2:226–230.

Page 176 Born in a small town . . . thrived at the plant: Martín Gil, interview by the author.

Page 176 argued for a workers' compensation payment: Report, Cuerpo Técnico de Investigación (hereafter CTI) Apartadó, June 18, 1997, *Gil* 1:269–279; Ariosto Milan Mosquera deposition, *Gil* 4:16–21.

Page 176 crack of a pistol rang out behind him: Giraldo, interview by the author.

Page 176 watched Gil's head snap backward: Manco, interview by the author.

Page 177 ten bullets . . . outside the gate: Gil autopsy report, December 10, 1996 (Diligencia de Necropsia, No. UCH-NC-96-412), *Gil* 1:87; photographs of Gil's body, *Gil* 1:243–246. Neither the Coca-Cola Company nor its bottlers have ever denied that Gil was killed at the plant. In initial reports, the company claimed that he died outside the gates; however, in more recent interviews, including the author's interview of Ed Potter, the company has conceded that he was killed inside the plant.

Page 177 Adolfo Cardona, ran to the body: Cardona, interview by the author; Cardona deposition, *Gil* 2:181–187.

Page 177 jumped on his own motorcycle . . . declare him dead: Gil, interview by the author.

Page 177 known as "El Diablo". . . safety of the police station: Cardona, interview by the author; Cardona deposition.

Page 178 Bebidas would buy plane tickets: Manco and Giraldo, interviews by the author.

Page 178 paramilitaries were busy breaking into the union hall: Letter from Javier Correa and Hernán Manco to Fiscalía, *Gil* 1:52; CTI Antioquia report, October 5, 1998, *Gil* 1, unidentified page; Complaint (1), *SINALTRAINAL v. Coke*, 21.

Page 179 "That kid was murdered at the plant": Manco, interview by the author.

Page 179 forty-five members signed letters or fled town: List prepared by Javier Correa, and resignation letters, *Gil* 2:100–150.

Page 179 wasn't an isolated occurrence: Javier Correa, interview by the author.

Page 179 SINALTRAINAL is unapologetically militant: Lesley Gill, interview by the author; SINALTRAINAL, *Una delirante ambición imperial* (Bogotá: Universo Latino, 2003).

Page 180 nothing to say about the situation: Amplification of deposition of William José Alberto Cruz Suarez, *Gil* 2:216–220; Alejandro García, interview by the author.

Page 180 learned about the murder days after: Mark Thomas, *Belching Out the Devil: Global Adventures with Coca-Cola* (New York: Nation Books, 2009), 351.

Page 180 fault of the paramilitaries: Detention order for Miguel Enrique Vergara Salgado, *Gil* 3:320–347.

Page 180 terminated for "abandoning their place of work": Lesley Gill, "Labor and Human Rights: 'The Real Thing' in Colombia," paper presented to the Human Rights Committee of the American Anthropological Association, Washington, D.C., November 28, 2004; amplification of deposition of William José Alberto Cruz Suarez, *Gil* 2:216–220.

Page 180 "You have to leave": Manco, interview by the author.

Page 181 threatened him at gunpoint: Giraldo, interview by the author.

Page 181 "No, we do not drink": Manco and Giraldo, interviews by the author.

Page 181 "Conducting business in the current environment": Jeffrey Distler, Consumer Affairs Specialist, The Coca-Cola Company, to Ellie Mitchell, United Steelworkers Union, October 24, 2001.

Page 182 established a code of ethics: The Coca-Cola Company, Supplier Guiding Principles, http://www.thecoca-colacompany.com/citizenship/pdf/SGP_Brochure_ENG.pdf.

Page 182 investigation into Gil's murder: Fiscalía General de la Nación, Unidad Nacional de Derechos Humanos, Radicado Preliminar No. 164 (*Gil*).

Page 182 identity of "Caliche": CTI report, October 5, 1998, *Gil* 1: 205–206; Ariel Gómez death certificate, *Gil* 1:280.

Page 182 identified as Enrique Vergara: Letter from Gloria Correa Martínez, Unidad Nacional de Derechos Humanos, August 1998, *Gil* 1:163.

Page 182 henchman of El Alemán: CTI report, June 19, 1998, *Gil* 1:313–324; CTI report, undated, *Gil* 1:327–330.

Page 182 Multiple witnesses . . . hang out with them: José Joaquín Giraldo Graciano deposition, *Gil* 2:24–29; José Heriberto Sierra Renfigo deposition, *Gil* 2:30–36; Gudnara del Socorro Osorio deposition, *Gil* 2:41–46.

Page 182 Marín let the paramilitaries: Joaquín Giraldo deposition, *Gil* 2:24–29; José Heriberto Sierra Renfigo deposition, *Gil* 2:30–34; Humberto de Jesús Peña deposition, *Gil* 2:35–40.

Page 182 Milan had resigned: Ariosto Milan Mosquera to Richard Kirby Kielland, November 28, 1996, *Gil* 3:17.

Page 182 Marín left six months later: Rigoberto Marín Restrepo to Peggy Ann Kielland, June 25, 1997, *Gil* 3:24.

Page 182 not only for Cepillo, but for Marín and Milan as well: Arrest warrants, February 10, 1999, *Gil* 2:233–250.

Page 183 "leaves not the slightest doubt": Orders for preventive detention, September 2, 1999, *Gil* 3:219–247.

Page 183 declared their innocence . . . collaborating with guerrillas himself: Ferenc Alain Legitime Julio (Milan's lawyer), undated letter, *Gil* 3:267–278; Ariosto Milan Mosquera deposition, *Gil* 4:16–21; Rigoberto Marín Restrepo deposition, *Gil* 4:22–26; Rigoberto Marín Restrepo amplification of deposition, *Gil* 4:124–130.

Page 183 it didn't have sufficient evidence: Decision, June 19, 2000, *Gil* 4:153–161.

Page 183 typical of the Colombian justice system: Dora Lucy, interview by the author.

Page 183 fewer than a hundred convictions: Human Rights Watch, *World Report 2009—Colombia*, January 14, 2009.

Page 183 public backlash: Human Rights Watch, "Attorney General Reno in Colombia, March 3–4," *Human Rights Watch Backgrounder*, March, 3, 1999.

Page 184 arrested General Alejo del Río: Human Rights Watch, "A Wrong Turn: The Record of the Colombian Attorney General's Office," *Colombia* 14, no. 3(B) (2002).

Page 169 sacked the head of the Human Rights Unit: Human Rights Watch, "A Wrong Turn," 2.

Page 184 "Osorio did severe damage": Adam Isacson, interview by the author.

Page 184 bases near Coca-Cola bottling plants: Steven Dudley, "War in Colombia's Oilfields," *The Nation*, August 5, 2002.

Page 184 met with AUC head Carlos Castaño: "Los paras contra Coca-Cola," *Cambio*, February 8, 1999.

Page 185 "I don't think it's valid": Maria McFarland, interview by the author.

Page 186 profits of $10 million a year: David J. Lynch, "Murder and Payoffs Taint Business in Colombia," *USA Today*, October 30, 2007.

Page 186 company insisted . . . banana plantations of Urabá: Sibylla Brodzinsky, "Chiquita Case Puts Big Firms on Notice," *Christian Science Monitor*, April 11, 2007.

Page 186 "Simply put": David J. Lynch, "Murder and Payoffs Taint Business in Colombia," *USA Today*, October 30, 2007.

Page 186 "peace and justice" law: "The Perils of 'Parapolitics,'" *The Economist*, March 23, 2007.

Page 186 "The companies that benefited": "'H.H.' se confiesa," *El spectador*, August 2, 2008.

Page 186 arrangement with Chiquita as well as Dole: José Gregorio Mangones Luno affidavit, October 29, 2009, *Does (1-44) v. Chiquita Brands International Inc. et al.*, United States District Court for the Southern District of Florida, 9:2008cv80465; Charlie Cray, "Hiring Death Squads Is Coming Back to Haunt U.S. Companies," AlterNet, February 16, 2010; Juan Smith, "Colombia; Ex-Paramilitary Implicates Two U.S. Companies in Murder of Trade Unionists," North American Congress on Latin America, December 14, 2009.

Page 186 Raúl Hasbún . . . ordering the deaths: "Las confesiones de Raúl Hasbún," *Semana*, October 4, 2008, English version.

Page 187 Isidro Gil . . . "collecting money for the guerrillas": Steven Dudley, "Colombian Paramilitary Tells How He Financed His Own Murder Inc.: Bananas," *Miami Herald*, March 21, 2009.

Page 187 Magdalena Medio . . . hundreds of bodies: Dudley, 41–43, 65; Kirk, 110, 125.

Page 187 Barrancabermeja was outside their control: Dudley, 18–19, 123.

Page 187 "The threats started in 2001": Juan Carlos Galvis, interview by the author.

Page 188 SINALTRAINAL had nearly two thousand members: William Mendoza, interview by the author.

Page 188 expanding throughout other South American countries: Panamerican Beverages Inc., Annual Report, 2003.

Page 188 acquired a 10 percent share . . . "anchor bottler": Panamerican Beverages Inc., Annual Report, 2003; "Panamerican Beverages and Panamco LLC Historical Timeline," submitted as exhibit to a deposition in *SINALTRAINAL v. Coke*, May 1, 2003; "Anchors Aboard: Coke Gives Panamco Larger Bottling Role in Latin America," *Beverage World*, December 1, 1995.

Page 188 25 percent by 1997: "Panamerican Beverages and Panamco LLC Historical Timeline," submitted as exhibit to a deposition in *SINALTRAINAL v. Coke*, May 1, 2003; "Panamco Merges with Coca-Cola y Hit de Venezuela; Strengthens Position as Leading Anchor Bottler," Business Wire, May 12, 1997.

Page 188 Panamco consolidated seventeen plants: Panamerican Beverages Inc., Annual Report, 2003.

Page 189 Some 6,700 Coke workers . . . cutting contracts with its workers: Gill, "Labor and Human Rights"; Lesley Gill, "Coca-Cola in Colombia: Increased Profits, Downsized Workforce," *Colombia Journal*, July 27, 2004.

Page 189 acquired by Mexico's Coca-Cola FEMSA: Panamco proxy statement, March 23, 2003; Coca-Cola FEMSA, S.A. de C.V., Annual Report, 2004.

Page 189 officials met directly with a member . . . spared any violence: Galvis and Mendoza, interviews by the author; Amnesty International, "Colombia: Killing, Arbitrary Detentions, and Death Threats—The Reality of Trade Unionism in Colombia," January 23, 2007.

Page 189 Galvis saw Rincón inside the company: Galvis and Mendoza, interviews by the author.

Page 189 arrested and convicted for conspiracy: "Por homicidio de tesorero de la USO cuatro condenados," Fiscalía, April 11, 2007, http://www.fiscalia.gov.co/PAG/DIVULGA/noticias2007/seccionales/SeccHomicidioAbr11.htm; "Aviso de citación a versión libre," Fiscalía, http://www.fiscalia.gov.co/justiciapaz/DetalleVersion.asp?ce=91422724; Galvis, interview by the author; Michael Lydon, "Interview: Juan Carlos Galvis Discusses Colombia's Fight Against Coca-Cola and Its Bitter Attacks on Himself and His Family," *Morning Star* (London), June 13, 2005.

Page 190 threats against Galvis . . . then her husband: Galvis, interview by the author.

Page 190 several men tried to pull . . . Mendoza declined: Mendoza, interview by the author; Final Report, "An Investigation of Allegations of Murder and Violence in Coca-Cola's Bottling Plants," NYC Fact-Finding Delegation on Coca-Cola in Colombia led by New York City councilman Hiram Monserrate, April 2004.

Page 191 witnesses reported that an armed robbery: Galvis, interview by the author.

Page 192 "He'll work a year" . . . "They are going to disappear me": Álvaro González, interview by the author.

Page 194 "I told them" . . . "We haven't done anything wrong": González and Domingo Flores, interviews by the author.

Page 194 earned the nickname "Chile": Luis Eduardo García, interview by the author.

Page 194 in death threats he is referred to by that nickname: García, interview by the author; undated death threat signed "Águilas Negras."

Page 195 When Chile first pulled into . . . pieces of candy: González, Flores, and García, interviews by the author.

Page 196 fired from their jobs: González, García, Flores, and Laura Milena García, interviews by the author.

Page 196 174 days in La Modelo: González, interview by the author.

Page 196 case started falling apart . . . ending the investigation: Fiscalía General de la Nación, Radicado No. 7834, San José de Cúcuta.

Page 196 prosecutors declined to press charges: Eduardo García and Alejandro García Salzedo, union lawyer for SINALTRAINAL, interviews by the author.

Page 196 In 2002, González's daughter . . . "I become another Álvaro": González, interview by the author.

Page 197 union has been decimated: Carlos Olaya, interview by the author.

Page 197 outsourcing of the workforce: Olaya, interview by the author.

Page 198 wages are even worse: Olaya, interview by the author.

Page 198 Coca-Cola now controls 60 percent: Olaya, interview by the author.

Page 198 threats against SINALTRAINAL continue: Human Rights Watch, *Paramilitaries' Heirs: The New Face of Violence in Colombia,* February 3, 2010.

Page 198 or even e-mailed: E-mail provided by Juan Carlos Galvis.

Page 198 paramilitaries kidnapped Flores's son: Flores, interview by the author; also reported by Colombia Solidarity Campaign, "Death Threat/Fear for Safety," October 5, 2007, http://www.colombiasolidarity.org.uk/index.php?option=com_content&task=view&id=129&Itemid=45.

Page 198 Chile's daughter Laura Milena García was targeted: Laura Milena García, interview by the author.

CHAPTER 8. THE FULL FORCE OF THE LAW

Page 202 "At a pretty young age": Dan Kovalik, interview by the author.

Page 202 has done nothing to stem cocaine production: U.S. Government Accountability Office Report 09-71, "Plan Colombia: Drug Reduction Goals Were Not Fully Met, but Security Has Improved; U.S. Agencies Need More Detailed Plans for Reducing Assistance," October 2008.

Page 203 began in Malaysia: Terry Collingsworth, interview by the author.

Page 205 provided enormous wiggle room to companies: Lance Compa and Jeffrey S. Vogt, "Labor Rights in the Generalized System of Preferences: A 20-Year Review," *Comparative Labor Law and Policy Journal* 22, no. 2/3 (2005), 199–238.

Page 205 Bill Clinton mediated a compromise: National Consumer League, "One Sweatshop Is Too Many: NCL Celebrates the 10th Anniversary of the White House Apparel Industry Partnership," press release, November 14, 1996.

Page 206 Global Sullivan Principles . . . "safe and healthy workplace": Global Sullivan Principles, "Charter Endorsers," "Frequently Asked Questions," "Principles," http://www.thesullivanfoundation.org/gsp/.

Page 206 principles against the use of child labor overseas: Don Melvin, "Child Labor Treaty Has Atlanta Backer," *Atlanta Journal-Constitution,* June 17, 1999.

Page 206 they were completely voluntary: The Coca-Cola Company, "Code of Business Conduct," http://www.thecoca-colacompany.com/ourcompany/pdf/COBC_English.pdf.

Page 206 a 2005 report by the company: David Teather, "Nike Lists Abuses at Asian Factories," *Guardian,* April 14, 2005.

Page 206 "At the end of the day": Terry Collingsworth, interview by the author.

Page 207 done for the benefit of two foreign companies: Phillis R. Morgan and R. Bradley Mokros, "International Legal Developments in Review: 2000," *International Lawyer*, Summer 2001.

Page 207 "You're a smart lawyer": Terry Collingsworth, interview by the author.

Page 207 "another example of imperialism": Tamar Lewin, "Judge Bars U.S. Suits on Bhopal," *New York Times*, May 13, 1986

Page 207 Alien Tort Claims Act: United States Code, Title 28, Part IV, Chapter 85, §1350.

Page 208 used exactly twice before 1980: Pamela J. Stephens, "Spinning *Sosa*: Federal Common Law, the Alien Tort Statute, and Judicial Restraint," *Boston University International Law Journal* 25, no. 1 (Spring 1997), 1–36.

Page 208 Joel Filártiga . . . Radovan Karadžić: Anne-Marie Slaughter and David L. Bosco, "Alternative Justice," *Crimes of War Project*, May 2001.

Page 208 $4.5 billion in damages: David Rhode, "Jury in New York Orders Bosnian Serb to Pay Billions," *New York Times*, September 26, 2000.

Page 208 no control over the Burmese military: David Moberg, "Burma Inc.; Keeping the Pressure on the Junta and Its Corporate Partners," *In These Times*, October 1, 2001.

Page 208 Unocal settled for an undisclosed amount: Lisa Girion, "Unocal to Settle Rights Claims," *Los Angeles Times*, December 14, 2004.

Page 209 suing ExxonMobil for funneling money: "Labor Fund Sues Exxon, Coke, Fresh Del Monte," *Social Issues Reporter*, September 2001.

Page 209 "hired, contracted with or otherwise": Complaint (1), *SINALTRAINAL v. Coke*, 4.

Page 210 In addition to the bottlers' agreements: Complaint (1), *SINALTRAINAL v. Coke*, 10.

Page 210 Coca-Cola Company's quarter share in Panamco: Complaint (1), *SINALTRAINAL v. Coke*, 15.

Page 210 could block the Kirbys from selling it: Complaint (1), *SINALTRAINAL v. Coke*, 15–16, 25.

Page 210 "I sought the permission": Richard Kirby Kielland deposition, *Gil* 2:200–204.

Page 210 "wherever we operate": "Colombian Union Sues Coke," United Press International, July 20, 2001.

Page 210 "the Coca-Cola Company does not": Nick Rosen, "Colombian Union to Sue Coca-Cola in Human Rights Case," Associated Press Worldstream, July 19, 2001.

Page 211 didn't deny that paramilitaries targeted: Juan Forero, "Union Says Coca-Cola in Colombia Uses Thugs," *New York Times*, July 26, 2001.

Page 211 "You don't use them": Garry M. Leach, "Coke Is It," *In These Times*, September 3, 2001.

Page 211 "For all we know": Transcript of motion to dismiss, June 6, 2002, *SINALTRAINAL v. Coke*.

Page 211 submitted a sample bottlers' agreement: Order on Motion to Dismiss for Lack of Subject Matter (103), *SINALTRAINAL v. Coke*, 11.

Page 212 Adolfo de Jesús Munera was shot dead: *Gladys Cecilia Rincón de Munera, et al. v. The Coca-Cola Company, et al.*, U.S. District Court for the Southern District of California, l:2006-cv-21412.

Page 212 Gil's murder wasn't a war crime: Order on Motion to Dismiss for Lack of Subject Matter (103), *SINALTRAINAL v. Coke*, 9–10.

Page 212 no control over the bottlers: Order on Motion to Dismiss for Lack of Subject Matter, *SINALTRAINAL v. Coke* (103); *SINALTRAINAL v. Coke*, 11–12.

Page 213 earliest education as an activist: Ray Rogers, interview by the author.

Page 214 "corporate campaign": "An Interview with Ray Rogers," *Working Papers*, January–February 1982. The first use of the term "corporate campaign" in a major newspaper is in a story about Rogers's campaign against J. P. Stevens: Jack Egan, "Stevens Director Resigns; Avon Chairman Resigns from Stevens Board," *Washington Post*, March 22, 1978.

Page 214 the company's 1977 shareholder meeting: "An Interview with Ray Rogers."

Page 215 threatening to pull out millions of dollars . . . bargaining table: Gail Bronson and Jeffrey H. Birnbaum, "Rogers' Tough, Unorthodox Tactics Prevail in Stevens Organizing Fight," *Wall Street Journal*, October 21, 1980; "An Interview with Ray Rogers"; Rogers, interview by the author.

Page 215 the "Ray Rogers Clause": "An Interview with Ray Rogers."

Page 215 "Because Stevens": "Labor's Blacklist," *Wall Street Journal*, March 24, 1978.

Page 215 "What the labor movement": "An Interview with Ray Rogers."

Page 215 goal of anyone wanting to change the world: Saul Alinsky, *Rules for Radicals: A Pragmatic Primer for Realistic Radicals* (New York: Vintage, 1989 [orig. pub. 1971]), 10.

Page 216 "rhetorical rationale": Alinsky, 13.

Page 216 "In a complex" . . . focused their efforts on Philip Morris: Alinsky, 130–132. For an excellent discussion of target selection based on Alinsky's work, see also Kim Fellner, *Wrestling with Starbucks: Conscience, Capital, Cappuccino* (New Brunswick, NJ: Rutgers University Press, 2008), 230–231.

Page 216 successful campaigns against Campbell's Soup and American Airlines: Daniel Benjamin, "Labor's Boardroom Guerrilla," *Time*, June 20, 1988; Ted Reed, "Union Hires Consultant for EAL Fight," *Miami Herald*, July 12, 1989; Larry Neumeister, "Zuckerman Takes Control of Daily News, Visits Newsroom," Associated Press, January 9, 1993; "American Agreement May Signal More Airline Labor Fights," Associated Press, December 24, 1987.

Page 217 650 people lost their jobs: Benjamin, "Labor's Boardroom Guerrilla."

Page 217 seeking confrontation and publicity: *American Dream*, directed by Barbara Kopple (DVD, Cabin Creek Films, 1990).

Page 217 "one of the labor movement's": Benjamin, "Labor's Boardroom Guerrilla."

Page 217 forced to relocate: Rogers, interview by the author; Doug Grow, "Labor Activist Bubbly over Coca-Cola Fight," *Star Tribune* (Minneapolis), April 25, 2004.

Page 218 A parade of union carpenters . . . challenged Coke's general counsel: David Kaplan and L. M. Sixel, "Human Rights, Salary at Issue for Coca-Cola," *Houston Chronicle*, April 17, 2003.

Page 218 kidnapping and beating of the son of Limberto Carranza: Final Report, "An Investigation of Allegations of Murder and Violence in Coca-Cola's Bottling Plants," NYC Fact-Finding Delegation on Coca-Cola in Colombia led by New York city councilman Hiram Monserrate, April 2004.

Page 218 SINALTRAINAL released a list of demands: "Seven Points to Settlement," Campaign to Stop Killer Coke, http://www.killercoke.org/sevpts.htm.

Page 219 yearlong boycott: César García, "Colombian Union Launches Boycott of Coca-Cola for Alleged Role in the Deaths of Plant Workers," Associated Press Worldstream, July 22, 2003.

Page 219 media reported it as such: Jim Lovell, "Students Call for Coke Boycott," *Atlanta Business Chronicle*, November 21, 2003.

Page 219 SunTrust Bank: Madeleine Baran, "Stop Killer Coke!" *Dollars & Sense*, November/December 2003; Rogers, interview by the author.

Page 219 owned some 50 million Coke shares: "SunTrust Sells Coca-Cola Shares It's Held 88 Years," CNBC.com, May 15, 2007, http://www.cnbc.com/id/18677410.

Page 220 casualties of a globalizing economy: See Klein, *No Logo*.

Page 220 protests at the WTO meetings: For an activists' perspective on the event, see David Solnit and Rebecca Solnit, *The Battle of the Story of the Battle of Seattle* (Edinburgh, Scotland: AK Press, 2009).

Page 220 patchouli-scented caravan of activists: See Naomi Klein, *Fences and Windows: Dispatches from the Front Lines of the Globalization Debate* (New York: Picador, 2002).

Page 220 removed Coke from its campus: Lovell, "Students Call for Coke Boycott"; "Boycott Killer Coke!" Colombia Action Network.

Page 220 Bard College in upstate New York followed suit: Lovell, "Students Call for Coke Boycott"; Baran, "Stop Killer Coke!"

Page 221 "Unfortunately, Bard College officials": Lovell, "Students Call for Coke Boycott."

Page 221 passed by fewer than sixty votes: Shane Hegarty, "Students Give Coke the Push," *Irish Times*, October 18, 2003.

Page 221 won by an even higher margin: Lovell, "Students Call for Coke Boycott."

Page 221 $100,000-a-year budget: Campaign to Stop Killer Coke grant requests, 2006 and 2007; Rogers, interview by the author.

Page 221 Coke's $30 billion: The Coca-Cola Company, Annual Report, 2010.

Page 221 mentioned the situation in Colombia: Paul Klebnikov, "Coke's Sinful World," *Forbes*, December 22, 2003.

Page 222 voted twelve to eight to remove Carleton's Coke machines: The details of this account stem solely from Rogers; however, independent sources corroborate the fact that he attended the meeting and debated Coke's representative. See Ian Werkheiser, "Killer Coke," *Z Magazine*, August 1, 2004, and Margaret Webb, "Human Rights Charges Still Gnaw at Coca-Cola," *Washington Post*, April 22, 2004.

Page 222 next campus to sever its ties with Coke: Avi Chomsky, interview by the author.

Page 223 honored as a civil rights pioneer: Brian C. Mooney, "Patrick's Path from Courtroom to Boardroom," *Boston Globe*, August 13, 2006.

Page 223 "from human rights violations": Letter from Terry Collingsworth to Equal Justice Works board members, October 2, 2003.

Page 223 "so we could see": Webb, "Human Rights Charges Still Gnaw at Coca-Cola."

Page 223 "sources close to the situation": Webb, "Human Rights Changes Still Gnaw at Coca-Cola."

Page 223 "confidence in the brand": Joan Vennochi, "Killer Coke's Charges Go Flat," *Boston Globe*, August 10, 2006.

Page 223 "either of two things": Mooney, "Patrick's Path from Courtroom to Boardroom."

Page 223 The company refused: Vennochi, "Killer Coke's Charges Go Flat."

Page 224 $2.1 million consulting contract: Mooney, "Patrick's Path from Courtroom to Boardroom."

Page 224 the campaign played a role in Daft's own retirement: Rogers, interview by the author.

Page 224 Rogers had a love-hate relationship: Rogers, interview by the author.

Page 224 "Coke has shown": Final Report, "An Investigation of Allegations of Murder and Violence in Coca-Cola's Bottling Plants," NYC Fact-Finding Delegation on Coca-Cola in Colombia led by New York city councilman Hiram Monserrate, April 2004.

Page 224 first-quarter profits of $1.13 billion: Scott Leith, "Coke's First-Quarter Profit Climbs 35 Percent," *Atlanta Journal-Constitution*, April 22, 2004.

Page 225 Daft addressed the Colombia situation . . . call for an independent investigation: The account of the 2004 shareholders meeting draws on video shown on *Democracy Now!*, April 27, 2004, "Killer Coke: Activist Disrupts Coca Cola Shareholders Meeting" (http://www.democracynow.org/2004/4/27/stream), as well as Ray Rogers, interview by the author, and the following contemporaneous news reports: Grow, "Labor Activity Bubbly over Coca-Cola Fight"; Scott Leith and Matt Kempner, "Scuffle, Catcalls Spice Coca-Cola's Annual Meeting in Delaware," *Atlanta Journal-Constitution*, April 22, 2004; and Webb, "Human Rights Charges Still Gnaw at Coca-Cola."

Page 225 hadn't intended the meeting to turn physical: Rogers, interview by the author.

Page 225 77,000 shares of common stock: The Coca-Cola Company, Proxy Statement,

March 4, 2004; The Coca-Cola Company, "Historical Price Lookup," http://ir.thecoca-colacompany.com/phoenix.zhtml?c=94566&p=irol-stocklookup.

Page 226 $5,000 check to Corporate Campaign, Inc.: Note from B. Wardlaw to Ray Rogers, April 23, 2004.

Page 226 refusal to investigate in Colombia: Betsy Morris, "The Real Story: How Did Coca-Cola's Management Go from First-Rate to Farcical in Six Short Years? Tommy the Barber Knows," *Fortune*, May 17, 2004.

CHAPTER 9. ALL THE WATER IN INDIA

Page 228 fecal coliform bacteria count of 600,000: "Up to Their Necks in It," *The Economist*, July 17, 2008.

Page 228 toxic soup of heavy metals: "Hazardous Heavy Metals Polluting Ganga," *Times of India*, June 4, 2009.

Page 228 "a cloudy brown soup of excrement": "Up to Their Necks in It."

Page 228 ambitious cleanup plan: Dipak Mishra, "Clean Ganga Water Still a Dream," *Times of India*, March 22, 2010; Samanth Subramanian, "The Monumental Decline of a Great River," *MINT*, September 1, 2009.

Page 228 Nearly half of those who bathe: "India's Ganges River Brings Disease, Pollution; Believers Scarcely Notice," Associated Press, May 9, 2002.

Page 229 "Lok Samiti follows": Nandlal Master, interview by the author.

Page 230 The plant here dates back to 1995: Nandlal, interview by the author; Shira Wolf, "Thanda-Hearted Matlab: Coca-Cola in India," University of Wisconsin College Year in India paper, 2003–2004.

Page 230 Coca-Cola India purchased the plant: Nandlal, interview by the author; Wolf, "Thanda-Hearted Matlab"; *Independent Third Party Assessment of Coca-Cola Facilities in India*, Project Report No. 2006WM21 (New Delhi: The Energy and Resources Institute, 2006), 219 (hereafter TERI report).

Page 230 clashing with the company: Nandlal, interview by the author.

Page 230 short-term contracts: Kalyan Ranjan, interview by the author.

Page 230 workers appealed to company management: Nandlal, interview by the author.

Page 230 "The first major problem": Urmika Vishwakarma, interview by the author.

Page 230 water pooled by the side of the highway: Nantoo Banerjee, *The Real Thing: Coke's Bumpy Ride Through India* (Kolkata, India: Frontpage, 2009), 79.

Page 231 "nothing would grow": Nandlal and Vishwakarma, interviews by the author.

Page 231 water shortages in 2002: Shankkar Aiyar, "The Impact: Thirst Aid," *India Today*, 2002; "Indian Economy: General Review," *Finance India*, March 2003; "Drought May Undo Govt's Plans for High GDP Growth," *Press Trust of India*, July 25, 2004.

Page 231 one of ninety-seven wells that Lok Samiti says: R. Chandrika, "Decreasing Water Levels: Status of Water Table in Mehdiganj and Surrounding Villages, Varanasi, U.P. (August 2006)," Lok Samiti Varanasi.

Page 231 villagers staged their first rally: Nandlal, interview by the author; Mukesh Prabhan, president of Nagepur village committee, interview by the author.

Page 231 ordered Coke to clean up: Nandlal, interview by the author; Banerjee, 79.

Page 231 canal overflowed into his fish pond: Local farmer, interview by the author.

Page 232 Coke uses only 3 percent of the area's groundwater: Ranjan, interview by the author.

Page 232 "We have never dispensed biosolids to farmers": *Press Trust of India*, July 31, 2003.

Page 233 "since 2003, we no longer distribute biosolids": "Coca-Cola India: Questions and Answers," www.cokefacts.com/India/facts_in_qa.shtml.

Page 233 problem persisted for months: Banerjee, 79.

Page 233 15 million liters during June: TERI report, 206.

Page 233 seven-step process of purification: Sanjay Bansal, interview by the author.

Page 234 tank containing two ground fish: Bansal, interview by the author.

Page 234 a lot of good for his village: Dudh Nath Yadav, interview by the author.

Page 234 more than 150 people protesting: Ranjan, interview by the author.

Page 234 thousands of people at a time protesting: See, for example, India Resource Center, "Police Attack Coca-Cola Protest, over 350 Arrested," press release, November 25, 2004; "UP Villagers Allege Coca-Cola of 'Poisoning' Their Drinking Water," *Hindustan Times*, October 5, 2006.

Page 235 Thums Up, a drier and fruitier cola: Tuck Business School of Dartmouth, *Coca-Cola India*, Case no. 1-0085, prepared by Jennifer Kaye, under the direction of Professor Paul A. Argenti, 2004 (hereafter, Tuck case).

Page 235 Coke simply bought up the company: Banerjee, 19.

Page 235 at least 49 percent of shares: Banerjee, 25.

Page 235 6 bottles per person per year: Tuck case.

Page 236 Coke languishes in third place: Banerjee, 43–46.

Page 236 stay of execution in divesting its shares: Banerjee, 28–32.

Page 236 10 percent of the company is Indian-owned: Banerjee, 33–42.

Page 236 Volume grew by nearly 40 percent: Tuck case.

Page 237 sank six bore wells: Coca-Cola India, "The Coca-Cola Company Addresses Allegations Made About Our Business in India," press release, June 1, 2004, www.thecoca-colacompany.com/presscenter/viewpoints_india.

Page 237 fast-tracked approval: A. Krishnan, Perumutty Gram Panchayat president, interview by the author.

Page 237 "When Coca-Cola first" . . . "Many villages have boycotted": R. Ajayan, interview by the author.

Page 237 distributed sludge for use as fertilizer: Ajayan, interview by the author; several anonymous villagers, interviews by the author.

Page 238 never enough water: Anonymous villagers, interviews by the author.

Page 238 bitter aftertaste: Taste test by the author.

Page 238 literacy rate of over 90 percent: Kerala Fact Sheet, 2005–2006, National Family Health Survey (NFHS-3), Ministry of Health and Family Welfare, Government of India, http://www.nfhsindia.org/pdf/KE.pdf.

Page 238 antibusiness climate had led to high unemployment: See Banerjee, 128–129.

Page 238 returned a portion of their ancestral lands: C. R. Bijoy, "Kerala's Plachimada Struggle" (Thiruvananthapuram [Trivandrum], India: Plachimada Coca-Cola Virudha Samara Samithi and Plachimada Struggle Solidarity Committee, November 2006), 4; C. R. Bijoy, interview by the author.

Page 239 "I told them their strength was in the local": Bijoy, interview by the author.

Page 239 around-the-clock sit-in: Bijoy and Veloor Swaminathan, interviews by the author; Bijoy, "Kerala's Plachimada Struggle," 7–10.

Page 239 "unfit for human consumption": Sangram Metals report, April 3, 2002; Bijoy, "Kerala's Plachimada Struggle," 10.

Page 239 "In the beginning": Krishnan, interview by the author.

Page 239 Indian branch of Greenpeace: D. Rajeev, "Coca-Cola's Cup of Woes Overflows," Inter Press Service, August 7, 2003.

Page 240 Sympathetic stories in the media: For example, "Kerala Villagers Up in Arms Against Coca-Cola," *Press Trust of India*, June 21, 2002.

Page 240 declared their support: "Communist Parties Throw Support," *Press Trust of India*, February 3, 2003.

Page 240 "They were just too arrogant": Krishnan, interview by the author.

Page 240 revoking the plant's operating license: Krishnan, interview by the author; Bijoy, "Kerala's Plachimada Struggle," 13; *Press Trust of India*, July 31, 2003.

Page 240 solid waste as fertilizer: "India Coca-Cola Investigation" (transcript), presenter John Waite, BBC Radio 4, July 25, 2003.

Page 240 useless as fertilizer: P. Venugopal, "Toxicity in Plachimada Sludge," *The Hindu*, July 27, 2003.

Page 240 toxic levels of lead and cadmium: BBC Test Results, "Analytical Results for Sample NGP03020"; Bijoy, "Kerala's Plachimada Struggle," 11; "Coke's 'Toxic Sludge' Raises Hackles in Kerala; State Pollution Control Board to Probe BBC Charge Against Coca-Cola," *India Abroad*, August 8, 2003.

Page 240 prostate and kidney cancer: National Toxicology Program, U.S. Department of Health and Human Services, "11th Report on Carcinogens," January 31, 2005.

Page 241 evidence from a respected British university: For an excellent exploration of modern India in all its complexity and contradictions, see Mira Kamdar, *Planet India: How the*

Fastest-Growing Democracy Is Transforming America and the World (New York: Scribner, 2007). For a discussion of cultural factors relating to the issue of pesticides in cola, see Neeraj Vedwan, "Pesticides in Coca-Cola and Pepsi: Consumerism, Brand Image, and Public Interest in a Globalizing India," *Cultural Anthropology* 22, no. 4 (2007), 659–684.

Page 241 **Kerala Pollution Control Board did its own tests:** *Press Trust of India*, July 31, 2003.

Page 241 **four times the tolerable limit:** *Press Trust of India*, August 6, 2003; Kerala State Pollution Control Board, "Presence of Heavy Metals in Sludge Generated in the Factory of M/S Hindustan Coca-Cola Beverages Pvt. Ltd., Palakkad, A Study Report," September 2003.

Page 241 **vowed to pursue legal action:** *Press Trust of India*, August 7, 2003.

Page 241 **pesticides at thirty-seven times the European standards:** Banerjee, 85–86; Ranjit Devraj, "Indian Coke and Pepsi Laced with Pesticides, Says NGO," Inter Press Service, August 5, 2003.

Page 241 **Coke's famous promise:** Vedwan, "Pesticides in Coca-Cola and Pepsi," 659–684.

Page 241 **banned the sale of soft drinks:** *Press Trust of India*, August 8, 2003.

Page 242 **tore down posters of Bollywood film stars:** "India to Test Coca-Cola Sludge," BBC News, August 7, 2003, http://news.bbc.co.uk/2/hi/south_asia/3133259.stm.

Page 242 **"Within days":** Banerjee, 94–95.

Page 242 **"we can safely assert":** Banerjee, 239, quoting ad from *Hindustan Times*, August 7, 2003.

Page 242 **not accredited highly enough:** "Green Body Claims Coke, Pepsi in India Contain Pesticides," *India Abroad*, August 15, 2003.

Page 242 **plummeted more than 30 percent:** "Toxic Effect: Coke Sales Fall by a Sharp 30–40%," *Economic Times*, August 13, 2003.

Page 242 **Joint Parliamentary Committee backed up CSE's findings:** Banerjee, 117.

Page 242 **CSE's own political agenda:** Banerjee, 98–100.

Page 242 **state-of-the-art water-intake treatment system:** Kushal Yadav, interview by the author.

Page 243 **pesticide story garnered more anti-Coke press:** Vedwan, "Pesticides in Coca-Cola and Pepsi."

Page 243 **organize college students to fight for environmental justice:** Amit Srivastava, interview by the author.

Page 244 **a budget of $60,000 a year:** Amit Srivastava, interview by the author; Steve Stecklow, "How a Global Web of Activists Gives Coke Problems in India," *Wall Street Journal*, June 7, 2005.

Page 244 **"The whole point":** Bijoy, interview by the author.

Page 245 **Coke's water use is an issue all over the world:** Srivastava, interview by the author.

Page 245 **new fire to the community in Mehdiganj:** Nandlal, interview by the author.

Page 245 reputation for being one of the more corrupt states: "Rampant Corruption in Uttar Pradesh's Government, Says Report," Indo-Asian News Service, February 18, 2010.

Page 245 arrested the regional head of the state pollution control board: "Pollution Control Board Officer Held for Taking Bribe," United News of India, March 27, 2009; Srivastava and Nandlal, interviews by the author; Amit Srivastava e-mail to the author, April 7, 2010.

Page 245 "The pollution control board": Nandlal, interview by the author; India Resource Center, "Fact Finding Team on the Coca-Cola Company's Franchisee Bottling Plant in Sinhachawar, Balia, Uttar Pradesh, India," June 4, 2007; "Pollution Board to Investigate Coke in Varanasi," *The South Asian*, September 23, 2006.

Page 245 study by the state pollution board in West Bengal: *Press Trust of India*, August 8, 2003.

Page 246 specially lined concrete landfills: "UP Village on Hunger Strike to Shut Down Coke plant," *Hindustan Times*, June 23, 2006.

Page 246 assessment of Plachimada's groundwater: Hazards Centre, "Ground Water Resources in Plachimada: Coca-Cola Stores Toxics for Future Generations" (New Delhi: People's Science Institute, June 2006).

Page 246 assessments of water conditions at five other Coke plants: Hazards Centre, "How Harsh Is Your Soft Drink?" May 2010.

Page 246 "two things are incontrovertible": Dunu Roy, interview by the author.

Page 246 The bioassay with the two fish: Roy, interview by the author.

Page 247 World Social Forum: India Resource Center, "More Than 500 Protest World Social Forum," press release, January 19, 2004.

Page 247 movement against water privatization: *Press Trust of India*, September 25, 2003.

Page 247 same slogan Gandhi used: "Conference Asks Soft Drink MNCs to End Water Exploitation," *The Hindu*, January 22, 2004.

Page 247 ten-day march of some one thousand villagers: India Resource Center, "Police Attack Coca-Cola Protest, over 350 Arrested," press release, November 25, 2004; Nandlal, interview by the author.

Page 248 vow of nonviolence: India Resource Center; "Police Attack Coca-Cola Protest, over 350 Arrested," press release, November 25, 2004; Nandlal, interview by the author; Vishwakarma, interview by the author.

Page 248 arrested more than 350 people: Nandlal, interview by the author.

Page 248 women who pushed to continue the protests: Vishwakarma, interview by the author.

Page 248 eight hundred people marched right up to the gates: India Resource Center, "Over 800 Protest Coca-Cola in India," press release, November 30, 2005.

Page 248 first declaring in December 2003: Judgement, *Perumatty Grama Panchayat v. State of Kerala*, The High Court of Kerala, W.P. (C) No. 34292 of 2003; V. M. Thomas, "Indian Village Claims Victory over Coke in Water Case," Associated Press, December 16, 2003;

Ranjit Devraj, "Greens Jubilant over Verdict Against Coke," Inter Press Service, December 17, 2003.

Page 248 council had acted without sufficient information: Krishnan and Bijoy, interviews by the author; "Investigations on the Extraction of Groundwater by M/S Hindustan Coca-Cola Beverages Private Limited at Plachimada," Final Report, filed before The Honourable High Court of Kerala, February 14, 2005; Judgement, *Hindustan Coca-Cola Beverages (P) Ltd. v. Perumatty Grama Panchayat*, The High Court of Kerala, 2005(2) KLT554, July 4, 2005.

Page 248 banned from extracting groundwater: *Press Trust of India*, March 22, 2004; V. M. Thomas, "India's Kerala State Bans Coke Plant from Using Groundwater," Associated Press, February 18, 2004.

Page 248 extract up to half a million liters a day: "This Kerala Village Fights Against Coke to Preserve Its Groundwater," *Hindustan Times*, April 16, 2005; "Shareholders Accuse Coca-Cola of Misleading Them on Adverse India Report," WebIndia123.com, April 23, 2005; "Coca-Cola Moves Kerala HC for Implementation of Its Order," *Press Trust of India*, May 16, 2005; S. Anand, "Don't Poison My Well," *Outlook*, May 16, 2005.

Page 249 "The thing is very simple": Krishnan, interview by the author.

Page 249 court order to renew the license: "Coke Set to Resume Production in Kerala," Indo-Asian News Service, June 7, 2005; "Panchayat Rejects Coke's Plea for Two-Year License," *Press Trust of India*, June 13, 2005.

Page 249 "divulge all of its ingredients": Krishnan, interview by the author.

Page 249 resist the reopening of the plant by any means necessary: Ajayan and Bijoy, interviews by the author.

Page 249 injuring six while arresting seventy: "Anti-Coke Protesters Lathicharged," *Press Trust of India*, August 15, 2005.

Page 249 plant couldn't reopen: "Kerala Pollution Board Orders Coke Plant to Close," *Hindustan Times*, August 20, 2005.

Page 250 "would at least win": Banerjee, 143.

Page 250 even more pesticides in Coke and Pepsi: "Pesticide Cocktail in Coke, Pepsi Brands, Says Study," *Press Trust of India*, August 2, 2006; Amelia Gentleman, "Pesticide Charge in India Hurts Pepsi and Coke," *New York Times*, August 22, 2006; "Soft Drinks, Hard Truths—II," Centre for Science and Environment, August 2, 2006.

Page 250 banned the sale of Coke and Pepsi: "Sale of Coke, Pepsi to Be Banned in Kerala," *Press Trust of India*, August 6, 2006; "Karna Bans Sale of Cola, Pepsi, Kerala Production," *Press Trust of India*, August 9, 2006; "Anti-Coke Lobby Rebukes US Statement on Cola Ban in India," *Hindustan Times*, August 18, 2006.

Page 250 "This kind of action": "Anti-Coke Lobby Rebukes US Statement on Cola Ban in India."

Page 250 no authority to ban imported products: "Kerala High Court Stays Government Ban on Sale of Coca-Cola and Pepsi," *Hindustan Times*, September 22, 2006.

Page 250 "Whatever the technical reasons": Ajayan and Bijoy, interviews by the author.

Page 250 When Neville Isdell took charge: Banerjee, 223–225; "Coke May Hive Off Bottling Business," *Times of India,* June 25, 2004.

Page 251 half of Rajasthan is fed by rivers: M. S. Rathore, Institute for Development Studies, Jaipur, interview by the author.

Page 251 built a bottling plant here: TERI report, 138.

Page 251 "Rajasthan is an important market": Ranjan, interview by the author.

Page 251 "I have been on roads": Sunil Sharma, interview by the author.

Page 252 less than 1 percent of water use: Ranjan, interview by the author.

Page 252 The system can recharge 1.3 million liters: Ranjan and Sharma, interviews by the author.

Page 253 upgraded Kala Dera's general hospital: "Coca-Cola India Helps to Restore Sarai Bawari," *Hindustan Times,* August 20, 2005.

Page 253 methods that use 70 percent less water: Ranjan, interview by the author; farmers at Farm Education Center, interviews by the author.

Page 253 protesters are "day laborers": Farmer and school principal, Kala Dera, interviews by the author.

Page 254 manipulating public opinion: Srivastava, interview by the author.

Page 254 loan of 150,000 rupees . . . for a new 225-foot bore well: Mahesh Yogi, interview by the author.

Page 255 every one of them raises a hand: Farmers, Kala Dera, interviews by the author.

Page 255 has owned this farm for five generations: Rameshwar Prasad Kuri, interview by the author.

Page 255 water level has gone down eight to ten feet a year: Kuri, interview by the author; this is consistent with data from India's Central Ground Water Department showing a decrease of 3.13 meters (10 feet) post-monsoon to 5.83 meters (19 feet) pre-monsoon in Kala Dera between 2007 and 2008, and 22 meters (73 feet) overall in the nine years between 2000 and 2009.

Page 256 two thousand people came to see Indian environmentalist Medha Patkar: "Protest March Against Coca-Cola Plant in Rajasthan," Indo-Asian News Service, September 25, 2004.

Page 256 local people had the right to groundwater: Sawai Singh, interview by the author.

Page 256 three hundred rainwater-harvesting structures: The Coca-Cola Company, "The Coca-Cola Company Pledges to Replace the Water It Uses in Its Beverages and Their Production," June 5, 2007.

Page 257 able to recharge 46,933 cubic meters per year: Coca-Cola India, "RWH Projects at Various Locations," document provided by Kalyan Ranjan.

Page 257 twenty-eight feet to nineteen feet belowground: Ranjan, interview by the author.

Page 257 level at the plant was eighty feet belowground: Hindustan Coca-Cola Beverages Private Limited ground water report, Annexure and Table A.

Page 257 average rainfall of 1,000 millimeters a year: Hindustan Coca-Cola Beverages Private Limited ground water report, Table A.

Page 257 half of the rain fell on one day: Nandlal and other activists, interviews by the author.

Page 257 more than ten feet between 2007 and 2008: Central Ground Water Department, Government of India.

Page 257 half of the prior year's total: Rathore, interview by the author.

Page 258 two or three rainy days total . . . recharging seventeen times: Rathore, interview by the author.

Page 258 groundwater gauge called a piezometer: Ranjan, interview by the author.

Page 258 lists Hindustan Coca-Cola among its clients: Integrated Geo Instruments & Services client list, http://www.igisindia.com/clientele_nongovt.htm.

Page 258 a representative confirms . . . $1,800 each: E-mail from Madhusudan Integrated Geo Instruments & Services to the author, April 10, 2010.

Page 259 $10 million it recently bequeathed: The Coca-Cola Company, "Local and Regional Foundations," http://www.thecoca-colacompany.com/citizenship/foundation_local.html.

CHAPTER 10. THE CASE AGAINST "KILLER COKE"

Page 260 "The Coca-Cola Company": Recording of Killer Coke address to UMass Radical Student Union, April 28, 2004, http://www.personal.kent.edu/~nsolinsk/.

Page 261 child labor in sugarcane plantations: Human Rights Watch, *Turning a Blind Eye: Hazardous Child Labor in El Salvador's Sugarcane Cultivation,* vol. 16, no. 2(B), June 9, 2004. For Coke's response to the allegations in El Salvador, see The Coca-Cola Company, "The Coca-Cola Company Response to the Human Rights Watch Report on Child Labor in El Salvador," Company Statements, June 13, 2005, at http://www.thecoca-colacompany.com/presscenter/company_statements.html. Also see *Dispatches: Mark Thomas on Coca-Cola* (London: Vera Films, 2007), part of a series produced for Channel 4 television in the United Kingdom, in which children are filmed cutting sugarcane for a Coke supplier.

Page 261 strike-busting in Russia and the Philippines: There have been only scattered news reports on Coke's union practices in Russia. See, for example, "Russian Coca-Cola Workers Demand Pay Hike, Fair Labour Rules," *Toronto Star,* May 21, 2005, and Boris Kagalitsky, "A New Era for Labor Unions," *Moscow Times,* December 6, 2007. In the Philippines, the union's battle against Coke has been led by an affiliate of the International Union of Food and Allied Workers (IUF); for more information, see for instance "Outsourced Coca-Cola Philippines Workers Fight for Regularization" (May 28, 2008), on the IUF website, http://www.iuf.org/cgi-bin/dbman/db.cgi?db=default&uid=default&ID=5064&view_records=1&en=1.

Page 261 31 percent of Coke workers in Colombia: Cokefacts.org website, June 22, 2004 (accessed through "Wayback Machine," web.archive.org); Sarah Greenblatt, "Coca-Cola War Escalates at Rutgers," *Home News Tribune* (East Brunswick, NJ), May 2, 2004.

Page 261 that rate applied only to official employees: See Killer Coke News Bulletin, August 31, 2005, http://www.Killercoke.org/nb0831.htm.

Page 262 Worker Rights Consortium: Liza Featherstone and United Students Against Sweatshops, *Students Against Sweatshops* (New York: Verso, 2002).

Page 262 a chance to directly affect a situation: Camilo Romero, interview by the author.

Page 262 take the campaign national: Jim Lovell, "Students Call for Coke Boycott," *Atlanta Business Chronicle*, November 21, 2003.

Page 263 a new generation of activists: Romero, interview by the author.

Page 263 "Always Rutgers, Always Coca-Cola": Greenblatt, "Coca-Cola War Escalates at Rutgers"; "Coke Wars," *Daily Targum*, April 10, 2000; Candice Choi, "Rutgers Group Voices Exploitation Concerns," *Daily Targum*, April 4, 2000.

Page 263 delay its decision until May 2005: Ray Rogers, interview by the author; Ken Tarbous, "Rutgers to Join the Pepsi Generation," *Home News Tribune* (East Brunswick, NJ), June 10, 2005.

Page 263 a giant inflatable Coke bottle: Kristen Hamill, "Students Form Coalition Against Coke Contract," *Daily Targum*, May 31, 2005.

Page 263 shock troops behind the scenes: Michael Blanding, "Coke: The New Nike," *The Nation*, March 24, 2005, http://www.thenation.com/doc/20050411/blanding.

Page 264 "It certainly catches your eye": Romero, interview by the author.

Page 264 "Maybe you don't like it": Rogers, interview by the author.

Page 264 ten-year, $17 million contract: Tarbous, "Rutgers to Join the Pepsi Generation"; Kelly Heybour, "At Rutgers, Pepsi's $17 Million Deal Is the Real Thing," *Star-Ledger* (Newark), May 14, 2005.

Page 264 "big blow to the company": Rogers, interview by the author; Heybour, "At Rutgers, Pepsi's $17 Million Deal Is the Real Thing."

Page 264 about a hundred vending machines: Crystal Yakacki, former organizer with anti-Coke campaign at NYU, interview by the author; Victoria Foltz and Barbara Leonard, "NYU Senate Bans Coke from Campus," *Washington Square News*, December 9, 2005; Brittani Manzo, "Possible Coke Ban to Take Effect at NYU," *Washington Square News*, November 28, 2005.

Page 264 USAS led the way: Romero, interview by the author; Barbara Leonard, "Coke Refuses NYU Request to Audit Workers' Rights Practices," *Washington Square News*," April 21, 2005.

Page 264 Students wrapped vending machines: Campaign to Stop Killer Coke "Student Protest Pics," www.killercoke.org/proteststud.htm.

Page 264 the student senate voted sixteen to four to ban Coke: "How NYU Chose Colombia over Coke," *BusinessWeek*, Online Extra, January 17, 2006, http://www.businessweek.com/magazine/content/06_04/b3968078.htm.

Page 264 a university-sponsored forum with the WRC: Jason Rowe, "Senate Must Challenge Coke," *Washington Square News*, March 10, 2005.

Page 265 The issue was tabled: Yakacki, interview by the author; "NYU Senate Is Impotent," *Washington Square News*, April 25, 2005.

Page 265 activists at . . . Michigan demanded that the school: Talia Selitsky, "Killer Coke Coalition Rallies at U. Michigan," *Michigan Daily*, February 10, 2005.

Page 265 the board ruled in the students' favor: Scott Leith, "University Says It Will Drop Coke Unless Colombia Charges Probed," *Atlanta Journal-Constitution*, June 18, 2005.

Page 265 "If they don't step up": Jeremy Davidson, "U. Michigan Adjusts Coca-Cola Contracts," *Michigan Daily*, June 20, 2005.

Page 265 Ed Potter had represented . . . new corporate code of conduct: Caroline Wilbert, "Trouble-shooter's Big Job Has Kept Him Traveling, from Colombia to China," *Atlanta Journal-Constitution*, April 16, 2006.

Page 265 spelling out the protections for workers: Ed Potter, interview by the author; The Coca-Cola Company, 2006 Corporate Responsibility Review; The Coca-Cola Company "Workplace Rights Policy," http://www.thecoca-colacompany.com/citizenship/pdf/workplace_rights_policy.pdf.

Page 266 a supposedly independent group: Cal Safety Compliance Corporation (CSCC) for The Coca-Cola Company, "Workplace Assessments in Colombia," 2005; Russ Childrey, vice president of CSCC, interview by the author.

Page 266 denying responsibility for the violence in Colombia: Author notes of shareholder meeting; Michael Blanding, "The Case Against Coke," *The Nation*, April 13, 2006.

Page 266 "felt more like a student protest rally": "Flat Coke," *Financial Times* (London), April 20, 2005.

Page 266 real negotiations began after the meeting: Potter and Romero, interviews by the author.

Page 266 Coke was soon setting its own rules: Notes from September 9, 2005, commission meeting by anonymous student.

Page 266 The students dismissed those demands: "How NYU Chose Colombia over Coke," *BusinessWeek*, Online Extra, January 17, 2006, http://www.businessweek.com/magazine/content/06_04/b3968078.htm.

Page 267 The university issued an ultimatum: Jacob Gershman, "University Senate at NYU Threatens to Oust Coca-Cola from Campus," *Sun* (New York), November 7, 2005.

Page 267 NYU . . . would begin removing Coke from campus: Patrick Cole, "NYU Bans Coca-Cola Products," Bloomberg News, December 9, 2005.

Page 267 "Certainly if there was any wrongdoing": Caroline Wilbert, "A Surprising Critic of Coke," *Atlanta Journal-Constitution,* January 28, 2006.

Page 267 new country: Turkey: Ali Riza Küçükosmanoğlu, president of Nakliyat-İş trade union, interview by the author; *Erol Türedi, et al. v. The Coca-Cola Company, et al.*, United States District Court, Southern District of New York, 05-CV-9635 (2005) (hereafter *Türedi v. Coke*).

Page 268 Coke had nothing to do with it: The Coca-Cola Company statement, "Lawsuit Regarding Protest in Turkey," November 15, 2005; Potter, interview by the author.

Page 268 "the flipside of being a big brand": Kenneth Hein, "Advertising: Big Ban on Campus for Coke Products," *Brandweek,* December 12, 2005.

Page 268 the union hadn't first exhausted its remedies: *Türedi v. Coke,* Decision and Order Granting Motion to Dismiss (39); Notice of Appeal (42).

Page 268 "investigate and evaluate": Donald R. Knauss, President, Coca-Cola North America, to Tim Slottow, Executive Vice President and CFO, University of Michigan, April 10, 2006.

Page 268 more conciliatory approach to negotiations . . . continued to throw cold water: "Why Does the IUF Attack SINALTRAINAL," http://www.killercoke.org/iufsinal.htm; "The Facts: The Coca-Cola Company and Columbia," The Coca-Cola Company press release, January 25, 2006; "Joint Coca-Cola and IUF Statement," March 15, 2005, http://www.iufdocuments.org/www/documents/coca-cola/jtstate-e.pdf.

Page 268 The anti-Coke campaign immediately cried foul: "University of Michigan Falls Prey to Another Coca-Cola PR Scam," Campaign to Stop Killer Coke news release, April 17, 2006.

Page 269 "There are 640 people": John J. Miller, "Fizzes and Fizzles," *National Review,* June 16, 2006.

Page 269 less of an explanation: Potter, interview by the author.

Page 269 "assessment of current working conditions": "University of Michigan Falls Prey to Another Coca-Cola PR Scam."

Page 269 "We have a document": Videocast, The Coca-Cola Company, Annual Meeting of Stockholders, April 19, 2006, http://events.streamlogics.com/pmtv/coke/apr19-06/auditorium/index.asp.

Page 269 "My message to you": Videocast, The Coca-Cola Company, Annual Meeting of Stockholders, April 19, 2006, http://events.streamlogics.com/pmtv/coke/apr19-06/auditorium/index.asp.

Page 269 activists raised red flags: Amit Srivastava, India Resource Center press release, "Coca-Cola Funded Group Investigates Coca-Cola in India," April 16, 2007.

Page 269 listed Coca-Cola as a sponsor: Confirmed from TERI website, April 16, 2006, www.teriin.org (accessed through Internet Archive, www.archive.org).

Page 269 had been paid by Coke: Confirmed by Ibrahim Rehman, Director, Social Transformation Division, The Energy and Resources Institute, in interview by the author.

Page 269 most responsible companies: Confirmed by Ritu Kumar, "Human Face of Corporates," *Times of India,* December 24, 2001.

Page 269 student campaign had "stalled": David Teather, "Has Coke Become the Next McDonald's?" *Guardian,* August 18, 2006.

Page 270 indifference, if not contempt: Order of Clarification as to Plaintiffs SINALTRAINAL and Juan Carlos Galvis (233), Order Granting Motion to Quash Attempted Service of Process (234), Order Reiterating Stay (237), *SINALTRAINAL v. Coke.*

Page 270 "If you didn't know any better": Status conference transcript, June 6, 2006.

Page 270 "unwarranted international fishing expeditions": Consolidated Omnibus Order Dismissing the Cases for Lack of Subject Matter Jurisdiction (322), *SINALTRAINAL v. Coke.*

Page 270 "We hope this decision": Duane D. Stanford, "Lawsuit vs. Coke Bottlers Tossed; Group Representing Colombian Workers May Appeal Ruling," *Atlanta Journal-Constitution,* October 4, 2006.

Page 270 denying the union proper discovery: Appellants' Opening Brief (1), *SINALTRAINAL, et al. v. The Coca-Cola Company, et al.*, on Appeal from the Decision and Final Order of the United States District Court for the Southern District of Florida, Case No. 06-15851-HH (hereafter *SINALTRAINAL v. Coke* Appeal).

Page 270 "Put aside Colombia, Coca-Cola": Terry Collingsworth, interview by the author.

Page 271 engaged a retired judge: Judge Daniel Weinstein (ret.), biography, http://www.jamsadr.com/weinstein/.

Page 271 call off the dogs: In re: TCCC's [The Coca-Cola Company's] Reply Brief, in Support of Motion for Sanctions and Related Relief, February 12, 2008. The documents and e-mail exchanges cited below are taken from exhibits to this brief.

Page 271 resumed criticizing Coke: Faith Gay to Judge Daniel Weinstein, re: TCCC Motion for Sanctions In re SINALTRAINAL Mediation, December 21, 2006.

Page 271 both sides refrain from public statements: Judge Daniel Weinstein e-mail to Faith Gay, Terry Collingsworth, et al., September 27, 2006.

Page 272 trolled Web and newspaper reports: Linda Spencer e-mails, October 2, 4, 9, and 27, 2006.

Page 272 they would have to resign from the union: Draft, "Colombia Settlement Agreement," October 13, 2006.

Page 273 "Every request we made for": Faith Gay to Terry Collingsworth, November 22, 2006.

Page 273 $120,000 in penalties: Order for Sanctions, January 8, 2007.

Page 273 "Look, don't waste my time": Terry Collingsworth, interview by the author.

Page 273 into the "lions' den": Duban Velez, secretary-treasurer of SINALTRAINAL, and Romero, interviews by the author.

Page 274 whatever the union leaders decided: Rogers, interview by the author.

Page 274 "We don't intend to give up our fight": *The Coca-Cola Case*, directed by Germán Gutiérrez and Carmen Garcia (Montreal: Cinema Politica and the National Film Board of Canada, 2009).

Page 274 a personal money grab: Romero, interview by the author.

Page 274 a bum deal: Romero, interview by the author.

Page 274 Finally Kovalik walked out: Romero, interview by the author.

Page 274 Collingsworth proposed . . . a breakthrough: Velez and Romero, interviews by the author.

Page 275 their elation turned to dismay: Velez, interview by the author.

Page 275 "It may be time": Ed Potter e-mail to Terry Collingsworth, April 22, 2007.

Page 275 contract at the University of Minnesota: Amit Srivastava, interview by the author; Jeff Shelman, "U Stands to Get Big Boost from Coke Contract," *Star Tribune* (Minneapolis), April 3, 2008; Ahnalese Rushmann, "U Renews Aramark, Coca-Cola Contracts," *Minnesota Daily*, April 14, 2008.

Page 275 "When you do something": Rogers, interview by the author.

Page 276 "ensur[e] that the Killer Coke Campaign": Draft Colombia Settlement Agreement, October 13, 2007.

Page 276 "Ladies and Gentlemen of The Coca-Cola Company": Letter from Javier Correa to The Coca-Cola Company, September 14, 2007.

Page 276 filing a complaint: SINALTRAINAL, "SINALTRAINAL Files Complaint Before the ILO," press release, September 28, 2007.

Page 276 "cause irreparable damage" . . . another fine: Faith Gay e-mail to Terry Collingsworth, September 24, 2007; Motion for Injunctive Relief and Sanctions in Order to Permit Parties to Hold Final Settlement Talks, October 15, 2007.

Page 276 told Weinstein that the union was pulling out: Terry Collingsworth to Judge Daniel Weinstein re: Joint Motion to Terminate Term Sheet, Response to Order to Show Cause, and Cross Motion for Sanctions, January 29, 2008.

Page 277 released a devastating report: India Resource Center, "Coca-Cola Continues Environmental Abuses in India," press release, June 4, 2007; India Resource Center, "Community Protests Coca-Cola Plant in India," press release, October 25, 2007.

Page 277 announced it was shuttering its doors: Letter from Brindavan Bottlers Limited to Uttar Pradesh Pollution Control Board, October 27, 2007; India Resource Center, "Coca-Cola Plant Shut Down in India," press release, August 14, 2008.

Page 277 with the TERI report: TERI report.

Page 278 "Enough is enough": India Resource Center, "Coca-Cola's Own Report Implicates Company for Abuses in India," press release, March 13, 2008.

Page 278 "community engagement framework": Jeff Seabright, Vice President, Environment and Water Resources, The Coca-Cola Company, to Tim Slottow, Executive Vice President and Chief Financial Officer, University of Michigan.

Page 278 "The easiest thing would be to shut down": Amelia Gentleman, "Coca-Cola Urged to Shut Down an Indian Plant to Save Water," *New York Times*, January 16, 2008.

Page 278 "dilapidated condition": TERI report.

Page 278 the surprising reason that TERI found no pesticides: The University of Michigan Dispute Review Board, memorandum to Tim Slottow re "Complaint Investigation and Resolution Recommendation Regarding SOLE's Allegations Against the Coca-Cola Company," June 13, 2005; Kelly Fraser, "Coke Cleared in India Investigation," *Michigan Daily*, January 15, 2008.

Page 279 much-vaunted ILO report: "Report: Evaluation Mission, Coca-Cola Bottling Plants in Colombia (June 30–July 11, 2008)," International Labour Organization, Geneva, October 3, 2008 (hereafter ILO report).

Page 279 The ILO reserved its highest criticism: ILO report, 44–48.

Page 279 never what the IUF had asked Coke to do: Ron Oswald, general secretary, International Union of Food and Allied Workers, interview by the author.

Page 280 "We said right from the beginning": Kari Tapiola, interview by the author.

Page 280 "I think there is a little dancing": Potter, interview by the author.

Page 280 The university senate held off the vote: Arielle Milkman, "Coke Ban Vote Pushed to Feb.," *Washington Square News*, December 1, 2008.

Page 281 "We really do not let go of these conversations": Potter, interview by the author.

Page 282 close defeat, twenty-eight to twenty-two: Sergio Hernandez, "Coke Ban Lifted," *Washington Square News*, February 5, 2009.

Page 283 Though he began to work . . . work stoppages or slowdowns: José Armando Palacios, interview by the author; José Armando Palacios asylum petition, June 19, 2006; Summons and Complaint, February 25, 2010, *José Armando Palacios, et al. v. The Coca-Cola Company, et al.*, Supreme Court of the State of New York, County of New York, Case No. 10102514 (hereafter *Palacios v. Coke*).

Page 283 started receiving threats: Palacios, interview by the author; asylum petition; *Palacios v. Coke.*

Page 283 did sign a statement with Palacios: Ministerio Público, República de Guatemala, undated document.

Page 283 working the graveyard shift . . . waited to be killed: Palacios, interview by the author; asylum petition; *Palacios v. Coke.*

Page 283 "totally damaging" to the company: Memorandum from Eduardo García to Colonel Efraín Aguirre, undated.

Page 284 the bottler fired him . . . The union protested: Palacios, interview by the author; asylum petition; *Palacios v. Coke*; "Petition to Remove Guatemala from the List of Beneficiary Developing Countries Under the Generalized System of Preferences," submitted by the Washington Office on Latin America (WOLA) and U.S./Labor Education in the Americas Project (US/LEAP), June 15, 2005.

Page 284 been in contact with Ed Potter: Ron Oswald e-mail, December 3, 2005.

Page 284 Oswald says that he was not involved: Ron Oswald, interview by the author.

Page 284 Coke Atlanta would fund a hefty "protection package": Stephen Coats e-mail to Bob Perillo, January 26, 2006, referring to protection offer by Stan Gacek, Virtus Advisors.

Page 284 killing him right in front of Palacios: Palacios interview; asylum petition.

Page 285 "approached by a certain D.C.-based lawyer": Ron Oswald e-mails to Bob Perillo, January 29 and February 2, 2006.

Page 285 arranged a meeting at a hotel: Rodrigo Romero e-mail to Bob Perillo, February 1, 2006.

Page 285 to confirm he offered money to Palacios: Rodrigo Romero e-mails to Bob Perillo, February 6 and 10, 2006.

Page 285 filed in New York Supreme Court in February 2010: Summons and Complaint, *Palacios v. Coke.*

Page 286 "The author describes": Potter, interview by the author.

Page 288 "too vague and conclusory": Opinion, *SINALTRAINAL v. Coke* Appeal, August 11, 2009.

Page 289 "We'd like to start with": The Coca-Cola Company, Annual Meeting of Stockholders, 2009, notes by the author.

Bibliography

Aaseng, Nathan. *The Unsung Heroes: Unheralded People Who Invented Famous Products.* Minneapolis: Lerner, 1989.

Acuff, Daniel S., and Robert H. Reiher. *Kidnapped: How Irresponsible Marketers Are Stealing the Minds of Your Children.* Chicago: Dearborn, 2005.

Adams, Samuel Hopkins. *The Great American Fraud: Articles on the Nostrum Evil and Quacks.* New York: P. F. Collier & Son, 1906.

Alinsky, Saul. *Rules for Radicals: A Pragmatic Primer for Realistic Radicals.* New York: Vintage, 1989 (orig. pub. 1971).

Allen, Frederick. *Secret Formula: How Brilliant Marketing and Relentless Salesmanship Made Coca-Cola the Best-Known Product in the World.* New York: HarperBusiness, 1994.

American Can Company. *Carbonated Beverages in the United States: Historical Review.* Greenwich, CT: American Can Company, 1971.

Armstrong, David, and Elizabeth Metzger Armstrong. *The Great American Medicine Show.* New York: Prentice Hall, 1991.

Atkins, Douglas. *The Culting of Brands: When Customers Become True Believers.* New York: Portfolio, 2004.

Bakan, Joel. *The Corporation: The Pathological Pursuit of Profit and Power.* New York: Simon & Schuster, 2004.

Banerjee, Nantoo. *The Real Thing: Coke's Bumpy Ride Through India.* Kolkata, India: Frontpage, 2009.

Barber, Benjamin R. *Consumed: How Markets Corrupt Children, Infantilize Adults, and Swallow Citizens Whole.* New York: W. W. Norton, 2007.

Barlow, Maude. *Blue Covenant: The Global Water Crisis and the Coming Battle for the Right to Water.* New York: New Press, 2007.

Barnet, Richard J., and Ronald E. Muller. *Global Reach: The Power of Multinational Corporations.* New York: Simon & Schuster, 1974.

Beatty, Jack, ed. *Colossus: How the Corporation Changed America.* New York: Broadway Books, 2001.

Berns, Gregory. *Satisfaction: The Science of Finding True Fulfillment.* New York: Henry Holt, 2005.

Beyer, Chris H. *Coca-Cola Girls: An Advertising Art History.* Portland, OR: Collectors Press, 2000.

Bhagwati, Jagdish. *In Defense of Globalization.* New York: Oxford University Press, 2007 (orig. pub. 2004).

Bingham, A. Walker. *The Snake Oil Syndrome: Patent Medicine Advertising.* Hanover, MA: Christopher, 1994.

Brodsky, Alyn. *Benjamin Rush: Patriot and Physician.* New York: Truman Talley, 2004.

Brown, John Hull. *Early American Beverages.* Rutland, VT: C. E. Tuttle, 1966.

Brownell, Kelly D., and Katherine Battle Horgen. *Food Fight: The Inside Story of the Food Industry, America's Obesity Crisis, and What We Can Do About It.* New York: McGraw-Hill, 2003.

Buckley, Christopher. *Thank You for Smoking.* New York: Random House, 1994.

Bullock, August. *The Secret Sales Pitch: An Overview of Subliminal Advertising.* San Jose, CA: Norwich, 2004.

Calhoun, Mary. *Medicine Show: Conning People and Making Them Like It.* New York: Harper & Row, 1976.

Campbell, William T. *Big Beverage.* Garden City, NY: Doubleday, 1952.

Campos, Paul. *The Obesity Myth: Why America's Obsession with Weight Is Hazardous to Your Health.* New York: Gotham Books, 2004.

Candler, Charles Howard. *Asa Griggs Candler.* Atlanta: Emory University Press, 1950.

Capparell, Stephanie. *The Real Pepsi Challenge: The Inspirational Story of Breaking the Color Barrier in American Business.* New York: Wall Street Journal Books, 2007.

Cardello, Hank. *Stuffed: An Insider's Look at Who's (Really) Making America Fat.* New York: HarperCollins, 2009.

Carson, Gerald. *One for a Man, Two for a Horse: A Pictorial History, Grave and Comic, of Patent Medicines.* Garden City, NY: Doubleday, 1961.

Charles, Barbara Fahs, and Robert Staples. *Dream of Santa: Haddon Sundblom's Vision.* Washington, DC: Staples & Charles, 1992.

Clark, Taylor. *Starbucked: A Double-Tall Tale of Caffeine, Commerce, and Culture.* New York: Little, Brown, 2007.

Clarke, Tony. *Inside the Bottle: Exposing the Bottled Water Industry.* Ottawa: Canadian Centre for Policy Alternatives, 2007 (orig. pub. 2005).

Cleland, Alan S., and Albert V. Bruno. *The Market Value Process: Bridging Customer and Shareholder Value.* San Francisco: Jossey-Bass, 1996.

Copley, Stephen, and Kathryn Sutherland, eds. *Adam Smith's Wealth of Nations: New Interdisciplinary Essays.* Manchester, England: Manchester University Press, 1995.

Coppin, Clayton A., and Jack High. *The Politics of Purity: Harvey Washington Wiley and the Origins of Federal Food Policy.* Ann Arbor: University of Michigan Press, 1999.

Critser, Greg. *Fat Land: How Americans Became the Fattest People in the World.* Boston: Houghton Mifflin, 2003.

Dalton, Sharron. *Our Overweight Children: What Parents, Schools, and Communities Can Do to Control the Fatness Epidemic.* Berkeley: University of California Press, 2004.

de Villiers, Marq. *Water: The Fate of Our Most Precious Resource.* Boston: Houghton Mifflin, 2007.

Dietz, Lawrence. *Soda Pop: The History, Advertising, Art and Memorabilia of Soft Drinks in America.* New York: Simon & Schuster, 1973.

Dudley, Steven. *Walking Ghosts: Murder and Guerrilla Politics in Colombia.* New York: Routledge, 2004.

Dufty, William. *Sugar Blues.* New York: Warner Books, 1976 (orig. pub. 1975).

Elliott, Charles. *"Mr. Anonymous": Robert W. Woodruff of Coca-Cola.* Atlanta: Cherokee, 1982.

Enrico, Roger, and Jesse Kornbluth. *The Other Guy Blinked: How Pepsi Won the Cola Wars.* Toronto: Bantam, 1986.

Erlbach, Arlene. *Soda Pop.* Minneapolis: Lerner, 1994.

Estes, Ralph. *Taking Back the Corporation.* New York: Nation Books, 2005.

Fast, Howard. *Being Red.* Boston: Houghton Mifflin, 1990.

Fellner, Kim. *Wrestling with Starbucks: Conscience, Capital, Cappuccino.* New Brunswick, NJ: Rutgers University Press, 2008.

Fishman, Charles. *The Wal-Mart Effect: How the World's Most Powerful Company Really Works—and How It's Transforming the American Economy.* New York: The Penguin Press, 2008.

Fox, Stephen. *The Mirror Makers: A History of American Advertising and Its Creators.* Urbana and Chicago: University of Illinois Press, 1997.

Frederick, William C., *Corporation, Be Good! The Story of Social Responsibility.* Indianapolis: Dog Ear, 2006.

Friedman, Thomas L. *The World Is Flat.* New York: Farrar, Straus & Giroux, 2007 (orig. pub. 2005).

Frundt, Henry J. *Refreshing Pauses: Coca-Cola and Human Rights in Guatemala.* New York: Praeger, 1987.

Gatehouse, Mike, and Miguel Angel Reyes. *Soft Drink, Hard Labour.* London: Latin American Bureau, 1987.

Gazzaniga, Michael S. *The Mind's Past.* Berkeley: University of California Press, 1998.

Gladwell, Malcolm. *Blink: The Power of Thinking Without Thinking.* New York: Little, Brown, 2005.

Glassner, Barry. *The Gospel of Food: Everything You Think You Know About Food Is Wrong.* New York: HarperCollins, 2007.

Goodrum, Charles A., and Helen Dalrymple. *Advertising in America: The First 200 Years.* New York: Harry N. Abrams, 1990.

Graham, Elizabeth Candler, and Ralph Roberts. *The Real Ones: Four Generations of the First Family of Coca-Cola.* Fort Lee, NJ: Barricade, 1992.

Greising, David. *I'd Like to Buy the World a Coke: The Life and Leadership of Roberto Goizueta.* San Francisco: John Wiley & Sons, 1998.

Haden-Guest, Anthony. *The Paradise Program: Travels Through Muzak, Hilton, Coca-Cola, Texaco, Walt Disney, and Other World Empires.* New York: William Morrow, 1973.

Hagstrom, Robert G. *The Warren Buffett Way.* Hoboken, NJ: John Wiley & Sons, 2005.

Haig, Matt. *Brand Failures: The Truth About the Biggest Branding Mistakes of All Time.* London: Kogan Page, 2003.

Haig, Matt. *Brand Royalty: How the World's Top 100 Brands Thrive & Survive.* London: Kogan Page, 2004.

Hayden, Tom, ed. *The Zapatista Reader.* New York: Nation Books, 2001.

Hays, Constance L. *The Real Thing: Truth and Power at the Coca-Cola Company.* New York: Random House, 2004.

Johnston, David Cay. *Perfectly Legal: The Covert Campaign to Rig Our Tax System to Benefit the Super Rich—and Cheat Everybody Else.* New York: Portfolio, 2003.

Kahn, E. J. *The Big Drink: An Unofficial History of Coca-Cola.* London: Max Reinhardt, 1960.

Kakabadse, Andrew, and Mette Morsing. *Corporate Social Responsibility: Reconciling Aspiration with Application.* Houndmills, England: Palgrave Macmillan, 2006.

Kamdar, Mira. *Planet India: How the Fastest-Growing Democracy Is Transforming America and the World.* New York: Scribner, 2007.

Kaufman, Francine R. *Diabesity: The Obesity-Diabetes Epidemic That Threatens America—and What We Must Do to Stop It.* New York: Bantam, 2005.

Kay, Ira T. *CEO Pay and Shareholder Value: Helping the U.S. Win the Global Economic War.* Boca Raton, FL: St. Lucie Press, 1998.

Kelly, Marjorie. *The Divine Right of Capitalism: Dethroning the Corporate Aristocracy.* San Francisco: Barrett-Koehler, 2003 (orig. pub. 2001).

Kennedy, Allan A. *The End of Shareholder Value.* Cambridge, MA: Perseus, 2002.

Kirk, Robin. *More Terrible Than Death: Massacres, Drugs, and America's War in Colombia.* New York: Public Affairs, 2003.

Klein, Naomi. *Fences and Windows: Dispatches from the Front Lines of the Globalization Debate.* New York: Picador, 2002.

Klein, Naomi. *No Logo: Taking Aim at the Brand Bullies.* New York: Picador, 1999.

Korten, David. *The Post-Corporate World: Life After Capitalism.* West Hartford, CT, and San Francisco: Kumarian Press and Berrett-Koehler, 1999.

Korten, David. *When Corporations Rule the World.* West Hartford, CT, and San Francisco: Kumarian Press and Berrett-Koehler, 1995.

Kotler, Philip, and Nancy Lee. *Corporate Social Responsibility: Doing the Most Good for Your Company and Your Cause.* Hoboken, NJ: John Wiley & Sons, 2005.

Kuisel, Richard. *Seducing the French: The Dilemma of Americanization.* Berkeley: University of California Press, 1993.

Lodge, George, and Craig Wilson. *A Corporate Solution to Global Poverty: How Multinationals Can Help the Poor and Invigorate Their Own Legitimacy.* Princeton, NJ: Princeton University Press, 2006.

Lofland, Cheryl Harris. *The National Soft Drink Association: A Tradition of Service.* Washington, DC: National Soft Drink Association, 1986.

López, Ann Aurelia. *The Farmworkers' Journey.* Berkeley: University of California Press, 2007.

Louis, J. C., and Harvey Yazijian. *The Cola Wars: The Story of the Global Corporate Battle Between the Coca-Cola Company and PepsiCo, Inc.* New York: Everest House, 1980.

Ludwig, David. *Ending the Food Fight: Guide Your Child to a Healthy Weight in a Fast Food/Fake Food World.* New York: Houghton Mifflin, 2007.

Martin, John D., and J. William Petty. *Value Based Management: The Corporate Response to the Shareholder Movement.* Boston: Harvard Business School Press, 2000.

Martin, Milward W. *Twelve Full Ounces: The Story of Pepsi-Cola.* New York: Holt, Rinehart and Winston, 1962.

Maupin, Melissa. *The Story of Coca-Cola.* Mankato, MN: Smart Apple Media, 2000.

McQueen, Humphrey. *The Essence of Capitalism: The Origins of Our Future.* Montreal: Black Rose Books, 2003.

Mentinis, Mihalis. *Zapatistas: The Chiapas Revolt and What It Means for Radical Politics.* London: Pluto, 2006

Michaels, David. *Doubt Is Their Product: How Industry's Assault on Science Threatens Your Health.* Oxford, England: Oxford University Press, 2008.

Mintz, Stanley W. *Tasting Food, Tasting Freedom: Excursions into Eating, Culture, and the Past.* Boston: Beacon, 1996.

Montague, Read. *Why Choose This Book? How We Make Decisions.* New York: Dutton, 2006.

Mooney, Chris. *The Republican War on Science.* New York: Basic Books, 2005.

Nash, June. *In the Eyes of the Ancestors: Belief and Behavior in a Maya Community.* New Haven, CT, and London: Yale University Press, 1970.

Nestle, Marion. *Food Politics: How the Food Industry Influences Health and Nutrition.* Berkeley and Los Angeles: University of California Press, 2007 (orig. pub. 2002).

Nownes, Anthony J. *Pressure and Power: Organized Interests in American Politics.* Boston: Houghton Mifflin, 2001.

Ogilvy, David. *Confessions of an Advertising Man.* New York: Atheneum, 1980 (orig. pub. 1963).

Ogilvy, David. *Ogilvy on Advertising.* New York: Crown, 1983.

Okie, Susan. *Fed Up: Winning the War Against Childhood Obesity.* Washington, DC: Joseph Henry, 2005.

Oliver, J. Eric. *Fat Politics: The Real Story Behind America's Obesity Epidemic.* New York: Oxford University Press, 2006.

Oliver, Thomas. *The Real Coke, the Real Story.* New York: Penguin, 1987.

Packard, Vance. *The Hidden Persuaders.* New York: Simon & Schuster, 1953.

Palacios, Marco. *Between Legitimacy and Violence: A History of Colombia, 1875–2002.* Durham, NC: Duke University Press, 2006.

Palazzini, Fiora Steinbach. *Coca-Cola Superstar.* New York: Barron's, 1988.

Patel, Raj. *Stuffed and Starved: Markets, Power, and the Hidden Battle for the World Food System.* Hoboken, NJ: Melville House, 2007.

Pearce, Fred. *When Rivers Run Dry: Water, the Defining Crisis of the Twenty-first Century.* Boston: Beacon, 2006.

Pendergrast, Mark. *For God, Country, and Coca-Cola: The Definitive History of the Great American Soft Drink and the Company That Makes It.* New York: Basic Books, 2000 (orig. pub. 1993).

Petretti, Allan. *Petretti's Coca-Cola Collectibles Price Guide,* 10th ed. Dubuque, IA: Antique Trader Books, 1997.

Pollan, Michael. *In Defense of Food: An Eater's Manifesto.* New York: The Penguin Press, 2008.

Pomeranz, Kenneth, and Steven Topik. *The World That Trade Created: Society, Culture, and the World Economy.* Armonk, NY: M. E. Sharpe, 2006.

Popkin, Barry. *The World Is Fat: The Fads, Trends, Policies, and Products That Are Fattening the Human Race.* New York: Avery, 2009.

Postrel, Virginia. *The Substance of Style: How the Rise of Aesthetic Value Is Remaking Commerce, Culture, and Consciousness.* New York: HarperCollins, 2003.

Prokosch, Mike, and Laura Raymond, eds. *The Global Activist's Manual: Local Ways to Change the World.* New York: Thunder's Mouth Press/Nation Books, 2002.

Randazzo, Sal. *The Myth Makers: How Advertisers Apply the Power of Classic Myths and Symbols to Create Modern Day Legends.* Chicago: Probus, 1995.

Rappaport, Alfred. *Creating Shareholder Value: A Guide for Managers and Investors.* New York: Free Press, 1998 (orig. pub. 1986).

Reichert, Tom. *The Erotic History of Advertising.* Amherst, NY: Prometheus, 2003.

Reis, Al, and Laura Reis. *The Origin of Brands: Discover the Natural Laws of Product Innovation and Survival.* New York: HarperBusiness, 2004.

Reis, Al, and Jack Trout. *The 22 Immutable Laws of Marketing.* New York: HarperBusiness, 1993.

Reitan, Ruth. *Global Activism.* New York: Routledge, 2007.

Riley, John J. *Organization in the Soft Drink Industry: A History of the American Bottlers of Carbonated Beverages.* Washington, DC: American Bottlers of Carbonated Beverages, 1946.

Rowland, Sanders, with Bob Terrell. *Papa Coke: Sixty-five Years Selling Coca-Cola.* Asheville, NC: Bright Mountain, 1986.

Royte, Elizabeth. *Bottlemania: How Water Went on Sale and Why We Bought It.* New York: Bloomsbury USA, 2008.

Rubin, Barry, and Judith Colp Rubin. *Hating America: A History.* London: Oxford University Press, 2004.

Schildt, Axel, and Detlef Siegfried, eds. *Between Marx and Coca-Cola: Youth Cultures in Changing European Societies, 1960–1980.* New York: Berghahn, 2006.

Schlosser, Eric. *Chew on This: Everything You Don't Want to Know About Fast Food.* Boston: Houghton Mifflin, 2006.

Schlosser, Eric. *Fast Food Nation: The Dark Side of the All-American Meal.* New York: Houghton Mifflin, 2002 (orig. pub. 2001).

Schofield, Robert E. *The Enlightenment of Joseph Priestley: A Study of His Life and Work from 1733 to 1773.* Philadelphia: Pennsylvania State University Press, 1997.

Schor, Juliet B. *Born to Buy.* New York: Scribner, 2004.

Schrank, Jeffrey. *Snap, Crackle, and Popular Taste: The Illusion of Free Choice in America.* New York: Dell, 1997.

Schutzman, Mady. *The Real Thing: Performance, Hysteria, & Advertising.* Hanover, NH, and London: Wesleyan University Press, 1999.

Shartar, Martin, and Norman Shavin. *The Wonderful World of Coca-Cola.* Atlanta: Perry Communications, 1978.

Shell, Ellen Ruppel. *The Hungry Gene: The Inside Story of the Obesity Industry.* New York: Grove Press, 2002.

Shiva, Vananda. *Water Wars: Privatization, Pollution, and Profit.* Cambridge, MA: South End, 2002.

Shulman, Seth. *Undermining Science: Suppression and Distortion in the Bush Administration.* Berkeley: University of California Press, 2006.

Silverstein, Michael J., and Neil Fiske, with John Butman. *Trading Up: The New American Luxury.* New York: Portfolio, 2003.

Simon, Michele. *Appetite for Profit: How the Food Industry Undermines Our Health and How to Fight Back.* New York: Nation Books, 2006.

Simontacchi, Carol. *The Crazy Makers: How the Food Industry Is Destroying Our Brains and Harming Our Children.* New York: Jeremy P. Tarcher, 2000.

Singer, Peter. *One World: The Ethics of Globalization.* New Haven, CT: Yale University Press, 2002.

Sivulka, Juliann. *Soap, Sex, and Cigarettes: A Cultural History of American Advertising.* Belmont, CA: Wadsworth, 1998.

Smith, Adam. *An Inquiry into the Nature and Causes of the Wealth of Nations.* London: T. Nelson & Sons, 1895 (orig. pub. 1776).

Snitow, Alan, and Deborah Kaufman, with Michael Fox. *Thirst: Fighting the Corporate Theft of Our Water.* San Francisco: John Wiley & Sons, 2007.

Solnit, David, and Rebecca Solnit. *The Battle of the Story of the Battle of Seattle.* Edinburgh, Scotland: AK Press, 2009.

Spurlock, Morgan. *Don't Eat This Book: Fast Food and the Supersizing of America.* New York: G. P. Putnam's Sons, 2005.

Standage, Tom. *A History of the World in 6 Glasses.* New York: Walker, 2005.

Stiglitz, Joseph E. *Globalization and Its Discontents.* New York: W. W. Norton, 2002.

Stiglitz, Joseph E. *Making Globalization Work.* New York: W. W. Norton, 2006.

Sullivan, Luke. *Hey Whipple, Squeeze This: A Guide to Creating Great Ads.* San Francisco: John Wiley & Sons, 2003 (orig. pub. 1998).

Summers, B. J. *B. J. Summers' Guide to Coca-Cola: Identifications, Current Values.* Paducah, KY: Collector Books, 2003.

Sutherland, Max, and Alice K. Sylvester. *Advertising and the Mind of the Consumer: What Works, What Doesn't, and Why.* St. Leonard's, Australia: Allen & Unwin, 2000 (orig. pub. 1993).

Tchudi, Stephen N. *Soda Poppery: The History of Soft Drinks in America.* New York: Charles Scribner's Sons, 1986.

Tedlow, Richard. *New and Improved: The Story of Mass Marketing in America.* New York: Basic Books, 1990.

Thomas, Mark. *Belching Out the Devil: Global Adventures with Coca-Cola.* New York: Nation Books, 2009.

Thomas, Susan Gregory. *Buy, Buy Baby: How Consumer Culture Manipulates Parents and Harms Young Minds.* Boston: Houghton Mifflin, 2007.

Tungate, Mark. *Ad Land: A Global History of Advertising.* London: Kogan Page, 2007.

Turner, E. S. *The Shocking History of Advertising!* New York: E. P. Dutton, 1953.

Veblen, Thorstein. *The Theory of the Leisure Class.* Amherst, NY: Prometheus, 1998 (orig. pub. 1899).

Vogel, David. *Fluctuating Fortunes: The Political Power of Business in America.* New York: Basic Books, 1989.

Wagnleitner, Reinhold. *Coca-Colonization and the Cold War: The Cultural Mission of the United States in Austria After the Second World War.* Chapel Hill: University of North Carolina Press, 1994.

Walker, Rob. *Buying In: The Secret Dialogue Between What We Buy and Who We Are.* New York: Random House, 2008.

Wansink, Brian. *Mindless Eating: Why We Eat More Than We Think.* New York: Bantam, 2006.

Watson, James L., and Melissa L. Caldwell, eds. *The Cultural Politics of Food and Eating.* Malden, MA: Blackwell, 2005.

Watters, Pat. *Coca-Cola: An Illustrated History.* Garden City, NY: Doubleday, 1978.

Weller, Worth H. *Conflict in Chiapas: Understanding the Modern Mayan World.* North Manchester, IN: DeWitt, 2000.

Wiley, Harvey Washington. *The History of a Crime Against the Food Law.* Washington, DC: Harvey W. Wiley, 1929.

Wilson, Timothy D. *Strangers to Ourselves: Discovering the Adaptive Unconscious.* Cambridge, MA: The Belknap Press, 2002.

Wolf, Martin. *Why Globalization Works.* New Haven, CT: Yale University Press, 2004.

Wrynn, V. Dennis. *Coke Goes to War.* Missoula, MT: Pictorial Histories, 1996.

Young, James Harvey. *The Toadstool Millionaires: A Social History of Patent Medicines in America Before Federal Regulations.* Princeton, NJ: Princeton University Press, 1961.

Young-Witzel, Gyvel, and Michael Karl Witzel. *The Sparkling History of Coca-Cola.* Stillwater, MN: Voyageur Press, 2002.

Zaltman, Gerald. *How Customers Think: Essential Insights into the Mind of the Market.* Boston: Harvard Business School Press, 2003.

Zyman, Sergio. *The End of Marketing As We Know It.* New York: HarperBusiness, 1999.

Index